GETTING REAL ABOUT RACE

*To my students, current and former, whose passion and curiosity
continually inspire me. And to my coeditor, whose courage and determination
continually humble me.*

— Stephanie M. McClure

*To my nephews and all future "Furbies"—may you inherit a world that is a little
kinder and understanding toward kids that look like you. To my students over the years
who have fought the good fight and decided to do the hard work of understanding
and fighting against inequality. And finally, to my coeditor, Steph, whose friendship
continues to be generous, patient, and amazing and whose brilliance
and passion are nothing short of inspiring.*

— Cherise A. Harris

GETTING REAL ABOUT RACE

HOODIES, MASCOTS,
MODEL MINORITIES,
AND OTHER CONVERSATIONS

Editors

STEPHANIE M. McCLURE
Georgia College

CHERISE A. HARRIS
Connecticut College

Los Angeles | London | New Delhi
Singapore | Washington DC

Los Angeles | London | New Delhi
Singapore | Washington DC

FOR INFORMATION:

SAGE Publications, Inc.
2455 Teller Road
Thousand Oaks, California 91320
E-mail: order@sagepub.com

SAGE Publications Ltd.
1 Oliver's Yard
55 City Road
London, EC1Y 1SP
United Kingdom

SAGE Publications India Pvt. Ltd.
B 1/I 1 Mohan Cooperative Industrial Area
Mathura Road, New Delhi 110 044
India

SAGE Publications Asia-Pacific Pte. Ltd.
3 Church Street
#10-04 Samsung Hub
Singapore 049763

Acquisitions Editor: Jeff Lasser
Developmental Editor: Eve Oettinger
Editorial Assistant: Nick Pachelli
Production Editor: Bennie Clark Allen and
                  Stephanie Palermini
Copy Editor: Diane DiMura
Typesetter: Hurix Systems Pvt. Ltd.
Proofreader: Kris Bergstad
Cover Designer: Gail Buschman
Marketing Manager: Erica DeLuca

Printed in the United States of America

*Library of Congress Cataloging-in-Publication
Data*

Getting real about race : hoodies, mascots,
model minorities, and other conversations /
edited by Stephanie M. McClure, Cherise A.
Harris.

pages cm
Includes bibliographical references.

ISBN 978-1-4522-5890-4 (pbk. : alk. paper) —
ISBN 978-1-4833-1246-0 (web pdf)

1. United States—Race relations. 2. Stereotypes
(Social psychology)—United States. 3. Race.
I. McClure, Stephanie M. II. Harris, Cherise A.,
1976-

E184.A1G43 2015
305.800973—dc23   2014002625

This book is printed on acid-free paper.

14 15 16 17 18 10 9 8 7 6 5 4 3 2

Contents

In this section, essay authors introduce key concepts and ideas regarding race and racial inequality. These include how race is socially constructed and how the construction process connects with questions of biology, history, and power. The essays also provide students with information about how and why we need to engage in meaningful, inclusive conversations about race in contemporary American society.

II. DEBUNKING INDIVIDUAL ATTITUDES 51

The essays in this section consider widespread individual attitudes and beliefs about the current state of racial inequality in the United States, including beliefs about color-blindness, meritocracy, and structures of opportunity. The authors compare these perceptions to social science research and information in psychology, sociology, history, and media studies. The information presented helps students consider the validity of these popular attitudes.

III. INSTITUTIONS, POLICIES, AND LEGACIES OF OPPRESSION 123

Following up on the history and attitudes discussed in the previous sections, these essays consider how misperceptions and beliefs about patterns of race and racial group differences manifest across social institutions. Some of the areas addressed include the family, schools, the state and public policy, and the criminal justice system. In this section, the authors consider the impact of legal history, individual perceptions and beliefs, and media representations of racial dynamics.

FAMILY

EDUCATION

POLITICS, SOCIAL POLICY, AND THE STATE

IV. RACE IN EVERYDAY INTERACTIONS   257

This final selection of essays returns students to the level of the individual and considers some of the key questions they may have as they look to engage in further conversation about race. The topics addressed encourage the kind of meaningful dialogue that is necessary to help students think more carefully about how they engage others.

Preface

Professors teaching introductory courses in race and ethnicity or "diversity" must not only communicate the long and complicated history, psychology, and sociology of these topics in just one semester but must also repeatedly respond to the myths and misperceptions of race that students bring with them into these courses. Some of these include the idea that race and racial classification systems are based on human biology or genetic variation; that systematic disenfranchisement by race ended with the culmination of the Civil War, the civil rights movement, or the election of the nation's first Black president; or that evidence for the persistence of racial discrimination is difficult to establish or does not exist. In teaching these topics semester after semester, it can become difficult for professors to summon the patience and empathy needed to engage students in early stages of critical awareness, particularly given how often we hear the same misperceptions. Furthermore, for instructors who may be wary of broaching these questions and discussing them in the classroom, a text that places the latest research at their fingertips can lead to essential learning in an area of sociology often fraught with controversy and silence.

Drawing from our experience of teaching race for nearly 20 years, we believe professors would find it useful to have an engaging text that comprehensively and succinctly addresses the most common misconceptions about race held by students (and by many in the United States, in general). In this book, we have put together a collection of short essays that draw on the latest sociological research on these topics. It is a "one-stop-shopping" reader on the racial topics most often pondered by students and derived from their interests, questions, and concerns. Many scholars write on these topics in various places (e.g., journal articles, books, readers), but what is often lacking is a systematic deconstruction of specific, widely shared myths repeated often by students. Moreover, with other readers, the professor is left to pull out the key pieces of information in each reading, provide the additional supporting information to debunk a particular myth, and create a consistency in a format that is understandable to students. However, the concise and topic-specific, short-essay format we use here aims to facilitate quicker movement from acknowledging misperceptions about race to examining and discussing sociological evidence. Each of our contributors has also provided excellent follow-up discussion questions for in-class work and suggested out-of-class activities that can help students apply their new knowledge to their everyday lives.

What we saw as necessary, and what drove us to put this collection together, is the work of "translation." The information contained in these essays is available in many other places, and given our space constraints, we point to those outside sources at the end of each essay. What we saw happen in our own courses was that students often had difficulty connecting the primary text readings to the specific kinds of misinformation and misunderstanding they brought with them. We have tried to build a reader that speaks both languages—the language of the commonly held myths and the language of social science—so that the two are together in one book. Our contributors are those who have written books and articles on these topics or who have been "in the trenches" teaching these topics on a regular basis. As scholars who consistently cover these issues in the classroom and in their scholarship, they are well versed in the latest scholarly literature on controversial racial topics such as these.

The primary target audience for this text is lower level or introductory race and ethnicity or diversity courses, especially those in the core or general education curriculum. Courses of this kind are taught every semester in colleges and universities across the country; approximate class sizes are between 30 and 60 students. Other courses where this text might be useful include education courses, social psychology of race or racism courses, introduction to higher education courses, and ethnic studies courses.

Our hope is that this reader will make the work of translation less difficult for the many excellent instructors all across the country engaging these topics in their classes every semester.

Suggested Additional Resource

Fox, H. (2009). *"When race breaks out": Conversations about race and racism in college classrooms.* New York, NY: Peter Lang.

Acknowledgments

Putting together an edited volume is no small task and requires the assistance of many. As we were deciding on which topics would be covered, we sought the advice of treasured colleagues and friends who gave us the benefit of their many years of experience in the classroom. We would like to thank Nikki Khanna, Keisha Edwards Tassie, Michelle Petrie, Ronald J. O. Flores, Afshan Jafar, Michallene McDaniel, Kelly Manley, Victoria Bruce, Michael Ramirez, and E. M. "Woody" Beck for their input and support during the early stages of our project and for the sage advice and wisdom they offered along the way. We would also like to thank Eve Oettinger, David Repetto, Jeff Lasser, Lauren Johnson, Diane McDaniel, Judith Newlin, Nick Pachelli, Stephanie Palermini, Diane DiMura, Bennie Clark Allen, and the rest of the team at SAGE who worked tirelessly to get this project off the ground and make our vision a reality.

This project is the product of teaching these topics to thousands of students in race and ethnicity courses over many years. In that time, we have witnessed and moderated many challenging discussions—discussions that remind us just how much there is left to know in this area and how important it is that instructors continue to do this difficult work, while having the tools to do so. We thank all of the students we have had over the years, as it is their questions and insights that fueled this anthology.

Finally, we would like to express our great appreciation and gratitude to the contributing authors for lending us their expertise and for writing essays that were better than we could have even hoped for when we first envisioned this project. We are honored and humbled to have you as colleagues and are beyond grateful for all you did to make this volume come to life.

PART I

Laying the Foundation

"But My Mother Says It's Rude to Talk About Race!"

How and Why We Need to Discuss Race in the United States

Cherise A. Harris
Connecticut College

Stephanie M. McClure
Georgia College

Cherise A. Harris is an associate professor of sociology at Connecticut College. She specializes in race, class, and gender, and teaches classes on the sociology of ethnic and race relations; the sociology of inequality; race, gender, and the mass media; and middle-class minorities. Her book, *The Cosby Cohort: Blessings and Burdens of Growing up Black Middle Class*, was published in 2013. She has also published in *Teaching Sociology, Sociological Spectrum,* and *Journal of African American Studies.*

Stephanie M. McClure is an associate professor of sociology at Georgia College. She teaches classes on racial stratification, social theory, and the sociology of education. Her research interests are in the area of higher education, with a focus on college student persistence and retention across race, class, and gender, and a special emphasis on postcollege student experiences that increase student social and academic integration. She has published in the *Journal of Higher Education, Symbolic Interaction,* and *The Journal of African American Studies.*

I n spite of our hesitance to talk about them, racial myths permeate our social world. They are frequently present in the mass media and public discourse as well as in our everyday conversations with each other. Perhaps in your dorm rooms, dining halls, workplaces, or on social media, you have heard a variation on the following statements:

- We have a Black president which means racism doesn't exist anymore.
- We need to look out for "real Americans" first, not immigrants.
- *Native American/Indian, Asian/Oriental, Latino/Hispanic.* Why does it matter what we call them?
- Asian Americans are doing very well. If other racial groups had their values, they would do well also.
- I know a minority who got worse scores than me and he got into a better college!
- I'm in favor of interracial dating and marriage but the children from these unions suffer.
- I don't know why people are so upset about team names like the *Washington Redskins.* It's really just a way of honoring Native American culture.

These kinds of statements reflect a great deal of the conventional wisdom around race. We define *conventional wisdom* as the received body of knowledge informally shared by a group or society that is often unstated, internally inconsistent, and resistant to change. This conventional wisdom is full of racial myths and misunderstandings. In this reader, we look at common racial myths that we and many sociology professors and race scholars have heard from their students in race courses. In this essay, we will give you the tools with which to navigate this reader and introduce some key ideas and questions to help you navigate discussions about race both inside and outside of the classroom.

Early in our schooling, we learn a simplified history of America's founding that ignores the significant levels of racial conflict and inequality that existed. For instance, it is often stated that America was founded on ideals of freedom and equality for all, an image that ignores the many groups who were excluded from that freedom and equality, namely people of color. We also tend to think that racial or ethnic strife happened sometime *after* that idealized founding. However, as sociologist Joe Feagin (2010) notes in his book, *The White Racial Frame: Centuries of Racial Framing and Counter-Framing,* "Racial oppression was not added later on in the development of [U.S.] society, but was the foundation of the original colonial and U.S. social systems, and it remains as a foundation to the present day" (p. vii). Yet, there is still a tendency in American society to gloss over this history or in other ways minimize the import of race. We see this minimization in the present day when political pundits and others in the media characterize our society as *post-racial,* asserting that race no longer determines one's life chances or determines them to a far lesser extent than it once did.

Indeed, since the election of President Barack Obama, we have been hearing more and more that we have moved beyond race, despite much evidence to the contrary. To be sure, the election of the nation's first Black president signaled a significant shift in the tenor of race relations in the United States. For this reason, you will see President Obama mentioned often in the essays in this volume because his election was a watershed moment in American race relations. Yet, his election has also been something of a miner's canary, signaling that perhaps we haven't come as far on the issue of race as we would like to think (see also Hughey, Essay 3). Unique occurrences that have happened during his presidency such as the "birtherism" movement or him being called a liar by a Congressman during a televised congressional address suggest that we are far from post-racial (see also Logan, Essay 17).

The move toward post-racialism and an emphasis on color-blindness are what Michael Omi and Howard Winant (1994) have referred to as *racial projects*. They are "simultaneously an interpretation, representation, or explanation of racial dynamics and an effort to reorganize and redistribute resources along particular racial lines" (p. 56). American history is replete with racial projects that have resulted in negative outcomes for people of color. The defining of Native Americans as *savages* that coincided with the violent removal of groups from their land, the current dehumanizing construct of Latinos (and Mexican Americans, specifically) as "illegal immigrants" thus prompting calls for stringent legislation and policy, or the branding of Black women as *welfare queens* undeserving of public assistance are all examples of racial projects and policies that have disenfranchised people of color. As Ted Thornhill explains in greater detail in Essay 5, the post-racial/color-blind discourse seems primarily to be a racial project designed to convince Americans that the restrictive racial barriers of the past have fallen (particularly with the election of a Black president) and thus to keep people from thinking or talking about the reality of race as it plays out in their day-to-day lives.

While empirical information about unequal outcomes in education, the criminal justice system, and the labor market clearly show all of the ways in which many Americans' lives are still affected by race, in the context of a supposedly post-racial and meritocratic society, when someone even mentions race, they are often subject to silencing and even ridicule. You may have heard the statement, "Why can't people just stop talking about race? If they stopped talking about it, it would just go away!" Perhaps you've even said it yourself. As difficult as it is to talk about, our ability to move toward greater social justice is severely limited by the silencing around race. Moreover, as Thornhill explains in Essay 5, "[D]ifferences in skin color are not the problem; racism, racial discrimination, White racial privilege, and racial inequality are." Silence only begets further misunderstanding and inhibits progress.

To get the discussion started, let's talk about the role race plays in the college experience and why you might be hearing more about race than you ever have.

The Impact of the College Experience on Racial Thinking

As Stephanie McClure (one of the editors of this volume) points out in Essay 14, the college experience has the potential to bring about a great deal of intellectual and personal growth and is an opportunity to obtain a degree, but also an opportunity for students to learn more about who they are as individuals and who they would like to become (see also Astin, 1993; Pascarella & Terenzini, 2005).

Sociologist Mary C. Waters (2013) writes that the college experience also often puts race in stark relief, where students find themselves thinking about race more than they did when they were younger:

> Sociologists and psychologists note that at the time people leave home and begin to live independently from their parents . . . they report a heightened sense of racial and ethnic identity as they sort through how much of their beliefs and behaviors are idiosyncratic to their families and how much are shared with other people. It is not until one comes into close contact with many people who are different from oneself that individuals realize the ways in which their backgrounds may influence their individual personality (p. 212; see also Aries, 2008; Tatum, 1997).

The effect of this experience may be even greater if the person has had very limited previous exposure to people of different races or ethnicities. Moreover, as Waters (2013) argues, prior to the college experience, many White students' relationship to their ethnicity is mostly symbolic, meaning that it is a voluntary relationship, that is often enjoyable, and expressed only intermittently (see also Gans, 1979). For instance, they may celebrate their distant Irish heritage on St. Patrick's Day, but otherwise rarely acknowledge it. Thus, their relationship to their race or ethnicity is fairly tenuous.

But "for all of the ways in which ethnicity [and race] does not matter for White Americans, it does matter for non-Whites" (Waters, 2013, p. 210). For students of color, and particularly those at predominantly White institutions (PWIs), race and ethnicity play a key role in their college experience. For example, in Elizabeth Aries's (2008, p. 36) study of race and class at an elite college, she found that race was something that almost every Black student in the study had thought about before arriving, while only half of the White students in the study had (see also Tatum, 1997). In addition, many of the White students in her study seemed unaware of the privileges that they possessed as a result of their race. One of those privileges is that college campuses are essentially built around White students' interests and needs—the food served in the dining halls, the membership and leadership of student organizations, the music played in dorm rooms and at campus parties, and even the course offerings at the college frequently center on the desires and interests of White students (see also Feagin & Sikes, 1995). In other words, the overall culture of the institution frequently reflects the things that Whites value. However, because Whiteness and White privilege is often made invisible (McIntosh, 2013), it is difficult for some White students to see.

Meanwhile, it is within this context that students of color must function. They may have grown up in a culture with different music, food, language, for example, or have different life histories, experiences, and concerns that they find difficult to have validated in the context of a White-dominated institution. Thus, it is challenging for these students to enjoy the full college experience. As Beverly Daniel Tatum (1997) writes, they also frequently find themselves the target of racial prejudice, discrimination, and isolation on campus and in the classroom:

Whether it is the loneliness of being routinely overlooked as a lab partner in science courses, the irritation of being continually asked by curious classmates about Black hairstyles, the discomfort of being singled out by a professor to give the "Black perspective" in class discussion, the pain of racist graffiti scrawled on dormitory room doors, the insult of racist jokes circulated through campus e-mail, or the injury inflicted by racial epithets (and sometimes beer bottles) hurled from a passing car, Black students [and other students of color] on predominantly White campuses must cope with ongoing affronts to their racial identity (p. 78; see also Feagin, 2010; Feagin & Sikes, 1994).

Recent events on college campuses bear out the nature of this hostility. For instance, in the last five years or so, a rash of "ghetto parties" have been held on college campuses where attendees are encouraged to dress up in clothes with "urban" labels (e.g., FUBU, Rockawear, etc.), athletic jerseys, and gold teeth. Similarly, in 2012, a White fraternity at a prestigious university allegedly held an Asian-themed party, complete with conical hats, geisha outfits, and misspellings on the invitation designed to convey an Asian accent (Quan, 2013; see also Kingkade, 2013).

As a result of these hostilities, Black, Asian, Latino, Middle Eastern, and Native American students may find solace in hanging out with other students who belong to their racial or ethnic group. They may even join a racial or ethnic affinity group like an Asian Student Union, a MeCHA group (Movimiento Estudiantil Chican@ de Aztlán) representing Chicano students, or a Black Greek Letter Organizations (BGLO) as a way of feeling safe and valued, while also feeling connected to the wider campus community. As McClure discusses in Essay 14, this process is known as *social integration* and is not only necessary for identity development, but also plays a key role in successful college completion. Yet, when White students enter a college campus and see racial affinity groups, they wonder why such things exist because their race or ethnicity has never been very important in their lives. They may even feel a sense of being left out when they see students of color gathering together (Aries, 2008) or see them in organizations built around their interests. This is one of the many ways in which the college experience highlights the salience of race.

Race is also highlighted in college classrooms in a way that it often isn't in high school classrooms. For example, college is frequently the first time that students are exposed to a history of the United States that analyzes race in a critical way. Historical accounts have long reflected an attempt "to sanitize this country's collective memories and to downplay or eliminate accurate understandings of our racist history" (Feagin, 2010, p. 17). For example, the story of contact between Native Americans and European settlers is often told (and represented in films like Disney's *Pocahontas*) as two communities who struggled to respect each other's differences rather than as a story of violent conflict and ultimate domination, colonization, and genocide on the part of White settlers. In another example, we are taught that true Black oppression ended with slavery or Jim Crow segregation, without looking at the legacy of systemic oppression and the destruction both of these systems left in their wake. In many cases, the college classroom is the first opportunity an individual has to seriously consider the true implications of race and the complicated and painful U.S. racial history. This can be a jarring and difficult experience.

Nonetheless, understanding the legacies of our racial history is a key emphasis of this book, for in understanding the history, we can disprove many common racial myths and move toward greater social justice. For instance, in Essay 6, Paula Ioanide disproves the commonly held myth that America is a meritocracy where anyone who works hard enough can get ahead. As Ioanide explains, Blacks and Whites with similar incomes, work histories, and family structures have "radically different relationships to wealth and inheritance," which is largely a function of Blacks' difficulty in accumulating wealth during restrictive social structures like slavery and Jim Crow. Thus, "hard work" isn't enough to overcome disparities that began long ago. The history of Jim Crow is also connected to persistent educational segregation and inequality, as discussed by Meanwell, Patel, and McClure in Essay 13 in this volume. Knowledge of these historical racial inequities in the American educational system are also necessary for understanding questions of affirmative action in higher education, as you'll read in Essay 15 by OiYan Poon, and in the labor market, a topic analyzed by Wendy Leo Moore in Essay 20.

Legacies of oppression also affect individual attitudes and interpersonal interactions. For example, when Black men are perceived as inherently criminal, every Black man becomes a suspect, as Sara Doude explains in her essay (Essay 19) on bias in perceptions of crime and criminals. Stereotypical thinking and what social psychologists refer to as "ultimate attribution error" contribute to how hooded sweatshirts (also known as "hoodies") are perceived very differently depending on the race of the wearer, a topic examined by Rashawn Ray (Essay 7). Legacies of racial oppression also live on in present day attitudes toward interracial dating as Nikki Khanna, author of *Biracial in America: Forming and Performing Racial Identity* (2011), discusses in her essay titled, "But What About the Children?' Contemporary Attitudes and Trends in Interracial Marriage" (Essay 11). Here, she demonstrates how racist attitudes toward interracial dating are disguised in concern about the children of these unions while also reflecting the country's long legacy of racial antipathy, particularly toward Blacks. In all of these ways, race and legacies of racial struggles resonate decades and even centuries later.

When White students are first exposed to the history of White oppression, some feel guilty or ashamed that the racial group of which they are a part has been responsible for colonization, domination, and global hegemony. For instance, once White students learn of this history, they sometimes become anxious to present themselves as "one of the good ones." They may even say, "I'm not racist! Some of my best friends are [Black, Asian, Latino, Native American, etc.] . . ." In reviewing the evidence from prominent sociologists like Eduardo Bonilla-Silva and Joe Feagin, Cherise Harris (coeditor of this volume) points out, in Essay 23, that often when people claim to have friends of other racial or ethnic backgrounds, their "friendships" lack depth; they may not even know their "friend's" name or the friendship disintegrates when the activity in which they have participated is over. They may also still harbor racist ideas despite their supposed friendship. While the friends defense is often an attempt by well-meaning Whites to present themselves as a racial ally, as Harris points out, being an ally is a far more complicated process that among other things involves taking proactive steps to confront one's own racism and the racist views and actions of other Whites. Through clearer understanding of our racial history and the nature of our racial dynamics and interactions, we have a far better chance of moving toward a society with greater social justice. That is one of several goals of this book.

Our Job and Your Job

Given the United States's varied, complicated, and difficult racial history, it is no great surprise that race is a challenging sociological topic. This is the case for three important reasons: (1) a good deal of our information about race and ethnicity includes conventional (or folk) wisdom that is frequently incorrect; (2) much of that conventional wisdom has been handed down to us by agents of socialization (e.g., parents, extended family, peers, the church, and media) whose opinions tend to weigh heavily upon us; and (3) there is an overall culture of silence around race that permeates the United States (see Tatum, 1997), thus prompting little critical analysis of that conventional wisdom. None of these should be underestimated in terms of their overall impact. For instance, it is problematic that conventional wisdom tends to reflect a sanitized racial history where our ugliest chapters are reimagined or deleted altogether (Feagin, 2010), yet repeated over and over again as truth in the media and in our everyday conversations. That they are frequently repeated by our agents of socialization is problematic because our tendency is to uncritically accept what they say in their role as significant others to whom we are closest and who have taught us many other important and meaningful life lessons. It is from them that we get many important cues about race. For example, perhaps there were points in your life where a parent, teacher, or friend suggested it was rude to mention race, let alone discuss it as a serious topic. The cue you might have gotten then is to silence any discussion about race. At other times, perhaps you received messages that minimized or dismissed its significance. If you are a person of color, the cue you might have gotten is not to mention race or racism for fear that you would be accused of being "angry" or "playing the race card"; perhaps worse, you remain silent because you fear that no one will care about your experience. For all of the above reasons, both Whites and people of color remain silent on racial issues and some are loathe to acknowledge its very existence. This is consistent with contemporary color-blind rhetoric, which leads to a dysfunctional national discourse on race.

The task of this volume is to open up critical discussions about racial topics and debunk many of the commonly held racial myths that college students often bring with them to race courses. Debunking involves unmasking and deconstructing some of our most commonly held notions and beliefs. As Peter Berger writes in *Invitation to Sociology* (1963),

The sociological frame of reference, with its built-in procedure of looking for levels of reality other than those given in the official interpretations of society, carries with it a logical imperative to unmask the pretensions and the propaganda by which [people] cloak their actions with each other. (p. 38)

A central premise of this reader is that debunking myths with accurate information and evidence can be an antidote to racism and racial prejudices. This is not an easy task, however. As Liz Grauerholz (2007), former editor of the journal *Teaching Sociology*, states, "All information that students learn is filtered through their prior understandings of the world and these preconceptions can present major barriers to gaining new knowledge about the social world" (p. 15).

To be clear, mere exposure to the information isn't sufficient. For good information to change attitudes, there must be a willingness to consider new information and an openness to change. As M. Neil Browne and Stuart M. Keeley (2001) discuss in their book, *Asking the Right Questions: A Guide to Critical Thinking,*

We bring lots of personal baggage to every decision we make—experiences, dreams, values, training, and cultural habits. If you are to grow, however, you need to recognize these feelings, and, as much as you are able, put them on the shelf for a bit. (p. 9)

Barriers to change exist for individuals in terms of their own ego and sense of identity and as well as our sense of the state of justice and fairness in the world. Indeed, we often perceive that we are being personally attacked when someone presents a position opposite to our own. The danger here is that "being emotionally involved in an issue prior to any active thought about it [means] that you may fail to consider potential good reasons for other positions—reasons that might be sufficient to change your mind on the issue if you would only listen to them" (Browne & Keeley, 2001, p. 9). Part of what you will need to do when considering the essays in this volume is engage your critical thinking skills. Critical thinking involves, among other things, identifying assumptions and value conflicts, evaluating evidence, assessing logic, identifying significant omitted information, coming up with alternative positions and ideas, and developing a reasonable conclusion (Browne & Keeley, 2001). It is through this process that many of our conventional notions about race are debunked.

Early in this volume, we debunk perhaps one of the most commonly held myths about race: that it is a biological entity that is fixed and unchangeable and that can even explain why, for instance, Blacks excel at particular sports. As Daniel Buffington in Essay 4 explains, citing scientific evidence where genotype is concerned, human beings are 99.9% identical when looking at nucleotide pairs, one of the building blocks of DNA. Indeed, genetic research suggests great similarity across racial and ethnic groups. When looking at this and other scientific research, Buffington (like most social scientists) concludes that race is mostly a social construct, where "the assignment of social importance to physical features occurred through social relations—such as migration and conquest, competition for scarce resources, and political challenges against the state." This is a key claim of this volume: *Race is a social construction.* Because it is a social construct, the explanations for racial dynamics are located in the social as well. Thus, the overrepresentation of Blacks in certain sports like basketball can be more directly attributed to social factors like more ample opportunity in those sports (e.g., access to basketball courts in neighborhoods and schools), coupled with limited opportunities in the occupational structure of the United States (e.g., limited employment opportunities particularly for Blacks located in neighborhoods with underfunded and under-resourced schools).

The essays in this volume similarly reflect critical perspectives on commonly held racial myths. As you read each essay, in addition to the questions raised by the author, consider the following questions: Where or from whom have you heard this myth? Do you believe it yourself? Why or why not? What evidence have you heard in support of this kind of conventional wisdom? How is the myth debunked by the author of the essay? What other information do you think would be useful for considering the questions raised in the essay and where could you locate this information? Finally, ask yourself, why is this myth so often perpetuated? In other words, whose purposes are served by keeping this myth alive and who is ultimately hurt by it? By considering these questions, you are deciding to make the effort to understand race in a critical fashion as opposed to blindly accepting the multitude of racial myths that dominate American society.

Final Thoughts

The essays in this volume share several key assumptions:

1. History matters.

2. Context matters.

3. Dialogue matters.

As students of U.S. racial history and racial dynamics, you have the opportunity to change the nature of the dialogue around race. But, that requires a comprehensive understanding of the context in which we live and also requires the courage, honesty, and good information needed to dispel conventional racial wisdom. Some of you may have been exposed to the information in this book already and you may have done the work necessary to modify your ideas and beliefs to fit this reality. As such, it might be difficult to watch your classmates and peers encounter information about race for the first time and not become frustrated and angry. Our hope is that having so much of the information needed to debunk the most common myths about race in the United States all in one place will be useful to you as you engage your classmates and peers in important conversation.

Suggested Additional Resources

Berger, P. L. (1963). *Invitation to sociology: A humanistic perspective.* New York, NY: Anchor Books.

Browne, M. N., & Keeley, S. (2001). *Asking the right questions: A guide to critical thinking.* Upper Saddle River, NJ: Prentice Hall.

Feagin, J. R. (2010). *The white racial frame: Centuries of racial framing and counter-framing.* New York, NY: Routledge.

Omi, M., & Winant, H. (1994). *Racial formation in the U.S.: From the 1960s to the 1990s.* New York, NY: Routledge.

Questions for Further Discussion

1. Prior to beginning college, how often had you thought about your race? When you did think about it, which events or occurrences prompted it?

2. How would you characterize what you learned about America's racial and ethnic history? For example, what is the conventional wisdom you have heard surrounding Whites, Blacks, Latinos, Asians, Native Americans, and Middle Easterners?

3. As you begin this course, what are some of your questions surrounding race? If they are not covered in this book, write them down and bring them to class to discuss with your classmates. What can the essays in this book tell you about the answer(s) to your question(s)?

Reaching Beyond the Color Line

Examining Your Attitudes Toward Race and Ethnicity: A Pretest and Posttest

Directions: At the beginning of the term, answer the questionnaire below. It is important to answer the questions as HONESTLY as possible, no matter how you think your answers may be perceived. After you have completed the course, look at your answers again to see if any have changed or if you now think of these questions in a different way. What do you now know about race and ethnicity that you didn't know before?

1. When you were a child, did your parents talk about race? What messages about race did you receive from them? What messages did you receive from other relatives or other agents of socialization (e.g., media, teachers, peers, religious figures, etc.)? What would you teach your children about race?

2. Do you think race is mostly about biology? Why or why not?

3. How do you define racism? Can anyone be racist?

4. How have your views about race changed in the last 10 years? Have they changed at all since you began college? In what ways?

5. How did the election of Barack Obama affect your sense of the American racial landscape? Do you think some people voted for him simply because he is Black? Is this problematic? Why or why not?

6. Do you think it's time for people to stop talking about racism? Explain your answer.

7. Do you believe it is okay to make judgments about people based on how they dress, like whether they are wearing a hoodie, hijab, or turban? Can making judgments based on people's appearance ever be justified?

8. Consider our use of cultural items typically associated with groups of color like hip-hop music and Native American or (ostensibly) Asian symbols. Where is the line between respecting or celebrating these cultures and appropriating or exploiting them?

9. How do you explain the large numbers of Black men in prison? Is this the result of bad choices or something else?

10. Do some racial or ethnic groups value marriage more than others or are there structural reasons that might account for any differences in marital rates?

11. Have we become more tolerant toward interracial relationships? Why or why not? Is the answer dependent on the racial or ethnic combination of the couple in question?

12. Do Asian Americans value education more than other racial or ethnic groups? Is this a positive stereotype or is it harmful to Asian Americans or other racial and ethnic groups in some way?

13. American culture subscribes heavily to the idea that with hard work, anyone can succeed. Do you think this is true? What should we glean from the successes of people like Barack Obama, Oprah Winfrey, or Bill Cosby? When figures like this promote meritocratic ideals, do you think that makes the American public cling harder to this notion? Why or why not?

14. Do you think that affirmative action is a good way to deal with racial or ethnic disparities in education or employment? Why or why not?

15. Consider the current debates over citizenship. Are our notions of citizenship based solely on documentation and paperwork? What other things might shape our understanding of who is and isn't a citizen or who should or shouldn't be a citizen?

16. Do you believe people are overly concerned with how we refer to racial or ethnic groups? Does it matter whether or not we use *African American* or *Black*, *Indian* or *Native American*, *Hispanic* or *Latino*?

17. Is it ever okay for non-Black groups to use the N-word? Why or why not?

18. Consider your campus community. Do students of different racial groups socialize with one another? Do you witness deep friendships across racial and ethnic lines? Why or why not?

19. Is it possible to be friends with someone of a different race and still be racist? Explain your answer.

20. What other questions would you add to this list?

References

Aries, E. (2008). *Race and class matters at an elite college*. Philadelphia, PA: Temple University Press.

Astin, A. W. (1993). *What matters in college? Four critical years revisited*. San Francisco, CA: Jossey-Bass.

Berger, P. L. (1963). *Invitation to sociology: A humanistic perspective*. New York, NY: Anchor Books.

Browne, M. N., & Keeley, S. (2001). *Asking the right questions: A guide to critical thinking*. Upper Saddle River, NJ: Prentice Hall.

Feagin, J. R. (2010). *The white racial frame: Centuries of racial framing and counter-framing*. New York, NY: Routledge.

Feagin, J. R., & Sikes, M. P. (1994). *Living with racism: The Black middle class experience*. Boston, MA: Beacon Press.

Feagin, J. R., & Sikes, M. P. (1995). How Black students cope with racism on White campuses. *The Journal of Blacks in Higher Education, 8*, 91–97.

Gans, H. (1979). Symbolic ethnicity: The future of ethnic groups and cultures in America. *Ethnic and Racial Studies, 2*, 1–20.

Grauerholz, L. (2007, Fall). Getting past ideology for effective teaching. *Sociological Viewpoints*, 15–28.

Omi, M., & Winant, H. (1994). *Racial formation in the U.S.: From the 1960s to the 1990s*. New York, NY: Routledge.

Kingkade, T. (2013, February 6). Duke University Kappa Sigma fraternity draws accusations of racism with "Asia Prime" party. *Huffington Post*. Retrieved from http://www.huffingtonpost.com/2013/02/06/duke-kappa-sigma-party_n_2630598.html

McIntosh, P. (2013). White privilege: Unpacking the invisible knapsack. In M. L. Andersen & P. H. Collins (Eds.), *Race, class, & gender: An anthology* (8th ed., pp. 49–53). Belmont, CA: Cengage Learning.

Pascarella, E. T., & Terenzini, P. T. (2005). *How college affects students: Volume 2: A third decade of research*. San Francisco, CA: Jossey-Bass.

Quan, K. (2013, February 7). Duke University fraternity suspended over Asian-themed "racist rager." *Time News Feed*. Retrieved from http://newsfeed.time.com/2013/02/07/duke-university-fraternity-suspended-over-asian-themed-racist-rager

Tatum, B. D. (1997). *Why are all the Black kids sitting together in the cafeteria?: And other conversations about race*. New York, NY: Basic Books.

Waters, M. C. (2013). Optional ethnicities: For Whites only? In M. L. Andersen & P. H. Collins (Eds.), *Race, class, & gender: An anthology* (pp. 209–217). Belmont, CA: Cengage Learning.

"What Is Racism Anyway?"

Understanding the Basics of Racism and Prejudice[1]

Beverly Daniel Tatum

Spelman College

> **Beverly Daniel Tatum** is the president of Spelman College in Atlanta, Georgia. For more than 20 years, Dr. Tatum has taught a course on the psychology of racism. She has also toured extensively, leading workshops on racial identity development and its impact in the classroom. Her latest book, *Can We Talk about Race? And Other Conversations in an Era of School Resegregation*, released in 2007, explores the social and educational implications of the growing racial isolation in public schools.

Early in my teaching career, a White student I knew asked me what I would be teaching the following semester. I mentioned that I would be teaching a course on racism. She replied, with some surprise in her voice, "Oh, is there still racism?" I assured her that indeed there was and suggested that she sign up for my course. Fifteen years later, after exhaustive media coverage of events such as the Rodney King beating, the Charles Stuart and Susan Smith cases, the O. J. Simpson trial, the appeal to racial prejudices in electoral politics, and the bitter debates about affirmative action and welfare reform, it seems hard to imagine that anyone

[1] This essay is an excerpt of Dr. Tatum's essay, "Defining Terms," Ch. 1 in *Why Are All the Black Kids Sitting Together in the Cafeteria?*" Copyright © January 17, 2003 Beverly Daniel Tatum. Reprinted by permission of Basic Books, a member of the Perseus Books Group.

would still be unaware of the reality of racism in our society. But in fact, in almost every audience I address, there is someone who will suggest that racism is a thing of the past. There is always someone who hasn't noticed the stereotypical images of people of color in the media, who hasn't observed the housing discrimination in their community, who hasn't read the newspaper articles about documented racial bias in lending practices among well-known banks, who isn't aware of the racial tracking pattern at the local school, who hasn't seen the reports of rising incidents of racially motivated hate crimes in America—in short, someone who hasn't been paying attention to issues of race. But if you are paying attention, the legacy of racism is not hard to see, and we are all affected by it.

The impact of racism begins early. Even in our preschool years, we are exposed to misinformation about people different from ourselves. Many of us grew up in neighborhoods where we had limited opportunities to interact with people different from our own families. When I ask my college students, "How many of you grew up in neighborhoods where most of the people were from the same racial group as your own?" almost every hand goes up. There is still a great deal of social segregation in our communities. Consequently, most of the early information we receive about "others"—people racially, religiously, or socioeconomically different from ourselves—does not come as the result of firsthand experience. The secondhand information we do receive has often been distorted, shaped by cultural stereotypes, and left incomplete.

Some examples will highlight this process. Several years ago one of my students conducted a research project investigating preschoolers' conceptions of Native Americans. Using children at a local day care center as her participants, she asked these three- and four-year-olds to draw a picture of a Native American. Most children were stumped by her request. They didn't know what a Native American was. But when she rephrased the question and asked them to draw a picture of an Indian, they readily complied. Almost every picture included one central feature: feathers. In fact, many of them also included a weapon—a knife or tomahawk— and depicted the person in violent or aggressive terms. Though this group of children, almost all of whom were White, did not live near a large Native American population and probably had had little if any personal interaction with American Indians, they all had internalized an image of what Indians were like. How did they know? Cartoon images, in particular the Disney movie *Peter Pan*, were cited by the children as their number-one source of information. At the age of three, these children already had a set of stereotypes in place. Though I would not describe three-year-olds as prejudiced, the stereotypes to which they have been exposed become the foundation for the adult prejudices so many of us have.

Sometimes the assumptions we make about others come not from what we have been told or what we have seen on television or in books, but rather from what we have *not* been told. The distortion of historical information about people of color leads young people (and older people, too) to make assumptions that may go unchallenged for a long time. Consider this conversation between two White students following a discussion about the cultural transmission of racism:

"Yeah, I just found out that Cleopatra was actually a Black woman."

"What?"

The first student went on to explain her newly learned information. The second student exclaimed in disbelief, "That can't be true. Cleopatra was beautiful!"

What had this young woman learned about who in our society is considered beautiful and who is not? Had she conjured up images of Elizabeth Taylor when she thought of Cleopatra? The new information her classmate had shared and her own deeply ingrained assumptions about who is beautiful and who is not were too incongruous to allow her to assimilate the information at that moment.

Omitted information can have similar effects. For example, another young woman, preparing to be a high school English teacher, expressed her dismay that she had never learned about any Black authors in any of her English courses. How was she to teach about them to her future students when she hadn't learned about them herself? A White male student in the class responded to this discussion with frustration in his response journal, writing "It's not my fault that Blacks don't write books." Had one of his elementary, high school, or college teachers ever told him that there were no Black writers? Probably not. Yet because he had never been exposed to Black authors, he had drawn his own conclusion that there were none.

Stereotypes, omissions, and distortions all contribute to the development of prejudice. *Prejudice* is a preconceived judgment or opinion, usually based on limited information. I assume that we all have prejudices, not because we want them, but simply because we are so continually exposed to misinformation about others. Though I have often heard students or workshop participants describe someone as not having "a prejudiced bone in his body," I usually suggest that they look again. Prejudice is one of the inescapable consequences of living in a racist society. Cultural racism—the cultural images and messages that affirm the assumed superiority of Whites and the assumed inferiority of people of color—is like smog in the air. Sometimes it is so thick it is visible, other times it is less apparent, but always, day in and day out, we are breathing it in. None of us would introduce ourselves as "smog-breathers" (and most of us don't want to be described as prejudiced), but if we live in a smoggy place, how can we avoid breathing the air? If we live in an environment in which we are bombarded with stereotypical images in the media, are frequently exposed to the ethnic jokes of friends and family members, and are rarely informed of the accomplishments of oppressed groups, we will develop the negative categorizations of those groups that form the basis of prejudice.

People of color as well as Whites develop these categorizations. Even a member of the stereotyped group may internalize the stereotypical categories about his or her own group to some degree. In fact, this process happens so frequently that it has a name, *internalized oppression.* Some of the consequences of believing the distorted messages about one's own group will be discussed in subsequent chapters.

Certainly some people are more prejudiced than others, actively embracing and perpetuating negative and hateful images of those who are different from themselves. When we claim to be free of prejudice, perhaps what we are really saying is that we are not hate-mongers. But none of us is completely innocent. Prejudice is an integral part of our socialization, and it is not our fault. Just as the preschoolers my student interviewed are not to blame for the negative messages they internalized, we are not at fault for the stereotypes, distortions, and omissions that shaped our thinking as we grew up.

To say that it is not our fault does not relieve us of responsibility, however. We may not have polluted the air, but we need to take responsibility, along with others, for cleaning it up. Each of us needs to look at our own behavior. Am I perpetuating and reinforcing the negative messages so pervasive in our culture, or am I seeking to challenge them? If I have not been exposed to positive images of marginalized groups, am I seeking them out, expanding my own knowledge base for myself and my children? Am I acknowledging and examining my own prejudices, my own rigid categorizations of others, thereby minimizing the adverse impact they might have on my interactions with those I have categorized? Unless we engage in these and other conscious acts of reflection and reeducation, we easily repeat the process with our children. We teach what we were taught. The unexamined prejudices of the parents are passed on to the children. It is not our fault, but it is our responsibility to interrupt this cycle.

Racism: A System of Advantage Based on Race

Many people use the terms *prejudice* and *racism* interchangeably. I do not, and I think it is important to make a distinction. In his book *Portraits of White Racism*, David Wellman (1977) argues convincingly that limiting our understanding of racism to prejudice does not offer a sufficient explanation for the persistence of racism. He defines *racism* as a "system of advantage based on race." In illustrating this definition, he provides example after example of how Whites defend their racial advantage—access to better schools, housing, jobs—even when they do not embrace overtly prejudicial thinking. Racism cannot be fully explained as an expression of prejudice alone (see Harris, Essay 23).

This definition of racism is useful because it allows us to see that racism, like other forms of oppression, is not only a personal ideology based on racial prejudice, but a *system* involving cultural messages and institutional policies and practices as well as the beliefs and actions of individuals. In the context of the United States, this system clearly operates to the advantage of Whites and to the disadvantage of people of color. Another related definition of racism, commonly used by antiracist educators and consultants, is *prejudice plus power*. Racial prejudice when combined with social power—access to social, cultural, and economic resources and decision-making—leads to the institutionalization of racist policies and practices. While I think this definition also captures the idea that racism is more than individual beliefs and attitudes, I prefer Wellman's definition because the idea of systematic advantage and disadvantage is critical to an understanding of how racism operates in American society.

In addition, I find that many of my White students and workshop participants do not feel powerful. Defining racism as prejudice plus power has little personal relevance. For some, their response to this definition is the following: "I'm not really prejudiced, and I have no power, so racism has nothing to do with me." However, most White people, if they are really being honest with themselves, can see that there are advantages to being White in the United States. Despite the current rhetoric about affirmative action and "reverse racism," every social indicator, from salary to life expectancy, reveals the advantages of being White.

The systematic advantages of being White are often referred to as White privilege. In a now well-known article, "White Privilege: Unpacking the Invisible Knapsack," Peggy McIntosh (1989), a White feminist scholar, identified a long list of societal privileges that she received simply because she was White. She did not ask for them, and it is important to note that she hadn't always noticed that she was receiving them. They included major and minor advantages. Of course she enjoyed greater access to jobs and housing. But she also was able to shop in department stores without being followed by suspicious salespeople and could always find appropriate hair care products and makeup in any drugstore. She could send her child to school confident that the teacher would not discriminate against him on the basis of race. She could also be late for meetings, and talk with her mouth full, fairly confident that these behaviors would not be attributed to the fact that she was White. She could express an opinion in a meeting or in print and not have it labeled the "White" viewpoint. In other words, she was more often than not viewed as an individual, rather than as a member of a racial group.

This article rings true for most White readers, many of whom may have never considered the benefits of being White. It's one thing to have enough awareness of racism to describe the ways that people of color are disadvantaged by it. But this new understanding of racism is more elusive. In very concrete terms, it means that if a person of color is the victim of housing discrimination, the apartment that would otherwise have been rented to that person of color is still available for a White person. The White tenant is, knowingly or unknowingly, the beneficiary of racism, a system of advantage based on race. The unsuspecting tenant is not to blame for the prior discrimination, but she benefits from it anyway.

For many Whites, this new awareness of the benefits of a racist system elicits considerable pain, often accompanied by feelings of anger and guilt. These uncomfortable emotions can hinder further discussion. We all like to think that we deserve the good things we have received, and that others, too, get what they deserve. Social psychologists call this tendency a "belief in a just world." Racism directly contradicts such notions of justice.

Understanding racism as a system of advantage based on race is antithetical to traditional notions of an American meritocracy. For those who have internalized this myth, this definition generates considerable discomfort. It is more comfortable simply to think of racism as a particular form of prejudice. Notions of power or privilege do not have to be addressed when our understanding of racism is constructed in that way.

The discomfort generated when a systemic definition of racism is introduced is usually quite visible in the workshops I lead. Someone in the group is usually quick to point out that this is not the definition you will find in most dictionaries. I reply, "Who wrote the dictionary?" I am not being facetious with this response. Whose interests are served by a "prejudice only" definition of racism? It is important to understand that the system of advantage is perpetuated when we do not acknowledge its existence.

Racism: For Whites Only?

Frequently someone will say, "You keep talking about White people. People of color can be racist, too." I once asked a White teacher what it would mean to her if a student or parent of color accused her of being racist. She said she would feel as though she had been punched in the stomach or called a "low-life scum." She is not alone in this feeling. The word racist holds a lot of emotional power. For many White people, to be called racist is the ultimate insult. The idea that this term might only be applied to Whites becomes highly problematic for after all, can't people of color be "low-life scum" too?

Of course, people of any racial group can hold hateful attitudes and behave in racially discriminatory and bigoted ways. We can all cite examples of horrible hate crimes which have been perpetrated by people of color as well as Whites. Hateful behavior is hateful behavior no matter who does it. But when I am asked, "Can people of color be racist?" I reply, "The answer depends on your definition of racism." If one defines racism as racial prejudice, the answer is yes. People of color can and do have racial prejudices. However, if one defines racism as a system of advantage based on race, the answer is no. People of color are not racist because they do not systematically benefit from racism. And equally important, there is no systematic cultural and institutional support or sanction for the racial bigotry of people of color. In my view, reserving the term *racist* only for behaviors committed by Whites in the context of a White-dominated society is a way of acknowledging the ever-present power differential afforded Whites by the culture and institutions that make up the system of advantage and continue to reinforce notions of White superiority. (Using the same logic, I reserve the word *sexist* for men. Though women can and do have gender-based prejudices, only men systematically benefit from sexism.)

Despite my best efforts to explain my thinking on this point, there are some who will be troubled, perhaps even incensed, by my response. To call the racially motivated acts of a person of color acts of racial bigotry and to describe similar acts committed by Whites as racist will make no sense to some people, including some people of color. To those, I will respectfully say, "We can agree to disagree." At moments like these, it is not agreement that is essential, but clarity. Even if you don't like the definition of racism I am using, hopefully you are now clear about what it is. If I also understand how you are using the term, our conversation can continue—despite our disagreement.

Another provocative question I'm often asked is "Are you saying all Whites are racist?" When asked this question, I again remember that White teacher's response, and I am conscious that perhaps the question I am really being asked is, "Are you saying all Whites are bad people?" The answer to that question is of course not. However, all White people, intentionally or unintentionally, do benefit from racism. A more relevant question is what are White people as individuals doing to interrupt racism? For many White people, the image of a racist is a hood-wearing Klan member or a name-calling Archie Bunker figure. These images represent what might be called *active racism*—blatant, intentional acts of racial bigotry and discrimination. *Passive racism* is more subtle and can be seen in the collusion of laughing when a racist joke is told, of letting exclusionary hiring practices go unchallenged, of accepting as appropriate the omissions of people of color from the curriculum, and of avoiding difficult race-related issues. Because racism is so ingrained in the fabric of American institutions, it is easily self-perpetuating. All that is required to maintain it is business as usual.

I sometimes visualize the ongoing cycle of racism as a moving walkway at the airport. Active racist behavior is equivalent to walking fast on the conveyor belt. The person engaged in active racist behavior has identified with the ideology of White supremacy and is moving with it. Passive racist behavior is equivalent to standing still on the walkway. No overt effort is being made, but the conveyor belt moves the bystanders along to the same destination as those who are actively walking. Some of the bystanders may feel the motion of the conveyor belt, see the active racists ahead of them, and choose to turn around, unwilling to go to the same destination as the White supremacists. But unless they are walking actively in the opposite direction at a speed faster than the conveyor belt—unless they are actively antiracist—they will find themselves carried along with the others.

So, not all Whites are actively racist. Many are passively racist. Some, though not enough, are actively antiracist. The relevant question is not whether all Whites are racist, but how we can move more White people from a position of active or passive racism to one of active antiracism? The task of interrupting racism is obviously not the task of Whites alone. But the fact of White privilege means that Whites have greater access to the societal institutions in need of transformation. To whom much is given, much is required.

It is important to acknowledge that while all Whites benefit from racism, they do not all benefit equally. Other factors, such as socioeconomic status, gender, age, religious affiliation, sexual orientation, mental and physical ability also play a role in our access to social influence and power. A White woman on welfare is not privileged to the same extent as a wealthy White heterosexual man. In her case, the systematic disadvantages of sexism and classism intersect with her White privilege, but the privilege is still there. This point was brought home to me in a 1994 study conducted by a Mount Holyoke graduate student, Phyllis Wentworth. Wentworth interviewed a group of female college students, who were both older than their peers and were the first members of their families to attend college, about the pathways that lead them to college. All of the women interviewed were White, from working-class backgrounds, from families where women were expected to graduate from high school and get married or get a job. Several had experienced abusive relationships and other personal difficulties prior to coming to college. Yet their experiences were punctuated by "good luck" stories of apartments obtained without a deposit, good jobs offered without experience or extensive reference checks, and encouragement provided by willing mentors. While the women acknowledged their good fortune, none of them discussed their Whiteness. They had not considered the possibility that being White had worked in their favor and helped give them the benefit of the doubt at critical junctures. This study clearly showed that even under difficult circumstances, White privilege was still operating.

It is also true that not all people of color are equally targeted by racism. We all have multiple identities that shape our experience. I can describe myself as a light-skinned, well-educated, heterosexual, able-bodied, Christian African American woman raised in a middle-class suburb. As an African American woman, I am systematically disadvantaged by race and by gender, but I systematically receive benefits in the other categories, which then mediate my experience of racism and sexism. When one is targeted by multiple isms—racism, sexism, classism, heterosexism, ableism, anti-Semitism, ageism—in whatever combination, the effect is intensified. The particular combination of racism and classism in many communities of color is life-threatening. Nonetheless, when I, the middle-class Black mother of two sons, read another story about a Black man's unlucky encounter with a White police officer's deadly force, I am reminded that racism by itself can kill.

Suggested Additional Resources

Lewis, A. (2003). *Race in the schoolyard: Negotiating the color line in classrooms and communities.* Piscataway, NJ: Rutgers University Press.

Tatum, B. D. (1997). *Why are all the Black kids sitting together in the cafeteria? And other conversations about race.* New York, NY: Basic Books.

Tatum, B. D. (2007). *Can we talk about race? And other conversations in an era of school resegregation.* Boston, MA: Beacon Press.

Questions for Further Discussion

1. What was the level of racial segregation in your own home community growing up? Does it fit the pattern identified by Tatum? Why or why not? What impact do you think this had on you?

2. What is *internalized oppression* as defined by this author? Why is this an important concept in the study of race and racism?

3. What is the difference between *fault* and *responsibility*? Why does the author argue that this difference is significant?

4. What are some of the costs of racism for White people? Do you think these are compelling? Why or why not?

Reaching Beyond the Color Line

1. Given the author's discussion of the impact of early education on ideas about race and racial groups, identify three or four kids in your social network (middle school or younger) and ask them what they know about Native Americans. What do their responses tell you about the content of their education?

2. In her piece, Tatum urges all of us to look at our own behavior and assess whether we are perpetuating and reinforcing negative messages about race or challenging them. Answer this question honestly, sharing your answers in a small, diverse discussion group. Is there anything uncomfortable about asking yourself this question or sharing your response? If so, why? What does this exercise tell you about the nature of race and racial dynamics in American society?

References

McIntosh, P. (1989, July/August). White privilege: Unpacking the invisible knapsack. *Peace and Freedom*, pp. 10–12.

Wellman, D. T. (1977). *Portraits of White racism*. Cambridge, UK: Cambridge University Press.

"They Should Get Over It!"

The End of Racial Discrimination?

Matthew W. Hughey

University of Connecticut

Matthew W. Hughey, PhD, is an associate professor of sociology and affiliate member of the Institute for African American Studies at the University of Connecticut. He is the author of, among other works, *White Bound: White Nationalists, White Antiracists, and the Shared Meanings of Race* (Stanford University Press, 2012). His research appears in academic journals like *Du Bois Review, Ethnic and Racial Studies, Ethnicities, Journal of Contemporary Ethnography, Social Problems,* and *Symbolic Interaction*. (Dr. Hughey's website is www.matthewhughey.com).

> *One is astonished in the study of history at the recurrence of the idea that evil must be forgotten, distorted, skimmed over. . . . The difficulty, of course, with this philosophy is that history loses its value as an incentive and example; it paints perfect man and noble nations, but it does not tell the truth.*
>
> –W. E. B. Du Bois, *Black Reconstruction in America,* 1935, p. 591

2014 was a watershed year for the United States. 395 years since the first Africans were forcibly brought to what is now Virginia, 149 years after the passage of the Thirteenth Amendment that curtailed slavery, and 50 years after the Civil Rights Act of 1964, the nation has witnessed nearly two full terms of its first Black presidency.

In reporting the momentous event in 2008, *The New York Times* ran the headline, "OBAMA. Racial Barrier Falls in Heavy Turnout" (Nagourney, 2008). *USA Today* penned the words, "The principle that all men are created equal has never been more than a remote eventuality in the quest for the presidency . . . that ideal is no longer relegated to someday. Someday is now" (Geller, 2008). And *The Wall Street Journal* (WSJ) boldly declared, "One promise of his victory is that perhaps we can put to rest the myth of racism as a barrier to achievement in this splendid country" ("President-elect Obama," 2008). Many interpreted the election of a Black man to the White House as the ultimate indication that the United States had become "post-racial" (Parks & Hughey, 2011; see also Logan, Essay 17). Many possess (or are frequently encouraged to hold) the opinion that racial inequality, racial segregation, and racial discrimination are relics of the past. Accordingly, when some people speak of racial discrimination in the search for employment, when people of color discuss the pride in their racial group for overcoming past oppression, or when Whites admit racial privilege or advantage when compared to some of their non-White counterparts, it seems that others often doubt their sincerity, believe they make a big deal out of nothing, or simply say: "They should get over it!"

Here, I challenge the naive belief that racial inequality, segregation, and discrimination are things of the past. I also argue that while race is strictly a social (rather than biological) reality, it is indeed a *social fact* that holds very real consequences for our identities, interests, institutions, ideologies, and interactions.

Who Believes the Hype?

In today's supposedly color-blind or post-racial world, more and more people seem to interpret discussions of racism as little more than non-Whites being "hyper-sensitive" or as "playing the race card"—what sociologist Eduardo Bonilla-Silva (2010, p. 29) calls the *minimization of racism*. In our contemporary moment, it is quite common to believe racial discrimination has all but disappeared and that race relations are now relatively unproblematic. This belief is reflected in polls and surveys gauging racial attitudes and trends.

Contemporary Racial Attitudes

In January of 2009, just after Barack Obama was first inaugurated as president, 45% of respondents in a NBC/WSJ poll said that Obama's election improved race relations, whereas 39% said it didn't change race relations (Murray, 2012). In another question, 72% said that race relations were "good" in the United States, which was up considerably from 2007 (58%) and 1995 (34%). In a larger, more representative sample by the General Social Survey (GSS),[1] adults were asked, "Do you agree strongly, agree somewhat, neither agree nor disagree, disagree somewhat,

---

[1] Run by the National Opinion Research Center, the survey has been conducted every year from 1972 to 1994 (except in 1979, 1981, and 1992), and since 1994 has been conducted every two years. The GSS contains race-related questions that provide a brief overview of key attitudes in the United States. Unfortunately, many of the responses do not include responses from racial groups other than Black and White (some include responses from the category "Other").

or disagree strongly with the following statement: Irish, Italians, Jewish and many other minorities overcame prejudice and worked their way up. Blacks should do the same without special favors." In 1994, 77.8% of Whites and 48.4% of Blacks either strongly or somewhat agreed with the statement. By 2006, 76% of Whites and 54.9% of Blacks either strongly or somewhat agreed with the statement (see Figure 3.1).

The GSS also asked, "On the average (Negroes/Blacks/African-Americans) have worse jobs, income, and housing than white people. Do you think these differences are mainly due to discrimination?" In 1985, 41.4% of Whites and 78.8% of Blacks said yes to this question. But by 2006, only 31.3% of Whites and 59.2% of Blacks answered yes (see Figure 3.2).

And finally, the GSS asked, "In the past few years, do you think conditions for black people have improved, gotten worse, or stayed about the same?" In 1994, 58.4% of Whites said conditions had improved, whereas 33.8% of Blacks said that. Just 8 years later in 2002, 68.8% of Whites and 58.4% of Blacks said that conditions had improved (see Figure 3.3).

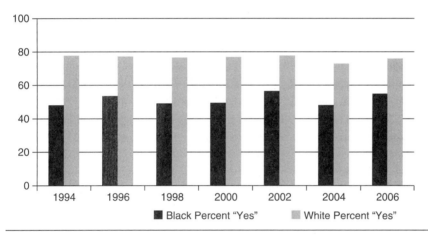

Figure 3.1 Blacks Should Overcome Prejudice Without Special Favors?

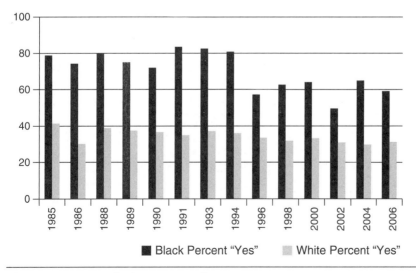

Figure 3.2 Are Blacks Worse Off Due to Discrimination?

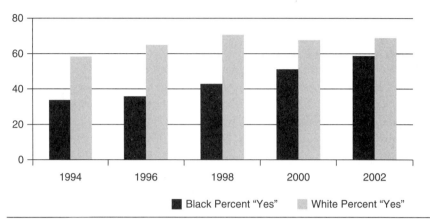

Figure 3.3 Have Conditions for Blacks Improved in Recent Years?

Responses to these polls and GSS questions provide a quick snapshot of a general trend: a growing belief that race does (and should) matter less than it used to in determining the quality of life for all people, and particularly for Black Americans. Interestingly, Blacks and Whites have come to share this general orientation over the years, with Blacks' attitudes moving closer to Whites.[2] These converging and positive attitude changes may be based on a range of evidence that indicates genuine improvement in some areas, such as the decline of overt forms of racial discrimination like the separate but equal laws and policies of the pre-1965 Jim Crow era.

If we turn again to Figure 3.1, we see a robust belief among Whites (and among increasing numbers of Blacks) that the Black experience with prejudice is no different than the experience of other White ethnics like Irish, Italians, and Jews. The attitude reveals a systemic lack of support for "special favors" for Blacks—the connotation being that if the Irish, Italians, and Jews worked hard, assimilated, and attained the "American dream" without "special favors" or "handouts," then so should Blacks. Accordingly, when reexamining Figure 3.2, we see that approximately two thirds of Whites (and again, increasing numbers of Blacks) believe that Black–White inequality is due to sources other than racial discrimination. Moreover, Figure 3.3 indicates that both Blacks and Whites are more likely to believe that Black social conditions are rapidly improving. These three measures of racial attitudes show that Whites (and increasing numbers of Blacks) believe that (1) Black and White experiences are similar, (2) Black inequality is not the result of discrimination, and (3) things are getting better for Blacks. Taken together, these attitudes altogether hinge on the assumption that racial discrimination is long gone. In this sense, these select GSS and polling questions do not gauge what *is,* but about what people think *might or should be.*

Given that insight, if we examine additional answers from the GSS, we get a more complete picture of people's attitudes toward discrimination. For example, Figure 3.4 below shows the results to the following question: "Do Blacks tend to be unintelligent

---

[2] I present this conclusion with a caveat. Survey methods are often singled out for portraying too rosy a picture of race relations. However, there are many survey measures (even within GSS) that demonstrate still entrenched racial animosities in addition to racist beliefs surrounding people of color's inherent moral dysfunctions and pathologies (cf. Bobo, Charles, Krysan, & Simmons, forthcoming).

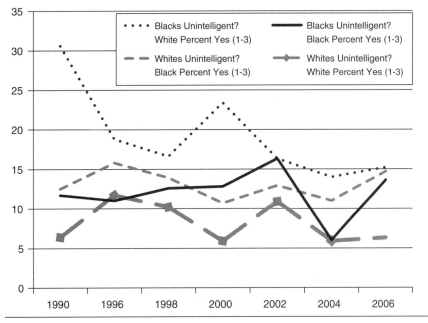

Figure 3.4 Are Whites/Blacks Unintelligent (1–3)?

or tend to be intelligent?"[3] Respondents then place their answer on a scale from 1 to 7 in which 1 equals "unintelligent," 7 equals "intelligent," and 4 is "neutral."

When asked if Whites are unintelligent, no more than 12% of Whites answered 1, 2, or 3. Compare that with the finding that no less than 14% of Whites answered 1, 2, or 3 for Blacks being unintelligent. This means that a nontrivial proportion of people believe that Whites are more intelligent than Blacks.

The GSS also asked about whether Whites or Blacks were hardworking or lazy. Respondents placed their answer on a scale from 1 to 7 in which 1 equals "hard-working," 7 equals "lazy," and 4 is "neutral" (see Figure 3.5).[4] Again, while the rates are trending toward neutral for Whites' attitudes on Black laziness, the last indication shows that almost of 34% of Whites answered 5, 6, or 7 (the side of the Likert scale for "lazy"). Taken together, these data show a robust belief in Black intellectual inferiority and laziness, especially when compared to White attitudes on White intellectualism and hard work ethics.

Additional answers to GSS questions reveal even more troubling attitudes that support discrimination. In 2008, 28% of Whites expressed the belief that it is an individual homeowner's right to discriminate on the basis of race when selling a

---

[3] This question is posed in two parts. First, there is a prequestion, "Do people in these groups tend to be unintelligent or tend to be intelligent?" Then respondents were asked, "Where would you rate Whites in general on this scale?" Then respondents were asked, "Blacks?" The answers are responses to a Likert scale series of answers of 1 through 7 (1 equals "unintelligent" and 7 equals "intelligent").

[4] This question was also posed in two parts. First, there is a prequestion, "The second set of characteristics asks if people in the group tend to be hard working or if they tend to be lazy." The literal question was then asked, "Where would you rate whites in general on this scale?" Then respondents were asked, "Blacks?" The answers are responses to a Likert scale series of answers of 1 through 7 (1 equals "lazy" and 7 equals "hardworking").

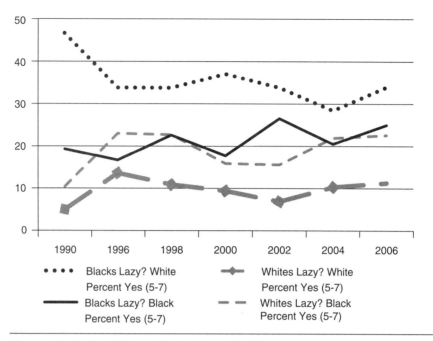

Figure 3.5 Are Whites/Blacks Lazy (5–7)?

home (General Social Survey [GSS], 2010). As recently as the 1990s, almost 40% of Whites objected to sending their children to a mostly Black school, and nearly 20% of Whites opposed sending their children to a school that is at least half Black.[5] And when asked if they were willing to live in a neighborhood where "half of your neighbors were blacks," 90% of Whites said they would not in 1990, and by 2008 only 20% said they would not. While this latter finding indicates some progress toward equality, it still means that 1 in 5 Whites do not favor living in a majority Black neighborhood today (GSS, 2010). Additionally, the prevalence and persistence of racial segregation stems largely from Whites' unwillingness to live in neighborhoods with high numbers of non-Whites (Card, Mas, & Rothstein, 2007). Research indicates that when White neighborhoods experience an influx of non-White residents, Whites will move away. That is, the tipping point of non-White residents to cause "White flight" ranges from 5% to 30% (Card et al., 2007).

In 1990, 65% of Whites opposed Black–White marriage. That number has also dropped over the years, but by 2010, 1 out of 4 Whites responded that they either "opposed" or "strongly opposed" a close relative or family member marrying a Black person (GSS, 2010; see also Khanna, Essay 11, and Harris, Essay 23). Taken as a whole, survey research on racial attitudes indicates that many Whites (at rates that still outpace non-White groups) continue to endorse segregationist and discriminatory views and practices. And so, we must be cautious with optimistic interpretations and investigate the continued significance of race in important areas of social life like housing, education, and the mass media.

---

[5] The GSS dropped these questions after 1996, but other research indicates that Whites still defend that attitude, consistent with the view that White segregation and discrimination attitudes are not simply an abstract racial prejudice but a protection of White resources (cf. Bobo & Tuan, 2006; Bobo, Charles, Krysan, & Simmons, forthcoming).

The Enduring Nature of Racial Discrimination

Racial Segregation in Housing

Housing segregation is on the decline. The index of dissimilarity (D) is a measure of segregation between two groups, and ranges from "0" for perfect integration to "100" for total segregation. If a metropolitan area is 40% Black and 60% White, a D of 100 indicates that every neighborhood (measured by U.S. census tract) was either 100% Black or 100% White. For example, in 2009, the Chicago–Naperville–Joliet metropolitan area had a D of 78, which means that 78% of the White or Black population would have to move to another U.S. census tract in order to have complete integration (D of zero). For the past three decades, the average level of segregation has fallen by approximately 10 points between 1970 and 1980 and another 10 points between 1980 and 2000 (Logan, Stults, & Farley, 2004). As of 2010, the index of dissimilarity was at its lowest level in a century (see Figure 3.6) (Glaeser & Vigdor, 2012). This trend, some argue, is largely the result of the Fair Housing Act (title VIII of the Civil Rights Act of 1968), whereby people of color are now less likely to be "redlined"[6] by realtors or denied housing loans by bank officials.

While the practice of overt racial housing segregation has declined on average, the largest cities in the United States remain highly segregated (Massey, Rothwell, & Thurston, 2009). Moreover, the often-hailed decline in racial segregation between 1980 and 2000 was the result not of a growth in mixed Black and White neighborhoods, but in the growth of multiethnic neighborhoods (Friedman, 2008). Discrimination appears to hold in place the remaining segregation. Between 2000 and 2002, the Department of Housing and Urban Development found that housing discrimination against Blacks, Latinos, Asians, and Native Americans (measured by almost 5,500 paired tests[7] in nearly 30 metropolitan locations) was rampant. Blacks

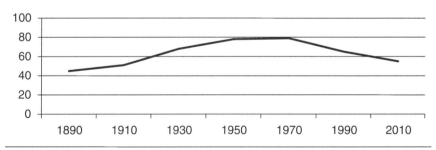

Figure 3.6 Index of Dissimilarity (Black/Nonblack Segregation)

---

[6] In the housing market, *redlining* is the practice of denying certain racial groups access to certain neighborhoods. The term was coined to refer to the practice of marking a red line on a map to delineate the area where banks would not invest or give loans to people of color.

[7] *Paired tests or audit studies* consist of sending in a White tester and a minority tester to seek housing and comparing their different outcomes.

and Latinos experienced the greatest and most consistent discrimination in housing searches, with Blacks encountering discrimination 20% of the time and Latinos encountering discrimination 25% of the time (Turner & Ross, 2003; Turner, Ross, Gaister, & Yinger, 2002).

As compared to similar White pairs, Black pairs received less information about units, fewer opportunities to view units, less assistance with financing, and experienced increased "steering" into poor neighborhoods with higher proportions of non-White residents (Pager & Shepherd, 2008). Such dynamics have created a situation in which, in 2012, the average White lives in a 78% White neighborhood (Glaeser & Vigdor, 2012). Even after housing is procured, research indicates that non-Whites are more likely than Whites to receive harassment or physical threats by managers or neighbors and are often subject to arbitrary and unequal enforcement of residential association's rules (Roscigno, 2007). Additionally, people of color are much more likely to be the targets of predatory, or subprime loans—loans typically made to borrowers with subprime credit histories, which carry higher or adjustable interest rates that soon rise dramatically—and increase the risk of home foreclosure. As Robert Stroup, Director of the Economic Justice Program at the NAACP Legal Defense and Educational Fund stated, "It's almost as if subprime lenders put a circle around neighborhoods of color and say, 'This is where we're going to do our thing'" (Fernandez, 2007).

Inequality in Education

In terms of education, many preach the decline of racial discrimination by pointing to a weakening of tracking by race. *Tracking* is the practice of taking students by racial group and placing them into stratified educational tracks (series of coursework) in which non-Whites are predominantly placed in lower ability classrooms where they receive a less rigorous and "highly repetitive" curriculum (Useem, 1990, p. 43). From 1999 to 2008, the total number of Black and Latino students taking an advanced placement (AP) exam tripled—from 94,000 to 318,000 students (Aud, Fox, & KewalRamani, 2010). Also, from 1998 to 2008, the population of SAT test takers saw increased participation among Black and Latino students. Latino students were 9% of the SAT in 1998 and 13% in 2008, while Black students were 11% of ACT test takers in 1998 and 14% in 2008 (Aud et al., 2010). Moreover, the number of Blacks with college degrees increased dramatically between 2000 and 2010 (U.S. Census Bureau, 2012). Forty-eight percent more Blacks (+25 in age) held at least a bachelor's degree by the end of the decade. That trend means that in 2010, 18.2 of every 100 U.S. Blacks in that age bracket (+25) had a bachelor's degree, compared to 14.3 of every 100 in 2000.

A closer look at education shows that racial discrimination still runs rampant. High achieving Black students are still less likely to be placed in college preparatory and advanced placement or honors courses than their White counterparts (Fenning & Rose, 2007; Kozol, 2006). Stark differences in the resources and quality of predominantly White and non-White schools still exist. More and better resources in White schools are believed to largely determine the high rates of high school graduation for Whites (Mickelson, 2003). Moreover, the 1978 to 2008 test scores for elementary and middle school students (what largely determines tracking) fluctuated in racial disparities (reaching the greatest point of equality in the 1980s when schools were most integrated) and have since risen in inequality along with schools' recent resegregation (Barton & Coley, 2010). So too, the rising rate of racial resegregation maps onto class inequality: by 2005, more than 60% of Black and Latino students attended high poverty schools, compared with 30% of Asians and 18% of Whites (Orfield & Lee, 2005, p. 18).

Racial Stereotypes in the Mass Media

As recently as the 1940s and 1950s, televisual media images were decidedly White, and the types of media images allowed for people of color were explicitly demeaning and overtly racist (Leab, 1975). By the 1960s, coverage of the civil rights movement brought hard-hitting issues of race and racism into White American living rooms. By the 1970s, "blaxploitation" films marketed a strong and independent image of Black confrontations with White racism, from Pam Grier's performances as "Foxy Brown" to Richard Roundtree as the indomitable "Shaft." This "Black-as-cool" image ushered in 1980s programs like *The Cosby Show* in which Black characters were not always regulated to criminals and hustlers, but were now middle-class doctors, lawyers, professors, and college students (Gray, 1995). In the 1990s, Black and White characters became on-screen friends and partners, in films like *Silver Streak, 48 Hrs., Beverly Hills Cop,* and *Lethal Weapon* (Donalson, 2005). And by the 2000s, people of color were playing strong, independent, and powerful characters, even that of God. Many translate such film and television diversity as evidence for the decline of racial discrimination in Hollywood and the media as a whole.

While televisual mass media has become more racially diverse over the past century, one must note that such visibility is not a guarantee of legitimacy or decency. People of color are frequently portrayed in negative roles associated with criminality, immorality, and laziness at rates much higher than Whites (Entman & Rojecki, 2001). Even strong and God-like, non-White characters often revolve around the White characters and hold a tone of contented servitude whose sole purpose is to redeem Whites (Hughey, 2009). When White characters play the "savior," they often interact with caricatured people of color that embody a host of racial stereotypes: from out-of-wedlock Latinas to Asian gangsters and their hand-wringing girlfriends to Black drug-dealers and hip-hop inspired dancers (Hughey, 2010).

Positive roles for people of color, especially Blacks, are not often rewarded. Between 1954 and 2012, only eighteen Black men and nine Black women were nominated for an Oscar for Best Actor or Actress in a Leading Role. Of those 28, only five received the coveted award—for roles playing a divine character sent to solve White problems: Sidney Poitier as a traveling handyman in *Lilies of the Field* (1963), Denzel Washington as a corrupt cop in *Training Day* (2001), Halle Berry as a hypersexual and abusive mother in *Monster's Ball* (2001), Jamie Foxx as musician Ray Charles in *Ray* (2004), and Forest Whitaker as the tyrannical dictator Idi Amin in *The Last King of Scotland* (2006).

There has also been a flood of overt racial discrimination in new media technology, from Facebook, to YouTube, to online news sites where discourse has come to resemble antebellum era–style racism (Hughey & Daniels, 2013). On the Internet, racism seems to erupt in discussions of events not overtly about race. And after the reelection of Barack Obama in 2012, researchers found a preponderance of Twitter users that tweeted words like *Obama, re-elected,* or *won* in conjunction with racist references, such as *nigger* or *monkey*. They geocoded the tweets to find that Alabama and Mississippi had the highest levels of racist discourse, followed closely by Georgia, Louisiana, and Tennessee. Yet, nearly as high levels of racism were also found in North Dakota, Utah, Missouri, Oregon, and Minnesota (Garber, 2012). Even on established and respected newspaper websites like *The New York Times* and *Wall Street Journal,* the presence of racial invective and stereotypes on comment fields are rampant (Hughey, 2012). Such dynamics may contribute to the famed "digital divide" rather than a divide over resources or knowledge (as it is often understood); the racial discrimination on mainstream websites may drive people of color away from digital technology (absence) or to safer sites (segregation) (Brock, 2006).

Conclusion

Despite evidence to the contrary, many Whites believe that they are unfairly victimized by race. In a recent study, Whites reported that racism against them had significantly increased while racism against Blacks deceased by the same margin. More and more Whites seem to see racism as a zero-sum game that they are now losing (Norton & Sommers, 2011). Some Whites are backlashing against earlier gains of the civil rights movement and believe that people of color are unfairly reaping social benefits at their expense. While this attitude is shared by an increasing number of mainstream Whites, some organize these worldviews into violent and dangerous groups like neo-Nazis, Klansmen, neo-Confederates, and White Nationalists—groups that have increased by 69% since 2000, and an astounding 755% (149 to 1,274) in the first three years (2008–2011) of the Obama administration (Southern Poverty Law Center, 2011). Many of these groups preach a message not just of overt racial hatred, but subtle insinuations that people of color are less than human and that their lower social status is due to genetic or cultural inability to learn, self-motivate, or act ethically.

The dehumanization of people of color is not just the product of card-carrying White supremacists; it is manifest in sundry locations throughout our society and takes aim at non-Whites (particularly Blacks and Latinos) regardless of their status or social power. For example, consider two Black men: President Barack Obama and Trayvon Martin. In regard to the former, during his candidacy and two presidential terms he was depicted as a monkey, an African tribal "savage" with a bone through his nose, and placed on a faux "food stamp" with pictures of KFC fried chicken, watermelon, spare ribs, and Kool-Aid—historical stereotypes associated with Black people (Hughey & Parks, 2014). Trayvon Martin was a 17-year-old, unarmed Black male who, under Florida's "stand your ground" laws, was shot and killed while walking through his gated neighborhood community while carrying a bag of skittles and a fruit drink, and wearing a hooded sweatshirt. His shooter described him as "cutting in-between houses . . . walking very leisurely . . . [and] looking at all the houses" (Fox News, 2012; see Ray, Essay 7 for further discussion). Shortly after Martin's death, Obama mentioned: "If I had a son, he'd look like Trayvon." By the next day, an Internet vendor was selling gun targets that mimicked Trayvon Martin's hoodie and his bag of Skittles—the vendor sold the entire inventory within a week (Coates, 2012). Such incidents demonstrate the continuing significance of race and the prescient power of anti-Black sentiment as a life-threatening practice, shared ideology, and consumer product.

Despite people's either well-intentioned hopes or their most honest delusions, racial discrimination is quite real and still a cornerstone of American social structure. Whether we look at survey attitudes, housing, education, the media, the White House, or gated communities—race matters in people's everyday lives. The persistence of racial disparities and discrimination across these multiple domains are intimately related and comprise an integrated system that shapes our ideologies, interests, institutions, interactions, and identities. But this should come as no surprise to those equipped with a robust sociological imagination that allows them to see through the smoke and mirrors of our now dominant "color-blind" discourse.

Suggested Additional Resources

Bonilla-Silva, E. (1997). Rethinking racism: Toward a structural interpretation. *American Sociological Review, 62*(3), 465–480.

Pager, D., & Shepherd, H. (2008). The sociology of discrimination: Racial discrimination in employment, housing, credit, and consumer markets. *Annual Review of Sociology, 34,* 181–209.

Parks, G. S., & Hughey, M. W. (2011). *The Obamas and a (post)racial America?* New York, NY: Oxford University Press.

Reskind, B. (2012). The race discrimination system. *Annual Review of Sociology, 38,* 17–35.

Questions for Further Discussion

1. Why do many people argue that society is racially equal, despite evidence to the contrary? What effect does this argument and belief have on efforts to bring about actual racial equality?

2. How do we change racial attitudes?

3. How should we best combat racial inequality in housing and education?

4. How can you explain the simultaneous presence of both racial inequality and discrimination (particularly anti-Black discrimination) and election of Barack Obama in 2008 and 2012?

Reaching Beyond the Color Line

1. Go to "Race 2012" (http://video.pbs.org/video/2289501021/) and watch the video. Then go to "Ethnic Studies in Arizona" (http://video.pbs.org/video/1699634973) and watch the video. In thinking about these two videos, answer the following question: How does the (not) recognizing of racial inequality and discrimination shape political debates, policy recommendations, laws, and leadership? In your answer, be sure to incorporate the debate over Arizona's law that bans the teaching of "ethnic studies" and what that debate signals about the future of race in the United States.

2. Go to "Where Race Lives" (http://www.pbs.org/race/006_WhereRaceLives/006_00-home.htm). Read all three stories: "Uncle Sam Lends a Hand," "A Tale of Two Families," and "The Downward Spiral." After reading these three stories, answer the following question: Does everyone have the same access to home ownership, good schools, and resources? In your answer, be sure to examine how government policies and past discrimination have made generating wealth easier for some Americans than others.

3. Go to "Gordon K. Hirabayashi" (http://www.historylink.org/index.cfm?DisplayPage=output.cfm&file_id=2070). Read about Hirabayashi and answer the following question: How has the nation rationalized the restriction of civil and human rights of citizens by race? In your answer, be sure to discuss not only the case of Japanese Internment camps during WWII, but more recent acts of discrimination, such as African American racial profiling by law enforcement or Middle Eastern, Arab, and Muslim discrimination in the post-9/11 era.

References

American Society of Newspaper Editors. (2012). *Total and minority newsroom employment declines in 2011 but loss continues to stabilize.* Retrieved from http://asne.org/content.asp?pl=121&sl=122&contentid=122

Aud, S. A., Fox, M. A., & KewalRamani, A. (2010). *Status and trends in the education of racial and ethnic groups* (NCES 2010015). Washington, DC: U.S. Department of Education, National Center for Education Statistics.

Barton, P. E., & Coley, R. J. (2010). *The Black-White achievement gap: When progress stopped.* Princeton, NJ: Educational Testing Service.

Bobo, L., Charles, C. Z., Krysan, M., & Simmons, A. D. (forthcoming). The real record on racial attitudes. In P. L. Marsden (Ed.), *Social trends in the United States, 1972–2008: Evidence from the General Social Survey.* Princeton, NJ: Princeton University Press.

Bobo, L., & Tuan, M. (2006). *Prejudice in politics: Group position, public opinion, and the Wisconsin treaty rights dispute.* Cambridge, MA: Harvard University Press.

Bonilla-Silva, E. (2010). *Racism without racists: Color-blind racism and racial inequality in contemporary America.* Lanham, MD: Rowman & Littlefield.

Brock, A. (2006). "Who do you think you are?" Race, representation and rhetorics in online spaces. *Poroi, 6*(1). Retrieved from http://ir.uiowa.edu/cgi/viewcontent.cgi?article=1013&context=poroi

Card, D., Mas, A., & Rothstein, J. (2007). Tipping and the dynamics of segregation. *Quarterly Journal of Economics, 123*(1), 177–218.

Coates, T. (2012, September). Fear of a Black president. *The Atlantic*. Retrieved from http://www.theatlantic.com/magazine/archive/2012/09/fear-of-a-black-president/309064

Donalson, M. (2005). *Masculinity in the interracial buddy film*. Jefferson, NC: McFarland & Company.

Du Bois, W. E. B. (1935). *Black reconstruction in America, 1860–1880*. New York, NY: Russell and Russell.

Entman, R., & Rojecki, A. (2001). *The Black image in the White mind*. Chicago, IL: University of Chicago Press.

Fenning, P., & Rose, J. (2007). Overrepresentation of African American students in exclusionary discipline. *Urban Education, 42,* 536–559.

Fernandez, M. (2007, October). Study finds disparities in mortgages by race. *The New York Times*. Retrieved from http://www.nytimes.com/2007/10/15/nyregion/15subprime.html?pagewanted=all

Fox News. (18 July 2012). *Exclusive: George Zimmerman breaks silence on "Hannity."* http://video.foxnews.com/v/1741879195001

Friedman, S. (2008). Do declines in residential segregation mean stable neighborhood racial integration in metropolitan America? A research note. *Social Science Research, 37*(3), 920–933.

Garber, M. (2012, November 9). Where America's racist tweets come from. *The Atlantic*. Retrieved from http://www.theatlantic.com/technology/archive/2012/11/where-americas-racist-tweets-come-from/265006

Geller, A. (2008, November 5). Obama's moment also a major juncture in US history. *USA Today*. Retrieved from http://www.usatoday.com/news/politics/2008-06-03-2497141011_x.htm

General Social Survey. (1972–2006). *The national data program for the sciences*. Chicago, IL: University of Chicago.

Glaeser, E., & Vigdor, J. (2012). The end of the segregated century: Racial separation in America's neighborhoods, 1890–2010. *Civic Report* 66. New York, NY: The Manhattan Institute for Policy Research.

Gray, H. (1995). *Watching race: Television and the struggle for "Blackness."* Minneapolis: University of Minnesota Press.

Hughey, M. W. (2009). Cinethetic racism: White redemption and Black stereotypes in "magical negro" films. *Social Problems, 56*(3), 543–577.

Hughey, M. W. (2010). The White savior film and reviewers' reception. *Symbolic Interaction, 33*(3), 475–496.

Hughey, M. W. (2012). Show me your papers! Obama's birth and the Whiteness of belonging. *Qualitative Sociology, 35*(2), 163–181.

Hughey, M. W., & Daniels, J. (2013). Racist comments at online news sites: A methodological dilemma for discourse analysis. *Media, Culture, and Society 35*(3): 332–347.

Hughey, M. W., & Parks, G. S. (2014). *The wrongs of the right: Race and the Republican party in the age of Obama*. New York, NY: New York University Press.

Kozol, J. (2006). *Savage inequalities: Children in America's schools*. New York, NY: Crown.

Leab, D. J. (1975). *From Sambo to Superspade: The Black experience in motion pictures*. Boston, MA: Houghton Mifflin.

Logan, J. R., Stults, B., & Farley, R. (2004). Segregation of minorities in the metropolis: Two decades of change. *Demography, 41*(1), 1–22.

Massey, D., Rothwell, J., & Thurston, D. (2009). The changing bases of segregation in the United States. *Annual American Academy of Political Social Science, 626,* 74–90.

Mauer, M., & King, R. S. (2007). *Uneven justice: State rates of incarceration by race and ethnicity*. Washington, DC: The Sentencing Project.

Mickelson, R. A. (2003). When are racial disparities in education the result of discrimination?: A social science perspective. *Teachers College Record, 105,* 1052–1086.

Murray, M. (2012, January). NBC/WSJ poll: Attitudes on race. *NBC News.* Retrieved from http://firstread.nbcnews.com/_news/2010/01/18/4427618-nbcwsj-poll-attitudes-on-race?lite

Nagourney, A. (2008, November 4). OBAMA. Racial barrier falls in heavy turnout. *The New York Times.* Retrieved from http://www.nytimes.com/2008/11/05/us/politics/05elect.html?pagewanted=all

Norton, M. I., & Sommers, S. R. (2011). Whites see racism as a zero-sum game that they are now losing. *Perspectives on Psychological Science, 6*(3), 215–218.

Orfield, G., & Lee, C. (2005). *Why segregation matters: Poverty and educational inequality.* Cambridge, MA: Civil Rights Project, Harvard University.

Pager, D., & Shepherd, H. (2008). The sociology of discrimination: Racial discrimination in employment, housing, credit, and consumer markets. *Annual Review of Sociology, 34,* 181–209.

Parks, G. S., & Hughey, M. W. (2011). *The Obamas and a (post)racial America?* New York, NY: Oxford University Press.

President-elect Obama: The voters rebuke Republicans for economic failure. (2008, November 5). *Wall Street Journal.* Retrieved from http://online.wsj.com/article/SB122586244657800863.html

Roscigno, V. J. (2007). *The face of discrimination: How race and gender impact work and home lives.* Lanham, MD: Rowman & Littlefield.

Southern Poverty Law Center. (2011, Spring). U.S. hate groups top 1,000. *Intelligence Report, 141.* Montgomery, AL: Author. Available at http://www.splcenter.org/get-informed/news/us-hate-groups-top-1000

Turner, M. A., & Ross, S. L. (2003). *Discrimination in metropolitan housing markets: National results from phase 2—Asians and Pacific Islanders.* Washington, DC: Department of Housing and Urban Development. Retrieved from http://www.huduser.org/publications/pdf/phase2_final.pdf

Turner, M. A., Ross, S. L., Gaister, G. C., & Yinger, J. (2002). *Discrimination in metropolitan housing markets: National results from phase 1 HDS 2000.* Washington, DC: Urban Institute, Department of Housing and Urban Development. Retrieved from http://www.huduser.org/portal/publications/pdf/Phase1_Report.pdf

U.S. Census Bureau Newsroom. (2012). *Black (African-American) history month: February 2012.* Washington, DC: Author. Retrieved from http://www.census.gov/newsroom/releases/archives/facts_for_features_special_editions/cb12-ff01.html

Useem, E. L. (1990). You're good, but you're not good enough: Tracking students out of advanced mathematics. *American Educator, 14*(3), 24–46.

"Blacks Are Naturally Good Athletes"

The Myth of a Biological Basis for Race

Daniel Buffington

University of North Carolina–Wilmington

Daniel Buffington is an assistant professor in the department of sociology and criminology at the University of North Carolina–Wilmington. He is the coauthor of "Racetalk and Sport: The Color Consciousness of Contemporary Discourse on Basketball," published in *Sociological Inquiry* in 2011. He researches in the area of race, sport, and culture.

Journalist Jon Entine opened his 2001 book, *Taboo: Why Black Athletes Dominate Sports and Why We Are Afraid to Talk About It*, with the following scenario:

Imagine an alien visitor chancing upon a basketball arena on a wintry night. It sees a curious sight: most of the faces of the extended tree trunks scampering around the court are black; the crowd, on the other hand, is almost all white. This alien would see much the same racial division at football games, boxing matches, and at track meets and running races around the world. Even in sports in which blacks are not a majority—baseball, soccer, rugby, cricket, even bobsledding in some countries—blacks are represented in a greater number than their share in the population. (p. 3)

Entine goes on to argue that genes are the primary explanation for athletes of African descent being overrepresented in elite levels of sport. He is hardly alone in making this claim. On the eve of the 2012 Summer Olympics, former gold medalist sprinter Michael Johnson contended that slavery caused people of African descent to have a "superior athletic gene" (Beck, 2012) that manifested in success in the 100 meter sprint. In doing so, he joined the likes of Al Campanis and Jimmy "The Greek" Snyder who have made similar comments. For Entine (and others coming from this perspective), skin color demarcates an unambiguous boundary between distinct populations, and thus explains a pattern of human social behavior. That an alien visitor would do the same would be as surprising as it would be unlikely. Yet, to a human being, especially one socialized within American culture, the idea that "Blacks are naturally good athletes" seems to make sense. That this myth exists to such a degree within our popular culture tells us a great deal about how the bio-physical diversity of our species has been (mis)understood. For this reason, it serves as a useful starting point for debunking the biological basis for race.

In contemporary biology, the term *race* refers to a unit of taxonomy—like kingdom or phylum—and is used synonymously with *subspecies* to indicate two or more biologically distinct populations within a species. For example, zoologists divide tigers into nine subspecies, including the Bengal, Siberian, and Sumatran types. They do so on the basis of genotypic and phenotypic traits, although the amount of variation necessary to constitute subspecies separation is not agreed upon and, therefore, the subject of debate (Keita & Boyce, 2001). *Genotype* refers to the genetic makeup of an organism including all genetic material inherited from one's parents or a portion of this material, such as chromosomes that code for eye color. *Phenotype* refers to the observable characteristics of an organism, such as body size, fingerprint pattern, or color of skin, hair, or feathers. While phenotype expresses an organism's genetic inheritance, it is also modified by environmental conditions, such as when exposure to sunlight darkens the color of human skin. Applying the biological meaning of race to humans suggests that our modern species, *Homo sapiens,* can be divided into a number of discrete, mutually exclusive subspecies based on phenotypic and genotypic differences, and that each subspecies will contain nearly uniform individuals who are more similar to each other than to members of other races.

If race strictly referred to a unit of taxonomy, it would be of no more than minor interest to sociologists. However, race has an even longer history of use outside biology. Although its origin is uncertain, the best evidence suggests the term entered the English language during the 16th century as a folk concept that referred to a breed of domesticated animals reproduced for specific behavioral or physical qualities (Smedley & Smedley, 2011). Over time, this meaning was applied to human beings so that race was used as a marker of social distinction, indicating membership in particular social groups. While physical appearance and ancestry played a crucial role in distinguishing between groups, so did behavior and social status. Indeed, as well-worn sayings such as "Blacks are naturally good athletes," "Asians are good at math," and "Whites can't dance" attest, in its more common, everyday usage, race was thought to influence a whole range of behaviors, from the athletic to the intellectual to the artistic. Even more, these different behavioral capacities were thought to naturally account for the unequal positions racial groups came to occupy in society.

A useful starting point, then, is to recognize at least two distinct uses and meanings of race. In the strictest biological sense, it refers to intraspecies variation measured by some unspecified amount of phenotypic and genotypic divergence, a meaning I will refer to as *biological race*. In contrast, the term *social race* will refer to its everyday use as a form of group identification, including how people identify themselves (self-identity) and how they are identified by others (social identity). This essay will focus on biological race, and in particular, whether or not the concept is useful for describing diversity within the human species.

Evidence for the Belief in a Biological Basis for Race

There is ample evidence that a significant portion of the general public believes that there are biologically discrete human races. For example, a survey of Georgia residents found that 61.3% of respondents agreed with the statement that "genetics plays a primary role in determining an individual's race" (Condit, Parrott, Harris, Lynch, & Dubriwny, 2004, p. 260). Further evidence can be deduced from questionnaires that ask about racial differences in more limited ways. For example, a survey conducted in 2001 found that 74% of White men and 65% of White women believed that genetics contributed to differences in athleticism across racial groups (Sheldon, Jayaratne, & Petty, 2007). While support for genetic explanations of racial differences tend to be higher for Whites than other racial groups regarding athleticism, intelligence, the drive to succeed, and tendency toward violence, non-Whites (like sprinter Michael Johnson) also express these views (Jayaratne et al., 2009). Open-ended questions show that beliefs about racial differences involve a complex mixture of biological, cultural, environmental, and personal explanations (Buffington & Fraley, 2011; Condit et al., 2004; Morning, 2011), with biology playing a particularly important role. Longitudinal evidence, however, suggests that these beliefs may be fading. In the 2010 version of the General Social Survey, only 10.3% of all respondents agreed that Blacks had lower socioeconomic status due to an "inborn disability" compared to 26% in 1977, the first year this question was asked. However, it is unclear whether this decline is due to an actual change in attitudes or increasing social stigma attached to such responses (Bonilla-Silva, 2010). Indeed, responses to surveys and interviews should be interpreted as a conservative estimate of the belief in a biological basis for race given the well-documented tendency for respondents to supply socially desirable answers.

It is clear then that a significant portion of the general public—including some minority group members—believe, to some degree, in the idea of biologically distinct human races. Yet, a number of scientists that specifically study human biodiversity (biologists, geneticists, and physical anthropologists) have questioned biological race's ability to accurately capture the type of variation found in the human species. In order to understand this doubt, we must return to the definition. Recall that race implies several things of note: that the human species can be divided into a number of distinct groupings on the basis of genotypic and phe-notypic differences; that these groupings are mutually exclusive (a person can fall into one, and only one, of these groupings); and that these subpopulations contain individuals who are only minimally different from each other. It is important, therefore, to examine the degree of genotypic and phenotypic diversity within the human species.

Reviewing the Evidence: Variation Within the Human Species

Considering genotype, humans are remarkably similar. On average, human beings are 99.9% identical in terms of nucleotide pairs (one of the building blocks of DNA), far more than many other species (Barbujani & Colonna, 2010). The vast majority of the remaining 0.1% variation (ranging from 80%–95% depending on the specific markers examined and samples used) is found within any local population, meaning two nonrelated individuals from the same population will, on average, be only slightly more genetically similar to each other than two unre-lated individuals from different continents. Furthermore, only a small portion of all alleles in the human genome are "private"—that is, found in only one region—and none of these are found with great frequency in the region where they occur (Rosenberg et al., 2002). This tremendous genetic similarity augments archeologi-cal evidence regarding the recentness of our species, suggesting there has not been much time for subspecies separation.

How is this minimal amount of diversity distributed across human popu-lations? Most of this genetic variation is *clinal* (Barbujani & Colonna, 2010; Cavilla-Sforza & Cavilla-Sforza, 1995; Rosenberg et al., 2005), that is, it varies gradually over geographic space in correspondence to transitions in environmen-tal conditions. Not surprisingly, phenotypic traits that are significantly impacted by climate also display this type of continuous variation (Relethford, 2009). The classic example is skin color, a trait that has been central to a number of racial classification systems, especially in the United States. Of course, there are human populations with relatively dark skin and those with relatively light skin. However, when we arrange all human beings from dark to light, we find gradual variation—that is, innumerable shades between the light and dark extremes. These differences correspond strongly to environmental conditions, so that darker skin is found most frequently in tropics where sunlight is particularly intense, and lighter colored skin is found nearer the poles (see Figure 4.1). Clinal variation leads to a general axiom: Populations differ by distance so that the further apart any two populations are in geographic space, the more genetically different they will be. Importantly, gradual variation poses a serious problem to attempts to divide humanity into separate units. Although individuals and groups will have distinctive traits in such a system, there are no obvious and clearly demarcated boundaries, meaning divisions will *always* be arbitrary and subjective, and the result of decisions made by human beings.

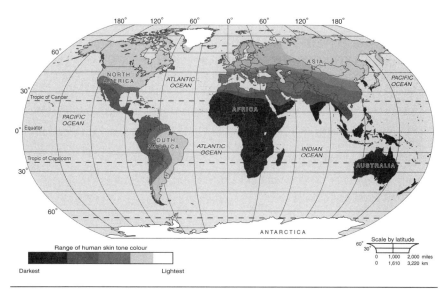

Figure 4.1 Worldwide Distribution of Skin Color Variation
Source: Worldwide distribution of skin color variation [Map]. In *Encyclopedia Britannica*. Retrieved from http://www.britannica.com/bps/media-view/106500/1/0/0.

That small portion of biodiversity that is not clinal is mostly the result of barriers that made reproduction between adjacent populations very difficult because of the presence of geographic boundaries like mountain ranges, deserts, large bodies of water, and narrow isthmuses that lie between these populations (Barbujani & Colonna, 2010; Cavilla-Sforza, 2000; Cavilla-Sforza & Cavilla-Sforza, 1995). As such, because the Mediterranean Sea is less difficult to cross than the Saharan desert, North Africans are more genetically similar to Southern Europeans than they are to sub-Saharan Africans despite these regions being of similar distance from each other. Social barriers—such as social preferences for mating with members of one's own social group—are also significant. Therefore, many of these differences in biodiversity appear at the borders between sociolinguistic groups (Cavilla-Sforza, 2000) or between groups that have strong social rules against intimate relationships, such as those between castes in India (Barbujani & Colonna, 2010).

Using multiple genetic markers simultaneously, researchers can examine these discontinuities and even classify an individual's geographic origins accurately (Bamshad, Wooding, Salisbury, & Stephens, 2004; Rosenberg et al., 2002), at least for those populations whose grandparents came from a single point of origin. Similarly, phenotypes that are minimally impacted by environmental conditions, such as skull size and shape, display a form of geographic clustering that allows researchers to accurately classify individuals using multiple measurements (Ousely, Jantz, & Freid, 2009; Relethford, 2009). However, the genetic similarities produced using this method are inconsistent and vary based upon the markers examined, the sample distribution, and method of analysis (Barbujani & Colonna, 2010). Furthermore, the groupings suggested by this method of clustering stray quite far from the general understanding of biological races as large, continent wide distinctions (Long, Li, & Healy, 2009).

For example, using multiple measurements of the skull, physical anthropologists can distinguish between the crania of American Whites and American Blacks with a very high degree of accuracy. However, this same technique can also distinguish with a similar level of accuracy between populations commonly thought to belong to the same racial group, such as Central and South Africans, northern and southern Native Americans, as well as northern and southern Japanese (Ousely et al., 2009; also see Relethford, 2009). Perhaps most surprising, the skulls of White males born in the mid-1800s and White males born in the mid-1900s display a similar amount of difference. Therefore, if the ability to group individuals on the basis of crania is taken as evidence of the existence of racial groups, there would be thousands of them.

What About Forensics and Medical Research on Biological Race?

At this point, some might argue that forensic anthropologists can determine the racial identity of unidentified skeletal remains at a better than random rate and that medical researchers use race to predict susceptibility to certain diseases. Forensicists in the United States are able to do so, in part, because the major population groups they deal with come from vastly different areas of the globe. Since differences in physical traits (i.e., phenotype) increase with geographical distance, accurate classification is possible using multiple measurements (Ousely et al., 2009). Still, identification only becomes accurate when compared against the known demographic composition of the location in which the remains are found (Konigsberg, Algee-Hewitt, & Steadman, 2009). This means that a set of bones found in rural Iowa and identified as White would be classified as Easter Island Polynesian if found in Hawaii. If found in Gary, Indiana, the same skeleton would be reported as Black.

Medical researchers are interested in race as a proxy for ancestry, and they are interested in ancestry as a way of predicting the likelihood of an individual possessing a genetic abnormality that can lead to illness. For example, individuals with ancestors from regions where malaria was frequent (including West Africa, India, the Middle East, and Southern Europe) are more likely to be carriers of the sickle-cell trait and therefore develop medical complications. Most studies of the relationship between race and disease rely on self-reported ancestry, which is problematic because the kinship systems used to trace ancestry are culturally (that is to say, socially) constructed. For example, the United States tends to practice a system of hypodescent (more commonly known as the one-drop rule) in which children of European–African sexual relations are socially designated as Black despite their mixed ancestry (Davis, 1991). This means that asking a descendant of one of these relationships his or her self-reported racial identity may provide only a partial understanding of the actual genetic ancestry. Still, medical researchers persist in using self-identity because it provides a rough (if imprecise) approximation of ancestry that is cheaper and less time consuming than the more accurate methods of detailed genealogical research or analysis of a person's entire genetic makeup (Bamshad et al., 2004; Collins, 2004). Clearly then, neither forensicists nor medical researchers have discovered something about race that was missed by other researchers.

The Sociological Perspective on Race

Given this, many students are curious as to why sociologists continue to use the word *race* and specific racial group designations like White, Black, and Native American as if these correspond to distinct entities. To argue that race is not biological is not the same thing as saying it does not exist. As already indicated, there is a "social" meaning of race distinct from its use in biology, and it is this meaning to which sociologists most frequently refer. Race in this sense refers to a type of social identification in which certain physical features have been assigned social importance. Importantly, this definition incorporates, rather than discounts, biological variation. As we have seen, human beings do differ in terms of physical traits, and these visible differences became the primary criteria for placing individuals into racial categories. However, this classification process only took place once humans came to believe that physical features were salient markers of differences. Although different theoretical perspectives within sociology disagree about the exact mechanisms, all concur that the assignment of social importance to physical features occurred through social relations—such as migration and conquest, competition for scarce resources, and political challenges against the state—that brought different populations into sustained contact with each other. It was only once social importance had been assigned to physical differences that people began to act on them, treating members of their perceived racial in-group different from members of their perceived racial out-group. The result has been the formation of more-or-less coherent social groups that differ in ways that matter a great deal to sociologists: in terms of identity, cultural practices, access to important societal resources, and treatment by the larger society. It is for this reason that sociologists continue to study and use the term *race*.

Explaining Differences in
Athletic Participation and Performance

Understanding the actual distribution of human biodiversity casts doubt on perspectives that rely on biological race as the primary explanation for behavioral differences, such as elite athletic performance. Conversely, recognizing that racial groups form through social interactions opens up the examination of a whole range of social forces. Considering athletic participation, it should be noted that Blacks are overrepresented in only a handful of sports[1], therefore a key question becomes why only these sports? Sociological explanations call attention to two social features shared by members of the Black category: the occupational structure of society and the opportunity structure within sport itself. The former emphasizes that as a minority group,

---

[1] Black participation rates exceeded their proportion of the overall U.S. population for only 8 of 38 NCAA-level sports during the 2009–2010 season, including men's and women's basketball, men's and women's indoor and outdoor track, football, and women's bowling (Irick, 2011). A similar pattern emerges when examining professional and Olympic-level competition (Phillips, 1993).

Blacks face limited employment prospects in many occupational fields. Conversely, the institution of sports was among the first to integrate and has subsequently offered a number of high-profile opportunities. These twin forces (ample opportunities in sport coupled with limited opportunities in other occupational fields) funnel a significant number of Blacks into elite sports participation (Coakley, 2009; Edwards, 1973). The opportunity structure within sports channels these participants into particular sports. A relative lack of material resources means that Black participation rates are highest in sports for which facilities, training, and competition are available in widely accessible social institutions like schools (Coakley, 2009; Phillips, 1993). Conversely, sports in which most training occurs in private clubs or through lessons (such as golf, tennis, and swimming) are the sports in which Black participation rates are low.

This is not to say that biology has no impact on an individual's ability to perform a particular activity. Both rules and tactical strategies mean that sports often favor particular phenotypes, such as height in volleyball and basketball. All other things being equal, a relatively tall individual will be at a distinct advantage in these endeavors. Because certain populations are taller on average than others, some groups would appear to have an advantage. However, because of the tremendous amount of diversity within any population, many members of relatively tall groups will not be tall at all. In addition, because of the high degree of shared genes across populations, many members of other groups—including those that are relatively short—would be quite tall. Finally, it must be remembered that phenotypes are malleable due to environmental factors (such as nutrition) and are acted on in social situations shaped by cultural preferences. The Dutch, the group with the tallest mean height in the world, have contributed very few elite basketball players because of this sport's lack of popularity. To the degree that an individual succeeds because of the contribution of particular genotype or phenotype, this would be because of their individual genetic inheritance, not biological features they share in common with members of their racial group.

Conclusion

By way of conclusion, reconsider how well biological race captures variation within the human species. As stated above, the clinal distribution of most of the variance within the human population makes the creation of distinct groupings difficult. Using sophisticated computer modeling focused on that small portion of human variation that is not clinal does allow for a reasonable classification scheme, however the corresponding categories are inconsistent and reveal thousands of biological divisions. Further, racial categories are not mutually exclusive, so a person cannot fall into one, and only one, classification. While the use of multiple genetic markers allows for a highly accurate classification of individuals, even these techniques fail to accurately classify everyone in their samples. Some individuals, and even entire groups, could be classified into multiple categories. If this is the case with samples whose recent ancestors all come from the same self-identified group, this suggests classification would be even more difficult for that significant and growing portion of the human populace that lives in multicultural societies where diverse ancestry is common. At best, biological race very crudely corresponds to diversity within the human species, misrepresenting this variation far more often than it enhances our understanding of it.

It is for this reason that sociologists have instead conceived of race as a social construction—that is, a way of assigning meaning to the social world. In the case of race, minor and primarily gradual biophysical differences between individuals and groups have become understood in everyday social interactions as deeply meaningful markers of boundaries between social groups. It is the actions based upon this assigned meaning, not the biophysical differences, that account for most of the differential outcomes among racial categories, including differences in sports participation. As such, biological race within the human species is most accurately described as a myth.

Suggested Additional Resources

Antrosio, J. (2012). *Part 1, biological anthropology: Human nature, race, evolution* [Web log comment]. Retrieved from http://www.livinganthropologically.com/anthropology/human-nature-race-evolution-biological-anthropology

Herbes-Sommers, C. (Writer & Director). (2003). Episode 1: The difference between us [Television series episode]. In L. Adelman (Producer), *Race: The power of an illusion*. San Francisco: California Newsreel.

Smedley, A., & Smedley, B. D. (2011). *Race in North America: Origin and evolution of a worldview* (4th ed.). Boulder, CO: Westview Press.

Questions for Further Discussion

1. What is clinal variation and why does it cast doubt on attempts to categorize humans into discrete racial groups?

2. Compare and contrast the biological and sociological explanations for different outcomes between racial groups, such as elite athletic participation.

3. If races are not biologically distinct groups, how do sociologists explain their existence in society? What factors does the author suggest contribute to the formation of racial groups? Can you think of others?

Reaching Beyond the Color Line

1. Examine the map in Figure 4.1. Do members of the same racial group share the same skin tone? Do members of different racial groups have distinct skin tones not shared by members of other racial groups? What are the implications of this activity for the biological basis of race?

2. Take the "race test" designed by Guido Barbujani in collaboration with Todd Disotell. In it, you will be asked to sort 35 people from around the world based on physical resemblance. (http://web.unife.it/progetti/genetica/Guido/index.php?lng=it&p=10). What do the results tell you about the social construction of racial categories?

References

Bamshad, M., Wooding, S., Salisbury, B. A., & Stephens, J. C. (2004). Deconstructing the relationship between genetics and race. *Nature Reviews Genetics, 5,* 598–608.

Barbujani, G., & Colonna, V. (2010). Human genome diversity: Frequently asked questions. *Trends in Genetics, 26*(7), 285–295.

Beck, S. (2012, June 30). Survival of the fastest: Why descendants of slaves will take the medals in the London 2012 sprint finals. *MailOnline.* Retrieved from http://www.dailymail.co.uk/news/article-2167064/London-2012-Olympics-Michael-Johnson-descendants-slaves-medals-sprint-finals.html#ixzz2q9LySGTZ

Bonilla-Silva, E. (2010). *Racism without racists: Color-blind racism and the persistence of racial inequality in the united states* (3rd ed.). Lanham, MD: Rowan & Littlefield.

Buffington, D. T., & Fraley, T. (2011). Racetalk and sport: The color consciousness of contemporary discourse on basketball. *Sociological Inquiry, 81*(5), 333–352.

Cavilla-Sforza, L. L. (2000). *Genes, peoples, and languages.* New York, NY: North Point Press.

Cavilla-Sforza, L. L., & Cavilla-Sforza, F. (1995). *The great human diasporas.* Reading, MA: Addison-Wesley.

Coakley, J. (2009). *Sports in society: Issues and controversies* (10th ed.). New York, NY: McGraw-Hill.

Collins, F. (2004). What we do and don't know about "race," "ethnicity," genetics and health at the dawn of the genome era. *Nature Genetics Supplement, 36*(11), S13–S15.

Condit, C. M., Parrott, R. L., Harris, T. M., Lynch, J., & Dubriwny, T. (2004). The role of "genetics" in popular understanding of race in the United States. *Public Understanding of Science, 13,* 249–272.

Davis, F. J. (1991). *Who is Black? One nation's definition.* University Park: Pennsylvania State University Press.

Edwards, H. (1973). *Sociology of sport.* Homewood, IL: Dorsey Press.

Entine, J. (2001). *Taboo: Why Black athletes dominate sports and why we are afraid to talk about it.* New York, NY: Public Affairs.

Irick, E., & National Collegiate Athletics Association. (2011). *NCAA race and gender demographics 1995–2011* [Data File]. Retrieved from http://web1.ncaa.org/rgdSearch/exec/main

Jayaratne, T. E., Gelman, S., Feldbaum, M., Sheldon, J. P., Petty, E. M., & Kardia, S. L. (2009). The perennial debate: Nature, nurture, or choice? Black and White Americans' explanations for individual differences. *Review of General Psychology, 13*(1), 24–33.

Keita, S. O., & Boyce, A. J. (2001). Race: Confusion about zoological and social taxonomies, and their places in science. *American Journal of Human Biology, 13,* 569–575.

Konigsberg, L. W., Algee-Hewitt, B. F., & Steadman, D. W. (2009). Estimation and evidence in forensic anthropology: Sex and race. *American Journal of Physical Anthropology, 139*(1), 77–90.

Long, J. C., Li, J., & Healy, M. E. (2009). Human DNA sequences: More variation and less race. *American Journal of Physical Anthropology, 139*(1), 23–34.

Morning, A. (2011). *The nature of race: How scientists think and teach about human difference.* Berkeley: University of California Press.

Ousely, S., Jantz, R., & Freid, D. (2009). Understanding race and human variation: Why forensic anthropologists are good at identifying race. *American Journal of Physical Anthropology, 139*(1), 68–76.

Phillips, J. C. (1993). *Sociology of sport.* Boston, MA: Allyn & Bacon.

Relethford, J. H. (2009). Race and global patterns of phenotypic variation. *American Journal of Physical Anthropology, 139*(1), 16–22.

Rosenberg, N. A., Mahajan, S., Ramachandran, S., Zhao, C., Pritchard, J. K., & Feldman, M. W. (2005). Clines, clusters, and the effect of study design on the inference of human populations structure. *PLoS Genetics, 1*(6), e70.

Rosenberg, N. A., Pritchard, J. K., Weber, J. L., Cann, H. M., Kidd, K. K., & Zhivotovsky, L. A. (2002). Genetic structure of human populations. *Science, 298,* 2381–2385.

Sheldon, J. P., Jayaratne, T. E., & Petty, E. M. (2007). White Americans' genetic explanations for a perceived race difference in athleticism: The relation to prejudice toward stereotyping Blacks. *Athletic Insight: The Online Journal of Sport Psychology, 9*(3), 31–56.

Smedley, A., & Smedley, B. D. (2011). *Race in North America: Origin and evolution of a worldview* (4th ed.). Boulder, CO: Westview Press.

PART II

Debunking Individual Attitudes

"If People Stopped Talking About Race, It Wouldn't Be a Problem Anymore"

Silencing the Myth of a Color-Blind Society

Ted Thornhill

Earlham College

Ted Thornhill received his PhD in sociology from the University of Massachusetts–Amherst and is currently an associate professor of sociology and African and African American studies at Earlham College. He teaches courses on racial stratification and crime and inequality. His research and writing focuses on the ways in which color-blind ideology and institutional policies and practices promote racial inequality, particularly in K-12 and higher education, the labor market, the criminal "justice" system, and the media.

Most White Americans firmly believe that race no longer matters and that in the United States anybody can get ahead if they work hard enough (Bonilla-Silva, 2014; Gallagher, 2012). This is one of the hallmarks of the color-blind perspective. In sociological terms, *color-blindness* actually has two meanings—one prescriptive, the other descriptive. The former suggests that it is both possible and preferable to think and act toward others without acknowledging skin color. The latter, sometimes called post-racialism, refers to the belief that race no longer determines individuals' life chances in contemporary U.S. society (Gallagher, 2012). Most Whites have internalized both of these meanings, allowing them to rest secure in the racial status quo, comforted by their post-racial illusion. Charles Gallagher (2012) explains it the following way,

> The rosy picture that colorblindness presumes about race relations and the satisfying sense that one is part of a period in American history that is morally superior to the racist days of the past is, quite simply, a less stressful and more pleasurable social place for whites to inhabit. (p. 93)

For most White Americans, it is those who would notice race and invoke it publicly (e.g., in policy discussions, classrooms, courtrooms, or the media) that are the real obstacles to a racially harmonious, color-blind society. This sentiment is frequently expressed in statements such as, "If people stopped talking about race, it wouldn't be a problem anymore." Yet, differences in skin color are not the problem; racism, racial discrimination, White racial privilege, and racial inequality are.

Color-Blindness: Whites' Illusion

National surveys show that the vast majority of Whites believe that the United States is a color-blind or post-racial society. A 2011 CBS News/New York Times poll found that 52% of Whites believe that Whites and Blacks have "about an equal chance of getting ahead in today's society" (9% actually believe that Blacks have a competitive advantage). A similar poll conducted the same year found that 77% of Whites believe that the Blacks living in their community have "just as good a chance as Whites" in finding employment (Gallup, 2011). And only 22% of Whites agree that "every possible effort to improve the position of Blacks and other minorities" should be made "even if it means giving them preferential treatment" (Pew Research Center, 2012). This is related to the fact that a majority of Whites (55%) believe that those "who can't get ahead in this country are mostly responsible for their own condition" (Time, 2008). That most Whites oppose race conscious policies as a means of redressing historical racial oppression is understandable, if not morally defensible, once we also consider that only 18% of Whites agree that racial bias is a "very serious" problem affecting the life chances of Americans of color today (Cable News Network, 2006).

In-depth interviews and focus groups with Whites show most strongly believe that Americans of color have an "equal opportunity" to succeed, need to stop dwelling on race, "playing the race card," and engaging in self-defeating behaviors (see for example Bonilla-Silva, 2014; DiTomaso, Parks-Yancy, & Post, 2003; Gallagher, 2012). Moreover, many Whites believe that the pendulum of racial preference has swung so far in the opposite direction that Americans of color are now the beneficiaries of "reverse discrimination or reverse racism" against Whites (Bonilla-Silva, 2014; DiTomaso et al., 2003; see also Moore, Essay 20). This sentiment is captured in the following quote by one White interviewee, "I think we find it sometimes going in the other direction. We bend over backwards for the minorities and the person that suffers is the White person" (DiTomaso et al., 2003).

Two additional locations where color-blind claims are commonly found are the comments sections of online news reports and blog postings. Even a cursory scanning of comments to articles or posts that address topics like affirmative action, bilingual or multicultural education (e.g., Arizona's ethnic studies ban in public schools), or crime (e.g., the killing of Trayvon Martin) reveal a color-blind ideology. Although there is not a reliable way to discern the racial identity of these individuals, except for profile pictures and self-reports within the body of the text, the tenor of their comments suggests most are White. Consider the following example.

In January 2012, a coalition of nonprofit organizations in Duluth, Minnesota, launched the Un-Fair Campaign, which was designed to promote awareness and initiate a conversation about White racial privilege and racism through the medium of roadside billboards. These billboards were intentionally provocative, with phrases like, "It's hard to see racism when you're White" written in bold letters on the faces of White women and men. The billboards sparked considerable controversy, locally and nationally. Opponents of the Un-Fair Campaign created a Facebook group in an effort to communicate their frustrations. Consider the following representative comment posted on the STOP Racist Unfair Campaign, *Facebook* Group site:

> Racism is Racism no matter how you slice it, and this ad campaign is RACIST! We all see color, how we react to all the colors we see in the world is up to each individual!! I was always taught to treat others as I would like to be treated, last time I looked an individual's color was not factored into what I was taught!!!!!! I will not apologize for being White and I would not ask anyone of color to apologize either!!! (2012)

This post is indicative of the problem with color-blindness; it assumes that we already inhabit a society where racial equality prevails. When White privilege and White racism are implicated as real barriers to racial equality, the tendency is for White Americans to summarily dismiss the well-established body of readily available evidence and respond with hollow claims of racism, particularly against Whites. Unfortunately, this practice is all too common. As mentioned earlier, broaching the topics of racial disparities between Whites and Americans of color in areas such as wealth, education, jobs, health care, and treatment by the criminal justice system is often cited as evidence of racism against Whites.

By now you may be wondering whether Americans of color advocate color-blindness, too. Some do, though not to the same extent as Whites. Sociologist Eduardo Bonilla-Silva (2014) explains this phenomenon in the following way:

> [A]n ideology is not dominant because it affects all actors in a social system in the *same* way and to the *same* degree. Instead, an ideology is dominant if *most* members (dominant and subordinate) of a social system must accommodate their views vis-à-vis that ideology [emphasis in original]. (p. 200)

In other words, since the ideology of color-blindness is hegemonic, some people of color will be persuaded by its claims.

So, what's wrong with color-blindness? It just means that you want to see people as human beings, not colors, right? Not exactly. The color-blind narrative omits crucial facts about how we arrived at the current racial reality in the first place. To begin with, the process of racialization is ignored. Racialization involves "creat[ing] difference where previously no phenotypical or biological difference existed" (Desmond & Emirbayer, 2010, p. 9). Europeans used certain physical features, most notably skin color, to classify non-Europeans as distinct "races," brand them as genetically and culturally inferior, and justify various forms of oppression against them, such as genocide, slavery, theft, and apartheid (Feagin, 2010a, 2010b). What are now considered distinct racial groups (e.g., Black, White, Asian, Native American) are actually social constructions originating from Europeans' desire to dominate those perceived as "other." Race is not a biological reality that, with focused effort, can be ignored and rendered inconsequential as the color-blind perspective suggests (see also Buffington, Essay 4). Instead, it is a social construct, contingent upon history, politics, geography, and *time.*

In reality, color-blindness is a powerful example of what sociologists Michael Omi and Howard Winant (1994) have called a "racial project," which they define as "*simultaneously an interpretation, representation, or explanation of racial dynamics, and an effort to reorganize and redistribute resources along particular racial lines*" [emphasis in original] (p. 56). As such, racial conflict of the past did not simply evaporate with the passage of the landmark civil rights legislation of the mid-20th century, it merely adapted to a different period. The overarching goal of the civil rights movement was to abolish the overt, state-sanctioned apartheid system that severely limited the life chances of Blacks, and other Americans of color, throughout the United States, particularly in the Southern states. Civil rights activists also demanded that Americans of color be accorded the same rights, privileges, and opportunities as Whites based on their common humanity and citizenship. The first goal was accomplished; the second goal has only been partially fulfilled.

Explaining Color-Blind Ideology

During the civil rights movement, activists often invoked the idea of a color-blind society—a sentiment embodied most strongly by Dr. Martin Luther King Jr.'s "I Have a Dream" speech (1963) where he envisioned a day where individuals "[would] not be judged by the color of their skin but by the content of their character." This phrase has since been co-opted by political conservatives in order to proselytize a rendering of post-civil rights America that is inconsistent with reality. These individuals, and an increasing number of liberals too, are steadfast in their mission to eliminate the very laws, programs, and policies meant to ensure that Americans of color would be fully incorporated into American society, unencumbered by the effects of historical White supremacy and its contemporary manifestations (Brown et al., 2003; Wise, 2010). Civil rights legislation has not eliminated the need for programs such as affirmative action that help offset the continued effects of state-sanctioned racial injustices of the past and contemporary forms of racism in the present.

While the civil rights movement did not eliminate racial inequality, it did initiate a reshaping of the discourse around race. One positive benefit of this restructuring is that the use of explicitly racist language has been eliminated from most public forums. The exception to this appears to be the Internet where some individuals use the anonymity of online chat rooms and forums, blogs, and e-mail to use racial epithets, promote racial stereotypes, and advocate White supremacy (Daniels, 2009; Steinfeldt et al., 2010). However, in most public forums, the discursive space around the topic of race is now dominated by the ideology of color-blindness.

Color-blindness is buttressed by several key assumptions. First, within the color-blind racial project, racism is conflated with racial prejudice. It fails to recognize that racism is a structural phenomenon that is "variable" and often takes on a different character in different historical periods (Bonilla-Silva, 1996, p. 470). When coupled with the sacrosanct color-blind imperative of "no race talk," it becomes impossible to address post-civil rights era racism and racial discrimination, which in the present is more often subtle, institutional, and at times, even unintentional. The color-blind perspective demands a permanent gag order against opponents of racial injustice and White supremacy (Guinier & Torres, 2002). And, in the flawed logic of color-blindness, merely suggesting that White racial privilege and White racism are real barriers to racial equality often results in the label of racial rabble-rouser for violating the color-blind imperative (see also Harris and McClure, Essay 1). This is problematic for several reasons, the most important of which is the fact that there are many institutional practices that produce negative and disparate outcomes by race, often without any overt racial animus or intent on the part of individual Whites. Under color-blind rhetoric, none of these issues can be addressed.

Consider the seemingly benign practice of many organizations of giving preference in hiring to the family members and friends of current employees. On the surface, this practice appears entirely nonracial. However, most Americans of color were barred from employment in nearly all historically White organizations through the better part of the 20th century. When coupled with the high level of racially endogamous marriages and peer groups among Whites, it is more likely than not that the family members and friends of White employees will be White. Color-blind rhetoric to the contrary, advocating for the dismantling of these types of racially unequal arrangements does not make one a racist, nor does a willingness to critically examine contemporary social issues (e.g., the Trayvon Martin killing or the federal government's response to Hurricane Katrina) from a race conscious perspective.

Another key assumption of color-blindness is that the civil rights movement was largely successful in dismantling all significant barriers to upward social mobility for Americans of color (i.e., contemporary racial discrimination is minimal; see also Hughey, Essay 3). Here, the claim is regularly made that *Brown v. Board of Education* along with the landmark civil rights legislation of the 1960s all but eliminated racial discrimination in education, housing, voting, and the labor market. As such, advocates of color-blindness believe that racial discrimination in these areas occurs only on rare or infrequent occasions because the practice is illegal. Martin Luther King Jr. succinctly addressed this White fallacy in his final book, *Where Do We Go From Here: Chaos or Community* (1968), where he wrote: "The recording of the law in itself is treated as the reality of the reform" (p. 5). Forty-six years since King penned these words, many Whites still seem disposed to this position. However, it does not hold water, as there are also federal and state laws and local ordinances that prohibit all sorts of behaviors (e.g., murder, theft, pollution, speeding, tax evasion, breach of contract, driving under the influence of drugs and alcohol). Yet, no one would claim that since we have laws and ordinances prohibiting these acts that they are not violated every day in the United States. Similarly, despite legal prohibitions against racial discrimination in areas such as housing, education, and employment, these laws are also violated every day in the United States. In 2012 alone, there were 33,512 employment-based racial discrimination complaints filed with the Equal Employment Opportunity Commission (EEOC). These complaints account for only a fraction of the actual number of violations, as most cases of racial discrimination in employment are likely to go unreported because most individuals are unaware that they have been victimized (Bendick, Jackson, & Reinoso, 1994). The claim that the modern civil rights movement eliminated racial discrimination or reduced it to the point of social insignificance is entirely inconsistent with the evidence.

The color-blind racial project is in essence the 21st-century equivalent of the ideology of White supremacy that prevailed in the United States prior to the achievements of the modern civil rights era. While the logic and presentation of these two belief systems are quite different, the effect remains the same: a racially unequal society where Whites are afforded greater life chances than Americans of color. This was the stated goal during the period when the ideology of White supremacy was dominant, but in the post-civil rights era, the ideology of color-blindness guarantees the same result.

It is important to note that the racially unequal status quo that is in large measure perpetuated by the ideology of color-blindness is not only harmful to people of color, it adversely affects Whites too. While a considerable body of research and writing has documented the numerous material and psychological benefits of White racial privilege (e.g., Jensen, 2005; Lipsitz, 1998; McIntosh, 2013), there are also costs associated with these unearned advantages. White racial privilege that is today buttressed by color-blind thinking can have the effect of enveloping its beneficiaries in "a bubble of unreality" that prevents an accurate understanding of "the way the world really works" (Wise, 2008, p. 155). Wise further states that it can also produce emotional and psychological costs that result from benefiting unjustly from racial advantages that harm other human beings (2008). This is particularly the case in an American society that pretends it is *the* archetype of meritocracy in the world.

There are also more tangible costs associated with White racial advantage. As Brown et al. (2003) claim,

> White Americans may win better jobs, better housing in better neighborhoods, a better shot at a high-quality education for their children. But they must also pay, and pay handsomely, for the prisons, police, mopping-up health care services, and other reactive measures predictably required by the maintenance of drastically unequal social conditions. (p. 249)

In his memoir *White Like Me: Reflections on Race From a Privileged Son,* anti-racist author Tim Wise (2008) asserts, "[r]acism and white privilege are dangerous to us, even as they pay dividends—sort of like a precious gem that turns out to be toxic if held too close" (p. 148). In essence, there are manifold reasons how the ideology of color-blindness can have indirect negative effects for Whites. Yet, the fact remains that people of color are inarguably those whose lives are most adversely and directly affected by a society that has permitted the chimera of color-blindness to become the popular understanding of race in America. That is, an understanding that race no longer matters. In the next section, I provide evidence that shows that the color-blind perspective is, in a word, wrong.

Race Still Matters: The Case of Education and the Labor Market

A concise review of the many ways in which, and social locations where, race continues to shape individuals' life chances would require a book-length treatment. However, a thorough repudiation of the myth of a color-blind society does not require such an exhaustive approach. Highlighting the falsity of this perspective only requires sufficient evidence that racism and racial discrimination remain durable and regular features of American society. Research has shown that racial inequities continue to exist in areas such as education, the labor market, housing, politics, health and health care access, the criminal justice system, exposure to industrial toxins, retail experiences, and media depictions to name but a few (see for example, Feagin, 2010a; Feagin & McKinney, 2003; Feagin & Sikes, 1994). In this section, I show how race affects Americans' experiences in the areas of education and the labor market. I focus on these two social areas because they are institutions in which nearly all Americans must interact fairly regularly throughout their lives, and because the law explicitly prohibits racial discrimination in both of them.

Race Matters in Education

Americans view education as the principal means of upward social mobility, a central pillar of the "American dream." In our "meritocratic" society, high academic achievement is supposed to grease the wheels of mobility and propel one forward toward occupational and financial success throughout life. This process tends to work marvelously for the average White student. Unfortunately, for some students of color, it operates in a wholly different manner due in large part to the poor quality of their schools.

In the United States, most children and adolescents attend schools based on where they live. However, the ghettoization of Blacks, Latinos, and Asians in cities and the forced relocation of indigenous peoples to reservations across the United States has ensured that children of color would not receive equal schooling, both prior to *Brown v. Board of Education* (because separate is *not* equal) and up to the present day (because separate is *still not* equal). Yet, because color-blind rhetoric prevails in public discourse, we pretend that Americans who find their children's schools unsatisfactory always have the option of moving to another location with better schools. Whether they decide to do so is entirely an individual decision. These types of statements ignore the overwhelming body of evidence showing that racially segregated urban ghettos were intentionally created by Whites through practices such as redlining, blockbusting and panic selling, threats and violence, and restrictive covenants. Today, racial residential segregation is maintained and expanded (either contiguously or noncontiguously) through such illegal practices as racially discriminatory lending and racial steering on the part of real estate agents as well as freedom of choice [read: White flight] (Lewis, Emerson, & Klineberg, 2011; Massey & Denton, 1993; Zubrinsky Charles, 2003). Where one lives matters for a variety of reasons including the availability of jobs, exposure to pollution (water, air, soil, noise), violent victimization, the availability of fresh fruits and vegetables, and most especially, the quality of schools that one's children will attend (McKoy & Vincent, 2008).

Due to the legacy of forced racial residential segregation, students of color, particularly Blacks and Latinos, are more likely than White students to attend inferior racially segregated schools, for example, with less qualified teachers and limited gifted, honors, and advanced placement classes (Kozol, 1991, 2005). This is partially due to social class differences by race. Yet, the social class advantage held by Whites is itself a product of White racism, both past and present (Feagin, 2010b). Even when students of color, especially Blacks, attend diverse schools, they are still more likely than White students to be "tracked low," independent of their abilities and aspirations and their parents' preferences (Diamond, 2006; Tyson, 2011). That is, they are disproportionately placed in developmental courses, dropout prevention, and vocational programs.

Students of color also routinely experience explicit and implicit racism on the part of some White teachers and students, which creates a significant disruption in their learning (see for example, Kailin, 1999, and Kohli, 2008). Examples of implicit racism include teachers and administrators subscribing to negative racial stereotypes about Black students having poor moral character and disliking academic pursuits. More overt forms of racism would include racially coded or not-so-veiled comments such as "come on Calvin (who is Black), you should know the answer to this question about slavery" or "Kim (who is Chinese American), how did your grandparents feel about the internment of Japanese Americans during World War II?" These types of statements and questions might come from teachers, administrators, or students. And, at the intersection of both explicit and implicit racial bias lies the well-documented lower expectations of many White teachers for Black and Latino students relative to White students (Landsman, 2004; Roscigno & Ainsworth-Darnell, 1999).

At this point, some might argue that students of color could overcome these barriers to academic excellence through hard work. Indeed, some of them do. However, pointing to examples of "motivated minorities" who attend poor schools, graduate at the top of their respective classes, and earn scholarships to prestigious colleges and universities, as an example of what is possible, is disingenuous. The "homeless to Harvard" and "jail to Yale" stories that appear in the popular media at seemingly regular intervals are extremely rare exceptions and, by definition, are far outside the norm. Further, given the differences in the educational experiences of White students and students of color it would be unrealistic to expect both groups to have comparable educational outcomes even if they worked equally hard, to say nothing of the social class advantages of White students. This begs the question: Why should a herculean effort be required of students of color in order to compensate for all of the educational inequities they experience? This doesn't comport with the widespread perception of education as "the great equalizer," or the claim of a color-blind society where race no longer has material consequences.

Race Matters in the Labor Market

Regarding the labor market, in terms of income, the U.S. Department of Labor (2012) reports Blacks and Latinos consistently earn less than their White and Asian counterparts across all major occupational groups (e.g., management, professional, service, and sales). The median income among Latinos (of any race) in 2011 was $15,136 compared to $31,708 among non-Hispanic Whites. Blacks fared only marginally better, earning a median income of only $17,981 in 2011. During the same year, Asian Americans earned a median income of $30,077, approximately $1,600 below that of Whites. While this is a positive sign given the magnitude of the Black–White and Latino–White income gaps, this seeming parity masks the great variation in income that exists among Asian ethnic groups. For example, the median incomes of Japanese, Filipino, and Hmong Americans in 2011 were $40,236, $29,238, and $11,502, respectively (U.S. Census Bureau, 2011). Moreover, members of those Asian ethnic groups with both higher and lower median incomes still pay a "race tax," as evidence reveals that they must be better educated and more experienced than their White counterparts to realize similar pay and promotion opportunities (Chou & Feagin, 2008; Woo, 2000). Unfortunately, Asian Americans' burden of having to be more qualified than their White colleagues to realize equal treatment in the workplace is widely ignored due to the invidious "model minority" myth (see Zhou, Essay 8).

From education to the labor market, research has shown that even among vocational school graduates, that is, those for whom marketable skills are of the utmost importance, the stigma of non-White skin color presents itself as a significant barrier to gainful employment. An important study by Deirdre Royster (2003) documented this phenomenon by following two groups of recent male graduates of a vocational school in Baltimore, Maryland, one Black and one White, similar in all relevant respects (i.e., motivation, grades, skill level, etc.), in order to assess their labor market experiences. She found that they had greatly disparate rates of success in the blue-collar labor market. The White graduates found more lucrative jobs in the areas in which they were trained and they did so relatively quickly. The Black graduates did not have the extensive networks of the White graduates due to historical racial discrimination in the blue-collar labor market and the exclusionary policies of most craft unions. Royster also found that Blacks' ability to develop these types of materially valuable social networks is stymied, in part, by the fallacious belief among White employers that Whites are routinely facing "reverse discrimination" and that they are "underdogs" in the labor market. Therefore, White employers found it necessary to look out for fellow Whites struggling to find employment in what they perceived to be a political climate overly concerned with issues of diversity and affirmative action. Royster (2003) concludes that

> [b]ecause older White men actively recruit and assist younger White men— even those who are not family members, to the virtual exclusion of young Black men—patterns that unfairly advantaged White men during the pre-civil rights era continue to do so now. (p. 177)

Conclusion

White Americans and Americans of color have significantly different opportunities in nearly every sphere of life. Color-blindness supports this racially unequal status quo and most Whites, and some people of color, buy into this ideology. So, how do we resolve this dilemma? Is there a viable alternative to color-blindness? Thankfully, there is. Rather than a color-blind society, we need to strive for a society that is both racism-free and racially equal. This first requires that we become race or color conscious. Anti-racist writer Tim Wise (2010) has suggested "illuminated individualism" as a way forward toward racial equity. Here, we must first acknowledge that individual identities matter; we are not simply raceless, generic Americans. Next, we need to realize that we have different lived experiences and be reflexive about how race has shaped those experiences. Lastly, it is imperative that we remain cognizant of the influence of historical and contemporary racism on the life chances of people of color in the United States. In essence, we need to adopt both a sociological and historical perspective. Without doing so we can never hope to achieve a society where race does not determine individuals' life chances. We *can* move forward together as Americans of all hues, but only after sincerely and completely addressing America's racist past, a commitment to address racism in the present, and a willingness to confront racism in the future when, not if, it rears it unsightly head.

Suggested Additional Resources

Bonilla-Silva, E. (2014). *Racism without racists: Color-blind racism and racial inequality in contemporary America* (4th ed.). Lanham, MD: Rowman & Littlefield.

Brown, M. K., Carnoy, M., Currie, E., Duster, T., Oppenheimer, D. B., Shultz, M. M., & Wellman, D. (2003). *Whitewashing race: The myth of a color-blind society.* Berkeley: University of California Press.

Feagin, J. R. (2010). *Racist America: Roots, current realities, and future reparations* (2nd ed.). New York, NY: Routledge.

Wise, T. (2010). *Color-blind: The rise of post-racial politics and the retreat from racial equity.* San Francisco, CA: City Lights Books.

Websites

Racism Review: http://www.racismreview.com:

"Racism Review is intended to provide a credible and reliable source of information for journalists, students and members of the general public who are seeking solid evidence-based research and analysis of "race," racism, ethnicity, and immigration issues, especially as they undergird and shape U.S. society within a global setting. We also provide substantive research and analysis on local, national, and global resistance to racial and ethnic oppression, including the many types of antiracist activism."

Tim Wise: http://www.timwise.org:

This is the personal website of anti-racist activist and author, Tim Wise. Many of his essays are posted here as well as interviews, speeches, and his speaking schedule.

White Privilege Conference [WPC]: http://www.whiteprivilegeconference.com:

This is the website of the annual White Privilege Conference [WPC]. This organization is dedicated to "examin[ing] challenging concepts of privilege and oppression and offers solutions and team building strategies to work toward a more equitable world." They also state that the conference is not "designed to attack, degrade or beat up on white folks" but rather to promote a "a philosophy of 'understanding, respecting and connecting.'"

Audio/Visual

Race: The Power of an Illusion (2003): This is a 3-part PBS documentary. The executive producer Larry Adelman writes, "Our hope is that this series can help us all navigate through our myths and misconceptions, and scrutinize some of the assumptions we take for granted. In that sense, the real subject of the film is not so much race but the viewer, or more precisely, the notions about race we all hold."

Colorblind: The Rise of Post-Racial Politics and the Retreat from Racial Equity (2011): "In this powerful lecture, anti-racist activist and author Tim Wise discusses the pitfalls of 'colorblindness' in the Obama era and argues for deeper color-consciousness in both public and private practice. Wise argues that we can only begin to move toward authentic social and economic equity by acknowledging the diverse identities that have shaped our perceptions and the role that race continues to play in the maintenance of disparities between whites and people of color in the United States today."

White Like Me: Race, Racism, & White Privilege in America (2013): "[B]ased on the work of acclaimed anti-racist educator and author Tim Wise explores race and racism in the U.S. through the lens of whiteness and white privilege. In a stunning reassessment of the American ideal of meritocracy and claims that we've entered a post-racial society, Wise offers a fascinating look back at the race-based white entitlement programs that built the American middle class, and argues that our failure as a society to come to terms with this legacy of white privilege continues to perpetuate racial inequality and race-driven political resentments today."

Questions for Further Discussion

1. Having learned about the problems with the color-blind perspective, do you still find that you are sympathetic to its claims? Why or why not?

2. Do you think a truly post-racial America is possible? Why or why not? If so, what do you think some of the preconditions might be for this to become a reality?

3. Why do you think some Americans of color endorse color-blindness, whereas other Americans of color strongly resist such claims?

Reaching Beyond the Color Line

1. If you are a White student, consider sharing with your White family members and friends how the color-blind perspective actually harms both White Americans and Americans of color. Would this be difficult to do? Why or why not? What steps might you take to become more comfortable talking about race and racial inequality?

2. If you are a student of color, think about how the color-blind perspective has shaped your understanding about race in both your own life and the larger society. How has the ideology of color-blindness played a role in how you interpret social issues?

3. If you have family members and friends of different races, make the decision to regularly talk with them about how race continues to be relevant.

References

Bendick, M., Jr., Jackson, C. W., & Reinoso, V. A. (1994). Measuring employment discrimination through controlled experiments. *The Review of Black Political Economy, 23*(1), 25–48.

Bonilla-Silva, E. (1996). Rethinking racism: Toward a structural interpretation. *American Sociological Review, 62*(3), 465–480.

Bonilla-Silva, E. (2014). *Racism without racists: Color-blind racism and racial inequality in contemporary America* (4th ed.). Lanham, MD: Rowman & Littlefield.

Brown, M. K., Carnoy, M., Currie, E., Duster, T., Oppenheimer, D. B., Shultz, M. M., & Wellman, D. (2003). *Whitewashing race: The myth of a color-blind society.* Berkeley: University of California Press.

Brown v. Board of Education, 347 U.S. (1954).

Cable News Network. (2006). *Survey by Opinion Research Corporation: CNN Poll # 2006-030: Bush administration/president election/racial bias, December 5–7, 2006.* iPOLL Databank, The Roper Center for Public Opinion Research, University of Connecticut. Retrieved from http://www.ropercenter.uconn.edu

CBS News, & The New York Times. (2011). *Survey by CBS News/New York Times Poll: Health Care/Environment/Gender and Race Relations, March 2–7, 2011.* iPOLL Databank, The

Roper Center for Public Opinion Research, University of Connecticut. Retrieved from http://www.ropercenter.uconn.edu

Chou, R. S., & Feagin, J. R. (2008). *The myth of the model minority: Asian Americans facing racism.* Boulder, CO: Paradigm.

Daniels, J. (2009). *Cyber racism: White supremacy online and the new attack on civil rights.* Lanham, MD: Rowman & Littlefield.

Desmond, M., & Emirbayer, M. (2010). *Racial domination, racial progress: The sociology of race in America.* New York, NY: McGraw-Hill.

Diamond, J. B. (2006). Still separate and unequal: Examining race, opportunity, and school achievement in "integrated" suburbs. *The Journal of Negro Education, 75*(3), 495–505.

DiTomaso, N., Parks-Yancy, R., & Post, C. (2003). White views of civil rights: Color blindness and equal opportunity. In A. W. Doane & E. Bonilla-Silva (Eds.), *White out: The continuing significance of racism* (pp. 189–198). New York, NY: Routledge.

Feagin, J. R. (2010a). *Racist America: Roots, current realities, and future reparations* (2nd ed.). New York, NY: Routledge.

Feagin, J. R. (2010b). *The White racial frame: Centuries of racial framing and counter-framing.* New York, NY: Routledge.

Feagin, J. R., & McKinney, K. D. (2003). *The many costs of racism.* Lanham, MD: Rowman & Littlefield.

Feagin, J. R., & Sikes, M. P. (1994). *Living with racism: The Black middle class experience.* Boston, MA: Beacon Press.

Gallagher, C. A. (2012). Color-blind privilege: The social and political functions of erasing the color line in post race America. In C. A. Gallagher (Ed.), *Rethinking the color line: Readings in race and ethnicity* (pp. 92–100). New York, NY: McGraw-Hill.

Gallup. (2011). *Survey by USA Today/Gallup Poll: August Wave 1—2012 Elections/Federal Debt/Race, August 4–7, 2011.* iPOLL Databank, The Roper Center for Public Opinion Research, University of Connecticut. Retrieved from http://www.ropercenter.uconn.edu

Guinier, L., & Torres, G. (2002). *The miner's canary: Enlisting race, resisting power, and transforming democracy.* Cambridge, MA: Harvard University Press.

Jensen, R. (2005). *The heart of Whiteness: Confronting race, racism, and White privilege.* San Francisco, CA: City Light Books.

Kailin, J. (1999). How White teachers perceive the problem of racism in their schools: A case study in "liberal" Lakeview. *Teachers College Record, 100*(4), 724–750.

King, M. L., Jr. (1963). I have a dream. In J. M. Washington (Ed.), *A testament of hope: The essential writings and speeches of Martin Luther King, Jr.* (pp. 217–220). New York, NY: HarperOne.

King, M. L., Jr. (1968). *Where do we go from here: Chaos or community?* Boston, MA: Beacon Press.

Kohli, R. (2008). Breaking the cycle of racism in the classroom: Critical race reflections from future teachers of color. *Teacher Education Quarterly, 35*(4), 177–188.

Kozol, J. (1991). *Savage inequalities: Children in America's schools.* New York, NY: HarperPerennial.

Kozol, J. (2005). *The shame of the nation: The restoration of apartheid schooling in America.* New York, NY: Three Rivers Press.

Landsman, J. (2004). Confronting the racism of low expectation. *Educational Leadership, 62*(3), 28–32.

Lewis, V. A., Emerson, M. O., & Klineberg, S. L. (2011). Who we'll live with: Neighborhood racial composition preferences of Whites, Blacks, and Latinos. *Social Forces, 89*(4), 1385–1407.

Lipsitz, G. (1998). *The possessive investment in Whiteness: How White people profit from identity politics.* Philadelphia, PA: Temple University Press.

Massey, D. S., & Denton, N. A. (1993). *American apartheid: Segregation and the making of the underclass.* Cambridge, MA: Harvard University Press.

McIntosh, P. (2013). White privilege: Unpacking the invisible knapsack. In M. L. Anderson & P. Hill Collins (Eds.), *Race, class, and gender: An anthology* (8th ed., pp. 49–53). Belmont, CA: Wadsworth/Cengage Learning.

McKoy, D. L., & Vincent, J. M. (2008). Housing and education: The inextricable link. In J. H. Carr & N. K. Kutty (Eds.), *Segregation: The rising costs for America* (pp. 125–150). New York, NY: Routledge.

Omi, M., & Winant, H. (1994). *Racial formation in the United States: From the 1960s to the 1990s.* New York, NY: Routledge.

Pew Research Center for the People and the Press. (2012, June 4). *Trends in American values: 1987–2012: Partisan polarization surges in Bush, Obama years.* Washington, DC: Pew Research Center for the People and the Press.

Roscigno, V. J., & Ainsworth-Darnell, J. W. (1999). Race, cultural capital, and educational resources: Persistent inequalities and achievement returns. *Sociology of Education, 72*(3), 158–178.

Royster, D. A. (2003). *Race and the invisible hand: How White networks exclude Black men from blue-collar jobs.* Berkeley: University of California Press.

Steinfeldt, J. A., Foltz, B. D., Kaladow, J. K., Carlson, T. N., Pagano, L.A., Jr., Benton, E., & Steinfeldt, M. C. (2010). Racism in the electronic age: Role of online forums in expressing racial attitudes about American Indians. *Cultural Diversity and Ethnic Minority Psychology, 16*(3), 362–371.

STOP Racist Unfair Campaign. (2012). In *Facebook* [Group page]. Retrieved July 12, 2012, from http://www.facebook.com/groups/Stopunfaircampaign

Time Magazine. (2008). *Survey by Time Magazine/Abt SRBI Poll # 2008-4556: Race, September 26–29.* iPOLL Databank, The Roper Center for Public Opinion Research, University of Connecticut. Retrieved from http://www.ropercenter.uconn.edu

Tyson, K. (2011). *Integration interrupted: Tracking, Black students, and acting White after Brown.* New York, NY: Oxford University Press.

U.S. Census Bureau. (2011). *American Community Survey 1-Year Estimates, 2011, Detailed Tables;* generated by Ted Thornhill; using American FactFinder. Retrieved August 12, 2013, from http://factfinder2.census.gov

U.S. Department of Labor. (2012). *Labor force characteristics by race and ethnicity, 2011* (Report No. 1036). Washington, DC: U.S. Bureau of Labor Statistics.

Wise, T. (2008). *White like me: Reflections on race from a privileged son.* Brooklyn, NY: Soft Skull Press.

Wise, T. (2010). *Color-blind: The rise of post-racial politics and the retreat from racial equity.* San Francisco, CA: City Lights Books.

Woo, D. (2000). *Glass ceilings and Asian Americans: The new face of workplace barriers.* Walnut Creek, CA: AltaMira Press.

Zubrinsky Charles, C. (2003). The dynamics of racial residential segregation. *Annual Review of Sociology, 29*, 167–207.

"Oprah, Obama, and Cosby Say Blacks Should Just Work Harder, Isn't That Right?"

The Myth of Meritocracy

Paula Ioanide

Ithaca College

Paula Ioanide is an assistant professor of comparative race and ethnicity studies in the Center for the Study of Culture, Race, and Ethnicity at Ithaca College in New York. Her research focuses on institutional forms of gendered racism in the post-civil rights era, including mass incarceration and policing, immigrant exclusion and detention, welfare reform, and warfare. Dr. Ioanide teaches courses about prisons, race and sexual politics, and social movements.

Often, when we hear Black celebrities promote the American ideals of hard work, merit, and individualism, our tendency is to cast them as authorities on "the Black experience" and racial realities in the United States, and thus we give their comments greater weight. Furthermore, iconic television sitcoms like *The Cosby Show* not only encourage Americans to believe that all dreams are achievable in U.S. society if a person simply works hard enough; they also popularize the notion that a person's race, gender, and class status do not present significant obstacles to realizing those dreams. Rags-to-riches stories of celebrities like talk show host Oprah Winfrey or rapper Jay Z tend to make people believe that U.S. society now has a structure of equal access and opportunity. Similarly, the 2008 election of President Barack Obama seemed to conclusively confirm the notion that U.S. society offers fair access and opportunity to anyone willing to pursue his or her goals. While people concede that poor people, people of color, and women continue to face some obstacles in U.S. society, the dominant belief is that they generally have a fair chance to achieve their goals. The perception is that if the Huxtables, Oprah Winfrey, Jay-Z, and President Obama managed to do so, other people of color and women should also be able to succeed. Under this logic, those who fail to achieve their dreams presumably have only themselves to blame.

Indeed, throughout its eight year run, *The Cosby Show* often advocated the values of hard work and personal responsibility. As a doctor and a lawyer, the Huxtables guided their children to do well in school, obtain a college degree, and establish themselves in professional careers in order to secure the stability and status afforded by wealth and income. The Huxtables upheld values that are central to popular American narratives and culture. Stories of immigrants who came to Ellis Island penniless and managed to reach the "American dream" because of their good work ethic and perseverance are prevalent. Whether that "American dream" involves owning a home, obtaining a well-paying job that provides for one's family, or the ability to acquire other symbols of wealth and success, many Americans believe that individuals who take the "personal responsibility" to obtain success are likely to reach their goals. What's more, people often assume that a person's success is a direct reflection of how hard that person worked to earn it.

Like all good narratives, there is some truth to such notions of meritocracy, hard work, and opportunity. Certainly, people who put little or no effort in pursuing their goals in education, work, business, or creative projects rarely reach their objectives. Personal experiences of overcoming obstacles to achieve particular aspirations similarly give legitimacy to the idea that hard work produces good results that are well deserved. The accomplishments of individuals like President Obama and the changing conditions of U.S. society cannot be discounted given that only one or two generations ago, the possibility of a Black person being elected president seemed inconceivable. Indeed, due to their agency and perseverance, a growing number of Black people have pursued new opportunities in education and employment that only a few decades ago were primarily reserved for Whites. Such perseverance has led to some measurable gains in Black people's class mobility (Lacy, 2007; Oliver & Shapiro, 1995).

When considering U.S. institutional structures and systems, however, the dominant belief that people are rewarded primarily on the basis of merit and that we live in a society of equal opportunity turns out to be much more myth than fact. An extensive body of sociological facts and empirical evidence shows that a person's life chances and opportunities in the United States—by which I mean people's ability to access and obtain home ownership, employment, education, good health, and economic security—continue to be severely shaped by a person's racial identity.

To be sure, a person's gender, class, sexual orientation, nationality, citizenship, religion, and other markers of identity intersect with a person's racial identity to further complicate the ways a person's life chances and opportunities are determined. But the relationship between race and life chances in the United States deserves particular scrutiny. As George Lipsitz (2011) argues, "[M]ore than four decades after the civil rights activism of the 1960s, and nearly one hundred and fifty years after the abolition of slavery, race remains the most important single variable determining opportunities and life chances in the United States" (p. 15).

This seems like a radical claim to make in an age that many have deemed "color-blind" or "post-racial." People often use these discourses to claim that institutional forms of racial exclusion and discrimination have largely been eliminated in today's society. To understand why this claim is unfounded and why life chances and opportunities are still severely skewed along racial lines, we must understand the historical connection between race and wealth in the United States. Specifically, we must consider how the wealth and inheritances of White Americans today originate directly from unfair gains and unjust advantages made possible by past racial discrimination.

Race and Wealth in the United States

Wealth and inheritance play a critical role in American's life chances. Sociologist Thomas Shapiro (2004) demonstrates that inheritance is more important than college degrees, number of children in the family, marital status, full-time employment, or household composition in giving a person opportunities to succeed economically in U.S. society (Lipsitz, 2011). This is because wealth and inheritance allow people to get a head start in accessing opportunities that subsequently yield the potential to build more wealth. People use wealth and inheritance to pay for private schools and college, to be able to buy homes in well-to-do neighborhoods, and to start small businesses. All of these things require work and perseverance, but the initial capital to start such initiatives make it so that the hard work of people who already have wealth is much more likely to yield economic rewards than the hard work of people who must use their entire income simply to manage bills and expenses.

Black and White people with similar incomes, work histories, and family structures have radically different relationships to wealth and inheritance. For example, "On the average, whites inherit $102,167 more than Blacks" (Lipsitz, 2011, p. 4). Because they tend to inherit significantly less money from their parents and grandparents, Blacks, Latinos, Native Americans, and other people of color are more likely to be asset poor. This means that they don't have savings to fall back on in the event a family member loses a job, experiences the onset of an illness or disability, or has to stop working in order to take care of children. According to Lipsitz (2011), "Only 26 percent of white children grow up in asset-poor households, but 52 percent of blacks and 54 percent of Latinos grow up in these economically fragile households" (p. 4).

Why are White Americans today much more likely to inherit wealth than Blacks, Latinos, Native Americans, and other people of color? The answer to this question has much less to do with White Americans' good work ethic than with policies and practices that purposefully and exclusively gave Whites opportunities to gain wealth in the past. Indeed, for most of U.S. history, racially discriminatory policies and practices did not simply produce disadvantages for Blacks, Latinos, Asian Americans, and Native Americans; they also produced calculable advantages for Whites. For example, 46 million Americans today can trace the origins of their family wealth to the 1862 Homestead Act, a federal policy that gave away farmland (typically of 160 acres) west of the Mississippi River to those who applied. Because the Homestead Act had restrictions that were expressly designed to exclude Black people, this land was overwhelmingly allocated to Whites, essentially producing intergenerational wealth advantages for millions of White Americans (Lipsitz, 2006). Such exclusive opportunities for White wealth accumulation were also facilitated by federal and state policies that dispossessed and forcibly removed Native Americans onto reservations west of the Mississippi, allowing White settlers to overtake and develop land in the northeast (Rogin, 1991).

White Americans today can also trace the origins of their wealth and inheritance to the trillions of dollars accumulated through the appreciation of home values that were secured through federally insured loans granted between 1932 and 1968. As part of Franklin D. Roosevelt's New Deal policies, Federal Housing Administration (FHA) mortgage loans enabled working-class people who previously would not have been able to afford to buy homes the benefits of wealth accumulation through home ownership. Once again, however, this opportunity was granted almost exclusively to Whites. As Lipsitz (2006) shows, "98 percent of FHA loans made during that era went to whites via the openly racist categories utilized in the agency's official manuals for appraisers" (p. 107). Because of the racially discriminatory practices in mortgage lending and real estate agencies, the American dream of owning a home, and the capital accumulated through the gradual increase in property values, means that White people were much more likely to reap the benefits of their hard work than people of color. As a cornerstone of racial inequality, residential segregation and the differential effects of homeownership means that middle-class Whites have between "3 and 5 times as much wealth as equally achieving blacks" (Lipsitz, 2011, p. 3).

Housing policies and practices were not the only mechanism through which Whites were given unearned economic advantages. New Deal policies like the 1935 Social Security Act, the Wagner Act, and the 1944 GI Bill of Rights were central to White working-class people's ability to climb the economic ladder (Roediger, 2005; see also Brown, 1988; Lipsitz, 2001; Williams, 2003). Although these policies were technically "race-neutral" and did not explicitly exclude people of color, their application in the larger context of racial inequality meant that they disproportionately granted taxpayer-subsidized advantages to White men. For example, the GI Bill offered some benefits to Black veterans and historically Black colleges, but the disqualification of Black men from military service as a consequence of segregated schools and poor health meant that they were underrepresented among GI Bill beneficiaries. As Linda Faye Williams (2003) notes, "In 1950, the first census year after World War II ended, of 15,386,000 veterans eligible for GI benefits, 920,000 or 6 percent, were African Americans, although they accounted for 10 percent of the adult male population" (p. 113).

It may seem that once overtly discriminatory and exclusionary policies were eliminated as a result of the racial justice struggles of the 1950s through the 1970s, the significance of race, wealth, and opportunity would diminish. But because assets transferred to subsequent generations tend to compound in value, the significance of White wealth advantages obtained as a result of past injustices actually become even more important in the present. A 2010 study showed that "the wealth gap between Blacks and Whites quadrupled between 1984 and 2007" (Lipsitz, 2011, p. 4). The baby boom generation is estimated to inherit between seven and nine trillion dollars between 1990 and 2020. Lipsitz (2011) writes that virtually all this money is

> rooted in profits made by whites from overtly discriminatory housing markets before 1968. Adult white wage earners routinely inherit money *from* parents, while adult non-white wage earners routinely send out money *to* their parents to compensate for the low wages and lack of assets they [the parents] possess because of racial discrimination. (pp. 3–4)

The racial wealth gap is also exacerbated by contemporary policies that are seemingly race-neutral or "color-blind." Reducing taxation on inheritance and capital gains, as well as granting deductions to local property taxes adds value to wealth created through past discrimination in lending and housing policies (Lipsitz, 2006). Moreover, the effects of subprime mortgage lending practices that are technically color-blind but applied in race-specific ways have produced disproportionate losses in wealth for people of color, particularly for Black and Latino people (Rugh & Massey, 2010). Subprime loans purportedly have higher interest rates and less favorable repayment terms to make up for some homebuyers' higher credit risk. Yet studies have found that even when people of color have similar income and debt characteristics as White applicants, they are disproportionately sold subprime loans (Lipsitz, 2011). A United for a Fair Economy Report titled "State of the Dream 2008: Foreclosed" found that people of color were more than three times more likely to be sold subprime loans. Based on federal data, the study estimated that high cost loans account for 55% of loans sold to Black people but only 17% of loans to Whites. Because of such racially discriminatory lending practices, people of color were disproportionately dispossessed of their wealth as the housing market began to collapse in 2007. The report estimated that people of color are expected to lose between $164 and $213 billion as a result of the subprime mortgage crisis. This represents the greatest theft of wealth in modern U.S. history. Although Whites also suffered economically as a result of the crisis, had subprime loans been distributed equitably, losses for White people would be 44.5% higher and losses for people of color would be about 24% lower (Rivera, Cotto-Escalera, Desai, Huezo, & Muhammad, 2008, p. vii). Numerous other studies, scholarly books, and policy evaluations also show that the shift to color-blind policies has not resulted in greater racial equality when it comes to wealth distribution (Bonilla-Silva, 2001, 2006; Feagin, 2000; Massey, 2007; Massey & Denton, 1993; Williams, 2003).

Economic capital is not the only unearned advantage Whites possess; social capital also facilitates White people's access to job opportunities. Social scientists have shown that personal contacts are the single most important advantage in obtaining employment. Moreover, most jobs in the United States are not listed in classified advertisements or conducted through publicly advertised searches (Lipsitz, 2006). Because White people dominate supervisory, hiring, and decision-making roles in most companies and institutions, White people often offer jobs to insiders in their social networks, creating a hidden advantage that is difficult to quantify or contest.

Although I have focused on the economic advantages White Americans obtain as a result of past and contemporary forms of discrimination, race is also enormously significant in determining other factors critical to obtaining well-being. The opportunity to obtain a good education, adequate health care, and safety are similarly shaped by the convergences between race and place. People of color systematically experience disproportionate vulnerability to environmental hazards, police violence, longer sentences and punishment in the criminal justice system, and health effects like asthma and lead poisoning in their neighborhoods, while White Americans are protected from these vulnerabilities due to privileges afforded by their skin color and suburban locales (Lipsitz, 2006, 2011; Massey & Denton, 1993).

Persistent Myths About Race and Wealth

Despite a growing body of evidence that race continues to be the single most significant factor in determining life chances and opportunities, the myths of meritocracy, hard work, personal responsibility, and equal opportunity continue to trump these facts. Indeed, even when presented with mountains of empirical evidence that White Americans' advantages are overwhelmingly rooted in past and present discriminatory practices, many people continue to believe that Whites tend to be at the top of the socioeconomic ladder as a result of merit and hard work. Today, common explanations for Black and Latino poverty rarely acknowledge the effects of past and present discrimination on the basis of race, citizenship, and ethnicity; instead, the low socioeconomic status of Black and Latino people tends to be attributed to "cultures of poverty" that purportedly encourage low aspirations for educational attainment, poor work ethic, family and sexual non-normativity (e.g., single-parent households or teenage pregnancy), and "welfare dependence." Such myths were reified during the 2012 presidential campaign when Republican candidates Rick Santorum, Newt Gingrich, and Mitt Romney made numerous racially explicit and implicit remarks that equated Black people with dependency, laziness, and unwillingness to work. Mitt Romney extended this notion of "welfare dependency" to President Obama's entire voter base. At a private fundraiser in Florida, Romney claimed that 47% of Americans would vote for Obama because they are "dependent upon government," consider themselves "victims," and don't take "personal responsibility and care for their lives." Consciously or unconsciously, Romney implied an elision between "welfare dependence" and the "browning/blackening" of America under the leadership of a Black president. In other words, voting for Obama was understood as a process of adopting a work ethic historically associated with Black people because of oft-repeated and unfounded racist ideologies.

What do we do when copious amounts of facts and evidence fail to make a difference in changing people's dominant beliefs and perceptions? And, why do people hold on to largely unfounded myths even when extensive evidence is presented to challenge and unravel these myths? Such denials, disavowals, and displacements suggest that people's investments in the myths of meritocracy and hard work are not simply based on ignorance. That is, people may hold on to false beliefs despite being exposed to evidence-based "correctives" because these mythologies provide a sense of ideological, psychological, and identity-based coherence.

For White people, holding on to these beliefs despite the extensive evidence of ongoing systemic racism often has to do with avoiding the guilt, pain, and moral questions raised by a violent history that continues to grant them unearned advantages and privileges. A White person may be avidly committed to stopping discrimination on the basis of race or ethnicity, but he or she still inherits some aspect of privilege and advantage by virtue of being White. Even poor White Americans who face significant economic obstacles are at the very least granted the privilege of not being constantly subject to discrimination on the basis of skin color.

When White Americans do accept the overwhelming evidence of White advantages and privileges yielded by a long legacy of racism, the worldviews, ideologies, and belief systems through which White folks are encouraged to understand themselves tend to crumble. If I believe that I got to the top of my class solely on the basis of my individual hard work, I may feel justified to consider myself superior to those who are lower than me in rank. If instead I consider all the unearned and unjust advantages I inherited by virtue of my race, my hard work has to be reconsidered in the context of these unjust advantages and disadvantages. By extension, I likely have to confront ethical questions about my role and responsibility in a system that gives me advantages through the exclusion, exploitation, and dispossession of people of color.

For people of color, investments in the myths of meritocracy and hard work are often rooted in something quite different. For the past 40 years, politicians, pundits, and media representations have blamed and demonized poor Native, Black and Latino people for high poverty rates, school dropouts, teenage pregnancies, criminality, and "welfare dependence" (Kim, 2000; Lee, 1999; Reeves, 1994; Springer, 2005). As a result, some people of color invest in notions of hard work, merit, and personal responsibility in order to dissociate themselves from these negative stereotypes, particularly from the stigmatization of dependence. Indeed, the demonized "Black urban underclass" was the unacknowledged stereotype that *The Cosby Show* implicitly worked so hard to dispel.

For Asian Americans who tend to be stereotyped as "the model minority," investments in the myth of meritocracy and hard work may be rooted in the desire to preserve a status that is relatively valorized in comparison to other groups of color. This often functions to socially divide groups who share experiences of racial discrimination and exclusion, emphasizing differences over similarities that could produce generative political alliances.

At times, people of color who obtain middle- and upper class status through education, entrepreneurship, or employment also adopt the rhetoric of blaming poor people of color for their class status and begin advocating the myth of meritocracy and hard work. They offer their own experiences of success as "proof" of other people's unwillingness to pursue opportunities. While there may be some truth to this correlation, such views often minimize the number of systemic obstacles poor people of color would have to overcome in order to reach economic ascendance *as a group.* In other words, the U.S. racial order has conceded class mobility for a small number of people of color. But if it were to allow the economic ascent of a majority of people of color, it would have to radically alter its wealth, opportunity, and social structure. White people would have to relinquish their long-term dominance in the domains of property and business ownership, employment, education, and political office and share these resources and opportunities with people of color.

Middle- and upper class people of color may also advocate notions of meritocracy and hard work in order to obtain or preserve higher positions of power. Such positions, particularly if they are situated in predominantly White institutions, often require that people of color adopt the values, rhetoric, and practices of those institutions. For example, it is not likely that people such as former Secretary of State Condoleezza Rice or Justice Clarence Thomas would have gained entry into such high governmental and judicial positions had they made public critiques of institutional racism in the United States.

When people of color advocate, defend, and invest in notions of hard work, personal responsibility, and equal opportunity without also revealing the ongoing significance of racial discrimination and inequality, the myth of meritocracy is reinforced. *The Cosby Show* introduced media representations of dignity, resilience, humor, and self-empowerment common in many families of color in the United States. Yet because these qualities were represented without also offering a critique of persisting color-blind reformulations of institutional racism, *The Cosby Show* and people of color who defended a pull-yourself-up-by-your-own-bootstraps ideology reinforced the myth of meritocracy in the post-civil rights era (Dyson, 2005; Gray, 1995; Hunt, 2005; Jhally & Lewis, 2005). Indeed, a study of White people's responses to *The Cosby Show* found that "acceptance of the Huxtables as an Everyfamily did not dislodge the generally negative associations White viewers have of 'black culture,' attitudes quickly articulated when other black TV sitcoms were discussed" (Jhally & Lewis, 2005, p. 86). In other words, while *The Cosby Show* was groundbreaking in humanizing Black people to predominantly White audiences, it did little to challenge the false notion that working-class Black people were economically impoverished as a result of their individual failings rather than long histories of purposeful and systemic disadvantage and discrimination.

Lipsitz (2006) reminds us that

we do not choose our color, but we do choose our commitments. We do not choose our parents, but we do choose our politics. Yet we do not make these decisions in a vacuum; they occur within a social structure that gives value to Whiteness and offers rewards for racism. (p. viii)

There is nothing inevitable about a White person complying with a system that continues to stratify advantages on the basis of racially unjust practices and policies. It is also not inevitable that a person of color will elect to fight such a system, though people of color have often spearheaded social justice movements that have collectively benefited the U.S. social fabric. But those who find justice irresistible and White supremacy intolerable always have the option to collectively organize in order to transform their society toward what W. E. B. Du Bois called "abolition democracy" (Du Bois, 1998). Abolition democracy does not mean opening up U.S. structures of opportunity so that people of color can simply compete better while leaving a radically hierarchal system intact. Instead, abolition democracy refers to democratization processes that undo the inherent hierarchies in wealth and opportunity this country has built along racial lines. It means changing the very structure of our socioeconomic system so that its conditions are increasingly conducive to communal health, safety, healing, and ethical integrity.

Suggested Additional Resources

Bonilla-Silva, E. (2006). *Racism without racists: Color-blind racism and the persistence of racial inequality in the United States* (2nd ed.). Lanham, MD: Rowman & Littlefield.

Dyson, M. E. (2005). *Is Bill Cosby right?: Or has the Black middle class lost its mind?* New York, NY: Basic Civitas Books.

Jhally, S., & Lewis, J. (2005). White responses: The emergence of "enlightened" racism. In D. M. Hunt (Ed.), *Channeling Blackness: Studies on television and race in America.* New York, NY: Oxford University Press.

Lee, R. G. (1999). *Orientals: Asian Americans in popular culture.* Philadelphia, PA: Temple University Press.

Lipsitz, G. (2006). *The possessive investment in Whiteness: How White people profit from identity politics* (Rev. and expanded ed.). Philadelphia, PA: Temple University Press.

Roediger, D. (2005). *Working toward Whiteness: How America's immigrants became White: The strange journey from Ellis Island to the suburbs.* New York, NY: Basic Books.

Shapiro, T. (2004). *The hidden cost of being African American: How wealth perpetuates inequality.* New York, NY: Oxford University Press.

Williams, L. F. (2003). *The constraint of race: Legacies of White skin privilege in America.* University Park: Pennsylvania State University Press.

Questions for Further Discussion

1. What role does the author believe hard work and personal responsibility play in life chances and outcomes? How invested are you in the idea of hard work and personal responsibility? How do these ideas affect the ways you act in school, at work, or in your family?

2. Does the evidence of racial discrimination and the root causes of wealth inequalities change your perception of "hard work" and the ways it is rewarded, or do you find yourself dismissing this evidence, needing further evidence? If so, why?

3. What are the differences between White students' investments in meritocracy and the investments of students of color? Based on this essay, what do you believe accounts for these differences?

Reaching Beyond the Color Line

1. Take some time to discuss family expectations and self-imposed expectations regarding achievement, success, educational attainment, and hopes for future employment. Are these expectations expressed differently by students of color and by White students? Why do you think these differences exist?

2. In a multiracial group, discuss whether White students and families acknowledge privileges and advantages on the basis of race. Also discuss the extent to which families and students of color expect to be faced with the obstacles and challenges of racial discrimination in college and beyond. What is the root of these different narratives and explanations?

References

Bonilla-Silva, E. (2001). *White supremacy and racism in the post-civil rights era.* Boulder, CO: L. Rienner.

Bonilla-Silva, E. (2006). *Racism without racists: Color-blind racism and the persistence of racial inequality in the United States* (2nd ed.). Lanham, MD: Rowman & Littlefield .

Brown, M. K. (1988). *Remaking the welfare state: Retrenchment and social policy in America and Europe.* Philadelphia, PA: Temple University Press.

Du Bois, W. E. B. (1998). *Black reconstruction in America, 1860–1880.* New York, NY: Free Press.

Dyson, M. E. (2005). *Is Bill Cosby right? Or has the Black middle class lost its mind?* New York, NY: Basic Civitas Books.

Feagin, J. R. (2000). *Racist America: Roots, current realities, and future reparations.* New York, NY: Routledge.

Gray, H. (1995). *Watching race: Television and the struggle for "Blackness."* Minneapolis: University of Minnesota Press.

Hunt, D. M. (Ed.). (2005). *Channeling Blackness: Studies on television and race in America.* New York, NY: Oxford University Press.

Jhally, S., & Lewis, J. (2005). White responses: The emergence of "enlightened" racism. In D. M. Hunt (Ed.), *Channeling Blackness: Studies on television and race in America.* New York, NY: Oxford University Press.

Kim, C. J. (2000). *Bitter fruit: The politics of Black-Korean conflict in New York City.* New Haven, CT: Yale University Press.

Lacy, Karyn R. (2007). *Blue-chip black: Race, class, and status in the new black middle class.* Berkeley, CA: University of California Press.

Lee, R. G. (1999). *Orientals: Asian Americans in popular culture.* Philadelphia, PA: Temple University Press.

Lipsitz, G. (2001). *American studies in a moment of danger.* Minneapolis: University of Minnesota Press.

Lipsitz, G. (2006). *The possessive investment in Whiteness: How White people profit from identity politics* (Rev. and expanded ed.). Philadelphia, PA: Temple University Press.

Lipsitz, G. (2011). *How racism takes place.* Philadelphia, PA: Temple University Press.

Massey, D. S., & Denton, N. (1993). *American apartheid: Segregation and the making of the underclass.* Cambridge, MA: Harvard University Press.

Massey, D. S. (2007). *Categorically unequal: The American stratification system.* New York, NY: Russell Sage Foundation.

Oliver, M., & Shapiro, T. M. (1995). *Black wealth/White wealth: A new perspective on racial inequality.* New York, NY: Routledge.

Reeves, J. (1994). *Cracked coverage: Television news, the anti-cocaine crusade, and the Reagan legacy.* Durham, NC: Duke University Press.

Rivera, A., Cotto-Escalera, B., Desai, A., Huezo, J., & Muhammad, D. (2008). *State of the dream 2008: Foreclosed.* Boston, MA: United for a Fair Economy. Retrieved from http://www.faireconomy.org/dream

Roediger, D. (2005). *Working toward Whiteness: How America's immigrants became White: The strange journey from Ellis Island to the suburbs.* New York, NY: Basic Books.

Rogin, M. P. (1991). *Fathers and children: Andrew Jackson and the subjugation of the American Indian.* New Brunswick, NJ: Transaction Publishers.

Rugh, J., & Massey, D. (2010). Racial segregation and the American foreclosure crisis. *American Sociological Review, 75*(5), 629–651.

Shapiro, T. (2004). *The hidden cost of being African American: How wealth perpetuates inequality.* New York, NY: Oxford University Press.

Springer, K. (2005). *Living for the revolution: Black feminist organizations, 1968–1980.* Durham, NC: Duke University Press.

Williams, L. F. (2003). *The constraint of race: Legacies of White skin privilege in America.* University Park: Pennsylvania State University Press.

"If Only He Hadn't Worn the Hoodie . . ."

Race, Selective Perception, and Stereotype Maintenance

Rashawn Ray

University of Maryland

Rashawn Ray is an assistant professor of sociology at the University of Maryland, College Park. He received a PhD in sociology from Indiana University in 2010. Ray's research interests are social psychology, race and ethnic relations, and race–class– gender. His work addresses three key areas: the determinants and consequences of social class identification, men's treatment of women, and how racial stratification structures social life. Ray is the editor of *Race and Ethnic Relations in the 21st Century: History, Theory, Institutions, and Policy.* His work has appeared in *Ethnic and Racial Studies, American Behavioral Scientist, Journal of Contemporary Ethnography, Journal of Higher Education,* and *Journal of African American Studies.*

On February 26, 2012, in Sanford, Florida, during halftime of the television viewing of the National Basketball Association's all-star game, 17-year-old Trayvon Martin (who was on the phone with a friend) was walking back from a local convenience store to his father's girlfriend's apartment with a bag of Skittles and a bottled iced tea. There was a light rain in the air and Martin had on a jacket with a hood, commonly called a "hoodie." George Zimmerman, who was the self-appointed neighborhood watchperson, thought Martin looked suspicious and began following him. Zimmerman then called 911 and reported that a police officer should be sent to the apartment complex because he saw a suspicious man walking around. When he reached a 911 operator, Zimmerman was specifically instructed to stop following Martin and wait for police to arrive. Minutes later, an altercation ensued between Zimmerman and Martin leaving Zimmerman bruised and bloodied and Martin shot dead.

Zimmerman, who had a gun permit and was previously arrested for assaulting a police officer, was arrested for questioning and later released under Florida's Stand Your Ground law. The law allows individuals to defend themselves by using deadly force if they feel their life is in danger (Cheng & Hoekstra, 2012). Zimmerman claimed he felt his life was in danger and had no other choice but to shoot Martin. For Martin, his body was initially labeled a "John Doe" and not identified until the following day when his father filed a police report. Calling this incident a national tragedy, President Barack Obama stated, "When I think about this boy, I think about my own kids . . . If I had a son, he'd look like Trayvon."

Following the shooting death of Martin, a national uproar with racial undertones ensued that ultimately led to Zimmerman being charged with second-degree murder. Zimmerman, who is perceived by some as phenotypically White, has a White father and Peruvian mother and identifies as Hispanic. Martin's mother and father are Black. Some in the media claimed that if Martin had not been wearing the hoodie, he would not have looked suspicious. Among those was Fox News host Geraldo Rivera (2012), who stated:

> I am urging the parents of Black and Latino youngsters particularly not to let their children go out wearing hoodies. I think the hoodie is as much responsible for Trayvon Martin's death as George Zimmerman was . . . Trayvon Martin, God bless him, an innocent kid, a wonderful kid, a box of Skittles in his hands. He didn't deserve to die. But I bet you money, if he didn't have that hoodie on, that nutty neighborhood watch guy wouldn't have responded in that violent and aggressive way.

Rivera's statement proved controversial in its effort to remove blame from Zimmerman and transfer it to Martin for choosing to wear a hoodie in drizzling weather.

As the case reached a level of national conversation, many argued that Zimmerman targeted Martin solely because he was Black. This argument asserts that there is something unique about being a Black male that results in individuals being perceived as suspicious, untrustworthy, and dangerous. Zimmerman refuted the claim that he targeted Martin because of his race but did report that a series of break-ins occurred in the complex and the perpetrators were believed to be Black males. As Benjamin Crump, lawyer for the Martin family claimed in a September 29, 2012 interview with the *Orlando Sentinel*, race was "the elephant in the room." A *Washington Post*–ABC Poll taken in April of 2012 ultimately supported his statement, as it found that 80% of Blacks believed that Martin's killing was unjustified, compared to about 40% of Whites. Concepts from the social psychology of race can help us better understand these kinds of significant racial differences in perceptions and attitudes.

The Social Psychology of Racial Stereotyping

Prominent sociologists, Michael Omi and Howard Winant (1994) note that we often use physical attributes including articles of clothing like a hoodie as mental shorthand for racial scripts. However, it is important to note that our racial cues are not limited to a hoodie or other articles of clothing. We use physical attributes, such as skin tone, facial features, and hairstyles to make racial assumptions. Accordingly, the social psychological processes described here relate to other forms of stereotypical thinking, such as assuming anyone who looks "Mexican" is "illegal," that all Asians are good at math, that most Arab Americans are terrorists, or that all Native Americans are alcoholics. These are *stereotypes* or oversimplified sets of beliefs about members of a particular group.

Negative attributes are often placed on Black men who wear hoodies because of their race and gender. In this context, the negative attribute in question is anticipated crime that leads to these group members being perceived as suspicious and dangerous to others. These attributes are not simply impromptu. Rather, they stem from intergroup attitudes that are formulated via broader sociohistorical contexts. In other words, the hoodie combined with Blackness and maleness triggers certain stereotypes based on preexisting "knowledge" about group members. Knowledge, in this context, does not refer to education, actual facts, or reality. Instead, it refers to the conventional wisdom that individuals use to make sense of personal interactions (see also Harris and McClure, Essay 1). I address this point more directly below.

Thomas F. Pettigrew's (1979) research suggests that individuals who perceive Black men with hoodies as a threat commit the *ultimate attribution error*. Ultimate attribution error asserts that undesirable characteristics exhibited by out-group members (i.e., Blacks and other people of color) are more likely to be perceived by those in the in-group (i.e., Whites) as innate and a part of one's personality. In other words, negative behaviors are perceived to be biological or rooted in the culture of the group (see Buffington, Essay 4; Meanwell, Patel, & McClure, Essay 13; and Zhou, Essay 8 for further discussion). On the other hand, positive characteristics (e.g., being a law-abiding citizen) are attributed to factors external to the individual like education. In addition, out-group members who are perceived positively are viewed as exceptions to the norm of "bad" behavior from their group.

Pettigrew (1998) highlights that attribution error occurs due to limited information about a particular group. As more information is obtained about out-group members, individuals are less likely to exhibit prejudiced attitudes because they come to view out-group members as more heterogeneous instead of more homogenous. As I will show later, the type and quality of information is key for changing prejudiced attitudes. Stereotypes about certain groups largely stem from public discourses. Public discourses can be conceptualized as mainstream narratives that become assumed facts about a particular group or how society operates. For example, during his 1976 presidential campaign, Ronald Reagan stating the following about an alleged woman on Chicago's South Side:

She has eighty names, thirty addresses, twelve Social Security cards and is collecting veteran's benefits on four non-existing deceased husbands. And she is collecting Social Security on her cards. She's got Medicaid, getting food stamps, and she is collecting welfare under each of her names. Her tax-free cash income is over $150,000.

Although the woman associated with this infamous overexaggeration was convicted of less than $10,000 in fraud, this statement led to Black women being stereotypically associated with the infamous "welfare queen" much more than White women (Gilliam,1999). Discourses transform language beyond the boundaries of words and sentences to have a real impact on policies and also on how individuals interact with each other.

Media play a dominant role in formulating stereotypical discourses in part because there is a limited amount of interaction across racial and social class divides. U.S. neighborhoods and schools are just as segregated today as they were in the 1950s (Dixon, 2006). Therefore, social media, television, movies, and music are dominant forms of public discourse that often portray people of color in stereotypical ways. For example, some movies suggest that the sexual predator a woman should be afraid of is a male stranger walking down a dark street possibly wearing a hoodie, when research shows that women are more likely to be raped by someone they know (Armstrong, Hamilton, & Sweeney, 2006). News media, in particular, can play a critical role in this perception. Communication scholars Robert Entman and Andrew Rojecki (2000) found that Black suspects and criminals are more likely to be featured on the news than White suspects and criminals. With limited interpersonal interactions across racial divides, these images lead to stereotypical thinking that all Black men are dangerous and threatening. For example, though more Whites commit violent crime, respondents estimated that Blacks commit 40% more violent crime than they actually do (see Entman & Rojecki, 2000).

Hogg (2000) highlights the importance of *subjective uncertainty,* which asserts that when there is minimal understanding about how someone should be categorized (e.g., individuals with hoodies or Black males), individuals express a "state of subjective uncertainty" where they infer stereotypes and, in turn, exhibit some form of discrimination against the person in question (Hogg, 2003). When individuals are categorized largely by group membership (under conditions of subjective uncertainty that are largely due to limited interpersonal interaction), others evaluate and interact with them based on the scripts perceived to be associated with that group.

Similarly, individuals engage in *selective perception* by only seeing the types of behaviors that confirm their stereotypes and not those that refute them. In other words, even when individuals encounter a man in a hoodie or a Black man walking down the street and nothing happens (or if they have a positive interaction), the combination of selective perception (i.e., only seeing what we want to see), subjective uncertainty (i.e., categorizing people inaccurately due to limited information about other groups), and ultimate attribution error (i.e., believing that undesirable characteristics are an innate part of out-group members such as "all Black men with hoodies are dangerous") mean that positive interactions mostly lead to in-group members ignoring that example or perceiving it as an "exception to the rule." This process is an attempt to avoid cognitive dissonance and maintain stereotypical thinking.

Defined as aligning one's beliefs in order to avoid disharmony or inconsistency Festinger & Kelly, (1951), *cognitive dissonance* can lead to irrational behavior. For example, individuals who hold prejudiced attitudes about Blacks being criminal may have a normal, satisfying, and uneventful social interaction with a Black man in a parking lot but not include this positive interaction into their knowledge base to evaluate the next Black man they encounter in a parking lot. Instead, their resolution of the cognitive dissonance will tell them to be afraid just as before. Another example is a person who interacts with a Latino person and finds out that person was born in the United States. Instead of thinking that the next Latino encountered could also be a U.S. citizen, the person continues to assume Latinos are "illegal" immigrants, failing to take the previous experience into account.

Taken together, all of these processes are connected to arguments about why Martin was followed by Zimmerman. Below, I dissect the arguments about whether Martin was followed because of a hoodie or his Blackness.

If He Hadn't Been Wearing a Hoodie . . .

In order to investigate the role the hoodie actually played in the Zimmerman case, we must examine a series of underlying assumptions and claims. The first claim is that a hoodie, and thus anyone wearing one, is suspicious. In other words, there is something about a hoodie that makes someone threatening. One approach to test this claim is to look at other social contexts where individuals wear hoodies to see if they are perceived as suspicious or innocuous. One person who wears a hoodie frequently is Facebook founder and CEO Mark Zuckerberg. Zuckerberg wears hoodies during casual encounters and even professional business meetings. However, he is not perceived as suspicious. Instead, as Benjamin Nugent's May 2012 CNN article states, "The hooded sweatshirt [is] a symbol of his independent-mindedness, his youth, his authenticity, his loyalty to the culture of Silicon Valley." At worst, Zuckerberg is regarded as "immature," but definitely not suspicious.

Another example is New England Patriots head football coach Bill Belichick who can be seen on the sidelines of every game in a hoodie. He is never regarded as suspicious or less than a coach because he wears a hoodie. In fact, he is evaluated only by his team's success and not his clothing or by the behavior of fans who may have on a hoodie and engage in violent or illegal behavior.

In addition to celebrities like Zuckerberg and Belichick, college students often walk around campuses with hoodies representing their university or favorite team. When it rains, snows, or is simply cold, individuals in public spaces wear hoodies to protect themselves from the weather. These groups of people are generally not regarded as suspicious or threatening unless there is another attribution placed on them that implies danger. We also know that Zimmerman, who was 28 at the time of the incident, thought Martin was older. As he said during his arraignment: "I did not know how old he was. I thought he was a little bit younger than I am, and I did not know if he was armed or not." Zimmerman's own statement implies that there was at least one additional attribute besides the hoodie that led to Martin looking suspicious. Even Rivera's statement about hoodies draws upon another attribute: race. In his statement, he specifically references "Black and Latino youngsters" and excludes White and Asian youth from his statement about who should and should not wear hoodies. While Asians have their own stereotypes such as being unassimilable, passive, and unable to lead, Blacks and Latinos are more likely to be stereotyped as criminal than Whites and Asians.

Collectively, the hoodie argument simply does not hold. Individuals wear hoodies regularly and are not followed or perceived as threatening. Instead, placing the focus on the hoodie not only moves the blame to Martin for wearing the hoodie, but it also allows individuals to avoid admitting their own racial prejudices.

Maybe It's Because Trayvon Was Black . . .

Given the previous discussion of racial stereotyping, a second claim that must be examined in looking at the role of the hoodie in the Zimmerman case is that perhaps the hoodie wasn't really the major factor in Martin being followed; perhaps Zimmerman targeted Martin because he was a Black male. Given that Blackness is at the center of this argument, one appropriate way to explore this perspective is to determine whether Black men not wearing hoodies are considered suspicious. Below, I provide examples where Black men are perceived as suspicious in various social contexts.

New York City (NYC) is notorious for its stop-and-frisk program (Center for Constitutional Rights, 2012; see also Doude, Essay 19). In 2011, NYC police officers performed nearly 700,000 stops. Blacks represented over one half of these stops compared to one third for Latinos and less than 10% for Whites. Over one half of all stops involved frisks. Of the nearly 140,000 times that force was used, Blacks represented roughly 55%. Obviously, we would assume from these statistics that the overwhelming majority of individuals who were stopped, frisked, and exposed to force were engaged in criminal activity. However, this is not the case. Only 2% of the nearly 700,000 stops resulted in the discovery of contraband (Center for Constitutional Rights, 2012). This means that over 9 out of 10 Black and Latino men stopped by the police were innocent and engaging in no wrongdoing.

Despite the very low numbers of individuals who are actually engaging in illegal activity during a stop-and-frisk, and the fact that in 2013 the stop-and-frisk program was ruled unconstitutional under the Fourth Amendment and the Equal Protection Clause of the Fourteenth Amendment, the perception is that Black and Latino men are dangerous. (As of publication, the Second U.S. Circuit Court of Appeals has put a hold on Scheindlin's District Court ruling of unconstitutionality; final disposition is pending.) In fact, NYC Mayor Bloomberg in a WOR-NY radio interview on June 28, 2013, stated, "I think, we disproportionately stop Whites too

much and minorities too little." As a result, some Black and Latino men have a difficult time engaging in activities that every U.S. citizen is granted—the ability to walk
down a street, breathe air, or catch a cab. In the early 2000s, former mayor Rudolph
Giuliani of New York introduced a sting operation to confirm the discrimination
Black men encounter when trying to catch a cab. Giuliani set up undercover opera-
tions to fine taxi drivers for passing Black riders. One may initially think, why is this
an issue? Well, cab drivers and Black men have a long, contentious history where cab
drivers have been suspected of skipping Black men as potential passengers because
they perceive they will be robbed. The sting operation implemented by Mayor
Giuliani stemmed from a lawsuit by actor Danny Glover (most known for his role
in *Lethal Weapon* films) after he claimed that at least five taxicabs passed him, his
daughter, and her roommate. Then, the taxicab that stopped refused to allow Glover
to sit in the front seat.

Some may still say, if Glover and other Black men had on hoodies, it is understandable that the cabs passed them up. They look suspicious. But what if the Black
men are wearing business suits? On the 2008 Presidential campaign trail, President
Barack Obama was continuously asked if he identified as Black. His response was a
colloquial, "The last time I tried to catch a cab in New York City . . . ." His statement
implies that he has difficulty catching a cab because he is a Black male. President
Obama is not the only notable Black man to make this claim. Dr. Cornel West, formerly of Harvard and Princeton Universities, wrote in the preface of his acclaimed
book, *Race Matters* (1994), that when he was going to finish his deal with the publisher, he was late for the meeting because he could not catch a cab while wearing a
suit. He mentions that 10 cabs passed by him. Below, I detail a few more examples
of Black men in different social contexts who did not have on a hoodie but were
considered suspicious, threatening, or dangerous.

In 2009, Dr. Henry Louis Gates, Harvard University W. E. B. Du Bois Professor of
African American Studies, returned from a research trip in China to find his front
door jammed shut. He and the driver of his car proceeded to force it open. A neigh-
bor called 911 to report a breaking and entering in progress. After police arrived,
events ensued that ultimately led to the arrest of Gates in his own home. This
incident culminated in what is now known as the "Beer Summit" where President
Obama invited Dr. Gates and the arresting officer to the White House for a beer to
discuss the incident and race relations more broadly.

In another example, in Murfreesboro, Tennessee, in 2012, police officers were in
pursuit of what was described as a young, Asian male. Officers came upon Joseph
Sushak, a Nigerian-born, 58-year-old graduate student, who was about to change
the oil of his truck in his driveway. Upon seeing Sushak, the police officers started
asking him a series of questions about his whereabouts. Within a matter of seconds,
Sushak was beaten, handcuffed, and face down on his own property. He suffered
injuries and had to go to the emergency room. When Sushak claimed he had been
a victim of police brutality, the case against the police was ultimately dismissed.

Finally, on December 31, 2008, at 2 a.m., Robbie Tolan, a Black minor league
baseball player, was driving home with his cousin from a night on the town celebrating the New Year. As they pulled into Tolan's driveway, a police car pulled up,
asked the men what they were doing there, and made them lie face down on the

ground. At this time, Tolan's parents came out of the house trying to determine what was going on and began explaining to the officers that their son lived there. One of the officers aggressively approached Tolan's mother. Tolan proceeded to get off the ground to protect his mother and was shot. Tolan's house was in a predominately White, upper middle-class neighborhood in Houston, Texas. The officer who shot Tolan was brought up on charges but ultimately acquitted.

Given these examples, it becomes clear that it is not the hoodie that made Trayvon Martin look suspicious. Similar to these men, it was his Blackness and maleness. As mentioned above, Black men are not the only ones who are victimized by stereotypical thinking. There are numerous incidents of Latino men being arrested, held in prison for months, or even killed for suspicion of "illegal" immigration (Golash-Boza, 2012). Furthermore, Asian Americans are victimized for posing an economic threat to some American workers. The tragic death of Chinese American Vincent Chin in 1982 highlights the most visceral type of stereotypical thinking. Chin was viciously murdered by White autoworkers in Detroit, Michigan, after being confused as Japanese at a time when Detroit was laying off its auto workers as a result of Japanese automakers' dominance in the market.

Since 9/11, Arab Americans have been profiled and discriminated against in airports and other public venues. In 2013, Atif Irfan and his wife Sobia Ijaz, along with six relatives, were trying to decide where to sit on an Air Tran flight from Washington, DC, to Orlando, Florida for a religious conference. Another passenger overheard this conversation and before the family knew it, they were escorted off the plane by security. Air Tran then removed all passengers to sweep the plane and rescreen all baggage. After hours of questioning and the children being unable to eat, the FBI released the family stating it was simply a misunderstanding. Air Tran refused to rebook the family on another flight (instead giving them a refund), thus forcing the family to book a flight on another airline for double the cost. All of the family members were born in the United States except one and Irfan is a lawyer from Detroit, Michigan. In these ways, many people of color find themselves the targets of racism and discrimination due to a variety of different attribution errors. As the Irfan and Ijaz case shows, there are many costs to individuals who are victimized this way, including financial costs. Yet, the costs may be far greater than this. In the next section, I use the role of criminalization in Black men's lives as a case study for how people of color are affected by these patterns.

Black Male Criminalization and Its Effects

Criminalization is the inability to separate a person from criminality based on the person's group identity. In this case, Black male criminalization is the inability to separate Black males from criminals (Muhammad, 2010). These stereotypes are evident when women clutch their purses when they see a Black man, or when Whites scurry to the other side of the street or out of purview of an approaching Black man (Feagin, 1991). Criminalization is something that is all too common for Blacks as Black mothers responded to Martin's death with statements such as "that could have been my son." Black men commonly made statements like "that could have been me." Following the Zimmerman verdict, in fact, President Obama stated, "Trayvon Martin could have been me, 35 years ago." In the case of Martin, his life ended tragically before his 18th birthday. However, even Black men who are not killed still suffer psychologically, educationally, economically, and physically from criminalization.

Psychologically, Black men have to deal with the effects of criminality and come to terms with the fact that socioeconomic status (as highlighted by the experiences of President Obama and Drs. West and Gates) does not protect them from being perceived as suspicious and threatening. As a result, they have worse mental health outcomes than similar Whites (Jackson, 1997). Educationally, Ferguson (2000) shows that Black boys in grade school are perceived by teachers as troublemakers, reprimanded more severely for the same behaviors as White students, and more likely to be suspended thus impacting their educational outcomes. Economically, Pager (2007) shows a staggering trend. Comparing the job prospects of Black and White men (some with a criminal record and some without), she found that not only were White men without a criminal record hired more often than Black men, but White men with a criminal record were hired more than Black men without a criminal record. Physically, Black men's health suffers. My research on the effects of the racial composition of neighborhoods on physical activity finds that Black men in predominately White neighborhoods are significantly less likely to be physically active than Black men in predominately Black neighborhoods. Black men in predominantly White neighborhoods are less likely to exercise because of their experiences with and fear of criminalization and the psychological processes with which they must engage when they leave their homes.

The question remains, what do we do about racial stereotyping? Research suggests that there are various ways to decrease stereotyping. Most of these ways involve some social interaction with people of different racial groups. For instance, *contact theory* asserts that when a sizable proportion of a minority group is present, there are increased opportunities for contact between majority and minority group members. Gordon W. Allport (1954) argues that the effects of contact on prejudice depend on the *quality of contact*: (1) Is the contact voluntary or involuntary? (2) When majority and minority group members come in contact, are they of equal status? and (3) Does the contact occur in competitive or collaborative environments? Contact that is voluntary, equal, and collaborative should lead to less prejudicial attitudes. Along these lines, the *type of contact* also matters. Friendships among majority and minority group members decrease prejudice, while acquaintanceships moderately decrease prejudice. Repetitive, positive, informal contact at times decreases prejudice (i.e., in a dorm or classroom of students), while the more rigorous conditions required for equal status contact are usually effective but rarely met.

Significantly, Jackman and Crane (1986) find that the effect of contact on reducing prejudicial attitudes varies by socioeconomic status. Specifically, Whites' negative attitudes toward Blacks become relatively obsolete when they have higher status Black friends. Unfortunately, as Jackman and Crane note, rarely do higher status Blacks interact with lower status Whites in meaningful ways. Additionally, having Black friends and acquaintances hardly affects Whites' policy attitudes about race-based policies. As a result, they conclude that the *diversity of contacts* is more important than the intimacy of contacts because diversity contributes to changing stereotypes of the entire group compared to just changing stereotypes of a particular individual. This distinction is important considering that Lawrence Bobo's (2012) research finds that Whites' positive interactions with Latinos and Asians alter their perceptions of the entire race, while positive interactions with Blacks only alter their perception of that individual (see Bobo & Hutchings, 1996). This finding further illuminates ultimate attribution error.

In sum, this research suggests that the quality, type, and diversity of contact across racial divides can facilitate meaningful conversations and knowledge exchanges about race relations. If contact facilitates more accurate knowledge about the lives of people of color, it will ultimately help Whites reassess their own group, form affective social networks with people of color, and perhaps decrease their prejudices and tendency to stereotype.

Conclusion

Ultimately, George Zimmerman was found not guilty of second-degree murder and manslaughter despite evidence that suggested he followed (or "profiled") Trayvon Martin. In the court of public opinion, however, Americans are still clearly conflicted. Zimmerman received an outpouring of financial support from individuals wanting to help with his defense. On the other hand, hundreds of thousands have marched or shown solidarity with the Martin family by wearing hoodies on specified days. The hoodie has been transformed into a symbol of protest even though it had very little to do with why Trayvon Martin was killed. The hoodie was simply a scapegoat for those trying to reconcile (their racial) cognitive dissonance. Most Black men, similar to most White men, are not criminals or untrustworthy; they are law-abiding citizens. Individuals must recognize significant and meaningful nonverbal cues and symbols, instead of ubiquitously categorizing Black men as dangerous. These changes in individuals' perceptions could contribute to reducing the criminalization of Black men and the stereotyping of all marginalized groups.

Suggested Additional Resources

Correll, J., Park, B., Judd, C.M., & Wittenbrink, B. (2002). The police officer's dilemma: Using ethnicity to disambiguate potentially threatening individuals. *Journal of Personality and Social Psychology, 83*(6), 1314–1329.

Katznelson, I. (2006). *When affirmative action was White: An untold history of racial inequality in the twentieth-century America.* New York, NY: W. W. Norton.

Mazzocco, P. J., Brock, T. C., Brock, G. J., Olson, K. R., & Banaji, M. R. (2006). The cost of being Black: White Americans' perceptions and the question of reparations." *Du Bois Review, 3,* 261–297.

Ray, R. (Ed.). (2010). *Race and ethnic relations in the 21st century: History, theory, institutions, and policy.* San Diego, CA: Cognella.

Websites

Center for Constitutional Rights: http://stopandfrisk.org
Harvard's Implicit Association Tests: https://implicit.harvard.edu/implicit/demo

Audio/Visual

Peters, W. (Director), & Cobb, C. (Writer). (1985, March 26). A class divided [Television episode]. *Frontline.* Boston, MA: Public Broadcasting System.

Questions for Further Discussion

1. What, if any, conversations have you had about the Zimmerman case? Have they included people whose background and racial group membership is different from your own? Why or why not?

2. Based on this review, do you think conflict is inevitable when distinct groups interact? Why or why not?

3. Given the author's discussion of contact, how do we encourage meaningful, equitable social interactions across racial groups?

4. How do we encourage candid conversations across racial groups about how race/ethnicity, racism, discrimination, and White privilege impact people's lives?

Reaching Beyond the Color Line

1. Consider examples from your own life and how stereotypical thinking might have shaped your perceptions. What could you do differently in the future, when faced with similar situations?

2. Watch these two scenes from the movie *Crash* and reflect on the social interactions.
   a. *"Hey Osama: I'm an American citizen!"*
      i. What is the conflict and source of conflict?
      ii. Does the gun store owner engage in subjective uncertainty?
   b. *"I want the locks changed in the morning: Your Amigo is going to sell our keys to one of his homies!"*
      i. Is the wife prejudiced or are her attitudes justified? Is she trying to be color-blind?
      ii. Did the wife perform ultimate attribution error?
      iii. What did this robbery do to the stereotypical thinking about Blacks/Latinos/Asians/Whites?

References

Allport, G. W. (1954). *The nature of prejudice.* New York, NY: Doubleday.

Armstrong, E., Hamilton, L., & Sweeney, B. (2006). Sexual assault on campus: A multilevel explanation of party rape. *Social Problems, 53,* 483–499.

Bobo, L. D. (2012). The *real* record on racial attitudes. In P. V. Marsden (Ed.), *Social trends in American Life: Findings from the General Social Survey since 1972* (pp. 38–83). Princeton, NJ: University Press.

Bobo, L. D., & Hutchings, V. L. (1996). Perceptions of racial group competition: Extending Blumer's theory of group position to a multiracial social context. *American Sociological Review, 61,* 951–972.

Center for Constitutional Rights. (2012). *Racial disparity in NYPD stops-and-frisks.* Retrieved from http://ccrjustice.org/stopandfrisk

Cheng, C., & Hoekstra, M. (2012). *Does strengthening self-defense law deter crime or escalate violence? Evidence from castle doctrine* (NBER Working Paper No. 18134). Retrieved from http://www.nber.org/papers/w18134

Dixon, J. C. (2006). The ties that bind and those that don't: Toward reconciling group threat and contact theories of prejudice. *Social Forces, 84,* 2179–2204.

Entman, R. M., & Rojecki, A. (2000). *The Black image in the White mind: Media and race in America.* Chicago, IL: University of Chicago Press.

Festinger, L., & Kelly, H. H. (1951). Changing attitudes through social contact. Ann Arbor, MI: Lithoprinted.

Ferguson, A. A. (2000). *Black boys: Public schools in the making of Black masculinity.* Ann Arbor: University of Michigan Press.

Gilliam, F. D., Jr. (1999). The "welfare queen experiment": How viewers react to images of African-American mothers on welfare. *Nieman Reports, 53*(2). Cambridge, MA: The Nieman Foundation for Journalism at Harvard University.

Golash-Boza, T. M. (2012). *Immigration nation.* St. Paul, MN: Paradigm.

Hogg, M. A. (2000). Subjective uncertainty reduction through self-categorization: A motivational theory of social identity processes. *European Review of Social Psychology, 11,* 223–255.

Hogg, M. A. (2003). Intergroup relations. In J. DeLamater (Ed.), *Handbook of social psychology* (pp. 479–502). New York, NY: Kluwer Academic/Plenum Publishers.

Jackman, M. R., & Crane, M. (1986). "Some of my best friends are Black . . .": Interracial friendship and Whites' racial attitudes. *The Public Opinion Quarterly, 50,* 459–486.

Jackson, P. B. (1997). Role occupancy and minority mental health. *Journal of Health and Social Behavior, 38,* 237–255.

Muhammad, K. G. (2010). *The condemnation of Blackness: Ideas about race and crime in the making of modern urban America.* Cambridge, MA: Harvard University Press.

Nugent, B. (2011). CNN article http://www.cnn.com/2012/05/16/opinion/nugent-facebook-zuckerberg/

Omi, M., & Winant, H. (1994). *Racial formation in the United States: From the 1960s to the 1990s* (2nd ed.). New York, NY: Routledge.

Pettigrew, T. F. (1979). The ultimate attribution error: Extending Allport's cognitive analysis of prejudice. *Personality and Social Psychology Bulletin, 5,* 461–476.

Pettigrew, T. F. (1998). Intergroup contact theory. *Annual Review of Psychology, 49,* 65–85.

Rivera, G. (2012, March 23). I am urging the parents of Black and Latino youngsters . . . . *Fox & Friends* (Television news broadcast). New York, NY: Fox Broadcasting.

West, C. (1994). *Race matters.* New York, NY: Vintage Books.

"Asians Are Doing Great, So That Proves Race Really Doesn't Matter Anymore"

The Model Minority Myth and the Sociological Reality[1]

Min Zhou

Nanyang Technological University

Min Zhou is currently Tan Lark Sye Chair Professor of Sociology and Director of the Chinese Heritage Centre at Nanyang Technological University, Singapore. She is also Professor of Sociology and Asian American Studies and Walter and Shirley Wang Endowed Chair in U.S.—China Relations and Communications at UCLA (on leave). Her main research interests include international migration, ethnic and racial relations, immigrant entrepreneurship, education and the new second generation, Asia and Asian America, and urban sociology. She is the author of *Chinatown: The Socioeconomic Potential of an Urban Enclave, Contemporary Chinese America: Immigration, Ethnicity, and Community Transformation*, and *The Accidental Sociologist in Asian American Studies*, and coauthor of *Growing Up American: How Vietnamese Children Adapt to Life in the United States*.

---

[1] This chapter was rewritten with much updated material from the published article "Are Asians Becoming White?" (Zhou, 2004).

> *I never asked to be white. I am not literally white. That is, I do not
> have white skin or white ancestors. I have yellow skin and yellow
> ancestors, hundreds of generations of them. But like so many other
> Asian Americans of the second generation, I find myself now the
> bearer of a strange new status: white, by acclamation. Thus it is
> that I have been described as an "honorary white," by other whites,
> and as a "banana" by other Asians . . . to the extent that I have
> moved away from the periphery and toward the center of American
> life, I have become white inside.*

(Liu, 1999, p. 34)

The "model minority" image of Asian Americans appeared in the mid-1960s, at the peak of the civil rights movement and the ethnic consciousness movements, but *before* the rising waves of immigration and refugee influx from Asia. Two articles in 1966—"Success Story, Japanese-American Style" by William Pettersen in the *New York Times Magazine,* and "Success of One Minority Group in U.S." by the *US News and World Report* staff—marked a significant departure from how Asian immigrants and their descendants had been traditionally depicted in the media. Both articles extolled Japanese and Chinese Americans for their persistence in overcoming extreme hardships and discrimination to achieve success, unmatched even by U.S.-born Whites, with "their own almost totally unaided effort" and "no help from anyone else."

Since then, Asian Americans have been celebrated as a "model minority" for their "superior" cultures that encourage a strong work ethic, a respect for elders, and a reverence for family. More importantly, they have been celebrated for their high rates of educational, occupational, and income attainment and low high school dropout rates as well as low rates of teen pregnancy and incarceration. They are declared to be on their way to becoming "White." These expectations are a burden and the predictions surely premature given the "foreigner" image Americans still have of Asians. In classrooms, as well as in society at large, the apparent success story of Asian Americans is often used to justify that race is no longer a determining factor in American life. This essay speaks both to the actual existing realities of the diverse range of communities encompassed by the panethnic "Asian American" label, and also considers the power and role of the model minority myth in the overall discourse of race and equality.

Issues of Terminology and Classification

Asian Americans have occupied an in-between status in America's racial hierarchy. They are often distinguished from other underrepresented racial groups, such as Blacks and Latinos, and are classified with Whites for equal opportunity programs. Although Asian Americans as a group have attained levels of education, occupation, and income equated with or even surpassing, those of

Whites[2], and although many have moved near to or even married Whites, they still remain culturally distinct and suspect in society.

At issue is how to define Asian American and White. The term *Asian American* was coined by the late historian and activist Yuji Ichioka during the ethnic consciousness movements of the late 1960s. To adopt this identity is to reject the Western-imposed label of *Oriental*. Today, "Asian American" is an umbrella category that includes both U.S. citizens and immigrants whose ancestors came from Asia east of Pakistan. Although widely used in public discussions, most Asian-origin Americans are ambivalent about this label, reflecting the difficulty of being American and still keeping some ethnic identity: Is one, for example, Asian American or Japanese American?

Similarly, "White" is an arbitrary label having more to do with privilege than biology. In the United States, groups initially considered non-White such as Irish and Jews have attained White membership by acquiring status and wealth. It is hardly surprising, then, that people of color would aspire to become "White" as a mark of and a tool for material success. However, becoming White can mean distancing oneself from people of color or selling out one's ethnicity. Panethnic identities—Asian American, African American, Latino—are one way the politically vocal in any group try to stem defections; these collective identities may restrain aspirations for individual mobility.

Varieties of Asian Americans

Privately, few Americans of Asian ancestry would spontaneously identify themselves as Asian, and fewer still as Asian American. They instead link their identities to specific countries of origin, such as Chinese, Japanese, Korean, Filipino, Indian, Vietnamese, and so on. In a study of Vietnamese youth in San Diego, for example, I found that 53% identified themselves as Vietnamese, 32% as Vietnamese American, and only 14% as Asian American, and that nearly 60% of these youth considered their chosen identity as very important to them (Zhou, 2001).

Some Americans of Asian origin have family histories in the United States longer than many Americans of Eastern or Southern European origins. However, they became numerous only after 1970, rising from 1.4 million to 17.3 million (including multiracials), or nearly 5.6% of the total U.S. population, in 2010. Before 1970, the Asian-origin population was largely made up of Japanese, Chinese, and Filipinos. Now, Americans of Chinese, Filipino, and Indian origin are the largest subgroups (at 3.8 million, 3.4 million, and 3.2 million, respectively), followed by Vietnamese (1.7 million), Koreans (1.7 million), and Japanese (1.3 million). Some 20 other national-origin groups, such as Cambodians, Pakistanis, Lao, Thai, Indonesians, and Bangladeshis were officially counted in government statistics only after 1980, and together amounted to more than 2.2 million in 2010.

---

[2] The 2010 U.S. census shows that 49.3% of Asian Americans age 25 and over had at least a college degree (20% had an advanced graduate degree), compared to 31% of non-Hispanic Whites. Also, 48% of Asian Americans age 16 and over held a professional occupation, compared to 40% of non-Hispanic Whites. Finally, the median family income for Asian American families was $78,152, compared to $69,531 for non-Hispanic White families.

The exponential growth of the Asian-origin population in the span of 40 years is primarily due to the accelerated immigration subsequent to the Hart–Celler Act of 1965, which ended the national origins quota system, and the historic resettlement of Southeast Asian refugees after the Vietnam War. Currently, about 60% of the Asian-origin population are foreign born (the first generation), another 30% are U.S. born of foreign-born parentage (the second generation), and just about 10% are born to U.S.-born parents (the third generation and beyond). The only exception to this pattern are Japanese Americans who have a fourth generation and many U.S.-born elderly.

Unlike earlier immigrants from Asia or Europe at the turn of the 20th century, who were mostly low-skilled laborers looking for work, new immigrants from Asia have more varied backgrounds and come for many reasons, such as to join their families, to invest their money in the U.S. economy, to fulfill the demand for highly skilled labor, or to escape war, political or religious persecution, and economic hardship. For example, Chinese, Taiwanese, Indian, and Filipino Americans tend to be overrepresented among scientists, engineers, physicians, and other skilled professionals, but less educated, low-skilled workers are more common among Vietnamese, Cambodian, Laotian, and Hmong Americans, most of whom entered the United States as refugees. While middle-class immigrants are able to start their American lives with high-paying professional careers and comfortable suburban living, low-skilled immigrants and refugees often have to endure low-paying menial jobs and live in inner-city ghettos. Asian Americans tend to settle in large metropolitan areas and concentrate in the West. California is home to about a third of all Asian Americans. But recently, other states such as Texas, Minnesota, and Wisconsin, which historically received few Asian immigrants, have become destinations for Asian American settlement. Traditional ethnic enclaves such as Chinatown, Little Tokyo, Manilatown, Koreatown, Little Phnom Penh, and Thaitown, persist or have emerged in gateway cities, helping new arrivals to cope with cultural and language difficulties in their initial stage of resettlement. However, affluent and highly skilled immigrants tend to bypass inner-city enclaves and settle in suburbs upon arrival, belying the stereotype of the "unacculturated" immigrant. Today, more than half of the Asian-origin population is spreading out in suburbs surrounding traditional gateway cities, as well as in new urban centers of Asian settlement across the country.

Differences in national origins, timing of immigration, affluence, and settlement patterns profoundly affect the formation of a panethnic identity. Recent arrivals are less likely than those born or raised in the United States to identify as Asian American. They are also so busy settling in that they have little time to think about being Asian or Asian American, or, for that matter, White. Their diverse origins evoke drastic differences in languages and dialects, religions, foodways, and customs. Many nationalities also brought to America their histories of conflict (such as the Japanese colonization of Korea and Taiwan, Japanese attacks on China, and the Chinese invasion of Vietnam). Immigrants who are predominantly middle-class professionals, such as the Taiwanese and Indians, or predominantly small business owners such as Koreans, share few of the same concerns and priorities as those who are predominantly uneducated, low-skilled refugees like Cambodians and Hmong.

Finally, Asian-origin people living in San Francisco or Los Angeles, among many other Asians and self-conscious Asian Americans develop sharper ethnic sensitivity than those living in, say, Latino-dominant Miami or White-dominant Minneapolis. A politician might get away with calling Asians "Oriental" in Miami but get into big trouble in San Francisco. All of these differences can create obstacles to fostering a cohesive pan-Asian solidarity. As sociologist Yen Le Espiritu shows in her research, pan-Asianism is primarily a political ideology of U.S.-born, American-educated, and middle-class Asians rather than of Asian immigrants, who are conscious of their national origins and overburdened with their daily struggles for survival.

Underneath the Model Minority: "White" or "Other"

The model minority has become a new stereotype imposed on Americans of Asian ancestry since the 1960s. On the surface, Asian Americans seem to be on their way to becoming White, just like the offspring of earlier European immigrants. But the model minority image implicitly casts Asian Americans as different from Whites. By placing Asian Americans above Whites, the model minority image also sets them apart from other Americans, White or non-White, in the public mind.

One consequence of this new form of stereotyping is to buttress the myth that the United States is devoid of racism and accords equal opportunity to all, and that those who lag behind do so because of their own poor choices and inferior culture (see also Meanwell, Patel, & McClure, Essay 13). Celebrating this model minority can help thwart other racial minorities' demands for social justice by pitting groups of color against each other. It can also pit Asian Americans against Whites.

Let me point to two less obvious effects. The model minority stereotype holds Asian Americans to higher standards, distinguishing them from average Americans. "What's wrong with being a model minority?" asked a Black student in a class I taught on race. "I'd rather be in the model minority than in the downtrodden minority that nobody respects." Whether people are in a model minority or a downtrodden minority, they are judged by standards *different* from average Americans. Also, the model minority stereotype places particular expectations on members of the group so labeled, channeling them to specific avenues of success, such as science and engineering, which in turn unintentionally reinforces barriers for Asian Americans in pursuing careers outside these designated fields. Falling into this trap, a Chinese immigrant father might be upset if his son told him that he had decided to change his major from engineering to English. Disregarding his son's passion and talent for creative writing, the father would rationalize his concern by saying, "You have a 90% chance of getting a decent job with an engineering degree, but what chance would you have of earning income as a writer?" This rationale reflects more than simple parental concern over career choices typical of middle-class families; it constitutes the self-fulfilling prophecy of a stereotype.

In the end, the celebration of Asian Americans as a model minority is based on the judgment that many Asian Americans perform at levels above the American average, which sets them apart not only from other people of color but also from

Whites. The truth of the matter is that the larger-than-average size of the middle- and upper middle class in some Asian-origin groups, such as the Chinese, Indian, and Korean, paves a much smoother path for the immigrants and their offspring to regain their middle-class status in the new homeland. The financial resources that immigrants brought with them to this country also help build viable ethnic economies and institutions, such as private afterschool programs, for the less fortunate group members to move ahead in society at a much faster pace than they would if they did not have access to these ethnic resources.

"It's Not So Much Being White as Being American"

In everyday reality, most Asian Americans seem to accept that "White" is mainstream, average, and "normal," and look to Whites as their frame of reference for attaining higher social position. Similarly, researchers often use non-Hispanic Whites as the standard against which other groups are compared, even though there is great diversity among Whites, too. Like most other immigrants to the United States, many Asian immigrants tend to believe in the American dream and measure their achievements materially. As a Chinese immigrant said to me in an interview, "I hope to accomplish nothing but three things: to own a home, to be my own boss, and to send my children to the Ivy League." Those with sufficient education, job skills, and money manage to move into White middle-class suburban neighborhoods immediately upon arrival, while others work intensively to accumulate enough savings to move their families up and out of inner-city ethnic enclaves. Consequently, many children of Asian ancestry have lived their entire childhood in White communities, made friends with mostly White peers, and grown up speaking only English. In fact, Asian Americans are the most acculturated non-European group in the United States. By the second generation, most have lost fluency in their parents' native languages. Sociologist David Lopez (1996) finds that in Los Angeles, more than three quarters of second-generation Asian Americans (as opposed to about one quarter of second-generation Mexicans) speak only English at home. Asian Americans also intermarry extensively with Whites and with members of other minority groups. Sociologists Jennifer Lee and Frank Bean (2010) find that more than one quarter of married Asian Americans have a partner of a different racial background, and 87% of intermarried Asians marry Whites; they also find that 12% of all Asian Americans claim a multiracial background, compared to 2% of Whites and 4% of Blacks.

Even though U.S.-born or U.S.-raised Asian Americans are relatively acculturated and often intermarry with Whites, they may be more ambivalent about becoming White than their immigrant parents. Many only cynically agree that "White" is synonymous with "American." A Vietnamese high school student in New Orleans told me in an interview, "An American is White. You often hear people say, hey, so-and-so is dating an 'American.' You know she's dating a White boy. If he were Black, then people would say he's Black." But while they recognize Whites as a frame of reference, some reject the idea of becoming White themselves. "It's not so much being White as being American," commented a Korean American student in my class on the new second generation. This aversion to becoming White is particularly common among the well-educated and privileged second-generation college student who have taken ethnic studies courses, or among Asian American community activists. However, most of the second generation continues to strive for the privileged status associated with Whiteness, just like their parents. For example, most U.S.-born or U.S.-raised Chinese American youth end up studying engineering, medicine, and law at college, believing that these areas of study would guarantee well-paying jobs and middle-class living and enhance social contact with Whites.

Second-generation Asian Americans are also more conscious of the disadvantages associated being non-White than their parents are, who as immigrants tend to be optimistic about overcoming the disadvantages. As a Chinese American woman points out from her own experience, "The truth is, no matter how American you think you are or try to be, if you have almond-shaped eyes, straight black hair, and a yellow complexion, you are a foreigner by default. . . . You can certainly be as good as or even better than Whites, but you will never become accepted as White." This remark echoes a common-felt frustration among second-generation Asian Americans who detest being treated as immigrants or foreigners. Their experience suggests that Whitening has more to do with the beliefs of White America than with the actual situation of Asian Americans. Speaking perfect English, effortlessly adopting mainstream cultural values, and even marrying members of the dominant group may help reduce this "otherness" at the individual level, but have little effect on the group as a whole. New stereotypes can emerge and "un-Whiten" Asian Americans anytime and anywhere, no matter how "successful" and "assimilated" they have become.

The stereotype of the "honorary White" or model minority goes hand-in-hand with that of the "forever foreigner." In the 21st century, globalization and U.S.–Asia relations, combined with continually high rates of immigration, affect how Asian Americans are perceived in American society. Many historical stereotypes, such as the "yellow peril" and "Chinese menace," have found their way into contemporary American life, as revealed in such highly publicized incidents as the murder of Vincent Chin, a Chinese American mistaken for Japanese and beaten to death by a disgruntled Michigan auto worker in the 1980s, the trial of Wen Ho Lee, a nuclear scientist suspected of spying for the Chinese government in the mid-1990s (eventually proven innocent), and the 2001 Abercrombie & Fitch T-shirts that depicted Asian cartoon characters in stereotypically negative ways—slanted eyes, thick glasses, and heavy Asian accents. Asian-looking Americans are still in an ambivalent position as neither White nor Black, and neither "American" nor "Asian." Ironically, the ambivalent, conditional nature of White acceptance of Asian Americans prompts them to organize panethnically to fight back—which consequently heightens their racial distinctiveness. So, becoming White or not is beside the point. Asian Americans still have to constantly prove they are truly loyal Americans, especially in times where U.S.–Asia relations are in the spotlight.

Suggested Additional Resources

Lee, W. H. (2002). *My country versus me: The first-hand account by the Los Alamos scientist who was falsely accused of being a spy.* New York, NY: Hyperion Books.

Park, L. (2007). A letter to my sister. In M. Zhou & J. V. Gatewood (Eds.), *Contemporary Asian America: A multidisciplinary reader* (2nd ed., pp. 425–430). New York, NY: New York University Press.

Maira, S. M. (2009). *Missing: Youth, citizenship, and empire after 9/11.* Durham, NC: Duke University Press.

Tuan, M. (1999). *Forever foreign or honorary White? The Asian ethnic experience today.* New Brunswick, NJ: Rutgers University Press.

Audio/Visual

Choy, C., & Tajima-Pena, R. (Directors). (1987). *Who killed Vincent Chin* [Documentary]. United States: Film News Now Foundation.

Lin, J. (Director), & Asato, J. (Producer). (2002). *Better luck tomorrow* [Motion picture]. United States: Paramount.

Nakamura, R. A. (Director). (1996). *Looking like the enemy* [Documentary]. United States: Japanese American National Museum.

Park, R. (Director). (2007). *Never perfect* [Documentary]. United States: Single Drop Films.

Sakya, S., Young, D., & Yu, K. (Directors). (2003). *Searching for Asian America* [Television documentary]. Public Broadcasting Service. United States: Center for Asian American Media (CAAM), KVIE.

Wong, C. (Director). (2010). *Whatever it takes* [Documentary]. United States: PBS Indies.

Questions for Further Discussion

1. What are the origins of the model minority stereotypes? How does this compare with previous depictions of Asian Americans as "yellow peril"? What, if anything, is significant about the evolution of these stereotypes over time? What, in your opinion, has prompted these changes in the model minority myth? Is it still utilized with the same political agenda in mind?

2. To what extent—if any—does the model minority myth factor into contemporary debates about Asian American identity? Can you think of any ways in which the media continue to perpetuate this stereotype? What negative effects does it continue to perpetuate for contemporary Asian Americans?

3. What are some stereotypical representations of Asian Americans on prime time television? What are some of the positive or neutral representations of Asian Americans that you've seen? How do the representations of Asian Americans compare to those of other racial groups? Why do you think there are discrepancies?

4. What do you think are the key mechanisms for stereotyping Asian Americans in American society? How would Asian Americans and the society as a whole act to counter the negative effects of stereotyping?

Reaching Beyond the Color Line

1. Consider the blog post at the link provided below:

   "Asian Americans respond to Pew: We're not your model minority" by Julianne Hing. http://colorlines.com/archives/2012/06/pew_asian_ american_study.html

   How does the controversy Hing describes connect to the issues raised in this essay? What does it add to your understanding of how and why the model minority myth is problematic?

2. Using the data provided by the American Community Survey FactFinder tool (http://factfinder2.census.gov/faces/nav/jsf/pages/searchresults.xhtml?refresh=t), locate the racial composition data on your home county and compare it to the United States overall. How do they compare? What does this tell you about the in-group variation hidden by the label *Asian American*. Why is this important?

References

Lee, J., & Bean, F. (2010). *The diversity paradox: Immigration and the color line in twenty-first century America*. New York, NY: Russell Sage Foundation.

Liu, E. (1999). *The accidental Asian: Notes of a native speaker*. New York, NY: Vintage.

Lopez, D. E. (1996). Language: Diversity and assimilation. In R. Waldinger (Ed.), *Ethnic Los Angeles* (pp. 139–159). New York, NY: Russell Sage Foundation.

Pettersen, W. (1966, January 9). Success story, Japanese-American style. *New York Times Magazine*.

US News and World Report. (1966, December 26). Success of one minority group in U.S. *US News and World Report*.

Zhou, M. (2001). Straddling different worlds: The acculturation of Vietnamese refugee children in San Diego. In R. G. Rumbaut & A. Portes (Eds.), *Ethnicities: Coming of age in immigrant America* (pp. 187–227). Berkeley, CA, & New York, NY: University of California Press & Russell Sage Foundation.

Zhou, M. (2004). Are Asian Americans becoming White? *Contexts, 3*(1), 29–37.

But Muslims *Aren't* Like Us!

Deconstructing Myths About Muslims in America[1]

Jen'nan Ghazal Read

Duke University

Jen'nan Ghazal Read is an associate professor in the sociology department and global health institute at Duke University. She is a Carnegie scholar studying the economic, political, and cultural integration of Muslim Americans and Arab Americans.

A decade after the terrorist attacks on U.S. soil catapulted Muslims into the American spotlight, concerns and fears over their presence and assimilation remain at an all-time high. In 2010, a Pew Research Poll of 1,003 Americans found that 38% of Americans have an unfavorable view of Islam, 35% believe Islam is more likely than other religions to encourage violence, and 51% objected to a mosque being built near the site of the World Trade Center. All this despite the fact that 55% admit they know very little about Islam (Pew Research Center, 2010). And yet Americans rank Muslims second only to atheists as a group that doesn't share their vision of American society (Edgell, Gerteis, & Hartmann, 2006).

These fears have had consequences. In 2001, the U.S. Department of Justice recorded a 1,600% increase in anti-Muslim hate crimes from the prior year, and these numbers rose 10% between 2005 and 2006. The Council on American-Islamic

---

[1] This essay, originally titled "Muslims in America," appeared in *Context* in 2008 (http://contexts.org/articles/fall-2008/muslims-in-america) and has been updated with most recent data.

Relations (CAIR) processed 2,647 civil rights complaints in 2006, a 25% increase from the prior year and a 600% increase since 2000. The largest category involved complaints against U.S. government agencies (37%). Since these years, Islamophobia has decreased somewhat, but data still indicate that the sentiment remains. In 2012, the Federal Bureau of Investigation's (FBI) Uniform Crime Report recorded that of the 1,166 hate crimes motivated by religious bias, nearly 13% were anti-Islamic. Moreover, a 2013 report from CAIR titled "Legislating Fear: Islamophobia and its Impact in the United States" documents the existence of at least 37 groups whose primary purpose is to promote prejudice against or hatred of Islam and Muslims and an additional 32 groups who regularly participate in this kind of activity. The report also finds that from 2011 to 2012, there were 51 recorded anti-mosque acts, further indicating the presence of anti-Muslim sentiment.

Clearly, many Americans are convinced Muslim Americans pose some kind of threat to American society and that they aren't like other Americans.

Two widespread assumptions fuel these fears. First, is that there's only one kind of Islam and one kind of Muslim, both characterized by violence and antidemocratic tendencies. Second, is that being a Muslim is the most salient identity for Muslim Americans when it comes to their political attitudes and behaviors, that it trumps their social class position, national origin, racial or ethnic group membership, or gender—or worse, that it trumps their commitment to a secular democracy.

Research on Muslim Americans themselves supports neither of these assumptions. Interviews with 3,627 Muslim Americans in 2001 and 2004 by the Georgetown University Muslims in the American Public Square (MAPS) project and Pew Research Center data collected in 2007 and 2011 all show that Muslim Americans are diverse, well integrated, and largely mainstream in their attitudes, values, and behaviors. They are also well aware and deeply affected by the degree of anti-Muslim sentiment that exists today. A majority (53%) report that it has become more difficult to be a Muslim in the United States. since the September 11th terrorist attacks and most (55%) believe that the government singles out Muslims for increased surveillance and monitoring (Pew Research Center, 2011). Arab Muslims have felt especially vulnerable, in part because the 9/11 acts were carried out by Arabs and because the subsequent U.S. war on terror focused on Iraq as much as Afghanistan. Arab Muslims have also had a long history dealing with anti-Arab stereotypes in the West, many of which continue to be used by anti-Muslim organizations to amplify their Islamophobic messages (Bail, 2012; Shaheen, 2009).

However, the data do not support the common belief that Muslims allow religion to dictate their behaviors and participation in American society. In fact, the data show that being a Muslim is less important for participating in American political and civic life than how Muslim you are, how much money you make, whether you're an African American Muslim or an Arab American Muslim, and whether you're a man or a woman.

The notion that Muslims privilege their Muslim identity over their other interests and affiliations has been projected onto the group rather than emerged from the beliefs and practices of the group itself. It's what sociologists call a *social construction*, and it's one that has implications for how these Americans are included in the national dialogue.

Some Basic Demographics

Let's start with who Muslim Americans really are. Pew Research Center demographers (2011) estimate that there are roughly 2.75 million Muslims of all ages living in the United States. Within that number is a great deal of variation in the social and demographic characteristics of the community.

Muslim Americans are the most ethnically diverse Muslim population in the world, originating from more than 80 countries on four continents. Sixty-three percent are first-generation immigrants to the United States, with 45% having arrived since 1990 (Pew Research Center, 2011). A little over a third (37%) were born in the United States. While the population largely consists of immigrants, it is important to note that 81% of Muslim Americans are U.S. citizens, including the 70% born abroad. About 4 in 10 first-generation, Muslim American immigrants are from the Middle East or North Africa, while a little over a quarter come from South Asian nations like Pakistan (14%), Bangladesh (5%), and India (3%). Others are from sub-Saharan Africa (11%), various countries in Europe (7%), Iran (5%), or other countries (9%). Also reflecting the diversity of the Muslim American population is that among the roughly 1 in 5 whose parents were born in the United States, 59% are Black and mainly converts. In fact, there is a great deal of racial diversity among Muslim Americans with 30% identifying as White, 23% as Black, 21% as Asian, 6% as Latino, and 19% as mixed race or Other (Pew Research Center, 2011).

Muslim Americans also tend to be highly educated, politically conscious, and fluent in English, all of which reflects the restrictive immigration policies that limit who gains admission into the United States. On average, in fact, Muslim Americans share similar socioeconomic characteristics with the general U.S. population: Twenty-six percent have a bachelor's degree or higher (as, compared to 28% of the general population), 22% live in households with incomes of $75,000 per year or more (versus 28% in the general population), and both 59% of the Muslim American population and the general public are employed either full-time or part-time. Nevertheless, some Muslims do live in poverty and have poor English language skills and few resources to improve their situations.

One of the most important and overlooked facts about Muslim Americans is that they are not uniformly religious and devout. Some are religiously devout, some are religiously moderate, and some are nonpracticing and secular, basically Muslim in name only, similar to a good proportion of U.S. Christians and Jews. Some attend a mosque on a weekly basis and pray every day, and others don't engage in either practice. Even among the more religiously devout, there is a sharp distinction between being a good Muslim and being an Islamic extremist (see also Pew Research Center, 2007, 2011).

None of this should be surprising. Many Muslim Americans emigrated from countries in the Middle East (now targeted in the war on terror) in order to practice—or not practice—their religion and politics more freely in the United States. And their religion is diverse. There is no monolithic Islam that all Muslims adhere to. Just as Christianity has many different theologies, denominations, and sects, so does Islam. And just like Christianity, these theologies, denominations, and sects are often in conflict and disagreement over how to interpret and practice the faith tradition. This diversity mimics other ethnic and immigrant groups in the United States.

Evidence from the Pew Research Center (2011) demonstrates that Muslim Americans are also more politically integrated than the common stereotypes imply. Consider some common indicators of political involvement, such as party affiliation, voter registration, and civic engagement. Compared to the general public, Muslim Americans are just slightly less likely to be registered to vote, reflecting the immigrant composition and voter eligibility of this group (66% compared to 79% of the general population). But they are as likely to have worked with others to fix neighborhood or community problems as the general population (33% vs. 38%, respectively). And, like other racial and ethnic minority groups, they are also more likely to affiliate with the Democratic Party (70% compared to 48% of the general population).

All these data demonstrate that, contrary to fears that Muslim Americans comprise a monolithic minority ill-suited to participation in American democracy, Muslim Americans are actually highly diverse and already politically integrated.

Attitudes, Values, and Variation

Muslim Americans, by and large, tend to be more conservative on social issues, while being more liberal on foreign policy matters. For example, Muslim Americans are somewhat more conservative on the issue of homosexuality than the general public where 39% of U.S. Muslims believe that homosexuality should be accepted by society versus 58% of the general public (Pew Center Research, 2011). They are also slightly more conservative than the general public when it comes to abortion: Forty-eight percent believe it should be illegal in all or most cases compared to 43% of the general population (Pew Research Center, 2008). In addition, Muslim Americans are more likely than the general public to believe that the federal government should do more to protect morality in society (59% vs. 37%, respectively; Pew Research Center, 2007).

In contrast to their more conservative views on American social policy, American Muslims are more liberal than the general public with regard to foreign policy, especially pertaining to the Middle East. In 2007, for example, the general public was nearly four times as likely to say the war in Iraq was the "right decision" and twice as likely to provide the same response to the war in Afghanistan (61% compared to 35% of Muslim Americans).

In short, these numbers tell us that Muslim Americans lean to the right on social issues but to the left on foreign policy. But these generalizations don't tell the whole story—in particular, these averages don't demonstrate the diversity that exists within the Muslim population by racial and ethnic group membership, national origin, socioeconomic status, degree of religiosity, or nativity and citizenship status.

Consider, for example, Muslim Americans' levels of satisfaction and feelings of inclusion (or exclusion) in American society—major building blocks of a liberal democracy. In examining how these perceptions vary by racial and ethnic group membership within the group, we see that African American Muslims express more dissatisfaction and feel more excluded from American society than Arab or South Asian Muslims (Project MAPS, 2004). They're more likely to feel the United States is fighting a war against Islam, to believe Americans are intolerant of Islam and Muslims, and to have experienced discrimination in the past year (whether racial, religious, or both is unclear). South Asians feel the least marginalized and Arab Muslims fall in between. These racial and ethnic differences reflect a host of factors, including the immigrant composition and higher socioeconomic status of the South Asian and Arab populations and the long-standing racialized and marginalized position of African Americans. Indeed, many (though not all) African Americans converted to Islam seeking a form of religious inclusion they felt lacking in the largely White Judeo-Christian traditions.

Incidentally, most African American Muslims adhere to mainstream Islam (Sunni or Shi'a), similar to South Asian and Arab Muslim populations. They should not be confused with the Nation of Islam, a group that became popular during the civil rights era by providing a cultural identity that separated Black Americans from mainstream Christianity. Indigenous Muslims have historically distanced themselves from the Nation of Islam in order to establish organizations that focus more on cultural and religious (rather than racial) oppression.

Before we can determine whether religion is the driving force behind all Muslims' political opinions and behaviors—whether Islam, as is popularly assumed, trumps Muslim Americans' other commitments and relationships to nationality, ethnicity, race, and even democracy—let's step back and place Muslim Americans in a broader historical context of religion and American politics.

When Religion Matters and Doesn't

Muslim Americans aren't the first religious or ethnic group considered a threat to America's religious and cultural unity. At the turn of the 20th century, Jewish and Italian immigrants were vilified in the mainstream as racially inferior to other Americans. Of course today, those same fears have been projected onto Hispanic, Asian, and Middle Eastern immigrants. The Muslim American case shares with these other immigrant experiences the fact that with a religion different from the mainstream comes the fear that it will dilute, possibly even sabotage, America's thriving religious landscape.

Yes, thriving. By all accounts, the United States is considerably more religious than any of its economically developed Western counterparts. In 2013, 92% of Americans said they believed in God or a universal spirit, 78% claimed affiliation with a specific religious denomination, and 59% reported membership in a church or synagogue (Gallup, 2013). The vast majority of American adults identify themselves as Christian (41% Protestant and 24% Catholic), with Judaism claiming the second largest group of adherents (2%), giving America a decidedly Judeo-Christian face (Gallup, 2013). There are an infinite number of denominations within these broad categories, ranging from the ultraconservative to the ultraliberal. And there is extensive diversity among individuals in their levels of religiosity within any given denomination, again ranging from those who are devout, practicing believers to those who are secular and nonpracticing.

This diversity has sparked extensive debates among academics, policymakers, and pundits over whether American politics is characterized by "culture wars," best summarized as the belief that Americans are polarized into two camps, one conservative and one liberal, on moral and ethical issues such as abortion and gay rights. Nowhere was the debate played out more vividly than the arena of religion and politics, where religiously based mobilization efforts by the Christian Right helped defeat liberal-leaning candidates and secure President Bush's reelection in 2004. In the 2008 and 2012 elections, these efforts were not as successful at the presidential level, but gains occurred on the state and local levels. So when does religion matter for politics and when doesn't it?

Here we come back to the Muslim American case. Like Muslim Americans, Americans generally have multiple, competing identities that shape their political attitudes and behaviors. For example, in 2008, 92% of Americans believed in God or a universal spirit but only 14% cited their religious beliefs as the main influence on their political thinking (Pew Research Center, 2008). In other words, just because most Americans are religiously affiliated doesn't mean most Americans base their politics on religion. To put it somewhat differently, the same factors that influence other Americans' attitudes and behaviors influence Muslim Americans' attitudes and behaviors. Those who are more educated, have higher incomes, higher levels of group consciousness, and who feel more marginalized from mainstream society are more politically active than those without these characteristics. Similar to other Americans, these are individuals who feel they have more at stake in political outcomes and thus are more motivated to try to influence such outcomes.

Muslims, on average, look like other Americans on social and domestic policies because, on average, they share the same social standing as other Americans, and on average, they are about as religious as other Americans. Both Christian Americans and Muslim Americans are quite religious, with 69% of U.S. Muslims saying religion is very important in their lives, compared to 70% of Christians (Pew Research Center, 2011). In addition, a sizeable proportion of Muslims attend services once a week or more, which is also on par with Christians (47% and 45%, respectively).

Again, these numbers tell only part of the story. What's missing is that religion's relationship to politics is multidimensional. In more complex analyses, it has become clear that the more personal dimensions of religious identity—or being a devout Muslim who prays every day—have little influence on political attitudes or behaviors, which runs counter to stereotypes that link Islamic devotion to political fanaticism.

In contrast, the more organized dimensions of Muslim identity, namely frequent mosque attendance, provide a collective identity that stimulates political activity. This is similar to what we know about the role of the church and synagogue for U.S. Christians and Jews. Congregations provide a collective environment that heightens group consciousness and awareness of issues that need to be addressed through political mobilization. Thus, it is somewhat ironic that one of the staunchest defenders of the war on terror—the Christian Right—may be overlooking a potential ally in the culture wars—devout Muslim Americans.

An Exceptional Experience

In many ways, these findings track closely with what we know about the religion–politics connection among other U.S. ethnic and religious groups, be they Evangelical Christians or African Americans. They also suggest that the Muslim experience may be less distinct than popular beliefs imply. In fact, Muslim Americans share much in common with earlier immigrant groups who were considered inassimilable even though they held mainstream American values (think Italian, Irish, and Polish immigrants).

At the same time, though, we can't deny that the Muslim American experience, particularly since 9/11, has been "exceptional" in a country marked by a declining salience of religious boundaries and increasing acceptance of religious difference. Muslim Americans have largely been excluded from this ecumenical trend. If we're going to face our nation's challenges in a truly democratic way, we need to move past the fear that Muslim Americans are un-American so we can bring them into the national dialogue.

Suggested Additional Resources

Further Reading

Abu-Lughod, L. (2002). Ethics forum: September 11 and ethnographic responsibility. Do Muslim women really need saving? Anthropological reflections on cultural relativism and its others. *American Anthropologist, 104*(3), 783–790.

Bail, C. A. (2012). The fringe effect: Civil society organizations and the evolution of media discourse about Islam. *American Sociological Review, 77,* 855–879.

Bakalian, A., & Bozorgmehr. M. (2009). *Backlash 9/11: Middle Eastern and Muslim Americans respond.* Berkeley: University of California Press. (One of the comprehensive assessments of the experiences of Middle Eastern Americans in the aftermath of 9/11.)

Foner, N. (2005). *In a new land: A comparative view of immigration.* New York, NY: New York University Press. (A thorough historical, comparative account of immigration in the United States.)

Gerstle, G., & Mollenkopf, J. (Eds.). (2001). *E Pluribus Unum? Contemporary and historical perspectives on immigrant political incorporation.* New York, NY: Russell Sage Foundation. (This edited volume places contemporary immigration politics in historical and comparative context.)

Jelen, T. J. (2006). Religion and politics in the United States: Persistence, limitations, and the prophetic voice. *Social Compass, 53,* 329–343. (A useful overview of the U.S. religion–politics connection situated in comparison to other western, industrialized nations.)

Kalkan, K. O., Layman, G. C., & Uslaner, E. M. (2009). "Bands of others"? Attitudes toward Muslims in contemporary American society. *The Journal of Politics, 71*(3), 1–16.

Tarlo, E. (2010). *Visibly Muslim: Fashion, politics, faith.* New York, NY: Bloomsbury Academic.

Audio/Visual

Jam Productions. (2004). *The aftermath: American-Muslims after September 11th* [Documentary]. Retrieved from http://www.youtube.com/watch?v=pKMoz--mFtw

Spurlock, M. (2005). Muslims and America [Television series episode]. *30 Days*. New York, NY: FX Network.

Questions for Further Discussion

1. What are the most common misconceptions about Muslims in America? Where do these come from? How do the data presented debunk these misconceptions?

2. What is the role of religious beliefs in shaping your own political values and ideas? What misconceptions do others have of you based on your own religious or nonreligious identity?

Reaching Beyond the Color Line

1. Given the variation discussed in this essay, take the opportunity over the next 2 weeks to attend religious services in a tradition that is new to you. Compare your observations and interactions with your previous ideas and write a brief reflection that connects these observations to the topics discussed in this essay.

2. Access the most recent Pew report on Muslim Americans at the Pew Research Center website (http://www.pewresearch.org). What changes does it show as compared to the 2007 survey? What other questions would you like to explore from this data? Write up a brief summary of the findings that are most intriguing to you.

3. Listen to the story of Sam Slaven and Yousef Radeef in *This American Life* (Episode 340), titled *The Devil in Me*, Act 1: And So We Meet Again (http://www.thisamericanlife.org/radio-archives/episode/340/the-devil-in-me). What can you learn from Sam and Yousef's story, in terms of your own college experiences and activities?

References

Bail, C. A. (2012). The fringe effect: Civil society organizations and the evolution of media discourse about Islam. *American Sociological Review, 77*, 855–879.

Council on American-Islamic Relations (CAIR). (2013). *Legislating fear: Islamophobia and its impact in the United States*. Retrieved from http://www.cair.com/islamophobia/legislating-fear-2013-report.html

Edgell, P., Gerteis, J., & Hartmann, D. (2006). Atheists as "Other": Moral boundaries and cultural membership in American society. *American Sociological Review, 71*, 211–234.

Gallup. (2013). *Religion: What is your religious preference?* Retrieved from http://www.gallup.com/poll/1690/Religion.aspx

Pew Research Center. (2007). *Muslim Americans: Middle class and mostly mainstream.* Retrieved from http://pewresearch.org/files/old-assets/pdf/muslim-americans.pdf

Pew Research Center. (2008). *U.S. religious landscape survey: Religious beliefs and practices.* Retrieved from http://www.pewforum.org/2008/06/01/u-s-religious-landscape-survey-religious-beliefs-and-practices

Pew Research Center. (2010). Public remains conflicted over Islam. *Pew Research: Religion & Public Life Project.* Retrieved from http://www.pewforum.org/2010/08/24/public-remains-conflicted-over-islam

Pew Research Center. (2011). *Muslim Americans: No signs of growth in alienation or support for extremism.* Retrieved from http://www.people-press.org/2011/08/30/muslim-americans-no-signs-of-growth-in-alienation-or-support-for-extremism

Project MAPS. (2004). *Muslims in the American Public Square: Shifting political winds & fall-out from 9/11, Afghanistan, and Iraq.* Retrieved from www.aclu.org/files/fbimappingfoia/20111110/ACLURM001733.pdf

Shahaeen, J. (2009). *Reel Bad Arabs: How Hollywood vilifies a people.* Northampton, MA: Olive Branch Press.

Uniform Crime Report. (2012). 2012 hate crime statistics. *Federal Bureau of Investigation.* Retrieved from http://www.fbi.gov/about-us/cjis/ucr/hate-crime/2012

"It's Just a Mascot!"

The Dark Side of Sports Symbols[1]

D. Stanley Eitzen

Colorado State University

Maxine Baca Zinn

Michigan State University

D. Stanley Eitzen, professor emeritus of sociology at Colorado State University, earned his PhD at the University of Kansas. Although he is well known for his scholarship on homelessness, poverty, social inequality, power, family, and criminology, he is best known for his contributions to the sociology of sport. In 1996, he was selected a Sports Ethics Fellow at the Institute for International Sport. His books on sport include: *Fair and Foul* (5th ed.; Rowman and Littlefield, 2012); *Sociology of North American Sport* (9th ed., co-authored with George H. Sage; Oxford University Press, 2013); and *Sport in Contemporary Society* (10th ed.; Oxford University Press, 2014).

Maxine Baca Zinn is professor emerita in the Department of Sociology at Michigan State University. She received her PhD in sociology from the University of Oregon. Her books include *Women of Color in U.S. Society* (with Bonnie Thornton Dill) and *Gender Through the Prism of Difference* (with Pierrette Hondagneu-Sotelo and Michael Messner). She is coauthor (with D. Stanley Eitzen) of *Social Problems* and *Diversity in Families,* both of which won McGuffey Awards for excellence over multiple editions from the Text and Academic Authors Association, and *Globalization: The Transformation of Social Worlds.*

---

[1] This article was originally titled "The Dark Side of Sport Symbols." Reprinted with permission from *USA Today Magazine,* January 2001. Copyright © 2001 by the Society for the Advancement of Education, Inc. All Rights Reserved.

The teams that played in the 1995 World Series were the Atlanta Braves and Cleveland Indians. Inside Atlanta Fulton County Stadium and Jacobs Field, the Braves' fans did the "tomahawk chop" and enthusiastically shouted "Indian" chants. Similarly, the fans of the Indians, united behind their symbol, Chief Wahoo, waved fake tomahawks and wore "war paint" and other pseudo-Native American symbols. Outside these stadiums, Native American activists carried signs in protest of the inappropriate use of their symbols by Anglos. (In less politically correct times, there was no such uproar when these same teams met in the 1948 World Series.)

A group's symbols serve two fundamental purposes—they bind together the individual members and separate one group from another. Each of the thousands of street gangs in the United States, for example, has a group identity that is displayed in its names, code words, gestures, distinctive clothing, and colors. The symbols of these gangs promote solidarity and set them apart from rivals.

Using symbols to achieve solidarity and community is common in American schools. Students, former students, faculty members, and others who identify with the institution adopt nicknames for its athletic teams, display the school colors, wave the school banner, wear special clothing and jewelry, and engage in ritual chants and songs.

A school's nickname is much more than a tag or a label. It conveys, symbolically, the characteristics and attributes that define the institution. In an important way, the symbols represent the institution's self-concept. Schools may have names that signify their ethnic heritage (e.g., the Bethany College Swedes), state history (University of Oklahoma Sooners), religion (Oklahoma Baptist College Prophets), or founder (Whittier College Poets). Most, though, utilize symbols of aggression and ferocity for their athletic teams—birds such as hawks, animals such as bulldogs, human categories such as pirates, and even the otherworldly such as devils (Franks, 1982; Fuller & Manning, 1987).

Although school names and other symbols evoke strong emotions of solidarity among followers, there is also a potential dark side to their use. The names, mascots, logos, and flags chosen may be derogatory to some group. The symbols may dismiss, differentiate, demean, and trivialize marginalized groups such as African Americans, Native Americans, and women. Thus, they serve to maintain the dominant status of powerful groups and subordinate those categorized as *others*. That may not have been the intent of those who decided on the names and mascots for a particular school, but their use diminishes these others, retaining the racial and gender inequities found in society. School symbols as used in sports, then, have power not only to maintain in-group solidarity, but to separate the in-group from the out-group and perpetuate the hierarchy between them.

Symbols of the Confederacy

At Nathan Bedford Forrest High School in Jacksonville, Florida, young African American athletes wear the Confederate Army's colors on their uniforms and call themselves the Rebels. The school they play for is named after the slave-trading Confederate general who became the original grand wizard of the Ku Klux Klan.

Within the neo-Confederate culture found in parts of the South, certain symbols such as the Rebel battle flag and the singing of "Dixie" are zealously promoted

(Britt, 1996). These symbols have two distinct meanings—one that promotes the South's heritage and another that symbolizes slavery, racial separation, and hate.

In 1948, the so-called Dixiecrats, rebelling against a strong civil rights plank in the Democratic platform, walked out of the party's convention. That year, the University of Mississippi adopted the Rebel flag, designated "Dixie" as the school's fight song, and introduced a mascot named Colonel Reb, a caricature of an Old South plantation owner. In 1962, James Meredith, despite the strong opposition of Governor Ross Barnett and other White leaders in the state, became the first Black student at the school. There were demonstrations at that time in support of segregation. Infused in these demonstrations was the showing of the Rebel flag and the singing of "Dixie" as symbols of defiance by the supporters of segregation (Edelson, 1991; Lederman, 1996; Nack, 1997).

Over the ensuing years, the use of these symbols at the University of Mississippi has caused considerable debate. On the one hand, they represented the state's heritage and as such were a source of pride, inspiration, and unity among its citizens. The opposing position was that these symbols represented a history of oppression against African Americans, noting that the Rebel flag was also a prominent symbol of the Ku Klux Klan. Opponents argued further that, since almost one third of Mississippians are African Americans, the flagship university of that state should not use symbols that recall the degradation and demeaning of their ancestors. Is it proper, they ask, to use the key symbol of the Confederacy and African American enslavement as a rallying symbol for the University of Mississippi's sports teams—teams composed of Whites and Blacks?

As a compromise, in 1983, 21 years after the University of Mississippi integrated, its chancellor ruled that the Rebel flag was no longer the official banner for the school. Chancellor Porter L. Fortune Jr. made it clear, however, that students would have the right to wave the flag at football games, and that they have done. Sports teams' names such as the Rebels as well as mascots like Colonel Reb and songs such as "Dixie" have continued as official school symbols.

The debate still rages. Charles W. Eagles, a University of Mississippi history professor, sums up the ongoing controversy:

> For some of us—those who believe in the University of Mississippi—the symbols prevent the university from being everything it can be. Others—those that are faithful to Ole Miss [the traditionalists]—think that if you took the symbols away, there wouldn't be anything there. The symbols are seen as a real burden for the university. But they're the backbone of Ole Miss. (Lederman, 1996, p. 132)

This debate demonstrates vividly the power of symbols, not only to unite or divide, but the hold they have on people, as seen in their resistance to change and in the organized efforts to remove those symbols interpreted as negative.

Native American Symbols

The use of Native American names such as *Redmen, Fighting Sioux, Utes,* and even *Savages* is common in high schools, community colleges, colleges, and universities.

Many professional teams have also adopted Native American names—in baseball, the Atlanta Braves and Cleveland Indians; in football, the Washington Redskins and the Kansas City Chiefs; in basketball, the Golden State Warriors; and in hockey, the Chicago Blackhawks.

Defenders of Native American names, logos, and mascots argue that their use is a tribute to the indigenous peoples. Native Americans, the argument goes, are portrayed as brave, resourceful, and strong. Native American names were chosen for sports teams precisely because they represent these positive traits.

Other defenders claim that their use is no different from those names and mascots that represent other ethnic groups such as the *Irish*, *Vikings*, or *Norse*. Because members of these ethnic groups accept the use of their names, Native Americans should also be proud of this recognition of their heritage, they maintain.

However, many Native Americans do object to their symbols being used by athletic teams. Since the early 1970s, individuals and organizations—such as the American Indian Movement (AIM)—have sought to eliminate the use of Native American names, mascots, and logos by sports teams. They use several key arguments, foremost among them being racial stereotyping. Names such as *Indian*, *Brave*, and *Chiefs* are not inherently offensive, but some names, logos, and mascots project a violent caricature of Native Americans ("scalpers," "savages"). Teams that use American Indian names commonly employ the tomahawk chop, war paint, and mascots dressed as Native Americans. This depiction of Native Americans as bloodthirsty warriors distorts history, since Whites invaded Indian lands, oppressed native peoples, and even employed and justified a policy of genocide toward them.

Some mascots are especially demeaning to Native Americans. Chief Wahoo of the Cleveland Indians is described by sportswriter Rick Telander as "the red-faced, big-nosed, grinning, drywall-toothed moron who graces the peak of every Cleveland Indians cap." Is such a caricature appropriate? Clyde Bellecourt, national director of AIM, summarizes the complaints:

> If you look up the word "redskin" in both the Webster's and Random House dictionaries, you'll find the word is defined as being offensive. Can you imagine if they called them the Washington Jews and the team mascot was a rabbi leading them in [the song] "Hava Nagila," fans in the stands wearing yarmulkes and waving little sponge torahs? The word "Indian" isn't offensive "Brave" isn't offensive, but it's the behavior that accompanies all of this that's offensive. The rubber tomahawks. The chicken-feather headdresses. People wearing war paint and making these ridiculous war whoops with a tomahawk in one hand and a beer in the other. All of these things have significant meaning for us. And the psychological impact it has, especially on our youth, is devastating. (Kravitz, 1992, p. 39)

Another problem is the imitation or misuse of symbols that have religious significance to some Native American peoples. Utilizing dances, chants, drummings, and other rituals at sporting events clearly tends to trivialize their meaning.

Also problematic is the homogenization of American Indian cultures. Native Americans are portrayed uniformly, disregarding the sometimes enormous differences among the tribes. Thus, through the use of Indian names and mascots, society defines who Native Americans are instead of allowing them to determine how society thinks of them.

A few colleges and universities—such as Stanford, Siena, Miami of Ohio, Dartmouth, and St. John's—have taken these objections seriously and changed their names and mascots. Most high schools and colleges, though, resist such a change. Ironically, they insist on retaining the Native American symbols even though those schools do not have an American Indian heritage or significant Native American student representation. The members of these schools and their constituencies insist on retaining their Native American names because they are part of their collective identities. This allegiance to their school symbols seems to have higher priority than insensitivity to the negative consequences produced by inappropriate depictions of Native Americans.

Sexist Names

Many studies have shown the varied ways in which language acts in the defining, deprecation, and exclusion of women (Eitzen & Baca Zinn, 1989, 1993; Henley, 1987; Thorne, Kramarae, & Henley, 1985). Names do this, too. Naming a women's and men's athletic team is not a neutral process. The names chosen often are badges of femininity and masculinity, hence of inferiority and superiority. To the degree that this occurs, the names of women's and men's athletic teams reinforce a basic element of social structure: gender division and hierarchy. Team names reflect this division as well as the asymmetry that is associated with it. Despite advances made by women in sports since the implementation of Title IX in 1971, widespread naming practices continue to mark female athletes as unusual, aberrant, or invisible.

We examined the names and accompanying logos and mascots of sports teams for females and males at 1,185 coeducational four-year colleges and universities. We identified eight gender-linked practices associated with names and/or logos that diminished and trivialized women:

- *Physical markers.* One common naming practice emphasizes the physical appearance of women, such as the Angelo State Rambelles. As Casey Miller and Kate Swift argue in *The Handbook of Nonsexist Writing*, this practice is sexist because the "emphasis on the physical characteristics of women is offensive in contexts where men are described in terms of achievement" (Miller & Swift, 1980, p. 87).
- The use of *girl* or *gal* stresses the presumed immaturity and irresponsibility of women, such as the Elon College Golden Girls. As Miller and Swift note, "Just as 'boy' can be blatantly offensive to minority men, so 'girl' can have comparable patronizing and demeaning implications for women" (Miller & Swift, 1980, p. 71).
- *Feminine suffixes.* This is a popular form of sexual differentiation found in the names of athletic, social, and women's groups. The practice not only

marks women, it denotes a feminine derivative by establishing a female negative trivial category. The devaluation is accomplished by tagging words with feminine suffixes like "ette." At Dillard University, for example, the men's team is the Blue Devils; the women's team, the Devilettes.

- *Lady.* This label has several meanings that demean women as athletes. "Lady," according to Miller and Swift, is used to "evoke a standard of propriety, correct behavior, and elegance" (Miller & Swift, 1980, p. 72), characteristics that are decidedly unathletic. Similarly, *lady* carries overtones recalling the age of chivalry. As Robin Lakoff (1975) maintains in *Language and Women's Place,* "This makes the term seem polite at first, but we must also remember that these implications are perilous: they suggest that a 'lady' is helpless, and cannot do things for herself" (Miller & Swift, 1980, p. 87). The use of *lady* for women's teams is common (e.g., the University of Florida Lady Gators). At Washington and Jefferson College, the men are Presidents and the women are First Ladies, which clearly marks the status of women's teams as inferior to that of the men.

- *Male as a false generic.* This practice assumes that the masculine in the language, word, or name choice is the norm, while ignoring the feminine altogether. Miller and Swift define this procedure as "terms used of a class or group that are not applicable to all members" (Miller & Swift, 1980, p. 9). The use of "mankind" to encompass both sexes has its parallel among men's and women's athletic teams that have the same name, for example, the Rams (Colorado State University) or the Hokies at Virginia Tech (a "hokie" is a castrated turkey). In *Man Made Language,* Dale Spender has called the practice of treating the masculine as the norm as "one of the most pervasive and pernicious rules that has been encoded" (Spender, 1980, p. 3). Its consequence is to make women invisible as well as secondary to men, since they are robbed of a separate identity.

- *Male name with a female modifier.* This practice applies the feminine to a name that usually denotes a male, giving females lower status. Examples among sports teams are the Lady Friars of Providence College and the Lady Gamecocks of the University of South Carolina (a "gamecock" is a fighting rooster). As we note in *Fair and Foul: Beyond the Myths and Paradoxes of Sport,* using such oxymorons "reflects role conflict and contributes to the lack of acceptance of women's sport" (Fuller & Manning, 1987, p. 64).

- *Double gender marking.* This occurs when the name for the women's team is a diminutive of the men's team name combined with *belle, lady,* or other feminine modifier. For example, at the University of Kentucky, the men's teams are the Wildcats and the women's teams are the Lady Kats. Compounding the feminine intensifies women's secondary status. In his 1986 book, *Grammar and Gender,* Dennis Baron argues that double gender marking occurs "perhaps to underline the inappropriateness or rarity of the feminine noun or to emphasize its negativity" (p. 115).

- *Male/female, paired polarity.* Women's and men's teams can be assigned names that represent a female/male opposition. When this occurs, the names of the men's teams embody competitiveness and other positive traits usually associated with sport, whereas the names for women's teams are lighthearted or cute. Successful athletes are believed to embody such traits as courage, bravura, boldness, self-confidence, and aggression. When the names given men's teams imply these traits, but those for women's teams suggest that females are playful and cuddly, women are trivialized and de-athleticized. For instance, the Mercer University men's teams are the Bears and the women are the Teddy Bears; at Fort Valley State College, the men's teams are the Wildcats and the women's teams are the Wildkittens.

Another grouping occurs when names that could be included in one of the above categories also incorporate race. This especially occurs with teams that adopt Native American symbols. The men's teams at Southeastern Oklahoma State University are the Savages and the women's teams are the Savagettes, utilizing the diminutive feminine suffix combined with a negative stereotype for the racial category. Similarly, at Montclair State College, the men are the Indians and the women are the Squaws. The word *squaw* also refers to a woman's pelvic area and means prostitute in some native languages. Vernon Bellecourt of the American Indian Movement says, "The issue itself is clear . . . The word 'squaw' has got to go in all its forms. It's demeaning and degrading to Indian women and all women" (Tomas, 1997, p. 11).

Our survey found that slightly over half of U.S. colleges and universities have sexist names, logos, or both for their athletic teams. Thus, the identity symbols for athletic teams at those schools contribute to the maintenance of male dominance within college sports. Since the traditional masculine gender role matches most athletic qualities better than the traditional feminine gender role, the images and symbols are male. Women do not fit into this scheme. They are "others," even when they do participate. Their team names and logos tend to perpetuate and strengthen the image of female inferiority by making them secondary, invisible, trivial, or unathletic.

Resistance to Change

It is important to note that many schools do not have team names, mascots, and logos that are racist or sexist. They use race- and gender-neutral names such as Bears, Eagles, Seagulls, Saints, or Blue Streaks. Schools that currently employ racist or sexist names could change to neutral ones that embody the traits desired in athletic teams such as courage, strength, and aggressiveness. For some, such a change would be relatively easy—dropping the use of *lady* or *ette* as modifiers, for example. Teams with Native American or male names (stags, rams, hokies, centaurs) must adopt a new name or eliminate the racism or sexism that is inherent in their present names. A few schools have done so over the past 15 years or so. Most schools, however, resist changing names with passion because a name change negates the school's traditions.

Tradition, above all, is always a barrier to change. Students, alumni, faculty, and athletes become accustomed to a particular name for their university and its athletic teams, and it seems "natural." This is the argument made on behalf of the many teams that continue to use American Indian names and symbols for their teams despite the objections of Native Americans. So, too, with names that are sexist. Even if a school team name has the force of tradition, is it justified to continue using that name if it is racist or sexist? If a sexist team name reinforces and socializes sexist thinking, however subtly, it should be changed. If not, the institution is publicly sexist.

Many see the naming issue as trivial. It is not trivial, though, to the group being demeaned, degraded, and trivialized. Some progressives argue that there are more important issues to address than changing racist or sexist names of athletic teams. This illustrates the contradiction that the naming of teams is at once trivial and important. For African Americans, whether the University of Mississippi fans sing "Dixie" and wave the Confederate flag is not as important as ending discrimination and obtaining good jobs. Similarly, for Native Americans, the derogatory use of their heritage surrounding athletic contests is relatively unimportant compared to raising their standard of living. For women, the sexist naming of athletic teams is not as significant as pay equity, breaking the glass ceiling, or achieving equity with men in athletic departments in resources, scholarships, and media attention.

Faced with a choice among these options, the naming issue would be secondary, but this sets up a false choice. We can work to remove all manifestations of racism and sexism on college campuses. Referring to language and relevant to the women's team names issue as well, the Association for Women in Psychology Ad Hoc Committee on Sexist Language has addressed and refuted the "trivial concern" argument:

> The major objection, often even to discussing changing sexist language, is that it is a superficial matter compared with the real physical and economic oppression of women. And indeed, women's total oppression must end; we are not suggesting any diversion of energies from that struggle. We are, however, suggesting that this is an important part of it. (1975, p. 16)

Symbols are extremely compelling in the messages they convey. Their importance is understood when rebellious groups demean or defame symbols of the powerful such as the flag. Names and other symbols have the power to elevate or put down a group. If racist or sexist, they reinforce and, therefore, maintain the secondary status of African Americans, Native Americans, or women through stereotyping, caricature, derogation, trivialization, diminution, or making them invisible. Most of us, however, fail to see the problem with symbols that demean or defame the powerless because these symbols support the existing power arrangements in society. Despite their apparent triviality, the symbols surrounding sports teams are important because they can—and often do—contribute to patterns of social dominance.

Colleges and universities, for the most part, are making major efforts to diversify their student bodies, faculties, and administrations by race, ethnicity, and sex. This laudable goal is clearly at odds with the existence of racist and sexist names and practices of their athletic teams. The leadership in these schools (boards of regents, chancellors, presidents, and faculty senates) must take a stand against racism and sexism in all its forms and take appropriate action. Removing all racist and sexist symbols such as names, mascots, flags, logos, and songs is an important beginning to this crucial project.

Suggested Additional Resources

Carstarphen, M. G., & Sanchez, J. P. (Eds.). (2012). *American Indians and the mass media.* Norman: University of Oklahoma Press.

Churchill, W. (2013). Crimes against humanity. In M. L. Andersen & P. H. Collins (Eds.), *Race, class, and gender: An anthology* (pp. 379–385). Belmont, CA: Thomson-Wadsworth.

Merskin, D. (2001). Winnebagos, Cherokees, Apaches, and Dakotas: The persistence of stereotyping of American Indians in American advertising brands. *The Howard Journal of Communications, 12,* 159–169.

King, C. R. (Ed.). (2010). *The Native American mascot controversy: A handbook.* Lanham, MD: Scarecrow Press.

Staurowsky, E. J. (2007). "You know, we are all Indian": Exploring White power and privilege in reactions to the NCAA Native American mascot policy. *Journal of Sport and Social Issues 31,* 61–76.

Websites

Change the Mascot.org: http://www.changethemascot.org

Campaign led by the Oneida Indian Nation to end the use of the racial slur "redskins" as the mascot and name of the National Football League (NFL) team, the "Washington Redskins." Campaign calls upon the NFL and it commissioner to "do the right thing and bring an end [to] the use of the racial epithet." Relatedly, see the September 8, 2013 *ABC News* article, "'Change the mascot' campaign hits Washington Redskins" (http://abcnews.go.com/US/sports-mascots-stir-controversy/story?id=20194389).

Granderson, L. Z. (2013, February 13). Prompting mascot change. *ESPN.com.* Retrieved from http://espn.go.com/nfl/story/_/id/8944042/history-alone-prompt-washington-change-nfl-mascot

Klatell, J. (2007, February 16). Fighting Illini say goodbye to the chief. *CBS News.* Retrieved from http://www.cbsnews.com/news/fighting-illini-say-goodbye-to-the-chief

National Coalition on Sports & Racism in Media: http://www.aimovement.org/ncrsm/index.html. The coalition is part of the American Indian Movement (AIM).

Audio/Visual

Rosenstein, J. (Producer). (1997). In whose honor? [Television series episode]. *POV.* Brooklyn, NY: American Documentary. Further information can be found at Public Broadcasting Service (http://www.pbs.org/pov/inwhosehonor).

Questions for Further Discussion

1. Before reading this article, how did you feel about Native American mascots or sexist mascots? Upon reading it, has your opinion changed? Why or why not? Does your race or gender inform your opinion on this issue?

2. Do you believe that teams with Native American names and mascots would lose fan support and funding if they changed their team name or mascot? How much should this be taken into consideration when considering changing team names or mascots?

3. Can you think of any other racist or ethnocentric traditions that we continue to uphold or celebrate? For instance, some argue that Thanksgiving is one such tradition. How should we think about these kinds of traditions? Should they be abolished altogether or can they be modified in some way?

Reaching Beyond the Color Line

1. Do an Internet search to find Native American tribal nations in your area. Research their histories and struggles. How does this knowledge shape your opinion of Native American mascots? Did any of the schools in your area use Native American team names or mascots? If so, what does this tell us about how we think about Native American people?

2. In small groups, research Native American team mascots in the National Collegiate Athletic Association (NCAA) and professional sports teams (e.g., Florida State Seminoles, Cleveland Indians, Atlanta Braves, Chicago Blackhawks, etc.). What information can you find about the origins of their mascot or team name? What do those origins tell us about how Native Americans exist in the public imagination? In your search, also look at how these teams have responded to the controversy over their mascots. What do their responses tell us about how Native Americans continue to exist in the public imagination? Has there been any change since the time that the mascot or team name was created?

References

Association for Women in Psychology Ad Hoc Committee on Sexist Language. (1975). Help stamp out sexism: Change the language! *APA Monitor, 6*(11), 16.

Baron, D. (1986). *Grammar and gender.* New Haven, CT: Yale University Press.

Blaubergs, M. S. (1980). An analysis of classic arguments against changing sexist language. *Women's Studies International Quarterly, 3,* 135–147.

Britt, B. (1996, December). Neo Confederate culture. *Z Magazine, 9,* 26–30.

Edelson, P. (1991, November). Just whistlin' Dixie. *Z Magazine, 4,* 72–74.

Eitzen, D. S., & Baca Zinn, M. (1989, December). The de-athleticization of women: The naming and gender marking of collegiate sport teams. *Sociology of Sport Journal, 6,* 362.

Eitzen, D. S., & Baca Zinn, M. (1993, April). The sexist naming of athletic teams and resistance to change. *Journal of Sport and Social Issues, 17,* 34–41.

Franks, R. (1982). *What's in a nickname? Exploring the jungle of college athletic mascots.* Amarillo, TX: Author.

Fuller, J. R., & Manning, E. A. (1987). Violence and sexism in college mascots and symbols: A typology. *Free Inquiry in Creative Sociology, 15,* 61–64.

Henley, N. (1987). This new species that seeks a new language: On sexism in language and language change. In J. Penfield (Ed.), *Women and men in transition* (pp. 3–27). Albany: State University of New York Press.

Kravitz, B. (1992, January 21). Aim of Native Americans' protest is true. *Rocky Mountain News*, 39.

Lakoff, R. (1975). *Language and woman's place*. New York, NY: Harper & Row.

Lederman, D. S. (1996). Old times not forgotten: A battle over symbols. In D. Stanley Eitzen (Ed.), *Sport in contemporary society* (5th ed., pp. 128–133). New York, NY: St. Martin's Press.

Miller, C., & Swift, K. (1980). *The handbook of nonsexist writing*. NY: Lippincott and Crowell.

Nack, W. (1997, November 3). Look away, Dixie land. *Sports Illustrated*, 114.

Spender, D. (1980). *Man made language*. London, UK: Routledge & Kegan Paul.

Thorne, B., Kramarae, C., & Henley, N. M. (1985). Language, gender, and society: Opening a second decade of research. In B. Thorne & N. M. Henley (Eds.), *Language, gender, and society* (pp. 7–24). Rowley, MA: Newbury House.

Tomas, L. (1997, October 19). What's in a name? *In These Times*, 11.

PART III

Institutions, Policies, and Legacies of Oppression

"But What About the Children?"

Understanding Contemporary Attitudes Toward Interracial Dating

Nikki Khanna

University of Vermont

Nikki Khanna received her PhD in sociology from Emory University and is currently an associate professor of sociology at the University of Vermont. Her work looks at racial identity among biracial and multiracial Americans and has been published in outlets such as *Social Psychology Quarterly, Ethnic and Racial Studies, Sociological Spectrum, The Sociological Quarterly, Sociology Compass,* and *Teaching Sociology.* Her recent book, *Biracial in America: Forming and Performing Racial Identity,* looks at Black–White biracial Americans and the underlying processes shaping their racial identities.

When Beth Humphrey, a 30-year-old White account manager, and Terence McKay, a 32-year-old Black welder, decided to wed in 2009, they were stunned when the local justice refused to sign their marriage license. The justice of the peace for Tangipahoa Parish's 8th Ward in Louisiana, Keith Bardwell, refused to do so, explaining that he had a personal policy against interracial marriage. When later questioned publicly about his controversial policy, Judge Bardwell defended himself: "I'm not a racist. . . . My main concern is for the children . . ." (Rentas, 2009). He added, "I think those children suffer and I won't help put them through it" (Interracial Couple Denied, 2010).

Without a doubt, Bardwell faced much public criticism. American approval of interracial marriage has increased substantially in the last 50 years—from 20% in 1968 to 86% in 2011—likely due to changing attitudes and generational replacement, that is, more socially progressive younger adults replacing less progressive older ones (Jones, 2011). Further, marriages between people of different races have increased steadily since the early 1960s—a time when many states criminalized interracial unions through anti-miscegenation laws. Indeed, there has been a shift in attitudes toward interracial dating, but as Judge Bardwell's statement indicates, there are still those who remain opposed to it and attempt to disguise their prejudices in alleged concerns for the children born of these unions. Looking at the history of anti-miscegenation laws can help us better understand and analyze this resistance to interracial dating and marriage.

History of Anti-Miscegenation Laws

At one time or another, 38 U.S. states criminalized interracial marriage through anti-miscegenation laws; four additional states had anti-miscegenation laws but repealed them prior to statehood (Fryer, 2007). *All* such laws prohibited marital and/or sexual unions between Whites and Blacks (Farley, 1999; Zack, 1993), clearly revealing which relationships Whites feared most. In many states, these laws were extended to other racial groups—including Native Americans, Asians (e.g., Chinese, Japanese, Koreans, Filipinos), Native Hawaiians, and in some states, *any* non-White group. For example, according to a 1927 Georgia statute, it was "unlawful for a white person to marry anyone but a white person" (Sohoni, 2007, p. 599). A *White person* was then carefully defined as anyone with "no ascertainable trace of either Negro, African, West Indian, Asiatic Indian, Mongolian, Japanese, or Chinese blood in their veins" (Sohoni, 2007, p. 599). Moreover, penalties for the violation of anti-miscegenation statutes varied state to state from having the marriage voided, paying a fine, and even imprisonment.

These laws primarily functioned to protect and preserve White racial purity; non-White "blood" was seen as a stain that corrupted White blood and defiled White racial integrity. In 1924, for instance, Virginia passed its Racial Integrity Act, which criminalized all marriages between Whites and non-Whites. Aimed at preserving White "racial integrity," it prohibited marriage between a White person and a person with *any* so-called admixture of non-White blood (Plecker, 1924). In the same year, Lonthrop Stoddard, a lawyer and eugenicist, argued that, "White race purity is the cornerstone of our civilization. Its mongrelization with non-white blood . . . would spell the downfall of our civilization."[1]

Efforts to curb interracial unions often centered on the "mongrel" offspring, and the threat they posed to "White racial purity." In 1878, John F. Miller, a future California senator, best articulated the West Coast anxiety regarding White–Chinese

---

[1] See Facing History website at http://www2.facinghistory.org/Campus/rm.nsf/0/6279243C0EEE444E8 5257037004EA259.

unions by saying, "Were the Chinese to amalgamate at all with *our* people, it would be the lowest, most vile, and degraded of *our* race, and the result of that amalgamation would be a hybrid of the most despicable, a mongrel of the most detestable that has ever afflicted the earth" (Childs, 2009, p. 23; emphasis added). In 1924, a California farmer further highlighted the problem of miscegenation in his statement before the U.S. Senate:

> Near my home is an eighty-acre tract of . . . land. On that tract lives a Japanese. With that Japanese lives a white woman. In that woman's arm is a baby. What is that baby? It isn't Japanese. It isn't white. . . . It is a germ of the mightiest problem that ever faced this state; a problem that will make the black problem of the South look white. (Kennedy, 2003, p. 268)

Anti-miscegenation laws were deemed necessary to preserve the White race and, relatedly, to keep power concentrated in the hands of Whites. Any mixing between Whites and people of color was perceived as a threat to the racial hierarchy that placed Whites comfortably at the top, and a threat to the power and resources they monopolized in their privileged position. Hence, there was little interest by White lawmakers to curb unions between non-White groups. Instead, anti-miscegenation laws primarily criminalized relationships (e.g., marital, sexual) between Whites and non-White groups including, for example, California (which prohibited marriages between Whites and "negroes, Mongolians, members of the Malay race, or mulattoes"), Nebraska (which prohibited marriages between Whites and anyone with "1/8th or more negro, Japanese, or Chinese blood"), and Alabama (which prohibited marriage between Whites and "any negro, or the descendent of any negro") Table 11.1 is an overview of American anti-miscegenation laws.

Table 11.1 Anti-Miscegenation Laws by State

State	Groups Whites Were Prohibited From	What Was Prohibited
Alabama	Negro or any descendent	Marriage, adultery, fornication
Arizona	Negro, Mongolian,[1] Malay, Hindu	Marriage
Arkansas	Negro, Mulatto	Cohabitation, birthing a mulatto child, marriage
California	Negro, Mongolian, Malay, Mulatto	Marriage
Colorado	Negro, Mulatto	Marriage
Delaware	Negro, Mulatto	Marriage
Florida	Negro, Mulatto, anyone with 1/8 or more Negro blood	Marriage, adultery, fornication, occupy the same room at nighttime
Georgia	Any non-White person	Marriage, sexual intercourse
Idaho	Negro, Mulatto, Mongolian	Marriage

(Continued)

Table 11.1   (Continued)

State	Groups Whites Were Prohibited From	What Was Prohibited
Illinois	Negro, Mulatto	Marriage
Indiana	Anyone with 1/8 or more negro blood	Marriage
Iowa	Negro, Mulatto	Marriage
Kansas	Negro, Mulatto	Marriage
Kentucky	Negro, Mulatto	Marriage
Louisiana	Aboriginal Indian race of America, Black, Colored	Concubinage, cohabitation
Maine	Negro, Indian, Mulatto	Marriage
Maryland	Negro, a person of Negro descent (to the third generation), Malay	Marriage
Massachusetts	Negro, Indian, Mulatto	Marriage
Michigan	Negro	Marriage
Mississippi	Negro, Mulatto, Mongolian, a person with 1/8 or more of Negro or Mongolian blood	Marriage
Missouri	Negro, a person with 1/8 or more of Negro blood, Mongolian	Marriage
Montana	Negro, Chinese, a person of Negro blood or in part Negro, Japanese	Marriage
Nebraska	A person with 1/8 or more Negro, Chinese, or Japanese blood	Marriage
Nevada	Ethiopian or Black, Malay or brown, Mongolian or yellow	Marriage, fornication, cohabitation
New Mexico	Negro, Mulatto	Marriage, cohabitation
North Carolina	Negro, a person of Negro descent to the third generation	Marriage
North Dakota	Negro	Occupying the same room, marriage
Ohio	Negro, or any person with any distinct and visible mixture of Negro or African blood	Intercourse, marriage
Oklahoma	Any person of African descent	Marriage
Oregon	Negro, Chinese, or any person having 1/4 or more Negro, Chinese, or Kanaka blood, or any person having more than 1/2 Indian blood	Marriage

Table 11.1   (Continued)

State	Groups Whites Were Prohibited From	What Was Prohibited
Pennsylvania	Negro	Cohabitation; fornication, adultery, marriage
Rhode Island	Negro, Indian, Mulatto	Marriage
South Carolina	Indian, Negro, Mulatto, Mestizo, or half-breed	Marriage
South Dakota	African, Korean, Malayan, Mongolian	Marriage, cohabitation
Tennessee	Negro, Mulatto	Marriage, cohabitation
Texas	Negro	Marriage
Utah	Negro, Mongolian, Malayan, Mulatto, Quadroon, Octoroon	Marriage
Virginia	Any non-White person	Marriage
Washington	Anyone with 1/4 or more of Negro blood or 1/2 or more Indian blood	Marriage
West Virginia	Negro	Marriage
Wyoming	Negro, Mulatto, Mongolian, Malay	Marriage

Source: Adapted from Fryer (2007) and http://www.lovingday.org/legal-map

Note: States that never had such laws: Alaska, Connecticut, Hawaii, Minnesota, New Hampshire, New Jersey, New York, Vermont, and Wisconsin.
1. "Mongolian" refers to Chinese, "Malay" refers to Filipino, "Hindu" refers to Asian Indian, "Mulatto" refers to anyone with Black and White ancestry, "Kanaka" refers to Native Hawaiian, "Quadroon" refers to someone who is 1/8 Black, "Octoroon" refers to someone who is 1/8 Black.

While rooted in colonial America, these laws flourished in the first half of the 20th century as White fears regarding miscegenation grew. Between 1900 and the late 1960s, 30 states had some form of anti-miscegenation legislation (Fryer, 2007). The taboo of interracial mixing was clearly evident even in Hollywood when the Motion Picture Association of America completely forbade the theme of miscegenation from the 1930s to the 1950s (Courtney, 2005; Sickels, 1972); in particular, depictions of sexual relationships between Whites and Blacks were strictly prohibited. In Alabama in the late 1950s, fear of Black–White marriage was readily apparent when a children's book, *The Rabbit's Wedding* by Garth Williams (1958), was removed from the shelves of the public libraries because the illustration portrayed one rabbit as White and the other as Black (Tucker, 2004). Nonetheless, the number of states with anti-miscegenation laws would decline in the 1950s and 1960s, but by 1966, 17 states still criminalized interracial marriage (all were in the southeast—as far west as Texas and Oklahoma, as far north as Maryland and Delaware, and as far south as Florida).

In 1967, a young couple from Virginia would challenge the constitutionality of such laws in the landmark case, *Loving v. Virginia*. Mildred Jeter, a Black woman, and Richard Loving, a White man, married nine years earlier in Washington, DC, where it was legal for them to do so. Upon returning to their home in Caroline County, Virginia, where they had spent most of their lives, they were arrested for violating the state's anti-miscegenation statute. After pleading guilty to the charges, they were sentenced to 1 year in jail. The trial judge, however, suspended their sentence on the condition that they leave the state of Virginia for 25 years (Zabel, 2000). In his opinion, the judge stated, "Almighty God created the races white, black, yellow, malay, and red, and he placed them on separate continents. . . . The fact that he separated the races shows that he did not intend for the races to mix" (Sollors, 2000, p. 28). Mildred Jeter and Richard Loving filed suit against the state, claiming that prohibition of marriage on the basis of race violated their Fourteenth Amendment right to equal protection under the law.

The Virginia Supreme Court upheld the state's anti-miscegenation law, claiming that the state had a right "to preserve the racial integrity of its citizens" and to prevent a "mongrel breed of citizens" (Sollors, 2000, p. 31). However, the case was soon appealed to the U.S. Supreme Court. In 1967, after nearly 10 years of marriage and the birth of three children (Sickels, 1972), the Court reversed the earlier decision and ruled anti-miscegenation laws unconstitutional; sixteen states were affected, including Virginia, but also Alabama, Arkansas, Georgia, Kentucky, Louisiana, Mississippi, Missouri, Tennessee, Texas, West Virginia, North Carolina, South Carolina, Florida, Oklahoma, and Delaware.

Interracial Marriage Today: Attitudes and Trends

Since *Loving v. Virginia* (1967), attitudes toward interracial marriage have become more favorable and rates of intermarriage have grown steadily, though these trends vary depending on many factors. A 2011 Gallup Poll of American attitudes toward Black–White interracial marriage found that those who were 65 years or older, less educated (high school or less), conservative, and Republican were less likely to approve of such marriages as compared to their younger, more educated, liberal, moderate, Democratic, and Independent counterparts (see Table 11.2 for a breakdown). The same poll revealed that the South is least likely to approve of intermarriage than any region of the country, and a 2012 survey of Republican voters found that 29% in Mississippi and 21% in Alabama still believed interracial marriage should be prohibited by law (The Economist, 2012). Notably, Alabama, in 2000, was the last state to lift its unenforceable ban on interracial marriage (Yen, 2012).

Moreover, *actual* rates of intermarriage, though growing, remain low. According to Jayson (2012), although interracial marriages reached an "all-time high" in 2010 (at 8.4% of all marriages), census data reveal that rates of intermarriage, like attitudes toward such unions, vary widely. Regarding region, Hawaii and Alaska have the highest share of mixed marriages, followed by Western states such as Oklahoma,

Table 11.2 Approval of Marriage Between Blacks and Whites

Subgroup	Percentage Approve
Men	87
Women	85
18–29 year olds	97
30–49 year olds	91
50–64 year olds	88
65 years +	66
East	90
Midwest	86
South	79
West	91
High school or less	78
Some college	91
College graduate only	92
Postgraduate	94
Liberal	95
Moderate	90
Conservative	78
Democrat	88
Independent	89
Republican	77

Source: Adapted from Jones, J. (2011). *Record-high 86% Approve of Black-White Marriages*. Retrieved from http://www.gallup.com/poll/149390/Record-High-Approve-Black-White-Marriages.aspx

Nevada, California, Oregon, New Mexico, Colorado, and Washington (Lofquist, Lugaila, O'Connell, & Feliz, 2012; Passel, Wang, & Taylor, 2010). States with the lowest share, according to a 2012 Pew Report, included Southern states, likely because of persistent segregation and prejudicial attitudes (e.g., Mississippi, Alabama, Louisiana), and homogenous, overwhelmingly White states where opportunity for outmarriage is low, for example, in Vermont and Maine; both states are 95% White (The Economist, 2012).

Further, a Pew analysis of new marriages in 2008 revealed that the majority of interracial marriages were between Latinos and Whites (41%).[2] Of the remaining interracial marriages, 16% were between two non-White partners, 15% were between Asians and Whites, and the smallest share (11%) were between Blacks

---

[2] It must be noted, however, that "Latino/Hispanic" is a panethnic label, and in census data those of Latino/Hispanic ancestry could be of any race, including White. Thus, these figures are somewhat misleading.

and Whites (Passel et al., 2010)—no doubt reflecting the taboo still surrounding Black–White marriages. Moreover, if we look at outmarriage rates among racial groups, Asians are most likely to marry outside their race (14%), followed by Blacks (5%), while Whites are the least likely group to marry outside their race (1%) (Fryer, 2007). Thus, although Whites showed a record high 84% approval rating of interracial marriage in 2011 (Jones, 2012), they remain least likely of all racial groups to actually marry outside their race. The disjuncture between the high approval rating and the low rate of outmarriage may in fact be explained by the concept of social desirability, as suggested by sociologist Daniel Lichter of Cornell University: "People don't want to reveal negative attitudes that might reflect badly on them, and they tend to tell the interviewers what they want to hear" (Jayson, 2012). Further, opportunity also influences intermarriage rates, and given that Whites are the majority group in the United States, many White Americans continue to have little day-to-day interaction with people of color in their neighborhoods, schools, and workplaces, thereby decreasing the impact of attitudes alone on actual behaviors.

Finally, a Pew analysis of interracial marriages finds that rates of intermarriage also vary by age, education, and gender (Passel et al., 2010). Not surprisingly, inter-marriage is strongly correlated with age; approximately 13% of those 25 years or younger have married outside their race as compared to 3% of those 75 and older, which is likely due to generational changes in racial attitudes (also keep in mind that for many older Americans, anti-miscegenation laws and segregation were the norm in their youth). As education increases, so does the likelihood of outmar-riage, though the differences are modest: Eleven percent of those with less than a high school degree married outside their race as compared to nearly 16% of those who have attended college. For Whites, there appears to be no gender difference regarding rates of outmarriage. However, gender is correlated with intermarriage for Blacks and Asians: Black men are much more likely to marry outside their race as compared to Black women (22% and 9%, respectively), and Asian women are far more likely to outmarry as compared to Asian men (40% and 20%, respectively). Thus, while studies reveal that attitudes toward interracial marriage have relaxed over the years, actual rates of intermarriage remain low and vary depending on many factors. These low rates point to the continuing significance of race in a "post-racial" society.

What About the Children?

Of those who disapprove of interracial marriage today, prejudicial attitudes likely play a key role, yet for some like Judge Bardwell of Louisiana, their explanations center on the *children* of interracial marriage: *I don't approve of interracial mar-riage because the children suffer.* Implicit in this reasoning is the assumption that the multiracial offspring of interracial couples are mixed-up, confused, and caught between two worlds, as exemplified by a biracial guest who appeared on the *Dr. Phil* show in 2003. With falling tears, the adult woman of Black and White ancestry said before millions of Americans watching at home: "There's no place for me," "I don't know who or what I am," and described herself throughout the segment as "lonely," feeling like "trash," "torn apart inside," "not good enough," "inferior," "strange," "different," "caught in the middle," and as having "no identity."[3]

Her story exemplified the "tragic mulatta" stereotype, a popular portrayal of Black–White biracial women during the slave and Jim Crow eras (also known more generally as the "tragic mulatto" stereotype). The tragic mulatta was depicted as confused, lost, self-loathing, lacking in self-esteem, and perpetually miserable (see Benshoff & Griffin, 2009). She was trapped in a permanent state of liminality— caught between two worlds without fully belonging to either. Her character was popularized in American novels, plays, and films, and more often than not, by the end of the story, she met a tragic and heartbreaking end—she suffered loss of social status, social isolation, violence, murder, and even suicide.[4] This tragic character is best exemplified by the concept of the "marginal man," which was first introduced by sociologist Robert Park in 1928 as "one whom fate has condemned to live in two societies and in two, not merely different, but antagonistic cultures" (Stonequist, 1937/1961, p. xiiii). He believed that mixed-race people were marginal and they lived "in two worlds," in both of which they were "strangers" (Park, 1928, p. 893). The question remains, however: To what extent does this "tragic marginal identity" accurately represent the experiences of multiracial people *today*? What do recent studies show?

According to Kathleen Korgen (1998), who examined identity among Black– White biracial Americans, there is an increasing acceptance of multiraciality today. Though some of her respondents sometimes felt like racial outsiders, she finds that "young biracial men and women today believe that the positive attributes of biracial identity outweigh the negative" and the overwhelming majority in her study "do not wish they were born any other way" (p. 79). In fact, she found that they believed they were more objective, more open minded, and better able to view others without "racial blinders" as compared to their monoracial counterparts (p. 78). Marion Kilson (2001), in her study of multiracial Americans, similarly finds that some of her respondents felt some measure of marginalization in adolescence, but most viewed their biracial heritage as unique and an "asset in which they take pride" (p. 167). In a more recent study, I found that most of my Black–White respondents expressed pride in their biracial backgrounds, and they claimed that their backgrounds made them feel "different and unique" (Khanna, 2011, p. 118).

Moreover, though studies frequently predict that mixed-race people suffer lower self-esteem, higher rates of depression, lower academic performance, or poor peer relations, empirical research actually shows that multiracial people tend to be "as well-adjusted as their monoracial peers on most psychological outcomes" (Shih & Sanchez, 2005, p. 569). In a review of more than 40 studies of multiracial Americans, Shih and Sanchez (2005) found very little evidence that multiracial individuals were dissatisfied, unhappy, or uncomfortable with their racial identities. Upon closer inspection, an analysis of the qualitative studies reveal both challenges and benefits for those with multiracial backgrounds; in some cases, they felt rejected by others

---

[3] Aired on the *Dr. Phil* show on March 15, 2003.
[4] To read more about this stereotype, see http://www.ferris.edu/htmls/news/jimcrow/mulatto.

because of their racial identity, while others cited benefits such as having access to and support from a larger number of racial and cultural communities. While the authors cite numerous studies that reveal issues with identity development, depression, problem behaviors (e.g., early sexual activity, alcohol or drug use), poor academic performance, and low self-esteem, the majority of these studies sampled clinical populations. This is problematic given the selectivity of the samples in question (i.e., study participants were already being treated in a clinical setting—often in therapy). Studies that sampled nonclinical populations generally found positive outcomes, such as pride in one's racial identity, happiness, success in school, and high self-esteem.

When reviewing quantitative studies, the authors found mixed results (see also Kahn and Denmon's 1997 review). For instance, they found multiracial adolescents exhibited slightly higher levels of problem behaviors (e.g., delinquency, marijuana use) than their monoracial counterparts, though this finding was based on a small number of studies and must, they warn, be interpreted with caution. Regarding school performance, some studies found no differences between multiracial adolescence and their White counterparts, and often studies suggested that multiracial adolescents fared better academically than their monoracial minority counterparts. Quantitative studies further reveal that multiracial adolescents develop good peer relations in terms of popularity and feeling accepted (which challenges the stereotype that they are socially isolated and marginalized), but there were mixed results regarding measures of self-esteem and depression. Some studies found that multiracial individuals show lower levels of self-esteem than their monoracial counterparts, while others find higher levels of self-esteem or no difference at all. And, studies that looked at depression suggest that multiracial individuals may possibly fare worse than their White peers, but not when compared to their monoracial minority peers—though this was based on only four studies and hence the trend should be viewed with caution.

Thus, according to Shih and Sanchez's (2005) review, previous studies reveal *no clear patterns* regarding the social and psychological adjustment of multiracial Americans. The mixed results are likely due to the fact that many studies drew respondents from clinical and therapeutic settings (which led to an early emphasis on problems), many relied on small, nonrepresentative samples, and some studies focused on one multiracial group, while others grouped all multiracials together regardless of racial background (Campbell & Eggerling-Boeck, 2006). The research, however, is ongoing, and in a more recent study of multiracial adolescents, Campbell and Eggerling-Boeck (2006) also ask, "What about the children?" Examining the mental health and social adjustment of more than a thousand multiracial adolescents of varying racial backgrounds in a large, nationally representative, nonclinical sample, they found "no pervasive disadvantage associated with a multiracial heritage" and they "do not find evidence that Park's 'marginal man' hypothesis is true today" (p. 168). They were able to examine multiracial groups separately (e.g., Black–White, Asian–White, American Indian–White) and together as a group, and they found no evidence that multiracial Americans differed significantly from their White counterparts in terms of depression, seriously considering suicide, feeling socially accepted, feeling close to others at school, and participating in extra-curricular activities.[5] While many Americans might hold particular concern about Black–White multiracial children, Campbell and Eggerling-Boeck (2006) further add, "It is especially noteworthy that Black-Whites face no pattern of particular hardships" given that "it is this group for whom most of the theories regarding the 'difficulty' of biracial status were developed" (p. 168). Clearly, more research is needed, though it appears from these data that we cannot assume that multiracial Americans today are the identity-confused, socially isolated, tragic characters commonly portrayed in early American history.

Conclusion

America has a 300-year history of anti-miscegenation legislation. Although these laws have since vanished and attitudes toward interracial marriage have relaxed, intermarriage rates remain low—even more so among certain segments of the American population. Attitudinal resistance to interracial marriage undoubtedly reflects lingering prejudicial attitudes, though frequently explanations center on the children of such marriages and the belief that they suffer as multiracial people living in a racialized world. Undeniably, multiracial Americans face unique challenges (and research does bear this out), yet studies also suggest that they are not necessarily maladjusted nor psychologically troubled as often believed. Though some studies do point to some negative social or psychological issues and these findings should not be ignored, studies also show that multiraciality is becoming more commonly accepted, and multiracial Americans are increasingly pointing to the positive aspects of having a multiracial ancestry. Moreover, as intermarriage becomes more common and less taboo and as the number of Americans with multiracial ancestry grows (as is projected to do so), the traditional challenges for children of multiracial ancestry will likely fade as well. Undoubtedly, during the height of the Jim Crow era and racial segregation their experiences may likely have mirrored the "tragic mulatto" stereotype, though recent scholarly evidence suggests that their experiences look quite different today.

These findings raise two important concerns. First, persistent negative stereotypes of multiracial people may be driving some of the observed disapproval ratings toward interracial relationships even in the present day. Lingering "tragic" stereotypes of multiracial children as confused and socially isolated, even if uncorroborated in research, may discourage many Americans from exploring interracial relationships and accepting those relationships in their families and in larger society. Certainly, some may object to interracial relationships out of apprehension for multiracial children and obstacles they perceive they might face in society.

Second, these findings also raise the question to what extent some Americans rely on the "multiracial-kids-suffer" argument to *mask* their own personal

---

[5] Only American Indian–White adolescents showed some negative outcomes compared to White students, but they resembled the outcomes of monoracial American Indians. Other multiracial groups (e.g., Black–White, Asian–White) were not shown to be disadvantaged compared to Whites.

prejudices against these unions. In other words, objections to interracial marriage under the pretense of concern for the well-being of multiracial children may very well be another form of hidden racism—a way to disguise one's true feelings toward interracial relationships in an era where overt racism has the potential to be met with backlash and criticism. Sociologist Eduardo Bonilla-Silva (2010) examines what he calls "color-blind racism," a new type of racism in contemporary America that, unlike earlier Jim Crow racism, which was overt and in-your-face (e.g., racial slurs, open discrimination), is by contrast "subtle" and "apparently nonracial" (p. 3). Yet, like Jim Crow racism, this new type of seemingly innocuous racism functions to maintain the racial status quo. In 2010, Bonilla-Silva writes:

> Compared to Jim Crow racism, the ideology of color blindness seems like "racism lite." Instead of relying on name calling (niggers, Spics, Chinks), color-blind racism otherizes softly ("these people are human, too"); instead of proclaiming God placed minorities in the world in a servile position, it suggests that they are behind because they do not work enough; instead of viewing interracial marriage as wrong on a straight racial basis, it regards it as "problematic" because of concerns over the children, location, or the extra burden it places on couples. Yet this new ideology has become a formidable political tool for the maintenance of the racial order. (p. 3)

Thus, for some Americans, multiracial children may arguably provide a scapegoat explanation for their own unfavorable attitudes toward interracial relationships and marriage. By focusing on the offspring of interracial unions, they can, as Bonilla-Silva puts it, "safeguard their racial interests without sounding 'racist'" (p. 4).

Suggested Additional Resources

Childs, E. C. (2005). *Navigating interracial borders: Black-White couples and their social worlds*. New Brunswick, NJ: Rutgers University Press.

Dalmage, H. M. (2000). *Tripping on the color line: Black-White multiracial families in a racially divided world*. New Brunswick, NJ: Rutgers University Press.

Kennedy, R. (2003). *Interracial intimacies: Sex, marriage, identity, and adoption*. New York, NY: Vintage Books.

Sollors, W. (2000). *Interracialism: Black-White intermarriage in American history, literature, and law*. New York, NY: Oxford University Press.

Questions for Further Discussion

1. In 1968, only 20% of Americans approved of interracial marriage, but by 2011 those numbers jumped to 86%. How might we explain these changing attitudes over time? (i.e., how can we explain declining prejudicial attitudes?) Furthermore, rates of intermarriage have also increased over

time. Other than declining prejudicial attitudes, what might be additional explanations for this trend?

2. Interracial couples may face unique challenges as compared to their same-race couple counterparts. What types of challenges, if any, might they face? In addition, what factors may affect the degree to which they face these challenges? (Hint: Think social context and the social characteristics of the couple, like their racial mix, social class, etc.)

3. To what extent do you think lingering negative stereotypes about multiracial people exist today? To what extent do you think they might contribute to some Americans' attitudes toward interracial marriage? Finally, the author argues that some Americans may rely on the "multiracial-kids-suffer" argument to mask their own personal prejudices against interracial unions. To what extent, if at all, do you think some use this argument as a form of hidden racism or color-blind racism?

4. Anti-miscegenation laws varied state to state, and in 1967, the Supreme Court ruled these laws unconstitutional because they violated the Fourteenth Amendment to the U.S. Constitution. What parallels, if any, exist between interracial marriage and same-sex marriage regarding the controversy and legislation?

Reaching Beyond the Color Line

1. As a class, explore contemporary attitudes toward interracial dating and marriage by collectively constructing a survey and distributing it to other students on campus (e.g., to students in another course, in the student center). In particular, ask questions about their attitudes toward interracial dating and marriage toward various racial groups (e.g., Whites, Blacks, Asians or Asian Americans, Native Americans), and collect information about the respondents—such as their race, gender, and political affiliation (and any other factor you deem potentially important). What do you find? Are there racial groups that students are more or less open to dating, marrying, or both? Are there differences in student perceptions of interracial dating versus interracial marriage? Are certain characteristics of the students (such as race, gender, or political affiliation) correlated with their attitudes?

2. For further research, go to http://www.lovingday.org/legal-map to view an interactive map of where interracial marriage was prohibited by law. Click on each state to read the anti-miscegenation legislation. Looking at the state you were born in and another state of your choosing, answer the following questions: Did an anti-miscegenation law exist? If not, why do you think this state was one of nine states that never had such laws? If yes, when was it created and repealed? If any, what type of union was prohibited in your state? Which racial groups were prohibited from intermarrying? What was the penalty for violating the law?

3. Consider one or more of the following questions for an in-class free-write activity: (a) What are your thoughts regarding interracial dating and marriage? What is beneficial about interracial unions? What is problematic about them? (b) Often people say they support interracial relationships until it comes to a member of their family dating or marrying outside his or her race. How do you think your family might react if you dated or married outside your race? How might you react if a sibling or other family member dated or married outside his or her race? Explain.

4. The portrayal of interracial relationships has a long history in Hollywood (though notably, the portrayal of Black–White relationships was prohibited from the 1930s to 1950s). Choose a film that features an interracial couple and answer the following questions in a short response paper: What year does the setting of the movie take place? How is the relationship portrayed (is it problematized or glamorized)? What is the family and societal reaction to the relationship (positive, negative, or neutral)? How close do you imagine the movie's portrayal of the relationship and reactions mirror reality during that time period and why? And finally, how might the portrayal look different today? Explain. Possible movies to analyze include: *Guess Who's Coming to Dinner* (1967), *Jungle Fever* (1991), *The Bodyguard* (1992), *Mississippi Masala* (1992), *Zebrahead* (1992), *Made in America* (1993), *Corrina, Corrina* (1994), *Monster's Ball* (2001), *Save the Last Dance* (2001), *Guess Who?* (2005), *Something New* (2006), and *Lakeview Terrace* (2008).

References

Benshoff, H. M., & Griffin, S. (2009). *America on film: Representing race, class, gender and sexuality at the movies.* Malden, MA: Blackwell.

Bonilla-Silva, E. (2010). *Racism without racists: Color-blind racism & racial inequality in contemporary America.* Lanham, MD: Rowman & Littlefield.

Campbell, M. E., & Eggerling-Boeck., J. (2006). What about the children? The psychological and social well-being of multiracial adolescents. *The Sociological Quarterly, 47*(1), 147–173.

Childs, E. C. (2009). *Fade to Black and White: Interracial images in popular culture.* Lanham, MD: Rowman & Littlefield.

Courtney, S. (2005). *Hollywood fantasies of miscegenation: Spectacular narratives of gender and race.* Princeton, NJ: Princeton University Press.

Farley, R. (1999). Racial issues: Recent trends in residential patterns and intermarriage. In N. J. Smelser & J. C. Alexander (Eds.), *Diversity and its discontents: Cultural conflict and common ground in contemporary American society* (pp. 85–128). Princeton, NJ: Princeton University Press.

Fryer, R. G. (2007). Guess who's been coming to dinner? Trends in interracial marriage over the 20th century. *Journal of Economic Perspectives, 21*(2), 71–90.

Interracial couple denied marriage license by Louisiana Justice of the Peace. (2010, March 18). *Huffington Post.* Retrieved January 15, 2013, from http://www.huffingtonpost.com/2009/10/15/interracial-couple-denied_n_322784.html?view=print&comm_ref=false

Jayson, S. (2012). U.S. rate of interracial marriage hits record high. *USA Today.* Retrieved September 16, 2012, from http://www.usatoday.com/news/health/wellness/marriage/story/2012-02-16/US-rate-of-interracial-marriage-hits-record-high/53109980/1

Jones, J. (2011, September 12). Record-high 86% approve of Black-White marriages. *Gallup.* Retrieved from http://www.gallup.com/poll/149390/Record-High-Approve-Black-White-Marriages.aspx

Kahn, J. S., & Denmon, J. (1997). An examination of social science literature pertaining to multiracial identification: A historical perspective. *Journal of Multicultural Social Work, 6,* 117–138.

Kennedy, R. (2003). *Interracial intimacies: Sex, marriage, identity, and adoption.* New York, NY: Vintage Books.

Khanna, N. (2011). *Biracial in America: Forming and performing racial identity.* Lanham, MD: Lexington Books.

Kilson, M. (2001). *Claiming place: Biracial young adults of the post-civil rights era.* Westport, CT: Bergin & Garvey.

Korgen, K. (1998). *From Black to biracial: Transforming racial identity among biracial Americans.* New York, NY: Praeger.

Lofquist, D., Lugaila, T., O'Connell, M., & Feliz, S. (2012). *Households and families: 2010.* United States Census Bureau. 2010 Census Brief. Retrieved September 16, 2012, from http://www.census.gov/prod/cen2010/briefs/c2010br-14.pdf

Loving v. Virginia, 388 U.S. (1967).

Park, R. (1928). Human migration and the marginal man. *American Journal of Sociology, 33*(6), 881–893.

Passel, J. S., Wang, W., & Taylor, P. (2010). *Marrying out: One-in-seven new U.S. marriages is interracial or interethnic.* Pew Research Center. Retrieved September 16, 2012, from http://www.pewsocialtrends.org/files/2010/10/755-marrying-out.pdf

Plecker, W. A. (1924, March). *Virginia health bulletin.* Retrieved from http://www.dnalc.org/view/10431--The-New-Virginia-Law-to-Preserve-Racial-Integrity-by-W-A-Plecker-Virginia-Health-Bulletin-vol-16-2-.html

Rentas, K. (2009). Removing a justice of the peace in Louisiana is no cakewalk. *CNN.com.* Retrieved January 15, 2013, from http://www.cnn.com/2009/CRIME/10/19/louisiana.interracial.marriage/index.html?iref=allsearch

The Republican primaries: Miscegenation and the South. (2012, March 13). *The Economist.* Retrieved May 23, 2012, from http://www.economist.com/blogs/democracyinamerica/2012/03/republican-primaries

Shih, M. D., & Sanchez, T. (2005). Perspectives and research on the positive and negative implications of having multiple racial identities. *Psychological Bulletin, 131,* 569–591.

Sickels, R. J. (1972). *Race, marriage, and the law.* Albuquerque: University of New Mexico Press.

Sohoni, D. (2007). Unsuitable suitors: Anti-miscegenation laws, naturalization laws, and the construction of Asian identities. *Law & Society Review, 41*(3), 587–618.

Sollors, W. (2000). *Interracialism: Black-White intermarriage in American history, literature, and law.* New York, NY: Oxford University Press.

Stonequist, E. (1961). *The marginal man.* New York, NY: Russell & Russell. (Original work published 1937)

Tucker, W. H. (2004). "Inharmoniously adapted to each other": Science and racial crosses. In A. S. Winston (Ed.), *Defining difference: Race and racism in the history of psychology* (pp. 109–128). Washington, DC: American Psychological Association.

Williams, G. (1958). *The rabbits' wedding.* New York, NY: HarperCollins.

Yen, H. (2012, February 16). Interracial marriage in the U.S. climbs to new high, study finds. *Huffington Post.* Retrieved June 1, 2012, from http://www.huffingtonpost.com/2012/02/16/interracial-marriage-in-us_n_1281229.html

Zabel, W. D. (2000). Interracial marriage and the law. In W. Sollors (Ed.), *Interracialism: Black-White intermarriage in American history, literature, and law* (pp. 54–60). New York, NY: Oxford University Press.

Zack, N. (1993). *Race and mixed race.* Philadelphia, PA: Temple University Press.

"Blacks Don't Value Marriage as Much as Other Groups"

Examining Structural Inequalities in Black Marriage Patterns

Dawne M. Mouzon

Rutgers University–New Brunswick

Dawne Mouzon, PhD, is a sociologist and assistant professor at the Edward J. Bloustein School of Planning and Public Policy at Rutgers University–New Brunswick. She is also a member of the core faculty at the Institute for Health, Health Care Policy, and Aging Research at Rutgers University. Her current research focuses identifying causal mechanisms to explain the "race paradox in mental health," or the unexpected finding that Blacks typically exhibit better mental health outcomes than Whites despite their lower socioeconomic standing and greater exposure to discrimination.

Most social scientists agree that there have been tremendous changes in what sociologist Dorothy Smith (1993) coined the *SNAF* or Standard North American Family. This ideological concept refers to a married heterosexual man and woman who live together with their biological children under one roof. However, contemporary families exhibit a far wider range of forms and flexibility. Even a brief historical glimpse into media representation of families over time reflects these societal changes. In the 1980s, two of the most popular sitcoms were *The Cosby Show* and *Family Ties*, which reflected the lives of solidly middle-class Black and White families that fit the SNAF mold. What we formerly viewed as "the family" has transformed into a mosaic of configurations, including stepfamilies, families raised by gay and lesbian couples, adoptive families, and interracial and interethnic unions, such as those represented in popular TV shows like *Modern Family* and *Grey's Anatomy*.

By far, the most important demographic change in the social institution of marriage over the past 50 years or so is the dramatic decline in the prevalence of marriage. Roughly 72% of all Americans were married in 1960 but only slightly more than half (53%) of all Americans were married in 2008 (Pew, 2010). This decline was also demonstrated among Whites; 74% of Whites were married in 1960 but only 56% were married in 2008. Latinos exhibit similar patterns (72% and 50%, respectively). The marriage decline has been far steeper among Blacks than any other racial or ethnic group in the United States. Almost 61% of Blacks were married in 1960 but this figure dropped to 32% by 2008 (Pew, 2010). Blacks also experience higher divorce rates and lower remarriage rates than Whites (Bramlett & Mosher, 2002). Scholars and the public have understandably been concerned about the universal marriage decline. After all, marriage historically provides myriad benefits to families. Individuals who are married have better physical and mental health, more social integration, have higher household incomes, accumulate more wealth, and raise children with more positive health and social outcomes than those who are unmarried (Waite & Lehrer, 2003). Because the marriage decline has been most amplified among Blacks, greater scrutiny has been directed toward this group in an effort to understand the fundamental question, "Why aren't more Black people married?" In part, this can be answered by looking at trends in marriage among Blacks over time.

The History of Black Marriage

The history of Black marriage in the United States is a complicated one. The transatlantic slave trade was initiated by European settlers in the early 17th century. During this process, White colonists captured, enslaved, and imported millions of Africans to the United States (among other places in the African Diaspora) in order to extract their free labor to aid in the agricultural and economic development of the new colonies. Because slavery was purely an economic system, African families were often forcefully separated from each other based on the labor and reproductive needs of plantation owners. Slaves were not considered citizens (or even fully human) and therefore were not legally eligible to marry. However, some plantation owners permitted their slaves to engage in symbolic Christian or African marriage ceremonies, often including rituals such as "jumping the broom." After almost 250 years of bondage, the institution of North American slavery was finally abolished at the end of the Civil War in 1865. Slavery was immediately followed by the development of new economic systems during Reconstruction (1865–1877) and the social marginalization of Blacks that characterized the Jim Crow Era (1877–1965).

In his landmark book, *The Black Family in Slavery and Freedom, 1750–1925*, historian Herbert Gutman analyzed an impressive array of data from sources such as birth records, census data, and marriage records from six large plantations. He concluded that during the period from 1850 to 1930, Black families were either equally likely or more likely to reside in married-couple households than native-born Whites. Moreover, roughly three quarters of slave unions were legally formalized after manumission (Gutman, 1977). Although recent work has suggested more modest marriage rates during this time, these data also show that at least half of Blacks were married between 1880 and 1940 (Ruggles, 1994). Taken together, these findings prove the unmistakable value that most Blacks placed on forging marital bonds both during and after slavery.

Influential scholars of Black family life have rightfully pointed out the historical strengths of Black families, including the incorporation of extended family members, strong biological and fictive kinship bonds, and flexible and egalitarian family roles, among other characteristics (R. Hill, 2003; S. Hill, 2005; Stack, 1974). Newer research suggests that historically abundant and supportive Black family networks have been partially eroded due to structural factors such as deindustrialization caused by globalization (and the ensuing flight of blue-collar jobs to developing countries), the disincentive to marry under mid-1990s welfare reform, and the War on Drugs, all of which primarily targeted people of color (Roschelle, 1997).

Marriage is a fundamental mechanism underlying health and social inequities, a major point that students begin to recognize in my courses. When asked to brainstorm about the factors underlying the contemporary Black marriage decline, one student will inevitably declare that, "Black people don't value marriage as much as Whites," a simple statement that echoes the sentiments of many scholars, policymakers, and the media. In other words, the assertion is that Blacks have certain cultural beliefs that devalue the importance of marriage to individuals, families, and the broader society as a whole. One of the first individuals to offer this argument was Daniel Patrick Moynihan, a sociologist turned Democratic senator who served the state of New York between 1976 and 2000.

Moynihan's theoretical framework—later coined the *culture of poverty* or the *tangle of pathology* approach—was first laid out in his 1965 research report titled *The Negro Family: The Case for National Action.* In this report, Moynihan argued that high poverty rates among Blacks could be easily traced back to their supposedly backwards cultural values. At the top of this list was Black women's presumed preference for the matriarchal family, an argument he supported by citing their disproportionately higher rates of nonmarital childbearing and low prevalence of marriage. At the outset of his chapter on "The Negro American Family," Moynihan professes this philosophy in no uncertain terms: "At the heart of the deterioration of the fabric of Negro society is the deterioration of the Negro family." In other words, Blacks devalue and therefore do not conform to the SNAF ideological code of a nuclear family consisting of a married man, woman, and their biological children co-residing in a single household. Because the nuclear family form is less prevalent among Blacks, Moynihan argues that they will be doomed to continue suffering from high rates of social problems such as nonmarital childbearing, crime, incarceration, and presumed welfare dependency. According to him, because these are alleged cultural values, they are even more troubling because they are destined to be passed down from generation to generation. By Moynihan's estimation, the intractable values of Black families mean that they will never progress in society and worse, it is their fault. The tangle of pathology approach is cultural determinism at its very worst and yet is still widely believed.

Answering the Question:
Do Blacks Value Marriage Less Than Whites?

Given the pervasiveness of belief in this idea, how well do empirical data support this culture of poverty argument? Do Blacks really value marriage less than Whites? Belinda Tucker, a social psychologist from the University of California–Los Angeles, used data from Whites, Blacks, and Mexican Americans residing in 21 U.S. cities to definitively answer this long-standing question. After examining 10 different values related to marriage (e.g., importance of marrying one day, importance of being married when having children, etc.), she found no race or ethnic differences among Whites, Blacks, and Mexican Americans on half of the measures. All groups had similar levels of values regarding the expectation of marriage, the importance of marrying someday, and the importance of being married when having children. Where there were differences, *Blacks actually valued marriage more than Whites* (Tucker, 2000).

The culture of poverty approach supposes that Black women prefer to head single-mother families—in other words, that they devalue the nuclear family. Yet, findings from the Pew Research Center (2010) cast serious doubt on that assumption. Blacks and Whites are equally critical of the trend of single motherhood; 74% of Blacks and 70% of Whites—yet only 58% of Latinos—reported that women having children without a male partner is "a bad thing for society" (Pew, 2010). When asked whether a child needs a home with both a mother and a father in order to grow up happily, 57% of Whites agreed with that statement. Despite their higher rates of nonmarital childbearing, more Blacks and Latinos agreed with that statement (65% and 72%, respectively). Moreover, among cohabiters, Blacks and Latinos are more likely than Whites to report that they intend to marry but less likely than Whites to ultimately marry their cohabiting partners (Guzzo, 2008).

If surveys indicate Blacks value marriage as much or more than Whites, what types of partners are they seeking? The Pew Research Center (2010) asked respondents to rate the importance of various factors when choosing a mate. When asked how important it is that a "good husband or partner provide a good income," 67% of Black women believed that it is very important, compared to half of Latinas and only 35% of White women. Roughly 55% of Black women and 54% of Latinas said it was very important for a husband or partner to be well educated, compared to only 28% of White women. When asked whether financial stability should be an important criterion for people to get married, 50% of Black women and 46% of Latina women agreed, versus only 25% of White women (Pew, 2010). A highly acclaimed ethnography from sociologists Kathryn Edin and Maria Kefalas, titled *Promises I Can Keep: Why Poor Women Put Motherhood Before Marriage* (2005), found that low-income Black and Latina mothers value marriage highly but perceive myriad financial barriers to becoming married. The fact that Black women place more emphasis on the role of socioeconomic status (SES) in deciding to marry yet many Black men experience socioeconomic disadvantage is one piece of the puzzle that can help explain the Black–White marriage gap.

Over the past 30 years, there has been a strong countermovement that seeks to change pervasive cultural assumptions about Black families. The crux of this movement focuses on structural—rather than cultural—impediments that hinder Blacks from becoming and remaining married. The underpinning of this argument is that the SNAF ideal was (and still is) harder for Blacks to attain given their marginalization in most mainstream social institutions.

Essentially, marriage stands at the intersection of many other social institutions. In other words, marriage and marital rates are greatly affected by the structure of the labor force, the educational system, and the criminal justice system. If, as we have just learned, Blacks value marriage and express a desire and intent to be married just as much as (if not more than) Whites, what explains their increasingly lower rates of marriage? In other words, are structural inequalities a more significant driving force behind the Black marriage decline than presumed cultural beliefs that devalue marriage?

Many scholars attribute the Black marriage decline to an imbalanced gender ratio. When considering the ratio of available (i.e., alive and noninstitutionalized) Black men to Black women, there were roughly 91 Black men for every 100 Black women in 2009 (U.S. Census Bureau, 2012). The corresponding gender ratio for Whites is 99 White men for every 100 White women. The gender ratio is actually reversed among Latinos, resulting in a gender ratio of 107 Latino men for every 100 Latina women. An analysis of low-income cities (Harknett & McLanahan, 2004) found that after taking employment into account, there were only 46 employed Black men for every 100 Black women (vs. roughly 82:100 ratio of employed White men to employed White women; corresponding figures for Mexicans and those of other Hispanic descent were 83 and 69 per 100, respectively).

Ralph Richard Banks (2011), a Stanford Law professor, recently offered a methodologically rigorous examination of the marriage decline (both overall and by race). In addition to pointing out these glaring disparities, he purported that interracial marriage may be one solution to increase the especially low rates of marriage among Black women. Although intermarriage is becoming a more common phenomenon across all groups, it is important to note that in 2010, more than twice as many Black men (24%) as Black women (9%) married interracially (Pew, 2012; see Khanna, Essay 11, for further discussion on interracial marriage). Therefore, an imbalanced gender ratio (further perpetuated by higher rates of interracial marriage among Black men) is a significant cause of the Black–White marriage gap. There are simply fewer Black men physically available for Black women to marry. This begs the question, where are Black men?

Where Are Black Men? Gender Ratios and "Marriageability"

There are two primary mechanisms to explain the relative dearth of available Black men in the community. First, Black men have the highest rate of incarceration of any other group. Black men had an incarceration rate of 4,347 per 100,000 in 2010, a rate that was six times higher than that of White men (678 per 100,000). The incarceration rate of Hispanic/Latino men was 1,775 per 100,000, half as high as that of Black men (U.S. Bureau of Justice Statistics, 2011; see also Doude, Essay 19). Even when prisoners are released from custody, they face extremely high levels of discrimination in the labor force, reflecting one of the most enduring stigmas and barriers to upward mobility in the United States. Given the high priority women of color place on the financial viability of potential partners, those with a criminal history will be considered less marriageable by potential partners, further driving down marriage rates in these groups.

Disproportionately high mortality rates and low life expectancy among Black men can also help to explain the imbalanced gender ratio (Xu, 2010). Black men die earlier than any other racial or ethnic and gender group. For example, White men and women can expect to live roughly 79 and 84 years, respectively. But Black women's life expectancy is roughly 78 years and Black men's life expectancy is only 71. Black men have a much higher age-adjusted death rate than White men (890 and 1,151 per 100,000, respectively) and a homicide death rate roughly 10 times higher than White men (37.1 and 3.7 per 100,000, respectively). Indeed, homicide—an important way in which bodies are prematurely removed from the marriage market—is the fourth leading cause of death for Black men and the eighth leading cause of death for Latino men but does not rank in the top 10 for White men at all (National Center for Health Statistics, 2011; Xu, Kochanek, Murphy, & Tejeda-Vera, 2010).

Clearly, there are fewer "warm bodies" whom Black women can marry, but what about the quality of Black men who *are* physically present in the dating and marriage markets? In his groundbreaking book, *The Truly Disadvantaged: The Inner City, the Underclass, and Public Policy* (1987/1990), sociologist William Julius Wilson set forth the argument that Black marriage decline was due to a shortage of "marriageable Black men." Marriageable men are those who exhibit qualities that are attractive to potential romantic partners in the marriage market. Women of all races and ethnicities prefer to date and marry men who are educated, earn a good income, and have a stable job (although, as described earlier, these characteristics are ironically most important to Black women—see Pew, 2010; Tucker, 2000). In a direct test of this theory, Wilson and Kathryn Neckerman (1986) found an inverse relationship between male employment and marriage rates; as male unemployment increased, marriage rates decreased. A similar study using longitudinal data from 1990 through 2009 found a strong inverse relationship between the rates of families headed by women and the quantity and the quality of men (Craigie, Myers, & Darity, 2012). In focusing on structural factors, William Julius Wilson's work (and subsequent work using this framework) stands in direct contrast to Moynihan's cultural argument.

Are there really fewer marriageable Black men than White men? Let's first consider unemployment rates. In 2010, 9.6% of White men were unemployed, compared to 18.4% of Black men (U.S. Bureau of Labor Statistics, 2011). Sociologists are well aware of the overlap between race or ethnicity and social class, a relationship that would imply that most of the race disparities in SES (in this case, unemployment) are because Blacks have less education than Whites. However, race disparities in unemployment persist even at the highest levels of education. Among the college educated, 4.4% of White men but fully 9.2% of Black men were unemployed in 2010, an even wider gap than the overall trend. This means that even after holding education constant—that is, comparing "apples to apples," or Black men with the same level of education as White men—Black men are still more likely to be unemployed than White men. When coupled with the aforementioned findings that Blacks place heavy emphasis on the role of finances when deciding whether to marry, these trends can help explain the Black–White marriage gap. It is quite clear that cultural values are not the problem, structural inequality is.

In examining the "marriageability" of Black men in terms of income, not surprisingly there is a race divide in median weekly earnings among men. In 2010, White men earned roughly $850 per week, while Black men earned $633 per week (U.S. Bureau of Labor Statistics, 2011). Can race differences in educational attainment explain why Black men earn so much less? That is, do Black men earn less than White men because they have lower educational attainment? As was the case with unemployment, the race wage gap is still present when comparing highly educated Black men to highly educated White men. The largest race wage gaps among men occur at the highest levels of education; college-educated White men earn $1,354 per week, while college-educated Black men earn only $1,010. Regardless of educational level, Black men earn roughly 25% less than White men (U.S. Bureau of Labor Statistics, 2011).

How does the socioeconomic standing of Black men compare with their likely romantic partners, Black women? For most racial and ethnic groups, women typically have lower SES than men. However, the socioeconomic standing of Black women is either equal to or higher than that of Black men. As an illustrative example, the gender wage gap is smaller among Blacks than Whites. Although White women earn only 80.5% of White men's annual earnings, Black women earn 93.5% of Black men's annual earnings, a much smaller gender difference (U.S. Bureau of Labor Statistics, 2011). Black women generally have higher educational attainment than Black men, a pattern that is not found among Whites. For example, a similar proportion of White men and White women hold at least a bachelor's degree (30.8% and 29.9%, respectively), but more Black women than Black men hold at least a bachelor's degree (21.4% and 17.7%, respectively; U.S. Census Bureau, 2012). Given their similar or higher levels of economic standing relative to Black men, Black women may perceive less economic benefit to marriage, which is another potential explanation for the Black–White marriage gap.

In an innovative study, Harknett and McLanahan (2004) simultaneously tested the cultural and structural arguments for why Black women are less likely than White women to marry after a nonmarital birth. They found that Black women had the strongest pro-marriage attitudes. Moreover, the overall gender ratio and an undersupply of employed men fully explained the Black mothers' lower likelihood of marriage. This analysis directly tested the culture-structure debate and provides convincing evidence that structure matters most and in fact, that Blacks neither suffer from nor perpetuate culturally deficiency mores that devalue marriage.

Conclusion

As the above empirical findings suggest, Blacks place similar or higher value on the institution of marriage, which definitively overturns the cultural argument that Blacks are less likely to get married because they don't value marriage as much as Whites. There instead appears to be strong evidence in support of two sets of structural factors to explain the Black marriage gap. First, the imbalanced gender ratio (due to higher incarceration and mortality rates among Black men) results in fewer Black men physically present in the marriage market. Second, the lower "marriageability" of Black men (who experience high rates of unemployment and lower earnings and educational attainment) reduces the economic benefit of marriage for Black women. Future research should put the cultural argument to rest and focus on finding policy solutions to increase the socioeconomic standing of Black men (Darity & Hamilton, 2012).

Suggested Additional Resources

Banks, R. R. (2011). *Is marriage for White people? How the African American marriage decline affects everyone.* New York, NY: Dutton.

Chambers, A. L., & Kravitz, A. (2011). Understanding the disproportionately low marriage rate among African Americans: An amalgam of sociological and psychological constraints. *Family Relations, 60*(5), 648–660.

Marsh, K., Darity, W. A., Cohen, P. N., Casper, L. M., & Salters, D. (2008). The emerging Black middle class: Single and living alone. *Social Forces, 86,* 735–762.

Patterson, O. (1999). *Rituals of blood: The consequences of slavery in two American centuries.* New York, NY: Basic Civitas Books.

Raley, R. K., & Sweeney, M. M. (2009). Explaining race and ethnic variation in marriage: Directions for future research. *Race and Social Problems, 1*(3), 132–142.

Questions for Further Discussion

1. Black marriage decline is often depicted as a function of cultural beliefs that devalue marriage. There has also been a similar culture-structure debate in the area of education, with some proposing that Blacks have worse educational outcomes because they value education less than Whites, an argument that has also been disproven (see also Meanwell, Patel, & McClure, Essay 13). Why do you think scholars and the media continue to portray Blacks' lower social standing to the notion that they have counterproductive cultural values?

2. Is the Black marriage decline/Black–White marriage gap a trend that deserves public policy attention? Based on the findings outlined in this chapter, what might be some effective policy solutions to address this gap?

3. Emerging sociological research (e.g., Marsh, Darity, Cohen, Casper, & Salters, 2008) has identified "The Love Jones Cohort," a relatively affluent group of Black Americans (primarily women) who are single and living alone (SALA), with neither a spouse nor children in the household. Research indicates that these households increasingly comprise a large proportion of the Black middle class. What are the implications of this cohort for companionship, childbearing, and caregiving across the life course? How might public policy best address this burgeoning segment of the Black population?

4. Other industrialized nations (e.g., Sweden) have begun the legal recognition of cohabiting unions, as opposed to the prior universal focus on implementing public policies that only benefit or protect couples who are legally married. Might this be a more appropriate solution for increasing the stability of Black romantic unions than universal marriage promotion policies? Why or why not?

5. In his 2011 book, *Is Marriage for White People? How the African American Marriage Decline Affects Everyone*, Stanford Law professor Ralph Richard Banks makes a strong case that structural barriers have caused the Black marriage decline. He proposes that Black women (who often face a lack of available or quality potential partners) should consider dating outside of their race. How do you feel about this recommendation? Would that solve the problem? What are the advantages and disadvantages of this approach?

6. Recent work finds that marriage rates are also declining among those with lower education. What might be some reasons for that decline? Does it deserve policy attention and if so, why?

Reaching Beyond the Color Line

1. Go to www.census.gov. Research the rates of interracial marriage. Which race or gender group has the highest rates of interracial or interethnic marriage? Which race or gender group has the lowest rates of interracial or interethnic marriage? How well do your findings mesh with Banks's (2011) recommendation that Black women consider marrying outside of their race?

2. Download data from the Pew Research Center Report on "The Decline of Marriage and Rise of New Families." Section 2 outlines racial and ethnic differences in perceptions of what makes a good partner. This chapter reviewed the findings regarding the importance of providing a good income. What other factors are important to Black, White, and Latina women? Are there similar findings for Black, White, and Latino men?

3. Pair up with a classmate. Research the marriage rates of Asians and Hispanics/Latinos over time. Compare them to the rates for Blacks. Are the patterns similar or different? What do you think makes these racial and ethnic groups distinct from Blacks?

References

Banks, R. R. (2011). *Is marriage for White people? How the African American marriage decline affects everyone.* New York, NY: Dutton.

Bramlett, M. D., & Mosher, W. D. (2002). *Cohabitation, marriage, divorce, and remarriage in the United States* (Ser. 23, Vol. 22). Atlanta, GA: Centers for Disease Control and Prevention, National Center for Health Statistics.

Craigie, T. L., Myers, S. L., & Darity, W. A. 2012. *The decline of marriageable males and female family headship revisited.* Retrieved from http://www.hhh.umn.edu/centers/rwc/conferences/fourth/pdf/craigie_myers_darity_draft8d.pdf

Darity, W. A., & Hamilton, D. (2012). Bold policies for economic justice. *The Review of Black Political Economy, 39*(1), 79–85.

Edin, K., & Kefalas, M. J. (2005). *Promises I can keep: Why poor women put motherhood before marriage.* Berkeley: University of California Press.

Gutman, H. (1977). *The Black family in slavery and freedom, 1750–1925.* New York, NY: Vintage Books.

Guzzo, K. B. (2008). Marital intentions and the stability of first cohabitations. *Journal of Family Issues, 30*(2), 179–205.

Harknett, K., & McLanahan, S. (2004). Explaining racial and ethnic differences in marriage among new, unwed parents. *American Sociological Review, 69*(6), 790–811.

Hill, R. B. (2003). *The strengths of Black families* (2nd ed.). Lanham, MD: University Press of America.

Hill, S. A. (2005). *Black intimacies: A gender perspective on families and relationships.* Walnut Creek, CA: AltaMira Press.

Moynihan, D. P. (1965). *The Negro family: The case for national action.* Washington, DC: U.S. Department of Labor, Office of Planning and Research.

National Center for Health Statistics. (2011). *Health, United States, 2010: With special feature on death and dying.* Hyattsville, MD: Centers for Disease Control & Prevention, National Center for Health Statistics.

National Center for Health Statistics. (2012). *Death in the United States, 2010.* Hyattsville, MD: Centers for Disease Control & Prevention, National Center for Health Statistics.

Pew Research Center. (2010, November 18). *The decline of marriage and rise of new families.* Washington, DC: Author.

Roschelle, A. R. (1997). *No more kin: Exploring race, class, and gender in family networks.* Thousand Oaks, CA: Sage.

Ruggles, S. (1994). The origins of African American family structure. *American Sociological Review, 59,* 136–151.

Smith, D. E. (1993). The Standard North American Family: SNAF as an ideological code. *Journal of Family Issues, 14*(1), 50–65.

Stack, C. B. (1974). *All our kin: Strategies for survival in a Black community.* New York, NY: Basic Books.

Tucker, M. B. (2000). Marital values and expectations in context: Results from a 21-city survey. In L. J. Waite & C. Bachrach (Eds.), *The ties that bind: Perspectives on marriage and cohabitation* (pp. 166–187). New York, NY: Aldine de Gruyter.

U.S. Bureau of Justice Statistics. (2011). *Correctional population in the United States, 2010.* Washington, DC: U.S. Department of Justice.

U.S. Bureau of Labor Statistics. (2011). *Labor force characteristics by race and ethnicity, 2010* (Report 1032). Washington, DC: U.S. Department of Labor.

U.S. Census Bureau. (2012). *The statistical abstract of the United States: The national data book.* Washington, DC: U.S. Department of Commerce. Retrieved from http://www.census.gov/compendia/statab/2012edition.html

Waite, L. J., & Lehrer, E. L. (2003). The benefits from marriage and religion in the United States: A comparative analysis. *Population and Development Review, 29*(2), 255–276.

Wilson, W. J. (1990). *The truly disadvantaged: The inner city, the underclass, and public policy.* Chicago, IL: University of Chicago Press. (Original work published 1987)

Wilson, W. J., & Neckerman, K. M. (1986). Poverty and family structure: The widening gap between evidence and public policy issues. In S. H. Danziger & D. H. Wienberg (Eds.),

Fighting poverty: What works and what doesn't (pp. 232–259). Cambridge, MA: Harvard University Press.

Xu, J., Kochanek, K. D., Murphy, S. L., & Tejeda-Vera, B. (2010, May 20). *National Vital Statistics Reports (NVSR), Deaths: Final data for 2007* (Vol. 58, No. 19). Hyattsville, MD: Centers for Disease Control and Prevention, National Center for Health Statistics.

"Well, That Culture Really Values Education"

Culture Versus Structure in Educational Attainment

Emily Meanwell
Indiana University

Hersheda Patel
Georgia State University

Stephanie M. McClure
Georgia College

Emily Meanwell is a doctoral candidate in sociology and the associate director of the Social Science Research Commons at Indiana University. She is also the study director for the Sociological Research Practicum. Her research focuses on culture and inequality, particularly political culture surrounding educational policies designed to reduce inequality. She has also explored the experiences of homeless shelter residents.

Hersheda Patel is a graduate student in the sociology program at Georgia State University. Her research interests are in the sociology of education, particularly the college choice process and the nature of campus racial composition.

Stephanie M. McClure is an associate professor of sociology at Georgia College. She teaches classes on racial stratification, social theory, and the sociology of education.

Her research interests are in the area of higher education, with a focus on college student persistence and retention across race, class, and gender, and a special emphasis on post-college student experiences that increase student social and academic integration. She has published in the *Journal of Higher Education*, *Symbolic Interaction*, and *The Journal of African American Studies*.

Public education is one of the most important institutions in American society and is considered a key mechanism of social mobility (Urban & Wagoner, 1996). Discussions of racial inequality in the United Sates frequently point to persisting differences in educational attainment (see Table 13.1). When attempting to explain these persisting differences, students often reach for cultural explanations, including the idea that high attainment on the part of Asian Americans is explained by shared cultural values. This belief is evident in popular culture, personal perceptions, and even academic conversations. From children's shows like *The Suite Life of Zack and Cody,* where Cody's Asian girlfriend Barbara takes "A.P. Lunch," to movies for an older crowd like *Harold and Kumar Go to White Castle* (2004) in which Kumar flawlessly performs advanced surgery despite his apathy toward medical school, stereotypical portrayals of highly academic Asian Americans appear and are even hyperbolized. The television series *Glee* drew on these stereotypes in an episode revolving around Mike Chang dealing with his father's anger after Chang receives an A-, or an "Asian F" on an exam. The Internet image macro series High Expectations Asian Father is another example of pop culture portrayals of Asians' value of education. When Asians aren't being used as stereotypical main or supporting characters, they are usually nothing more than shadows of the stereotype, such as the Asian nerds in the movie *Mean Girls* (2004), the technology-producing Asians of District Three in *The Hunger Games* (2012), the straight-A student Chang Triplets from the Disney TV show *The Proud Family,* or the NBC TV show *Community*'s all-Asian Math Club.

Occasionally, Asians are portrayed in roles that are the exact opposite of the stereotypical nerdy Asian. This too, however, plays into the stereotype, because the irony of the character's disconnect from the stereotype becomes a constant part of the storyline and the character is never seen as an individual, only as a response to a stereotype. In *Harold and Kumar Go to White Castle* (and subsequent films in the series), the pot-smoking duo are often compared to "normal" Asians.

These popular portrayals of Asian Americans are rooted in stereotypical perceptions of Asians in real life. Even Harkaran Singh (2011), a writer for the *Berkeley Political Review* (a magazine from the University of California) writes that Asians value education more than Americans because of the importance of gaining respect for one's family in society. He also asserts that Americans do not value education and are more likely to idolize the class clown than the scholar (Singh, 2011). In order to consider whether Asian educational attainment can be explained by the idea that "Asian culture really values education," and the

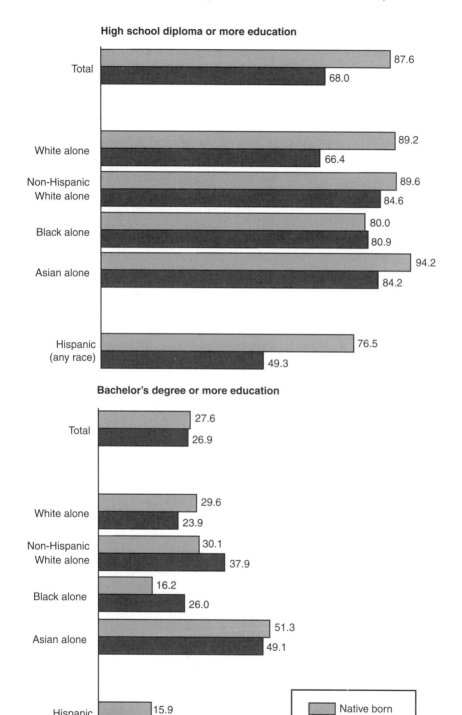

High school diploma or more education

Bachelor's degree or more education

Figure 13.1 Educational Attainment of the Population Aged 25 and Over by Race, Hispanic Origin, and Nativity Status: 2007 (in percent)

Source: U.S. Census Bureau, American Community Survey, 2007.

corresponding belief that lower levels of attainment among Blacks and Latinos are explained by lack of cultural value for education, we must first define and unpack some key terms used in these claims: *education, Asian, Black, Latino, culture,* and *value.* While at first glance these terms may appear straightforward and easily definable, upon further examination, we see that their meanings are often quite murky, which significantly complicates the nature of these claims and ultimately debunks them.

Clarifying the Terms

To begin, in most of the research that has engaged these issues, *education* has been defined as either "educational attainment" and measured by category (high school, college, postcollege) or with a continuous measure (years of education), or it has been defined as "achievement" and measured using standardized test scores. But on both of these measures, it is true that Black and Latinos have lower levels of education, whether defined by attainment, category of education, or years of education. The question is: Why is this the case? And what can further examination of terms like *Asian, Black, Latino,* and *culture,* tell us about the differences in how racial groups really think about education?

Terms like *Asian, Black,* and *Latino* require further examination because these are socially constructed categories that contain individuals from widely different backgrounds. For instance, the term *Asian* refers most overtly to the world's largest continent, from which many people who have immigrated to the United States originate. It is important to note that on the Asian continent, almost no one refers to themselves as "Asian"; they may refer to themselves by national identity (e.g., Chinese, Japanese, Korean), or by a more specific regional identity (e.g., Han, Zhuang, or Man). The use of the term *Asian* to refer to this widely diverse group is most often deployed in the United States, where it is attached to *American* to form the panethnic label, *Asian Americans.* This label was originally developed by the U.S. government (particularly the Census Bureau) but has subsequently come to be used by people within the group as well. The process of panethnic identity development has been explored in some depth by several authors (Espiritu, 1993; Liu, 1998; Wu, 2003) and is well worth exploring further (see suggestions for further reading at the end of this chapter). For our purposes, it is important to note that the label *Asian American* is socially constructed, generated by the immigrant experience, and encompasses an incredibly diverse group of people with different histories, backgrounds, and immigration experiences (see also Zhou, Essay 8).

Thus, one of the problems with the stereotype that all Asians as a panethnic group are high educational achievers is that it obscures the fact that this stereotype does not hold across all Asian students. For example, Baker, Keller-Wolff, and Wolf-Wendel (2000) find that Asian and Pacific Islander students have higher math performance than Whites, but that there are major differences between subgroups of Asian students—with Filipino and Pacific Islander students (e.g., students of indigenous Hawaiian heritage, Samoans, Guamanians, and Tahitians), showing significantly lower levels of math achievement (though Filipino students outperform other Asian subgroups in reading achievement). Another analysis finds that Pacific Islanders are falling behind other Asian groups in obtaining bachelor's degrees (UC AAPI Policy Initiative, 2006; see also Lee & Kumashiro, 2005). These differences are important to consider when looking at differences in educational attainment and how Asian Americans have fared as a whole.

The terms *Black* and *Latino* are equally complicated and also reflect panethnic racial categories that include individuals from very different places whose reasons for being in the United States can be quite distinct. Further discussions of the development and diversity of these groups are available in Omi and Winant (1994), Davis (1991), De Genova and Ramos-Zayas (2003), and Rodriguez (2000); more of this diversity is also discussed below. All of these terms form a sort of racial shorthand that can be deployed for various purposes (e.g., government data collection, social science description, political collective action), most of which are somewhat neutral. Nonetheless, it is important to keep in mind their internal diversity and socially constructed nature. This variation is particularly salient as we move to the next term: *culture*.

Culture has been defined by social scientists in diverse ways. For our purposes, we will use one of the most common definitions, which fits with what is implied by the myth itself: that culture is a set of attitudes, values, beliefs, and practices that form a way of life for a particular group of people. With that definition in hand, and given our previous discussion of the panethnic racial labels, we see the first problem with this myth. Given the great variation contained in the group we call "Asian Americans," it isn't reasonable to assume that all of the people within it share the same attitudes, values, beliefs, and practices. The assumption of within-group homogeneity is one of many problems with shorthand racial labels as they are used in everyday conversation. Determining who "values" education and how we can detect that "valuing" through data collection is even more difficult. When we try to decide who values education and who doesn't using racial group categories, we are required to account for some of that within-group variation.

Additionally, while people in a given group may share certain experiences, there are many individual-level differences that greatly affect their values, lifestyle, and educational achievement. These variables create a great deal of variance within the group, making universal assumptions about values and achievement of the entire group inaccurate. These variables include, but are not limited to: parents' occupations, parenting styles, educational attainment of parents, family structure, number of books and other resources in the home, and Internet access (Fuligni, 1997; Kao, 1995; Portes & Zhou, 1993; Teachman, 1987). Two parents with well-paying jobs and college degrees who encourage positive educational practices in a nice house with books and Internet access is the ideal background for promoting high levels of educational achievement, but the presence of these characteristics varies both by group and within groups (Kao, 1995). Knowing this variety exists, the idea that all people in any group value or do not value education becomes problematic.

Finally, the positive educational outcomes often attributed to "Asian values" have been found in other immigrant groups. For example, West Indian immigrants show higher levels of education, higher socioeconomic status, and higher standards of living than nonimmigrant Americans (Model, 1995, 2011). One can hardly make the argument that West Indian immigrants share Asian culture and values. It is more plausible that we find higher levels of educational success among immigrant groups due to the nature of individuals that self-select into the immigration process and possibly the nature of immigration itself (Xie & Goyette, 2003). In fact, some evidence suggests that the risks and challenges associated with immigration may contribute to increased pressure on first-, 1.5-, and second-generation immigrants to succeed academically in order to achieve upward social mobility. This pressure can come directly from families or through shared knowledge of the hardships that accompany immigration (Waters, 1996). This pressure crosses racial and ethnic lines and is evident in all American immigrant groups across time (Portes & Rumbaut, 2001). Over generations, we find that immigrants show equal levels of academic success as nonimmigrant Americans. It seems that once the intensity of the immigrant experience becomes diluted, the pressure associated with it lessens, leading to "normal" levels of academic achievement. This finding allows us to consider other variables that may explain differing levels of academic achievement across groups that do not rely on culturally essentialist explanations.

Determining who values education ultimately requires collecting data at two levels: (1) the individual level—such as information on family economic resources, parental educational attainment, and immigrant status (e.g., first or second generation, age at time of immigration, legal vs. undocumented, or visa status), and (2) the collective or group level, which takes into consideration, for example, whether the group is a voluntary or an involuntary immigrant group, the historical timing of their arrival in the United States, reception on arrival, geographic concentration, and overt structural barriers to education. When we take these factors into account, simplistic narratives of which group values education more, and how that valuing is causally related to educational attainment, become more complex. For example, what were the resources immigrants brought with them from their country of origin (including money, education, connections to people already in the United States), and what kinds of aid did they receive on arrival? These factors are rarely taken into account when considering who values education, and instead, we have come to rely on cultural explanations. This is particularly evident in the discourse surrounding Black Americans and education.

Cultural Explanations of Black Educational Achievement

The persistent differences in academic achievement between Black students and their peers are particularly troubling. Despite the centrality of education to the civil rights movement's agenda, one of the most common ways this achievement gap has been explained is by pointing to *cultural factors* and a supposed devaluing of education among Blacks. Even President Obama has employed detrimental cultural explanations. For example, in a speech on July 27, 2004, then-Senator Obama stated

Go into any inner city neighborhood, and folks will tell you that government alone can't teach kids to learn . . . children can't achieve unless we raise their expectations and . . . eradicate the slander that says a Black youth with a book is acting White.

Obama's reference to the idea that Black students who put forth academic effort are derided by peers for "acting White" connects to a theory that has been researched and debated by scholars for over 30 years, under the umbrella of *oppositional culture theory.*

Anthropologist John U. Ogbu's oppositional culture explanation for racial differences in academic achievement emphasizes academic disengagement among Blacks (Fordham & Ogbu, 1986; Ogbu, 1978). Ogbu distinguished between different types of minorities in the United States, particularly between voluntary immigrant minorities who came to America in search of prosperity, and involuntary, subordinate minorities like Blacks who were brought to the United States against their will. While members of voluntary immigrant groups have an optimistic attitude toward schooling, Ogbu argued, Blacks do not. Faced with and frustrated by substandard schools, discrimination, and limited opportunities for success in the job market, he argued that Blacks, over generations, developed coping mechanisms and adaptations—including a cultural orientation toward education that leads to a lack of effort and underachievement. Fordham and Ogbu (1986) argued that academic achievement was further discouraged by negative sanctioning from Black peers, who labeled academic effort and good grades as "acting White."

As this cultural explanation of academic achievement gaps between different racial and ethnic groups became more popular, some of its original points became muddied or lost. While Ogbu emphasized that oppositional culture was an adaptation to social structural conditions, subsequent discussions tended to focus on problematic Black culture while overlooking the structural roots Ogbu emphasized. Thus, there was a tendency to explain racial achievement gaps by attributing them to a lack of valuing of education while ignoring the societal conditions that Ogbu said produced academic disengagement in the first place. This is a history and structure that must be taken into account when looking at Blacks' and also Latinos' relationship with education.

Beyond Cultural Explanations: The Role of History and Structure in Education

A major problem with cultural explanations of educational achievement is that they disregard structural barriers to achieving success. *Structure* refers to the patterns and relationships among social institutions, social networks, and other participants in a society that affect the behaviors of all members of the society. Structure is both created by and regulates the actions, behaviors, attitudes, and beliefs of individuals. Therefore, structural barriers are those roadblocks enacted by social institutions, social networks that are outside of the immediate control of any single person in any racial or ethnic group.

Different racial and ethnic groups within the United States have faced these structural barriers with varying levels of resources (such as education and occupational training and skills). For example, most documented Asians that have come to America in the past 60 years have possessed high levels of education and training and have been able to replicate their success in America both in terms of education and occupation (Steinberg, 2001). Similarly, in the late 19th century and early 20th century, White ethnic groups were able to successfully assimilate and integrate into mainstream society because of the industrial skills they brought with them from Europe (Blauner, 2001; Steinberg, 2001). On the other hand, Blacks were heavily concentrated in the South during this time and mainly had agricultural skills. During the Industrial Revolution, Blacks moved to the North equipped with the most basic of skills and facing a 200-year-old system of racism and prejudice (Blauner, 2001; Steinberg, 2001). In the North, White ethnics were hired at higher rates than Blacks. When Blacks were hired in large numbers, it was a result of strikes by White ethnic groups, which meant Blacks were paid much lower wages (Steinberg, 2001). All of these historical and structural factors contributed to the inability of Blacks to achieve success and overcome the economic barriers to gaining widespread access to higher education at the same levels as White ethnics and Asians.

College educations were long reserved for White, upper class, Protestant males (Rudolph, 1962/1990). While times have changed and other groups have gained access to higher education, many college campuses remain predominantly White (U.S. Census Bureau, 2012). Historical research indicates that many early Asian immigrant populations achieved educational parity with Whites between the First and Second World Wars (Hirschman & Wong, 1986; Wong, 1980). Census data suggest that there was no educational disadvantage between Whites and native-born Japanese Americans at least as far back as 1910. For Chinese Americans, parity seems to have arrived by 1920, and for Filipino Americans, by 1940 (Hirschman & Wong, 1986). This early parity significantly influences intergenerational patterns at the group level today. In other words, higher educational attainment for any group is intimately connected to the educational attainment of previous generations.

On the other hand, prior to the mid-20th-century civil rights movement, Black participation in predominantly White institutions across the country was extremely limited. Between 1865 and 1895, approximately 194 Blacks graduated from Northern colleges, 75 from Oberlin (Ohio) alone, with the other 119 attending 52 other schools, for an average of little more than two per school. There is also evidence of some Blacks graduating from Southern colleges before their admittance was made illegal at the end of this period (Bowles & DeCosta, 1971). This Southern restriction was relatively consistent through 1953, with the exception of some minimal movement among primarily border state universities after key court cases in the 1930s (Bowles & DeCosta, 1971). However, Bowles and DeCosta (1971) write that Northern schools were not much better in this period:

> The difference between the passive discrimination of the Northern colleges which, while permitting a few Negro students to enter, were by reason of financial requirements or social isolation, or both, discouraging to most Negro prospective students, and the active discrimination of the white Southern colleges was, essentially, only a difference in degree. (p. 40)

Beginning in the 1960s and influenced by a changing political climate, universities exhibited a rising concern with the participation of people of color in higher education. This led to the development of admissions policies designed to increase the number of students of color on campus, which was relatively successful at increasing Black student enrollment (Allen, Epps, & Haniff, 1991; see also Poon, Essay 15). However, this varied significantly by region. Many Southern states adopted a position of "massive resistance" to integration, including the signing of the Southern Regional Education Compact on February 8, 1948, by 14 states trying to avoid the desegregation of their institutions of higher education and the Southern Manifesto, signed on March 12, 1956, by over 100 Southern senators, which denounced the 1954 *Brown v. Board of Education* (47 U.S. 483) decision that declared separate as inherently unequal.

In spite of this history, the idea that group-level value for education explains differences in attainment persists. In particular, the idea that Blacks and Latinos do not value education has been present both in American society generally and in academic research (see Coontz, 1992, on myths about Black families' culture more generally). As mentioned above, this myth does not square with the emphasis on access to education that has been central throughout Blacks' long fight for equality (Anderson, 1988; Bowles & DeCosta, 1971). For example, the landmark ruling in *Brown v. Board of Education,* in which the Supreme Court ruled that separate schools could not be equal, was one of the most important steps in the civil rights movement (see Tushnet, 1987). This decision removed some of the most crucial structural barriers that denied Black children equal educational opportunity and set the long process of integrating schools into motion. Yet, over 50 years later, the promise of equal education hasn't come to fruition.

What the Research Shows: Lack of Support for Cultural Explanations

Scholars have researched the oppositional culture theory for more than a quarter century. Researchers have looked at attitudes toward education among different racial groups, as well as evidence of stigmatization of high-achieving Black students as "acting White." This work has produced mixed findings but, overall, little empirical support for the cultural explanations of differences in academic achievement proposed by Ogbu's theory. First, researchers have found that Black students hold positive attitudes toward education. Research has found that education is valued by Blacks as the chief pathway to upward social mobility (Cole & Omari, 2003). Theoharis (2009) similarly finds that Black and Latino students are committed to education and see it as holding promise even as they attend a failing urban school in which they perceive some adults to think they are not capable of success. In one study that used data from a national survey, Black students reported more pro-school attitudes than White students (Ainsworth-Darnell & Downey, 1998; for similar findings see Cook & Ludwig, 1997; A. L. Harris, 2006, 2008). While these studies used survey data of older students, another study using ethnographic data found positive attitudes toward education among younger Black students at two all-Black elementary schools (Tyson, 2002).

Second, research has also explored the idea that Black students' peer culture stigmatizes academic success. Ainsworth-Darnell and Downey (1998) found that Blacks who were seen by their peers as good students were *more* likely to be popular than Whites seen as good students; Datnow and Cooper (1996) found similar results for Black students at a predominantly White elite school. These findings contradict the idea that successful Black students are stigmatized by peers as "acting White." Some research has, though, found an increased likelihood for Black students who report being "very good" students to also report being put down by peers (Farkas, Lleras, & Maczuga, 2002; see also a response from Downey & Ainsworth-Darnell, 2002). Other research found that in some schools, Black students may be mildly socially penalized for certain public expressions of academic engagement or effort in the classroom—a "weak" version of the acting White hypothesis (Wildhagen, 2011).

Recent work on the "acting White" phenomenon gives a nuanced view that is instructive for considering the daily, lived experiences of students. One study found that when students talk about "acting Black," "acting Spanish," and "acting White," they were related to ethnic or racial cultural tastes and styles, and not really about opposition to education or stigmatizing academic achievement (see also C. A. Harris, 2013). Another study found some evidence that high achievement among Blacks is stigmatized, but only in one of the eight schools the researchers studied (Tyson, Darity, & Castellino, 2005). In addition to being relatively uncommon, the researchers also found that while the stigma of "acting White" was a painful experience for high-achieving Black students, it did not keep those students from pursuing academic achievement.

Tyson et al. (2005) in fact find important similarities between the experiences of high-achieving Black *and* White students. The authors found three types of oppositional culture to high academic achievement: a general type, labeling high-achieving students of any race as "nerds"; a racialized version (with race-based labels like "acting White" or "Oreo," i.e., Black on the outside but White on the inside); and a class-based version that stigmatized high-achieving students of any race as "high and mighty" or acting like they're better than others (Tyson et al., 2005). This work highlights the similar experiences of high-achieving students across different racial and even class groups.

Additionally, in the few cases where the racialized version of oppositional culture was present, the authors found that it was related to particular school environments and experiences: The "acting White" stigma occurred in the context of racially mixed (but predominantly White) schools where high-achieving Black students in advanced classes were isolated from other Black students (Tyson, 2011), and is more likely to be part of local school culture when students see stark differences in socioeconomic status between Blacks and Whites and perceive them as corresponding to academic achievement and class placement within the school (Tyson et al., 2005). This research thus points to the importance of the school context and structural factors—like tracking or ability grouping and the resulting racial isolation in some schools—in shaping the "acting White" phenomena, more than the cultural values students bring with them to school. Instead of attitudes toward education shaping achievement, then, Tyson et al. (2005) emphasize how experiences at school can shape attitudes toward education.

Ogbu's theory of oppositional culture has also been used to discuss academic achievement gaps between White and Latino students—particularly Mexican American students, whom Ogbu (1978) argued were involuntary minorities—conquered in what is now the Southwest United States, with later immigrants from Mexico being given the same status as a conquered minority. Research on oppositional culture among Mexican Americans has been less widespread but has thus far found little support for the idea that Mexican American or Latino youth do not value education (see Valencia, 2011; Valencia & Black, 2002). For example, alongside the Black civil rights movement was a Mexican American fight for equal schools (Donato, 1997; San Miguel, 1987). Studies found that in actuality, Mexican American and Latino parents value education, hold high expectations for their children's educational attainment, and may even emphasize higher education more than White parents (Immerwahr & Foleno, 2000; Valencia & Black, 2002). Carter (2005) found heterogeneous experiences but overall high rates of pro-school attitudes among low-income Latino youth; while students did talk about "acting White" versus "acting Spanish," these ideas were not related to academic achievement (and instead tended to focus on dress and linguistic style).

Conclusion

As a whole, this work challenges the myth that racial differences in academic achievement simply result from differences in the value placed on education across racial and ethnic cultures. The lack of empirical evidence for cultural explanations suggests that educators and policymakers need to look at other factors to understand and close the achievement gap. Tyson's work (2011) points to the importance of structural arrangements of schooling in America––including the racialized nature of ability tracking in many schools—and their impact on student cultures. Research also shows Black students are significantly more likely to be taught by inexperienced teachers than their White peers, contributing to differences in achievement (Clotfelter, Ladd, & Vigdor, 2005). A. L. Harris and Robinson (2007) point to racial differences in prior skills—cognitive skills developed before students enter high school—as the key underlying factor contributing to poor achievement among Black students in high school, regardless of their behaviors during high school (while in comparison, Asian American students' achievement in high school is statistically explained mostly by their behaviors during high school).

As these brief paragraphs indicate, access to and success in education has a long and complex racial history. Belief that culture itself is a sufficient explanatory variable in regard to education requires a vast oversimplification of the concept of culture itself, as well as blindness to the impact of history and structural opportunity that shape the outcomes of individuals and groups. It may be a comforting simplification, and it is certainly widespread, but it does not square with empirical reality. Continued commitment to the idea of a monolithic Asian culture or a monolithic Black or Latino culture does little to forward our understanding of variation in intergroup educational attainment.

Suggested Additional Resources

Carter, P. L. (2005). *Keepin' it real: School success beyond Black and White.* New York, NY: Oxford University Press.

Liu, E. (1998). *The accidental Asian: Notes of a native speaker.* New York, NY: Vintage Books.

Tyson, K. (2011). *Integration interrupted: Tracking, Black students, and acting White after Brown*. New York, NY: Oxford University Press.

Wu, F. (2003). *Yellow: Race in America beyond Black and White*. New York, NY: Basic Books.

Audio/Visual

Hampton, H., Vecchione, J., Fayer, S., Bagwell, O., Crossley, C., DeVinney, J. A., . . . Bond, J. (2006). *Eyes on the prize* [Television Series; American Experience special broadcast.] Alexandria, VA: Public Broadcasting Service. (Especially "Fighting Back" [on school desegregation post-*Brown*] and "The Keys to the Kingdom" [on school desegregation in Boston in 1974]).

Palos, A. L. (Director). (2011). *Precious knowledge* [Documentary]. Tucson, AZ: Dos Vatos Productions.

Questions for Further Discussion

1. Why do you think this myth that some cultures simply value education more than others has persisted, despite evidence to the contrary?

2. If cultural differences did explain differences in educational attainment, what kinds of policy changes would be necessary? If, on the other hand, the authors are correct in asserting that culture is not a sufficient explanation, how does that change the kinds of policies necessary to decrease group-level differences in educational attainment?

Reaching Beyond the Color Line

1. The authors give several examples of these myths in popular culture. Choose a television show or movie mentioned in the essay and analyze the portrayal of the myth that some cultures just value education more than others. Look at the portrayals of race, inequality, and structural and cultural factors. Where do cultural factors come into play? What about structure? You can find examples at the following website (which also assumes a cultural explanation): http://tvtropes.org/pmwiki/pmwiki.php/Main/AsianAndNerdy

References

Ainsworth-Darnell, J. W., & Downey, D. B. (1998). Assessing the oppositional culture explanation for racial/ethnic differences in school performance. *American Sociological Review, 63*(4), 536–553.

Allen, W. R., Epps, E. G., & Haniff, N. G. (Eds.). (1991). *College in Black and White: African American students in predominantly White and in historically Black public universities*. Albany: State University of New York Press.

Anderson, J. D. (1988). *The education of Blacks in the South 1860–1935*. Chapel Hill: University of North Carolina Press.

Baker, B. D., Keller-Wolff, C., & Wolf-Wendel, L. (2000). Two steps forward, one step back: Race/ethnicity and student achievement in education policy research. *Educational Policy, 14*(4), 511–529.

Blauner, B. (2001). *Still the big news: Racial oppression in America*. Philadelphia, PA: Temple University Press.

Bowles, F., & DeCosta, F. A. (1971). *Between two worlds: A profile of Negro higher education*. New York, NY: McGraw-Hill.

Brown v. Board of Education, 347 U.S. (1954).

Carter, P. L. (2005). *Keepin' it real: School success beyond Black and White*. New York, NY: Oxford University Press.

Clotfelter, C., Ladd, H., & Vigdor, J. (2005). Who teaches whom? Race and the distribution of novice teachers. *Economics of Education Review, 24*(4), 377–392.

Cole, E. R., & Omari, S. R. (2003). Race, class and the dilemmas of upward mobility for African Americans. *Journal of Social Issues, 59*(4), 785–802.

Cook, P. J., & Ludwig, J. (1997). Weighing the "burden of 'acting white'": Are there race differences in attitudes toward education? *Journal of Policy Analysis and Management, 16*(2), 256–278.

Coontz, S. (1992). *The way we never were: American families and the nostalgia trap*. New York, NY: Basic Books.

Datnow, A., & Cooper, R. (1996). Peer networks of African American students in independent schools: Affirming academic success and racial identity. *Journal of Negro Education, 656*(4), 56–72.

Davis, J. F. (1991). *Who is Black? One nation's definition*. University Park: Pennsylvania State University Press.

De Genova, N., & Ramos-Zayas, A. (2003). Latino racial formations in the United States: An introduction. *The Journal of Latin American Anthropology, 8*(2), 2–17.

Donato, R. (1997). *The other struggle for equal schools: Mexican Americans during the civil rights era*. Albany: State University of New York Press.

Downey, D. B., & Ainsworth-Darnell, J. W. (2002). The search for oppositional culture among Black students. *American Sociological Review, 67*(1), 156–164.

Espiritu, Y. L. (1993). *Asian American panethnicity: Bridging institutions and identities*. Philadelphia, PA: Temple University Press.

Farkas, G., Lleras, C., & Maczuga, S. (2002). Does oppositional culture exist in minority and poverty peer groups? *American Sociological Review, 67*(1), 148–155.

Fordham, S., & Ogbu, J. U. (1986). Black students' school success: Coping with the "burden of 'acting White.'" *The Urban Review, 18*(3), 176–206.

Fuligni, A. (1997). The academic achievement of adolescents from immigrant families: The roles of family background, attitudes, and behavior. *Child Development, 68*(2), 351–363.

Harris, A. L. (2006). I (don't) hate school: Revisiting oppositional culture theory of Blacks' resistance to schooling. *Social Forces, 85*(2), 797–833.

Harris, A. L. (2008). Optimism in the face of despair: Black–White differences in beliefs about school as a means for upward social mobility. *Social Science Quarterly, 89*(3), 629–651.

Harris, A. L., & Robinson, K. (2007). Schooling behaviors or prior skills? A cautionary tale of omitted variable bias within oppositional culture theory. *Sociology of Education, 80*(2), 139–157.

Harris, C. A. (2013). *The Cosby cohort: Blessings and burdens of growing up Black middle class*. Lanham, MD: Rowman & Littlefield.

Hirschman, C., & Wong, M. (1986). The extraordinary educational attainment of Asian-Americans: A search for historical evidence and explanations. *Social Forces, 65*(1), 1–27.

Immerwahr, J., & Foleno, T. (2000). *Great expectations: How the public and parents—White, African American, and Hispanic—view higher education.* New York, NY: Public Agenda.

Kao, G. (1995). Asian Americans as model minorities? A look at their academic performance. *American Journal of Education, 103*(2), 121–159.

Lee, S., & Kumashiro, K. (2005). *A report on the status of Asian Americans and Pacific Islanders in education: Beyond the "model minority" stereotype.* Washington, DC: National Education Association.

Model, S. (1995). West Indian prosperity: Fact or fiction? *Social Problems, 42*(4), 535–553.

Model, S. (2011). *West Indian immigrants: A Black success story?* New York, NY: Russell Sage Foundation.

Ogbu, J. U. (1978). *Minority education and caste: The American system in cross-cultural perspective.* New York, NY: Academic Press.

Oliver, M., & Shapiro, T. (2006). *Black wealth/White wealth: A new perspective on racial inequality* (2nd ed.). New York, NY: Routledge.

Omi, M., & Winant, H. (1994). *Racial formation in the United States: From the 1960s to the 1990s.* New York, NY: Routledge.

Portes, A., & Rumbaut, R. (2001). *Legacies: The story of the immigrant second generation.* Berkeley: University of California Press and Russell Sage Foundation.

Portes, A., & Zhou, M. (1993). The new second generation: Segmented assimilation and its variants. *Annals of the American Academy of Political and Social Science, 530,* 74–96.

Rodriguez, C. E. (2000). *Changing race: Latinos, the census, and the history of ethnicity in the United States.* New York, NY: New York University Press.

Rudolph, F. (1990). *The American college & university: A history.* Athens: University of Georgia Press. (Original work published 1962)

San Miguel, G., Jr. (1987). *"Let all of them take heed": Mexican Americans and the campaign for educational equality in Texas, 1910–1981.* Austin: University of Texas Press.

Singh, H. (2011, November 22). [Web log message]. Retrieved from http://bpr.berkeley .edu/2011/11/why-do-asian-americans-dominate-education

Steinberg, S. (2001). *The ethnic myth: Race, ethnicity, and class in America* (3rd ed.). Boston, MA: Beacon Press.

Teachman, J. (1987). Family background, educational resources, and educational attainment. *American Sociological Review, 52*(4), 548–557.

Theoharis, J. (2009). "I hate it when people treat me like a fxxx-up": Phony theories, segregated schools, and the culture of aspiration among African American and Latino teenagers. In G. Alonso, N. S. Anderson, C. Su, & J. Theoharis (Eds.), *Our schools suck: Students talk back to a segregated nation on the failures of urban education* (pp. 69–112). New York, NY: New York University Press.

Tushnet, M. (1987). *The NAACP's legal strategy against segregated education, 1925–1950.* Chapel Hill: University of North Carolina Press.

Tyson, K. (2002). Weighing in: Elementary-age students and the debate on attitudes toward school among Black students. *Social Forces, 80*(4), 1157–1189.

Tyson, K. (2011). *Integration interrupted: Tracking, Black Students, and acting White after Brown.* New York, NY: Oxford University Press.

Tyson, K., Darity, W. A., Jr., & Castellino, D. (2005). "It's not a Black thing": Understanding the burden of acting White and other dilemmas of high achievement. *American Sociological Review, 70*(4), 582–605.

UC AAPI Policy Initiative. (2006). *Pacific Islanders lagging behind in higher educational attainment: Analytical brief of new Census data.* Retrieved from http://www.aasc.ucla .edu/archives/PIEducationAttainBrief.pdf

U.S. Census Bureau. (2012). *Table 5: Type of college and year enrolled for college students 15 years old and over, by sex, age, race, and Hispanic origin: 1980 to 2009* [chart]. Retrieved from http://www.census.gov/hhes/school/data/cps/2012/tables.html

Urban, W. J., & Wagoner, J. L., Jr. (1996). *American education: A history.* New York, NY: Routledge.

Valencia, R. R. (Ed.). (2011). *Chicano school failure and success: Past, present, and future* (3rd ed.). New York, NY: Routledge.

Valencia, R. R., & Black, M. S. (2002). "Mexican Americans don't value education!"—On the basis of the myth, mythmaking, and debunking. *Journal of Latinos and Education, 1*(2), 81–103.

Waters, M. (1996). Ethnic and racial identities of second-generation Black immigrants in New York City. In A. Portes (Ed.), *The new second generation.* New York, NY: Russell Sage Foundation.

Wildhagen, T. (2011). What's oppositional culture got to do with it? Moving beyond the strong version of the acting White hypothesis. *Sociological Perspectives, 54*(3), 403–430.

Wong, M. G. (1980). Changes in socioeconomic status of the Chinese male population in the United States from 1960 to 1970. *International Migration Review, 14*(4), 511–524.

Wu, F. (2003). *Yellow: Race in America beyond black and white.* New York, NY: Basic Books.

Xie, Y., & Goyette, K. (2003). Social mobility and the educational choices of Asian Americans. *Social Science Research, 32*, 467–498.

"They Don't Want to Be Integrated, They Even Have Their Own Greek Organizations"

History, Institutional Context, and "Self-Segregation"

Stephanie M. McClure
Georgia College

Stephanie M. McClure is an associate professor of sociology at Georgia College. She teaches classes on racial stratification, social theory, and the sociology of education. Her research interests are in the area of higher education, with a focus on college student persistence and retention across race, class, and gender, and a special emphasis on postcollege student experiences that increase student social and academic integration. She has published in the *Journal of Higher Education, Symbolic Interaction,* and *The Journal of African American Studies.*

When discussing issues of race on campus, students often correctly recognize that racial segregation in residence halls, dining halls, and student organizations on campus indicates the amount of work that needs to be done around race in society as a whole (Saenz, Ngai, & Hurtado, 2007). Such segregation is the result of a range of social forces connected to many of the topics discussed in this book. However, in a search for easy scapegoats for this segregation, students often turn their attention to campus sororities and fraternities, Greek-letter organizations or GLOs (Collison, 1987; Crain & Ford, 2013; Dziadosz, 2006; Vendituoli & Grant, 2013). On most campuses throughout the United States, the composition of GLOs is noticeably racially homogenous. While this is true across the color line, many students regularly single out for attention and questioning those that are historically Black. These questions regularly come up on college campuses and in introductory courses on race, including in the comments of my own students, as is referenced in the quote in the title of this essay. Yet, the history of Black Greek-letter organizations (BGLOs) on campuses and their impact on their members is rarely familiar to college administrators, much less to college students themselves (Hughey, 2007). It is worth considering this history and impact in more depth in order to debunk common misperceptions. We can also ask how and why White students often call attention to these specific organizations, even as racial segregation occurs in many other on-campus settings.

College is potentially a time of great intellectual and personal growth. Students not only spend time on campus engaging in the process of attaining a degree, but also in learning about who they are as individuals and figuring out who they want to become (Astin, 1993; Pascarella & Terenzini, 2005). Research shows that this process is most successful where students are able to develop meaningful friendships and get involved in clubs and organizations that they enjoy (Braxton, 2000). That is, in order to experience the full value of a college experience, all students must be able to locate a group of people with whom they feel safe and valued, and through whom they feel connected to the wider campus community. This process is known as social integration and is not only necessary for identity development, but is in fact fundamental to successful college completion (Braxton, 2000; Tinto, 1993, 2006). This is true for all students, but research has clearly demonstrated that it can be particularly challenging for students of color on predominantly White campuses (Black, Belknap, & Ginsberg, 2005; Feagin, Vera, & Imani, 1996; Patton, Bridges, & Flowers, 2011). Social integration has recently been related to a concept called "sense of belonging," which several studies have demonstrated is an important predictor of whether or not students stay in and graduate from college (Museus & Maramba, 2011). Self-reported "sense of belonging" is often lower for Black, Latino, and Asian American students on predominantly White campuses (Johnson et al., 2007).

As any college student can tell you, campuses are made up of a variety of different subcultures or communities that are effective at integrating different types of students into the life of the college. The greater the variety of campus communities available, the more likely it is that a greater range of students "will be able, if they so desire, to become integrated and establish competent intellectual and social membership" in the institution (Tinto, 1993, p. 124). The integrative effectiveness of these various communities is largely dependent on having a critical mass of diverse students on campus, including students with different social class backgrounds, geographic origins, unique interests, and racial or ethnic group membership (Tinto, 1993; Willie, 2003). But involvement in extracurricular organizations is unequivocally linked to higher levels of student satisfaction and college graduation (Fischer, 2007; Jackson & Swan, 1991).

For example, Samuel D. Museus (2008) conducted an interview study with 24 Black and Asian American undergraduate students at a large public university that was 85% White. His data revealed that for students in both groups, their membership in "ethnic student organizations" gave them connections, emotional support, and space for identity exploration, which increased their sense of comfort on campus. Museus did not find that this membership also facilitated increased contact with faculty, another important factor for student success, although this has been a finding in other research (e.g., Guiffrida, 2003).

For students of all racial backgrounds, Greek membership is one way to achieve this kind of successful social integration. All GLOs are characterized by restricted membership, as a specific type of voluntary association (Knoke, 1986). The student organizations that evolved to become the GLOs we know today were literary and study groups that attempted to provide avenues for discussion, academic development, and social outlets within a pretty restrictive, almost monastery-like, higher education environment (Jones, 2004; Rudolph, 1962/1990). These organizations also provided students with housing, built-in study groups, and social support, as well as the benefit of helping students find others who shared common interests and goals. Beginning in the late 19th century, sororities were organized along the same lines, with the first collective organization occurring in 1902. These Greek organizations were also always race and class selective at a time when American higher education itself was primarily, although not exclusively, available to only a very select proportion of the U.S. population, namely upper-class Whites (Handler, 1995). They particularly remained closed to the small numbers of African Americans on predominantly White campuses at the turn of the 20th century (Kimbrough, 2003; Washington & Nuñez, 2005).

That these organizations were completely White at the time is revealed in a 1968 story from the University of Georgia campus newspaper regarding the experiences of Deborah Williams, an African American student who participated in sorority rush (the recruitment period for National Panhellenic Conference [NPC] organizations). Ms. Williams described the shock and surprise of the White members who greeted her at the various sorority houses. Although she was invited back to three sororities, she did not receive an invitation to join any of them. Several of the sorority women did tell her that they "thought a black sorority would be good for the campus, that it would give black students the chance they wanted to identify" (Baugh, 1968).

While most fraternities or sororities moved to rid themselves of overtly racially restrictive clauses around the middle of the last century, this was a complex and controversial process. It most often took the form of conflict between current members who were in favor of removing official clauses but without changing racially marked pledging practices, and national offices that were run by alumni who resisted any policy change whatsoever, particularly when it was demanded by campus administrators (Hughey, 2007). For instance, this was the case at both the University of Minnesota and the University of Michigan, and of the Theta Chi fraternity at Dartmouth (Lee, 1955). It was in 1963 that all social organizations were mandated to remove any remaining racially restrictive membership clauses (Whipple, Grady, & Baier, 1991). It is important to keep in mind that, under whatever circumstances, the removal of specific clauses was rarely associated with change in new member recruitment practices or the overall racially marked character of these organizations (Crain & Ford, 2013; Hughey, 2010; Lee, 1955). While none of the national governing organizations collects official data on the racial composition of their chapters, single institution data from a range of studies confirms racial homogeneity observed by students on campus (Hughey, 2010; Stains, 1994; Vendituoli & Grant, 2013).

Black GLOs were founded, starting at the turn of the 20th century, in part to offer a Greek option for Black students who were banned from joining those existing White organizations. However, they differ significantly from their historically White counterparts not only in their history of racial restrictions but also in mission. There are currently nine national Black Greek organizations under the National Pan-Hellenic Council (NPHC). Black students on both the campuses of Historically Black Colleges and Universities (HBCUs) and predominantly White institutions (PWIs) founded fraternal organizations to enhance their college experiences and to deal with political and social issues facing the Black community (Rodriguez, 1995). While the major breeding ground for BGLOs was Howard University, an HBCU where five of the nine organizations were founded, three of the nine were founded on predominantly White campuses. These include Alpha Phi Alpha fraternity (Cornell University in 1906), Kappa Alpha Psi fraternity (Indiana University in 1911), and Sigma Gamma Rho sorority (Butler University in 1922).

BGLOs have from the start been more focused on sociopolitical goals, including racial equality and community service. This activism can clearly be seen in many of the initial major service programs that were established as the organizations grew to be national and international in scope. These include Phi Beta Sigma's Bigger and Better Business Program, which was established in the 1920s and worked to empower Black business owners; the Guide Right program established by Kappa Alpha Psi in 1922, which works to encourage academic achievement among high school seniors; the Voting Rights Program developed by Alpha Phi Alpha, which worked to register African Americans to vote at a time of widespread disenfranchisement; the National Library Project created in 1937 by Delta Sigma Theta, which helped to develop local libraries for African Americans; and the Zeta Phi Beta Housing project of 1943, where the sorority worked with the National Housing Association to locate housing vacancies for WWII war workers (Berkowitz & Padavic, 1999; Ross, 2000). Moreover, it is important to note that there are many cases where White students who shared these goals have joined these groups (Hughey, 2007).

For many Black students on predominantly White campuses, even those who are not Greek members, BGLOs are a primary source of social activities, in a setting where few such resources are available (Kimbrough & Hutcheson, 1998). White students often respond to this information by suggesting that social clubs and events that are predominantly White are in fact open to students of all races and that students of color are welcome at these events. While this is nominally the case, research suggests that at many such events, particularly those where alcohol is involved, the risk of racist comments and behavior can be quite high, creating an unwelcoming, even hostile environment in a nominally race-neutral setting

(Black et al., 2005). Research on the impact of campus racial climate, defined as a combination of the racial history of an institution, its racial demography, and the average attitudes and behaviors of current students, confirms what my own students report (Hurtado, Enberg, Ponjuan, & Landremann, 2002). As a White student of mine wrote of his adjustment to the college party scene [and why he left it], "I used to hear so much racist language from other people at the parties. I remember being shocked . . ." The experience of social integration may be virtually impossible for a Black student who has multiple experiences with discrimination on campus. It is difficult to come to share the norms and values of a community when those seem to include a lack of value for someone from your racial background (see Mendoza-Denton, Downey, Purdy, Davis, & Pietrzak, 2002). This kind of discrimination often takes organizational form in White GLOs, particularly in the form of racially insensitive party themes, including "ghetto" parties and "tacos and tequila" (Hughey, 2010; Stains, 1994; Whaley, 2009).

In addition, as discussed above, several studies found that participation in same-race organizations did not increase isolation for Black and other minority students, as commonly believed, but actually made them feel more a part of the campus community (McClure, 2006; Moran, Yengo, & Algier, 1994; Murguia, Padilla, & Pavel, 1991; Taylor & Howard-Hamilton, 1995). Students use these enclaves to scale down a large campus and deal with it more effectively, particularly as it relates to issues of discrimination on campus. It is in this function that the Black Greek organization can most clearly be seen as unique from White Greek organizations. Based on the overall campus environment and the needs and experiences of students of color, same-race organizations create a unique integrating niche for these students.

As these organizations often function as a kind of supportive enclave for minority students, they can actually facilitate increased cross-race interaction for their members. Because they generate a sense of meaningful membership in the larger campus community members are encouraged to participate in other non-Black student organizations that promote equal status contact (McClure, 2006; Murguia et al., 1991). Equal status contact is one of the most effective prejudice reduction mechanisms and requires long-term contact among individuals of equal social status who voluntarily work toward a cooperative goal under the supervision of a legitimate authority (Wittig & Grant-Thompson, 1998).

Conclusion

For White students who believe race does not play a role in campus life and who believe they are open to being friends with students of all races, several questions could be considered. First, while you may not say negative things about students of other races, do you ever hear them in all-White social settings, particularly where alcohol is involved? If yes, when you hear these things, are they immediately followed by negative social sanctions (glares, verbal recrimination, stony silence), which indicate they are not approved of by other White students? Or, do you and your peers often do as the student quoted above admitted, "most of the time I took the path of least resistance and ignored it"?

It is also worth reflecting on why the question of "self-segregation" repeatedly comes up in campus discussions of race. Often, the question itself is a distancing mechanism. For those of us who were and are members of predominantly White Greek organizations (including this author), the question justifies the racial homogeneity of our own organizations and lets us off the hook for taking action to change that reality. For non-Greek White students, the question may be related to a wider strategy of denial and resistance, which seeks to define a problem as the result of someone else's choices. The issue then becomes unrelated to any action or inaction we may take in our own day-to-day college activities. This is in spite of the fact that on many campuses, students of color regularly spend time in environments where they are the minority, while this happens only rarely for White students.

Given the apparent openness of most campus events, it is possible for White students with a sincere interest in moving past highly segregated social spaces to take the initiative to attend alone or with a few friends events that are sponsored or organized by minority student groups on campus, including those of BGLOs. This decision is a powerful individual act that moves past verbal and written accusation into the realm of action. That is, instead of using the existence of minority-marked events as a justification and rationalization for our own racially homogeneous social networks, White people have the opportunity to put into action the very thing that they indicate they desire in people of color.

Suggested Additional Resources

On the History of Greek Organizations

Kimbrough, W. M. (2003). *Black Greek 101: The culture, customs, and challenges of Black fraternities and sororities.* Madison, NJ: Fairleigh Dickinson University Press.

Ross, L. C., Jr. (2000). *The divine nine: The history of African American fraternities and sororities.* New York, NY: Kensington.

Syrett, N. L. (2009). *The company he keeps: A history of White college fraternities.* Chapel Hill: University of North Carolina Press.

On the Experiences of Students of Color on Predominantly White Campuses

Aries, E. (2008). *Race and class matters at an elite college.* Philadelphia, PA: Temple University Press.

Chavous, T. M. (2000). The relationships among racial identity, perceived ethnic fit, and organizational involvement for African American students at a predominantly White university. *Journal of Black Psychology, 26*(1), 79–100.

Feagin, J. R., Vera, H., & Imani, N. (1996). *The agony of education: Black students at White colleges and universities.* New York, NY: Routledge.

Hu, S., & St. John, E. P. (2001). Student persistence in a public higher education system: Understanding racial and ethnic differences. *Journal of Higher Education, 72*(3), 265–286.

Willie, S. S. (2003). *Acting Black: College, identity and the performance of race.* New York, NY: Routledge

Websites

North-American Interfraternity Council: http://www.nicindy.org
National Panhellenic Conference: http://www.npcwomen.org/index.aspx
National Pan-Hellenic Council: http://www.nphchq.org

Questions for Further Discussion

1. Have you ever thought about the concept of "self-segregation" as it relates to your campus? What information in the essay do you believe best challenges the assumption that minority student organizations self-segregate? What other information do you think might be useful?

2. If BGLOs do not exist (or exist in great numbers) on your campus, consider organizations like the Black Student Union or the Latino Alliance. How are they different from the Greek organizations discussed here or from other student organizations on campus? How and why might this vary with campus racial composition?

3. What (if any) student organizations are you involved with? What is the overall racial composition of these groups? Does it reflect the racial composition or social dynamics described in this essay? How or why?

Reaching Beyond the Color Line

1. For White students, following this discussion, locate and attend an on-campus event where you believe you will be one of the few White people in attendance. For students of color, if you are involved in a student organization like those described above (where there may be relatively few White people in attendance), ask a White friend or classmate to attend an organizational event or meeting with you. For all students, take some time to reflect on how you felt about this experience and whether or not you would likely do the same thing again. Why or why not?

References

Astin, A. W. (1993). *What matters in college? Four critical years revisited.* San Francisco, CA: Jossey-Bass.

Baugh, C. (1968). Describes reactions as "priceless." *Red & Black, 11,* 1–68.

Berkowitz, A., & Padavic, I. (1999). Getting a man or getting ahead: A comparison of Black and White sororities. *Journal of Contemporary Ethnography, 27*(4), 530–557.

Black, T., Belknap, J., & Ginsberg, J. (2005). Racism, sexism, and aggression: A study of Black and White fraternities. In T. L. Brown, G. S. Parks, & C. M. Phillips (Eds.), *African American fraternities and sororities: The legacy and the vision* (pp. 363–392). Lexington: University Press of Kentucky.

Braxton, J. M. (Ed.). (2000). *Reworking the student departure puzzle.* Nashville, TN: Vanderbilt University Press.

Collison, M. N. E. (1987, April 22). Black fraternities on White campuses, accused of separatism, say they are just misunderstood. *The Chronicle of Higher Education, 35.*

Crain, A., & Ford, M. (2013, September 11). The final barrier: 50 years later, segregation still exists. *The Crimson White.* Retrieved from http://cw.ua.edu/2013/09/11/the-final-barrier-50-years-later-segregation-still-exists

Dziadosz, A. (2006, November 30). After years of self-segregation, Greeks say it's time to shake up the system. *Michigan Daily.* Retrieved from http://www.michigandaily.com/content/after-years-self-segregation-greeks-say-its-time-shake-system?page=0,1

Feagin, J. R., Vera, H., & Imani, N. (1996). *The agony of education: Black students at White colleges and universities.* New York, NY: Routledge.

Fischer, M. J. (2007). Settling into campus life: Differences by race/ethnicity in college involvement and outcomes. *The Journal of Higher Education, 78*(2), 125.

Guiffrida, D. A. (2003). African American student organizations as agents of social integration. *Journal of College Student Development, 44,* 304–319.

Handler, L. (1995). In the fraternal sisterhood: Sororities as gender strategy. *Gender & Society, 9*(2), 236–256.

Hughey, M. W. (2007). Crossing the sands, crossing the color line: Non-Black members of Black Greek letter organizations. *Journal of African American Studies 11,* 55–75.

Hughey, M. W. (2010). A paradox of participation: Nonwhites in White sororities and fraternities. *Social Problems, 57*(4), 653–679.

Hurtado, S., Enberg, M., Ponjuan, L., & Landremann, L. (2002). Students' pre-college preparation for participation in a diverse democracy. *Research in Higher Education 43*(2), 163–186.

Jackson, K., & Swan, L. (1991). Institutional and individual factors affecting African American undergraduate student performance. In W. R. Allen, E. G. Epps, & N. Z. Haniff (Eds.), *College in Black and White: African American students in predominantly White and in historically Black public universities* (pp. 127–142). Albany: State University of New York Press.

Johnson, D. R., Solder, M., Leonard, J. B., Alvarez, P., Inkelas, K. K., Rowan-Kenyon, H. T., & Longerbeam, S. D. (2007). Examining sense of belonging among first year undergraduates from different racial/ethnic groups. *Journal of College Student Development, 48*(5), 525–542.

Jones, R. L. (2004). *Black haze: Violence, sacrifice, and manhood in Black Greek-letter fraternities.* Albany: State University of New York Press.

Kimbrough, W. M. (2003). *Black Greek 101: The culture, customs, and challenges of Black fraternities and sororities.* Madison, NJ: Fairleigh Dickinson University Press.

Kimbrough, W. M., & Hutcheson, P. A. (1998). The impact of membership in Black Greek-letter organizations on Black students' involvement in collegiate activities and their development of leadership skills. *The Journal of Negro Education, 67*(2), 96–105.

Knoke, D. (1986). Associations and interest groups. *Annual Review of Sociology, 12,* 1–21.

Lee, A. M. (1955). *Fraternities without brotherhood: A study of prejudice on the American campus.* Boston, MA: Beacon Press.

McClure, S. M. (2006). Facilitating student involvement and cross-race contact: The impact of membership in a Black Greek organization. In R. M. Moore III (Ed.), *African Americans and Whites: Changing relationships on college campuses* (pp. 77–88). Lanham, MD.: University Press of America.

Mendoza-Denton, R., Downey, G., Purdy, V., Davis, A., & Pietrzak, J. (2002). Sensitivity to status-based rejection: Implications for African American students' college experience. *Journal of Personality and Social Psychology, 83,* 896–918.

Moran, J., Yengo, L., & Algier, A. (1994). Participation in minority oriented co-curricular organizations. *Journal of College Student Development, 35,* 143.

Murguia, E., Padilla, R. V., & Pavel, M. (1991, September). Ethnicity and the concept of social integration in Tinto's model of institutional departure. *Journal of College Student Development, 32,* 433–439.

Museus, S. D. (2008). The role of ethnic student organizations in fostering African American and Asian American students' cultural adjustment and membership at predominantly White institutions. *Journal of College Student Development, 49*(6), 568–586. Retrieved from http://search.proquest.com/docview/195183067?accountid=11078

Museus, S. D., & Maramba, D. C. (2011). The impact of culture on Filipino American students' sense of belonging. *Review of Higher Education, 34*(2), 231–258. Retrieved from http://search.proquest.com/docview/854040759?accountid=11078

Pascarella, E. T., & Terenzini, P. T. (2005). *How college affects students: Volume 2. A third decade of research.* San Francisco, CA: Jossey-Bass.

Patton, L. D., Bridges, B. K., & Flowers, L. A. (2011). Effects of Greek affiliation on African American students' engagement: Differences by college racial composition. *College Student Affairs Journal, 29*(2), 113–123,177–179. Retrieved from http://search.proquest.com/docview/903807619?accountid=11078

Rodriguez, R. (1995, November 30). Pledging relevance: From the Million Man March to education budget cuts, Black and Latino fraternities and sororities lock step with their communities. *Black Issues in Higher Education,* 32–34.

Ross, L. C. (2000). *The divine nine: The history of African American fraternities and sororities.* New York, NY: Kensington.

Rudolph, F. (1990). *The American college & university: A history.* Athens: University of Georgia Press. (Original work published 1962)

Saenz, V. B., Ngai, H. N., & Hurtado, S. (2007). Factors influencing positive interactions across race for African American, Asian American, Latino, and White college students. *Research in Higher Education, 48*(1), 1–38.

Stains, L. A. (1994). Black like me. *Rolling Stone, 678,* 69.

Taylor, C. M., & Howard-Hamilton, M. F. (1995). Student involvement and racial identity attitudes among African American males. *Journal of College Student Development, 36*(4), 330–336.

Tinto, V. (1993). *Leaving college: Rethinking the causes and cures of college student attrition.* Chicago, IL: University of Chicago Press.

Tinto, V. (2006). Research and practice of student retention: What next? *Journal of College Student Retention, 8*(1), 1–19.

Vendituoli, M., & Grant, M. (2013, September 19). College changes sorority rush process amid racism claims. *USA Today College.* Retrieved from http://www.usatoday.com/story/news/nation/2013/09/18/sorority-rush-changed-racism/2833079

Washington, M., & Nuñez, C. L. (2005). Education, racial uplift, and the rise of the Greek-letter tradition: The African American quest for status in the early twentieth century. In T. L. Brown, G. S. Parks, & C. M. Phillips (Eds.), *African American fraternities and sororities: The legacy and the vision* (pp. 137–179). Lexington: University Press of Kentucky.

Whaley, D. E. (2009). Links, legacies, and letters: A cultural history of Black Greek-letter organizations. In C. L. Torbenson & G. S. Parks (Eds.), *Brothers and sisters: Diversity in college fraternities and sororities* (pp. 46–82). Cranbury, NJ: Associated University Presses.

Whipple, E. G., Baier, J. L., & Grady, D. L. (1991). A comparison of Black and White Greeks at a predominantly White University. *NASPA Journal, 28*(2), 140–148.

Willie, S. S. (2003). *Acting Black: College, identity and the performance of race.* New York, NY: Routledge.

Wittig, M. A., & Grant-Thompson, S. (1998). The utility of Allport's conditions of intergroup contact for predicting perceptions of improved racial attitudes and beliefs. *Journal of Social Issues, 54*(4), 795–812.

"I Had a Friend Who Had Worse Scores Than Me and He Got Into a Better College"

The Legal and Social Realities of the College Admissions Process

OiYan Poon

Loyola University–Chicago

OiYan Poon is an assistant professor in the higher education program at Loyola University Chicago's School of Education and a Research Fellow at the Asian American and Pacific Islander Research Coalition (ARC). Her research interests include Asian Americans in education, college access and admissions policies, civic engagement, and participatory democracy. She has served as an undergraduate admissions reviewer at University of California–Davis and a scholarship application reviewer for the Gates Millennium Scholars Program.

A college degree, especially from a selective postsecondary institution, is commonly valued as prerequisite to an upwardly mobile lifestyle. With limited seats available, selective institutions have their pick of an overabundance of highly qualified students each year. In the zero-sum game of selective college admissions, many qualified applicants denied admissions may question the fairness of the selection process. For example, a YouTube video[1] presents the following scenario, in which a White female applicant is denied admissions to a college where her Black acquaintance with lower grades and test scores was admitted, drawing the unfounded conclusion that the Black applicant was racially privileged in the admissions process:

> Look at Sara, a white female high school student applying for college. Throughout high school, she achieved good grades in challenging classes and earned good test scores. She applied to one of the best universities in her state, only to be denied admission a few weeks later. She later found out that her friend Emily, an African American student, was accepted to the same school with lower grades and test scores. Unfortunately, Sara was negatively affected by affirmative action. If the standard college application simply did not include race, there would be no room for inequality.

Two key misconceptions underlie the video's argument. First, it presumes that affirmative action is an unfair system of racial quotas that defies principles of equality. It incorrectly frames the goal of the civil rights movement as color-blindness, and thus race-conscious admissions policies as counter to principles of racial justice. Secondly, it assumes that selective institutions utilize a simplistic process of college admissions that applies the same basic criteria of test scores and grades for evaluating student achievement, aptitude, and merit. In this misconception, test scores and grades are incorrectly viewed as unquestionably reliable measures of achievement.

In reality, admissions processes are complex evaluation methods that necessarily include criteria beyond tests and grades to gauge the fit between students and a given selective institution. Admissions committees begin by answering the question: How does this university or college define "merit" in the admissions process? Among selective higher education institutions, there are many ways to define merit for admissions. According to *Merriam-Webster's, merit* is defined as "character or conduct deserving reward" (Merit, 2011). Although "merit" is commonly assumed to mean high test scores and grades, students' character and conduct extend beyond simplistic measures of academic achievement and promise. Indeed, selective institutions include more than test scores and grades in determining selection criteria that align with how they define "merit" because students are more than just what numbers can reveal. Research demonstrates that test scores and grades are significantly limited in their ability to predict how successful a student will be in college and beyond (Sedlacek, 2010). They are also inadequate measures of student talents, gifts, achievements within specific contexts of opportunity, and other unquantifiable characteristics.

Unique institutional missions and interests inform each college and university's admissions policies and procedures, resulting in the development and utilization of a large array of selection criteria. Given the complexities and diversity of institutional interests, it is false to assume that test scores, grades, and race are, or even should be, the *only* three criteria considered. It is also problematic to assume that tests and grades are objective, reliable, and race-neutral measures of a student's achievements and aptitude (Santelices & Wilson, 2010).

---

[1] See http:// www.youtube.com/watch?v=UdBMWpu2Opo.

Common Misconceptions

Myths surrounding race-conscious admissions policies often emerge from under-lying concerns over fairness in the generally opaque process of admissions in top schools. Anxiety over the mysterious selective college admissions process is under-standable given the intense public discourse on increasing competition in selective college admissions (Steinberg, 2003). Moreover, this anxiety can be fed by a general perception that the prestige of the institution attended can have direct effects on one's future well-being and earning potential (Lareau, 2011).

Misconception 1: Affirmative action consists of racial quotas and reverse discrimination.

Contemporary opponents of affirmative action policies misleadingly claim that it is a system of racial quotas. *Quotas* are defined as an articulated allotment of a limited resource assigned to specific groups; in this case, a finite number of enrollment offers at selective colleges. Quotas have historically acted as a cap limiting certain groups from accessing elite institutions like those placed on Jews by Ivy League schools in the early 20th century (Brodkin, 1998; Karabel, 2005). Conversely, quotas are also minimum targets for certain groups; as in the case of the Ivy League Jewish quota, the limitation of Jews allowed for the assurance of a minimum target allotment of admission for White Anglo-Saxon Protestants. The practice of utilizing quotas in college admissions was declared unconstitutional by the U.S. Supreme Court in the 1978 *Bakke v. Regents of the University of California*. However, the Court distinguished between the use of quotas and the consideration of race in selective admissions. In selecting students, admissions offices cannot legally utilize racial quotas, but they can continue to consider race as one of many factors in reviewing applications. Therefore, claims that current-day practices of affirmative action are racial quotas are misleading and false.

Opponents of race-conscious admissions also argue that affirmative action represents "reverse discrimination," which defies values of hard work and merit. According to a 1974 opinion piece published in *The Harvard Crimson,* affirma-tive action, "provoked an outcry of 'reverse discrimination' from whites who say blacks and other minorities don't have to work as hard to get into college" (Leonard, 1974). Arguing that affirmative action actually serves as a source of rac-ism, a more recent opinion piece in *The Daily Texan* states, "The biggest problem with affirmative action is simple. Using discrimination to combat discrimination encourages racial hatred in our society" (McGarvey, 2012). While Whites have been the supposed targets of "reverse discrimination," some also claim that Asian Americans are harmed by affirmative action policies (Brief for the Asian American Legal Foundation, 2012). Inherently, this view frames Whites and Asian Americans as hard workers that deserve admissions at top schools, while Black, Latino, and other students of color are stereotyped as undeserving students who generally do not work hard. While some have claimed that the elimination of affirmative action would lead to overwhelming Asian American majorities in elite college under-graduate enrollments (Espenshade & Chung, 2005), such studies do not account for the removal of suspected negative action[2] practices that would increase admissions for Asian American. Unlike affirmative action, negative action limits the admission of Asian Americans in favor of White applicants (Kidder, 2005), similar to earlier Ivy League quotas against Jews (Golden, 2007). Moreover, studies like Espenshade's often assume that admissions criteria only include test scores and grades, which is an incomplete and deficient understanding of the admissions selection process.

Opponents of race-conscious admissions policies also argue that affirmative action is also a system of unfair racial preferences. At least as early as 2003, conservative student organizations have staged "anti-affirmative action bake sales" charging different prices determined by a given customer's racial identity (Potter, 2003). They compare the unequal pricing schema to admissions policies that include race as a factor. Ward Connerly, a prominent, Black affirmative action opponent, has explained that his stance emerged from his commitment to civil rights. Invoking the words of Dr. Martin Luther King Jr., Connerly (2005) states, "the success of [Dr. King's] children should be based on their individual accomplishments and merit and their right to equal treatment" (see also Thornhill, Essay 5 for further discussion). The misappropriation of Dr. King's words is disturbing, since the late reverend was clearly not color-blind in leading a movement that acted to affirmatively confront systems of racial inequality (Turner, 1996). Bonilla-Silva (2006) has incisively argued how color-blind ideology serves to maintain racism by ignoring persistent racial injustices.

Misconception 2: Race-blind admissions policies are fair.

Finally, opponents of affirmative action believe that a race-blind admissions process is both possible and the only fair system of college admissions. They argue that race-blind admissions policies would be tantamount to charging everyone the same price for a cupcake regardless of social identity. In reference to the *Fisher v. University of Texas* U.S. Supreme Court case (2013), Megyn Kelly, a correspondent on *The O'Reilly Factor*, stated, "in this case you have a white student who was denied admission to the University of Texas saying, 'the reason I didn't get in is because kids who have lower GPAs, lower test scores than I did were admitted because of the color of their skin'" (O'Reilly, 2012).

In addition to incorrectly assuming that test scores, grades, and race are the only admissions criteria, anti-affirmative action advocates also presume that tests and grades are racially neutral in their evaluative power. However, these quantitative measures can be tainted by bias, making them unfair gauges of student potential especially if they are the only factors for admissions. The evaluative power of high

---

[2] According to Kang (1996), "negative action against Asian Americans is in force if a university denies admission to an Asian American who would have been admitted had that person been white" (p. 3). For example, since the 1980s, there have been notable controversies and concerns that elite institutions restrict the admission of Asian Americans in order to maintain and increase the admissions rates of White applicants (Poon, 2009; Liu, 2007; Kang, 1996; Nakanishi, 1995).

school GPA can be limited by implicit and explicit biases influencing how schools and teachers treat diverse students, creating barriers to high school academic achievement by race (Conchas, 2006; Tenenbaum & Ruck, 2007). Moreover, SAT results have been found to correlate with socioeconomic backgrounds of test takers, leading to critical questions about the reliability of such tests to fairly evaluate applicants' academic achievement and potential (Geiser, 2008; Santelices & Wilson, 2010). Consequently, some highly competitive colleges have even decided to de-emphasize or not require tests scores, including institutions like Bates College, Colby College, New York University, and Pitzer College.

Ultimately, it is essential to understand that selective evaluation methods for admissions are constructed to fit the unique interests of diverse institutions in how they define what merits a student's admission. Therefore, narrow quantitative measures like test scores and grades are severely limited in what they can tell admissions officers about students. Taken alone, they can hinder admissions review processes from a fair and full evaluation of fit between a student and institution. Below is a glimpse into the selective college admissions process, which is a systemic approach to evaluating large numbers of highly qualified applicants for student–institutional fit.

What Goes in to an Admissions Process and Why?

The first step to constructing an informed opinion about the fairness of admissions review criteria is to gain a basic understanding of the complicated nuts and bolts of selective college admissions. A wide range of selection criteria are used in the admissions process to evaluate whether a student will help an institution fulfill its specific interests and goals, which may include the advancement of financial health, campus traditions, athletic teams, and geographic, economic, cultural, and racial diversity. Subsequently, criteria for admissions may include preferences for geographic locations of hometowns, legacies and relatives of donors, and student athletes, among many other criteria. Race can serve as one of many factors in the process of admissions review, but legally it cannot serve as a singular criterion.

In the next section, I present an overview of the role and function of admissions offices, a brief description of some selection criteria connected to institutional goals, and key legal principles that limit how race can be used in admissions decisions.

Evaluating for Institutional Interests and "Fit"

Specific institutional values, missions, and interests determine the methods and criteria for undergraduate admissions at selective postsecondary institutions (Steinberg, 2003). Admissions officers represent and apply their respective institutional missions, values, and goals in recruiting applicants, constructing criteria and review procedures for the evaluation of applicants, and enrolling students (Hossler, 2011). They work to ensure a strong fit between their institution's characteristics and interests and those of incoming students. Much like in a healthy relationship, student and institution should complement each other's interests.

Admissions processes at different schools reflect the diversity of institutional values and interests, resulting in different mixes and weighting of multiple criteria in admissions policies and practices (Steinberg, 2003). These factors and their weighting are subject to change depending on specific institutional interests and goals (Rashid, Hurtado, Brown, & Agronow, 2009). While it is impossible to provide a comprehensive list of admissions criteria at both private and public institutions, because private schools are not obligated to release details on their selection criteria, it is interesting to note the similarities in criteria between selective public universities like the University of California (UC) and the University of Texas (UT). Based on the highly selective nature of these two revered institutions, it is possible to speculate that the criteria used at these two universities might share some similarities with those at elite private institutions.

The UC (2012), which consists of nine undergraduate campuses, has defined 14 criteria for admissions review for undergraduate admissions:

- Academic grade point average
- Test scores
- Number of, content of, and performance in academic courses
- Number of and performance in honors or advanced placement classes
- High school class ranking
- Quality of the senior-year program, including the number and type of academic classes in progress or planned
- Quality of academic performance relative to the educational opportunities offered at the student's high school
- Outstanding work in one or more subjects
- Outstanding work in one or more special projects in any academic field of study
- Recent, marked improvement in academic performance as demonstrated by GPA and quality of courses completed or in progress
- Special talents, achievements, or awards in a particular field
- Completion of special projects undertaken in the context of a student's high school curriculum or in conjunction with special school events, projects, programs
- Academic accomplishments in light of student's life experiences and special circumstances
- Location of student's secondary school and residence

The admissions offices at each undergraduate UC campus work with their respective campus leaders to determine the evaluation method for each criterion in accordance with their individual university ethos. Therefore, how UC Davis, UCLA, or UC San Diego each evaluate quality of senior-year program or special talents may greatly differ. Due to the passage of Proposition 209 in 1996, affirmative action practices are not allowed by state law in California.

Unlike the UC, the University of Texas continues to legally consider race among many other factors in its admissions process, but only for a small proportion of the applicant pool. In 1997, the State of Texas established a law that required the university to automatically offer admission to Texas high school seniors who ranked in the top 10% of their high school classes. In 2009, the state amended the law to automatically admit enough Texas high school graduates to fill 75% of available slots for Texas residents. With state population outpacing available slots for new students in the state's higher education system, Texas adjusted the class ranking threshold to the top 8% in 2013. For the remaining 25% of incoming classes, UT engages in a holistic review of qualifications for every applicant. In holistic review, the university considers "a variety of both academic and personal achievement factors, as well as special circumstances that can help to put an applicant's achievement into context" (University of Texas, 2013). To evaluate academic achievement, UT considers students' class ranks, test scores, and high school coursework. To assess personal achievement, the University reviews students' written essays, information about student activities, and letters of recommendation. It also considers special circumstances, "to get a clearer picture of the applicant's qualifications." These include socioeconomic status of family, single-parent home, language spoken at home, family responsibilities, overcoming adversity, cultural background, race and ethnicity, and other information included in student files. This information can be provided by students in an optional essay or letters of reference.

By taking a look at these two universities' admissions criteria, we can see they recognize that prospective college students are much more than just their test scores and grades. In constructing complex evaluation methods, selective colleges and universities intentionally select the mix of information they require to make informed admission decisions. Indeed, tests and grades are not the only means for evaluating academic merit, and are limited in their capacity to evaluate and understand who students are and what they bring to a campus community.

In constructing an admissions review method, it is important to understand what each item adds to the process and how it contributes toward the evaluation of a student according to institutional criteria for determining a student's merit. While some assume that test scores are the best measures of academic merit, research has found that standardized tests are reliable in predicting only about 6% of the variance in college GPA (Atkinson & Geiser, 2009; Sedlacek, 2005). In other words, the SAT and ACT have the power to predict a very small amount of difference in students' academic potential. High school grades have been found to be a stronger predictor of college freshmen year grades than test scores but are also very limited in what they say about a student (Hoffman & Lowitzki, 2005).

Logically then, tests and grades should not be the only standards of merit. Given the severe inadequacies of tests and grades, a fair assessment of merit must include a wide range of criteria to provide a holistic assessment of applicants. Even "The College Board has long felt that the SAT was limited in what it measured and should not be relied upon as the only tool to judge applicants" (Sedlacek, 2005, p. 177). A range of criteria should be used to understand who students are and what they bring to a campus environment. These criteria, such as those used by the UC and the UT, may include place of residence and secondary school, language spoken at home, socioeconomic background (including race), ability to overcome adversity, special talents, and accomplishments.

In pursuit of fairness in selective college admissions, opponents of affirmative action are often silent about the ways in which U.S. systems of education are riddled with racial barriers (McDonough, 1994) that prevent fairness in competition for diverse college-bound students. While some criticize the use of race and ethnicity as one factor for admissions, few of these critics are as vocal about the use of legacy preferences, which privileges children of alumni in admissions. Legacy applicants at Harvard have been found to have a 40% admission rate compared to the 11% admission rate for the general applicant pool even with lower test scores and grades compared to other applicants (Howell & Turner, 2004; Shadowen, Tulante, & Alpern, 2009). To date, there has been no lawsuit confronting the practice of legacy preferences. Private institutions may defend the use of legacy preference in admissions as a tool for preserving institutional tradition and to encourage alumni donations supporting institutional financial interests (Golden, 2007; Howell & Turner, 2004).

Generally, a student's chances of admission at a given institution depend on a number of factors that represent institutional interests. In any given year, an institution may be seeking particular types of students to contribute toward the campus character. In addition to academic interests, colleges and universities may want to satisfy alumni demands in exchange for financial donations. For institutions with competitive NCAA sports teams, talented student-athletes may be evaluated for their academic promise as well as their athletic talents. Therefore, the captain of a state championship volleyball team or nationally or internationally ranked tennis player might have lower test scores and grades than his or her peers, yet be admitted to contribute his or her unique talents to the campus. Indeed, much more than just tests, grades, and race go into admissions decisions to evaluate fit between students and selective institutions.

Racial Diversity: A Compelling Interest

Among the various institutional interests to be met in the college admissions process, campus racial diversity is but one compelling interest. Legally, race can be one of many factors in college admissions processes through affirmative action practices. In the 1978 *Bakke* decision, the U.S. Supreme Court allowed for the use of race as one of many factors in college admissions, and banned the use of racial quotas. This practice of affirmative action was affirmed in the 2003 Supreme Court decision in *Grutter v. Bollinger*. In that case, the University of Michigan Law School successfully demonstrated that the educational benefits of racial diversity represented a compelling state interest. Based on a large and growing body of empirical research, racial diversity on campus can lead to positive educational outcomes for all students (Gurin, Dey, Hurtado, & Gurin, 2002), student growth and development in skills for democratic citizenship and participation (Gurin, Nagda, & Lopez, 2004), and is generally linked to the educational and civic mission of higher education (Hurtado, 2007). Therefore, to fulfill legitimate educational goals, some selective institutions justifiably implement limited racial preferences, alongside a number of other preferences and criteria, in their admissions processes.

Consequently, affirmative action practices in college admissions are legally justified as long as they pass the strict scrutiny test. According to Winkler (2006), strict scrutiny consists of a two prong test in which

Courts first determine if the underlying governmental ends, or objectives, are "compelling." . . . If the governmental ends are compelling, the courts then ask if the law is a narrowly tailored means of furthering those governmental interests. Narrow tailoring requires that the law captures within its reach no more activity (or less) than is necessary to advance those compelling ends. (p. 800)

According to the 2013 U.S. Supreme Court *Fisher v. University of Texas* decision, diversity remains a compelling state interest justifying affirmative action in admissions.

Conclusion

The inclusion of race as one of many criteria in selective college admissions processes is justified in fulfilling institutional and public interests in racial diversity and equity. Without racial diversity, college campuses can be hindered from preparing and educating all students to become socially responsible leaders, socially engaged citizens with cultural competencies in an increasingly global society faced with significant challenges. Given the educational interests and benefits of racial diversity, the compelling public interest in addressing persistent racial inequalities (Zamani-Gallaher, Green, Brown, & Stovall, 2009), and traditional civil rights principles of advancing racial justice and equity, the use of race, as one factor in admissions, is necessary.

Aspiring college students come from all walks of life. Their varied life experiences, which result from social differences, can endow them with an array of unique perspectives, talents, and skills representing the strengths of diversity in the United States. Many college applicants are proven community leaders, budding scientists, talented artists, gifted athletes, brilliant musicians, future teachers, caring and integral members of their families and communities. They have passions, talents, and vocational callings that span an immense range of fields. Test scores and GPAs cannot fairly represent the totality of any given student's qualities and strengths. With such divergent qualifications found among large and talented pools of applicants, selective colleges and universities have the difficult task of constructing methods to understand and evaluate how each student would fit into the specific school's mission.

Thus, "merit" becomes the demonstration of characteristics that fit an institution's values and interests. Merit is not measured in a uniform way. Consequently, selective colleges and universities determine their own mix of criteria for assessing applications. These criteria are chosen for their relevance and reliability in evaluating students for fit with institutional values and goals. While test scores and high school grades serve as limited tools in predicting college GPAs, colleges and universities that value racial diversity, equity, diverse student skills, talents, and potentials above and beyond book learning and multiple-choice test taking must include other criteria.

Accordingly, selective admissions processes represent complex methods of student evaluation involving multiple measures. Returning to the video presented at the beginning of this essay, the narrator's assertion that Sara was negatively impacted by affirmative action is groundless, given the wide range of goals and criteria in college admissions at different schools. Moreover, the full details of Sara's and Emily's applications are not provided in the case. Did Emily win a statewide academic award? Has she been recognized for leading a successful countywide service project? Was Emily's grandfather an important donor to the university? Many factors may have contributed to the decision to admit Emily and reject Sara, but we don't know what those factors are. There are many factors that lead to various outcomes in selective college admissions. The inclusion of race as one among many factors in admissions has become a tepid policy to advance racial diversity and equity, and yet it remains under attack. In an effort to prepare future college graduates for a multicultural and racially diverse world and to confront pervasive and persistent racial inequalities in U.S. education systems, selective institutions are justified in using race as one of many criteria in their efforts to affirmatively and intentionally pursue racial diversity and equity.

Suggested Additional Readings

Chang, M., Witt, D., Jones, J., & Hakuta, K. (2003). *Compelling interest: Examining the evidence on racial dynamics in colleges and universities.* Stanford, CA: Stanford University Press.

Espenshade, T. J., & Radford, A. W. (2009). *No longer separate, not yet equal: Race and class in elite college admission and campus life.* Princeton, NJ: Princeton University Press.

McDonough, P. M. (1997). *Choosing colleges: How social class and schools structure opportunity.* Albany: State University of New York Press.

Zamani-Gallaher, E. M., & Green, D. O. (2009). *The case for affirmative action on campus: Concepts of equity, considerations for practice.* Sterling, VA: Stylus.

Reaching Beyond the Color Line

You are a member the admissions committee at Catalina College, a selective institution that values the pursuit of knowledge, social justice, and leadership in service to humanity. Based on this three-part mission, construct criteria with which you will evaluate the following four applicants. Using the criteria you construct, select two students to accept for admission.

Student 1:

- Captain of tennis team; lettered in three sports (tennis, basketball, and cheerleading)
- 3.7 GPA (weighted)
- Has taken 7 of 23 (30%) AP courses offered by high school
- SAT: 740 (CR); 690 (Math); 780 (Writing)

- Attended Middlebury College summer school (costs $8,000 for 8 weeks)
- Grandparents are alumni of Catalina who have contacted the institution because they are considering giving the school a large donation
- White female; upper middle class

Essay: Ever since I was very young, I have had the privilege of traveling all over the world. By the time I was 15, I had been to over 25 countries. I've always been amazed by the diversity of cultures, and had the opportunity to try all kinds of foods that I wouldn't normally have had the chance to. When I entered high school, I knew I wanted to better understand the world around me through an academic lens. I also wanted to serve people who are not as privileged as me. So during the summer after my junior year of high school, I was accepted to Middlebury College Summer School. It was a chance to practice being a college student. I took great classes on philosophy and biology. Most importantly, I was able to confront and overcome the adversity of having a roommate with Multiple Sclerosis. She was wheelchair bound, and depended on people to help her in and out of bed. A lot of that responsibility fell on me. At first it was really burdensome for me because it took away from my time in the morning and at night to get my work done. After a while, I realized that I was lucky to not have a physical disability, and learned to help my roommate when I had time. Even though I had a lot on my plate, I came to an epiphany that it is important to help people. It helped me learn to balance responsibilities, and most importantly it made me feel good.

Student 2:

- Works 35 hours a week at a fast food restaurant to save money for college
- 3.75 GPA (weighted)
- Has taken 3 of 3 (100%) AP courses offered by high school
- SAT: 620 (CR); 750 (Math); 690 (Writing)
- Asian American female; working class; first-generation college student

Essay: I haven't always been someone who thought college was possible. My parents were constantly struggling to make ends meet, and fighting over finances. They worked all the time to keep their store open. My earliest memories are of playing on the floor of their convenience store. The other memories after that are of being physically and verbally abused by my parents. They were always mad about not being able to make ends meet, about rude customers, and about how life in America wasn't a dream. When I was 12, the abuse I took at home became apparent at school, and I was taken away from my parents, and placed in the foster care system. Over the last six years, I've lived in 5 different homes. Thankfully, they've all been in the same city, close to the high school I go to now. When I started high school, I met Mrs. Kane who somehow saw something in me, and took me under her wing. She told me about Upward Bound, and for the next few years I learned how college offered a pathway for a better life. To make ends meet, I started working 35 hours a week, so I could save money for college. I'm grateful that I had some great teachers who cared and a stable school community, where I started the South Asian Student Association. Last year, we raised money to support the earthquake victims in northern India. I know that I've benefited from support from people like Mrs. Kane and the staff at Upward Bound. Without people like them, I would not have been prepared to succeed in college. I probably wouldn't have even known the first thing about applying to college. In my future, I plan to "pay it forward." In college, I want to be a tutor and mentor underprivileged youth, and give back to the Upward Bound program. After college, I'm thinking about pursuing a career that would allow me to help young people in the foster care system. I hope to also find reconciliation with my parents, and let them know that I forgive them.

Student 3:

- 4.1 GPA (weighted)
- Has taken 9 of 15 (60%) AP courses offered by high school
- SAT: 770 (CR); 800 (Math); 760 (Writing)
- Elected leader in eight different activities—Key Club, Spanish Club, Chess Club, school newspaper, student government, speech and debate, Academic Decathlon, and band
- Asian American male; middle class

Essay: For as long as I can remember, my parents have been my heroes. They immigrated to the U.S. with almost nothing, and have become very successful in providing everything that my siblings and I would need. They're even founders and leaders of our church, which keeps growing every year. My parents came to the U.S. as international graduate students. Shortly after they arrived, they found out they were pregnant with my older sister. Life as graduate students was very difficult, and raising a child on grad student salaries was going to be even harder. Several years later, when I was 3, my parents graduated from their doctoral programs, and we moved to northern California. Even with their limited English skills and cultural barriers, they knew they had to find a place to live that had good schools for their children. Last year, when we visited the ancestral villages in China on both sides of my family, I was struck by their humble beginnings. The villages were extremely poor, and only a few houses had modern plumbing. My parents' story, where they've come from and how they've made themselves into community leaders, inspires me to be the best that I can be. They've taught me that hard work in America is always rewarded.

Student 4:

- 3.4 GPA (weighted)
- Has taken 5 of 15 (33%) AP courses offered by high school
- Member of a U.S. Olympic team; came in 5th place in event.
- SAT: 580 (CR); 610 (Math); 550 (Writing)
- Mixed race African American and American Indian; middle class

Essay: It's 4 a.m., and my alarm has gone off. I feel like I just went to bed a couple hours ago, and well . . . I actually did. It's time for practice again. My schedule looks like this: 3 hours of practice every day before school; school; 4 hours of practice after school; dinner; homework until about 1 a.m.; and sleep. On Saturdays, I have 6 hours of practice. I have one rest day—Sunday. You could say I don't have a normal teenage schedule, but I have a dream. Ever since I first saw the Olympics on television, I knew that I wanted to be an Olympian. I have been competing nationally and internationally since I was ten years old, and finally became an Olympian. I try to bring the same intensity to my academics, but with my schedule it's been a challenge. However, I know that the skills I've developed as an Olympian have cultivated strong leadership skills and a commitment to achieving all my goals in life. College will be the first time I will be able to control my schedule and explore non-athletic endeavors. I am excited about the possibilities of being involved in campus leadership programs, studying abroad, and even just meeting new people with diverse interests. I bring a unique perspective to my classes and to the campus community and am anxious to learn from my peers and accomplished faculty.

Questions for Discussion:

1. What criteria and institutional interests did you use to review and select students for admission?

2. Which two students did you select? Why?

3. Did you admit students with lower grades or test scores than another applicant? Why or why not?

4. Was your process fair to all students and meet institutional interests?

5. Do you feel that anyone can understand who you are, your accomplishments and potentials by just looking at your test scores and high school grades? Why or why not?

References

Atkinson, R. C., & Geiser, S. (2009). *Reflections on a century of college admissions tests* (No. CSHE.4.2009). Research and Occasional Papers Series (pp. 1–21). Berkeley, CA: Center for Studies in Higher Education. Retrieved from http://cshe.berkeley.edu/publications/docs/ROPS-AtkinsonGeiser-Tests-04-15-09.pdf

Bonilla-Silva, E. (2010). *Racism without racists: Color-blind racism and the persistence of racial inequality in the United States.* Lanham, MD: Rowman & Littlefield.

Brief for the Asian American Legal Foundation and the Judicial Education Project as Amici Curiae in support of Petitioner, Abigail Noel Fisher v. University of Texas at Austin, et al. (No. 11–345).

Brodkin, K. (1998). *How Jews became White folks & what that says about race in America.* Brunswick, NJ: Rutgers University Press.

Conchas, G. Q. (2006). *The color of success: Race and high-achieving urban youth.* New York, NY: Teachers College Press.

Connerly, W. (2005, April 15). On the defensive: Quota defenders are having a tough time. *Old National Review*. Retrieved from http://old.nationalreview.com/document/connerly200504150756.asp

Espenshade, T. J., & Chung, C. Y. (2005). The opportunity cost of admission preferences at elite universities. *Social Science Quarterly, 86*(2), 293–305.

Geiser, S. (2008). *Not so fast! A second opinion on a University of California proposal to endorse the new SAT* (No. CSHI.16.2008). Research and Occasional Papers Series (pp. 1–11). Berkeley, CA: Center for Studies in Higher Education. Retrieved from http://cshe.berkeley.edu/publications/docs/ROPS-Geiser-SAT-11-12.pdf

Golden, D. (2007). *The price of admission: How America's ruling class buys its way into elite colleges—and who gets left outside the gates.* New York, NY: Three Rivers Press.

Grutter v. Bollinger, 539 U.S. 306 (2003).

Gurin, P., Dey, E. L., Hurtado, S., & Gurin, G. (2002). Diversity and higher education: Theory and impact on educational outcomes. *Harvard Educational Review, 72*(3), 330–366.

Gurin, P., Nagda, B. A., & Lopez, G. E. (2004). The benefits of diversity in education for democratic citizenship. *Journal of Social Issues, 60*(1), 17–34.

Hoffman, J. L., & Lowitzki, K. E. (2005). Predicting college success with high school grades and test scores: Limitations for minority students. *The Review of Higher Education, 28*(4), 455–474.

Hossler, D. (2011). From admissions to enrollment management. In N. Zhang (Ed.), *Rentz's student affairs practice in higher education* (4th ed., pp. 63–95). Springfield, IL: Charles C Thomas.

Howell, C., & Turner, S. (2004). Legacies in Black and White: The racial composition of the legacy pool. *Research in Higher Education, 45*(4), 325–351.

Hurtado, S. (2007). Linking diversity with the educational and civic missions of higher education. *Review of Higher Education, 30*(2), 185–196.

Kang, J. (1996). Negative action against Asian Americans: The internal instability of Dworkin's defense of affirmative action. *Harvard Civil Rights-Civil Liberties Law Review, 31*, 1–48.

Karabel, J. (2005). *The chosen: The hidden history of admission and exclusion at Harvard, Yale, and Princeton.* New York, NY: Houghton Mifflin.

Kidder, W. C. (2005). Negative action versus affirmative action: Asian Pacific Americans are still caught in the crossfire. *Michigan Journal of Race & Law, 11*, 605–624.

Lareau, A. (2011). *Unequal childhoods: Class, race, and family life.* Berkeley: University of California Press.

Leonard, H. J. (1974, February 8). The "reverse discrimination" backlash. *The Harvard Crimson*. Retrieved from http://www.thecrimson.com/article/1974/2/8/the-reverse-discrimination-backlash-pminority-enrollment

Liu, A. (2007). Affirmative action & negative action: How Jian Li's case can benefit Asian Americans. *Michigan Journal of Race & Law, 13*, 391–432.

McDonough, P. M. (1994). Buying and selling higher education: The social construction of the college applicant. *The Journal of Higher Education, 65*(4), 427–446.

McGarvey, S. (2012, March 19). Affirmative action: Racist by nature. *The Daily Texan*. Austin, TX. Retrieved from http://uwire.com/2012/03/20/column-affirmative-action-is-racist-by-nature

Merit. (2011). *Merriam-Webster.com.* Retrieved from http://www.merriam-webster.com/dictionary/merit

Nakanishi, D. T. (1995). A quota on excellence? The Asian American admissions debate. In D. T. Nakanishi & T. Nishida (Eds.), *The Asian American educational experience* (pp. 273–284). New York, NY: Routledge.

O'Reilly, B. (2012, February 23). Supreme Court to hear affirmative action case. *The O'Reilly Factor. Fox News*. Retrieved from http://nation.foxnews.com/supreme-court/2012/02/24/supreme-court-hear-affirmative-action-case

Poon, O. (2009). Haunted by negative action: Asian Americans, admissions, and race in the "colorblind era." *Harvard University Asian American Policy Review, 18.* Retrieved from http://www.hks.harvard.edu/aapr/AAPR.pdf#page=81

Potter, W. (2003, February 28). Chewing over affirmative action. *The Chronicle of Higher Education,* p. A8.

Rashid, M., Hurtado, S., Brown, M., & Agronow, S. (2009). *A response to: "Not so fast! A second opinion on a University of California proposal to endorse the new SAT."* Research and Occasional Paper Series. Berkeley, CA: Center for Studies in higher Education. http://cshe.berkeley.edu/publications/publications.php?id=330

Santelices, M. V., & Wilson, M. (2010). Unfair treatment? The case of Freedle, the SAT, and the standardization approach to differential item functioning. *Harvard Educational Review, 80*(1), 106–134.

Sedlacek, W. E. (2005). The case for noncognitive measures. In W. Camara & E. W. Kimmel (Eds.), *Choosing students: Higher education admissions tools for the 21st century* (pp. 177–194). Mahwah, NJ: Lawrence Erlbaum.

Sedlacek, W. E. (2010). Noncognitive measures for higher education admissions. In P. L. Peterson, E. Baker, & B. McGaw (Eds.), *International encyclopedia of education* (3rd ed., pp. 845–849). Amsterdam, The Netherlands: Elsevier.

Shadowen, S. D., Tulante, S. P., & Alpern, S. L. (2009). No distinctions except those which merit originates: The unlawfulness of legacy preferences in public and private universities. *Santa Clara Law Review, 49,* 51–136.

Steinberg, J. (2003). *The gatekeepers: Inside the admissions process of a premier college.* New York, NY: Penguin Books.

Tenenbaum, H. R., & Ruck, M. D. (2007). Are teachers' expectations different for racial minority than for European American students? A meta-analysis. *Journal of Educational Psychology, 99*(2), 253–273. doi:10.1037/0022-0663.99.2.253

Turner, R. (1996). The dangers of misappropriation: Misusing Martin Luther King, Jr.'s legacy to prove the colorblind thesis. *Michigan Journal of Race & Law, 2,* 101–130.

University of California. (2012). *How applications are reviewed.* Retrieved from http://www.universityofcalifornia.edu/admissions/freshman/how-applications-reviewed/index.html

University of Texas. (2013, July 11). *Application review factors: What we consider.* Retrieved from http://bealonghorn.utexas.edu/freshmen/after-you-apply/factors

Winkler, A. (2006). Fatal in theory and strict in fact: An empirical analysis of strict scrutiny in the federal courts. *Vanderbilt Law Review, 59,* 794–871.

Zamani-Gallaher, E. M., Green, D. O., Brown, M. C., & Stovall, D. O. (2009). *The case for affirmative action on campus: Concepts of equity, considerations for practice.* Sterling, VA: Stylus.

"Black People Voted for Obama Just Because He's Black"

Group Identification and Voting Patterns

Veronica L. Womack and James Bridgeforth
Georgia College

Bre'Auna Beasley
Virginia Commonwealth University

Veronica L. Womack is an associate professor of political science and public administration at Georgia College. She received her bachelor's in communications, as well as an MPA and PhD in political science and public administration with a concentration in African American studies from the University of Alabama. She currently serves as the director of the Office of Institutional Equity and Diversity and special assistant to the president at Georgia College. Dr. Womack's research efforts include publications on public policy, leadership, and diversity. She also teaches diversity within the public sector and works on issues of diversity within the larger community.

James Bridgeforth is a recent graduate of Georgia College, with bachelor's degrees in political science and sociology. His main areas of interest include political parties and elections, minority student persistence and retention in higher education, and the effects of the growth of the charter school movement in urban cities in the United States. Currently, James serves as a regional admissions counselor for Georgia College with plans to pursue graduate studies at The University of Georgia in Fall 2014.

Bre'Auna Beasley is a doctoral student in the Public Policy and Administration program at Virginia Commonwealth University, where she holds a graduate teaching assistant post. Her scholarship focuses on the intersections of race, socioeconomic class, and gender within the field of public policy and the allocation of public health resources in marginalized communities.

The 2008 presidential election saw the rise of Barack Obama as the first viable African American presidential candidate and eventually, the first to be elected president. Despite the United States's troubled racial history, Obama built a coalition of supporters that transcended racial, socioeconomic status, gender, and generational boundaries—a coalition that reelected him in 2012. Both elections saw record numbers of voters with 131 million votes in the 2008 presidential election and 126 million votes in the 2012 election, indicating a drastic increase in voter participation. The two preceding elections yielded just 123 million votes (in 2004) and 105 million votes (in 2000). However, both the 2012 election, as well as the 2008 election, proved to be "over-performing" elections for Blacks who make up 12% of the voting population but accounted for 13% of all votes cast in both elections (Taylor, 2012). Indeed, Blacks were highly motivated in both elections and played a critical role in them. However, the central question raised by the media in particular centered on how much identity politics would and did play a role in these two elections, but specifically the landmark 2008 election.

Indeed, identity politics played a key role early on in the media and among political analysts of the 2008 primary, where the election was often framed in terms of gender (i.e., Hillary Clinton) and race (i.e., Barack Obama). The consistent question was whether America was ready for a Black president or a woman president? Yet voting patterns highlighted the fact that the simplified formula promoted by the media was inadequate. According to data collected by the Pew Research Center in 2007, Black Democratic voters ranked candidates Clinton (52%) and Obama (50%) very favorably (Dimock, 2007). In fact, the primary election showed Blacks were a diverse group of people with differing ideas, values, and hopes, instead of a monolithic voting force. In a *New York Times* op-ed, Juan Williams (2007) highlighted the differences among Blacks by showing that Blacks with at least some college education were more likely to think that Obama shared the values and interest of all Blacks as compared to only 41% of Blacks with a high school education or less.

Nevertheless, many, including students in our classes, wondered whether Blacks voted for Obama solely because he was Black, a theory not used to explain White voting behavior. Before the 2008 election, in our classes, students typically talked about policy as a reason why people backed certain candidates, but during the Obama candidacy the focus was on race. However, there was little to no discussion of race-based voting patterns for Hillary Clinton or John McCain. Based on these observations, some students believed that Black people vote based on race, but

Whites do not. To be sure, this implication echoes a long-held stereotype of Blacks as unintelligent, uncritical, and sheeplike in their choices while simultaneously casting Whites as far more critical voters who are never influenced by a candidate's race. Unfortunately, this was a sentiment held by many and was even reflected in mainstream media coverage.

The media and general public alike suggested that Blacks would vote for Obama solely on the basis of his race. For example, Kevin Jackson, author of *The Big Black Lie,* told Fox News, "Racists that they are, [Blacks] voted for [Obama] because he's Black, not because he's qualified" (quoted in Touré, 2012). Conservative author Ron Christie echoed him, saying Blacks voted for Obama because of "straitjacket solidarity" (quoted in Touré, 2012). However, Touré, cohost of MSNBC's *The Cycle,* and others have pointed out that this alleged racial solidarity does not extend to Black politicians like Herman Cain, Allen West, or Alan Keyes who, although they are Black, do not promote the policy agenda of most Blacks, and thus receive little support from them. This inconsistency reveals some of the problems with the myth of Black race-based voting patterns and demonstrates that Blacks, like most voters, look beyond race when choosing a candidate.

Voting Patterns in the 2008 and 2012 Elections

The early days of the 2008 primary election served as an initial indication that Blacks wouldn't be voting for Obama simply because he was Black. Originally, the Black electorate largely supported Hillary Clinton and not Barack Obama. As Adia Harvey Wingfield and Joe Feagin (2009) argue in *Yes We Can: White Racial Framing and the 2008 Presidential Campaign,* "the fact that Black voters initially strongly supported Hillary Clinton and did not mobilize around Obama until many months into his candidacy indicates that African Americans did not blindly, automatically support Obama due to nothing more than shared racial status" (p. 165). In fact, in a February 2007 poll, Clinton led Obama in the Black vote, 41% to 17% (Balz & Cohen, 2007). Even civil rights leaders such as John Lewis publicly supported Hillary Clinton in the early days of the 2008 primary election. This early rift between Obama and traditional Black leadership casts further doubt on Blacks' alleged blind support for Obama.

After his success in the 2008 Iowa Primary, Obama became a real voting option for Blacks and Whites. Not only were White voters carefully studying the feasibility of voting for both Obama and Clinton, but they showed that they were indeed willing to vote for a Black presidential candidate. In comparing Obama's White support to other Democratic presidential candidates, he registered very strong White support. In fact, Jimmy Carter's White support was only four points higher than Obama's. Obama also equaled Bill Clinton's White support in 1996. Remarkably, his support among young White voters was more than any other Democratic presidential nominee in over 30 years (Kuhn, 2008).

Given our country's troubled racial history, Obama's support among Whites was more than a foregone conclusion. Headlines and op-eds such as "Fear of a Black President," "Is Obama the End of Black Politics[?]," and "Who's to blame for the race politics[?]," revealed the existence of the color line in the United States. Many pollsters wondered early on whether the *Bradley Effect* would ultimately derail Obama's message of hope and post-racial politics. Named after former Los Angeles Mayor Tom Bradley, the effect suggests that White voters will lie to pollsters regarding their support for a Black candidate because they do not want to appear racially prejudiced. In 1982, Bradley ran for the governorship of California and the preelection polls showed him with a nine point or more lead, yet he lost to Republican George Deukmejian by a little more than one point. This phenomenon also occurred in the 1989 Virginia gubernatorial race of Douglas Wilder, a Black man, who was shown to have at least a 10-point lead against his opponent, but won by less than one point. That same year, New York mayor David Dinkins, also Black, was shown to have led his opponent by more than 12 points, but won by less than three points. A year later in a North Carolina senatorial race between White senator Jesse Helms and his Black opponent Harvey Gantt, the issue of race became the center of the campaign and although the polls predicted a win by Gantt, Helms won the election by six points (Keeter & Samaranayake, 2007). These examples of unsuccessful polling due to hidden racial attitudes were often mentioned as Obama led in 2008 polls. However, the polls proved accurate as his White support materialized into tangible votes and a victory.

Obama's strong support among Whites was only bolstered by strong support among Blacks. Yet, that support is greatly attributable to Blacks' propensity to vote Democratic, as they have for several decades. Gallup polling estimated that the previous White Democratic candidates John Kerry (2004 election) and Al Gore (2000 election) received 93% and 95% of the Black vote, respectively. Evidence suggests that it is this voting pattern, rather than racial allegiance, that better explains Black voting preference for Obama (see Newport, 2008). In general, many Blacks believe that the Democratic party shares more of their interests and values than the Republican party and first began voting Democrat in large numbers during Franklin Roosevelt's election. By the time John F. Kennedy was elected and subsequently Lyndon Johnson, the trend of Blacks voting Democrat had been firmly established and extended into both the 2008 and 2012 elections.

Obama's success included overwhelming support from other groups as well. For example, he was able to link an extraordinary coalition of voters from across the age and class spectrum. Exit polls in 2008 revealed Obama received 68% of voter support from 18- to 24-year-olds compared to McCain's 30%. Voters in the 25- to 29-year-old category supported Obama 69% to McCain's 29%. In fact, Obama was able to beat or tie McCain in every age bracket except for voters age 65 or older (CNNPolitics, 2008). He also led or tied among voters in every income category, registering a support level of 60% among those making $50,000 or less, the median income in the United States. Some of his highest levels of support in 2008 came from women of color, with 96% of Black women but also 68% of Latinas supporting Obama (CNNPolitics, 2008).

The above patterns beg the question, which groups supported the Republican candidate, John McCain in 2008? McCain won 55% of the White vote, leading in every age category except with young White voters. He also won the support of White women, but only at a margin of 53% to 46%. In addition, McCain won the support of White college graduates 51% to 47%, but took White working-class voters 59% to Obama's 40% (Kuhn, 2008). These patterns highlight the intersection of race and class in the United States.

The geographic location of voters also proved an interesting determinant of Obama's support in 2008. The South played a significant role in his victory; there were notable increases in voting percentages in the Southern states of Mississippi, Georgia, North Carolina, and Louisiana, which is understandable as the South houses a large percentage of the country's Black population. Yet, although Obama was able to build multiracial coalitions that typically transcended geographical locations, it proved more difficult to rise above geographical Whiteness in the South. Robert J. Kruse (2009) discusses the spatial geography of Whiteness, focusing on Obama's ability to successfully navigate the world of Northern Whites based on his educational attainment and economic status and his representation of post-racialism. In fact, he was supported by a vast majority of Northern states. However, he failed to transcend race for many Southern Whites, thus revealing the geographical difference in Obama's White support and perhaps long-standing patterns of race relations in the South. Unlike in other regions where a multiracial coalition was developed, in the South, this coalition movement was not feasible because of marginalized Southern Whites who had long ago abandoned the Democratic Party. In these ways, the election revealed interesting cleavages within the American electorate based on racial attitudes, stereotypes, and the changing complexity of racism. The 2012 election yielded similar results as the South remained overwhelmingly Republican.

In fact, the 2012 exit polls continued many of the above patterns, although Obama lost support from some groups. He again received 60% of voter support from 18- to 24-year-olds, compared to Mitt Romney's 36%. Voters in the 25- to 29-year-old category supported him 60% to Romney's 38%. However, Romney was able to beat Obama in all age brackets over 40 years of age (Exit Poll, 2012). Obama again received 60% of the votes among those making $50,000 or less, while Romney won all income categories above $50,000. Obama was able to sustain or increase his level of support from women of color, maintaining 96% of Black women and increasing his support to 76% among Latinas.

As mentioned above, perhaps most revealing was the political participation and voter turnout of people of color during both the 2008 and the 2012 presidential elections. These proved to be the most racially and ethnically diverse elections in American history. According to one study, Black voters had a higher turnout rate than all other minority groups in 2012, and may have voted at a higher rate than Whites for the first time in U.S. history. In 2008, racial minority groups accounted for approximately 1 in 4 voters. More specifically, Black voter turnout rates almost matched those of White voters, with Black turnout at 65.2% and White voter turnout at 66.1%. This extremely high voter turnout was supplemented by the increased participation of Black women. In fact, for the first time in American history, Black women had the highest voter turnout among any population subgroup (Lopez & Taylor, 2009). In addition, participation among Blacks ages 18 to 29 proved extraordinary as they were shown to have the highest voter turnout (58%) compared with other same age peers (51%). Among racial and ethnic minorities, the percentages were even more astonishing as Obama received 96% of the Black vote, 67% of the Latino vote, and 63% of the Asian vote (CNNPolitics, 2008). Preliminary 2012 exit polls revealed that Obama maintained or increased his minority support, receiving 93% of the Black vote, 71% of the Latino vote, and 73% of the Asian vote (CNNPolitics, 2012).

Some researchers propose that this increase in voting among people of color in general, and Blacks in particular, was not coincidental but was due to intentional efforts. Philpot, Shaw, and McGowen (2009) used the National Black Election Studies database at the University of Michigan to analyze Black voter participation and mobilization during the 2008 election and found that over 45% of the Black voters were self-identified as nonhabitual voters, but over 62% of those respondents voted in the 2008 election. The authors attribute the increase in Black voter participation to party mobilization by the Obama campaign and the Democratic Party. Obama supporters mobilized Black voters through extraordinary door-to-door contact. These efforts resulted in nearly 79% of Black respondents reportedly having been contacted by the Democratic Party in 2008. Thus, Philpot et al. dispel the notion that the political interest and voter turnout of Blacks was heightened solely by the presence of a Black candidate, where the Obama campaign's serious and purposeful voter outreach likely played a significant role in increasing Black voter participation.

Obama also targeted Blacks for intentional campaigning in 2012, launching his efforts with a video addressed to Blacks on the first day of Black History Month. In addition, according to a Huffington Post article, *African Americans for Obama* was part of Operation Vote, the campaign's outreach arm to select voting blocs, which included Blacks, Latinos, Jews, LGBTQs (Lesbian, Gay, Bisexual, Transgender, Queer/Questioning), youth, and older voters. *African Americans for Obama* included a number of programs geared toward Blacks, including one to engage barbershop and beauty salon owners as "opinion leaders" and volunteer recruiters in the community. Other initiatives included programs to empower and engage Black business leaders, civic organizations, and students at historically Black colleges and universities. In February 2012, a campaign spokesperson said of the effort, "Our goal is to provide a platform for the community to get involved—we plan on stressing the importance of voter education and registration" (African Americans for Obama, 2012). Again, significant voter outreach played a critical role in support for Obama among people of color.

The increase in minority voting did not manifest in support for the Republican party candidate in 2012. That year, 88% of Romney's voters were White (Scocca, 2012). This fact is in great contrast to the multiracial support received by Obama. Romney's candidacy highlights the monolithic White voting bloc that supported the Republican candidate in 2012 and serves as a cautionary tale of future elections if Republican candidates are unable to broaden their base to reflect the changing demographics of American society. If most Black voters vote Democratic, it is also the case that most Republican voters are White.

While Obama's extensive outreach efforts are evidence of the skilled political maneuvers of the campaign, it is worth noting that the candidate himself appealed to a range of voters. Malik Simba (2009) discusses how, unlike other Black presidential candidates, Obama did not self-identify as a "Black candidate." In fact, according to Simba, "Obama described himself as a post-civil rights, multi-cultural 'Horatio Alger' " (p. 186). He portrayed race relations in an almost idealistic way that emphasized unity and strength, and promoted the idea that regardless of race or ethnicity, one could make it if he or she worked hard enough. This is the classic "America Dream" ideology. With this message, Obama was able to build a strong coalition of "youth, Blacks, Hispanics, and the distressed White middle class, both rural and urban" (Simba, 2009, p. 187). According to Kruse (2009), Obama learned to adjust his racial identification throughout his childhood, as a means of assimilating into various geographical cultures. The author concluded that Obama's ability to remain a viable presidential candidate could be attributed to his learned racial fluidity and ability to transcend into spaces of Whiteness.

Shifting Perspectives of Race in Politics

While monolithic race-based voting patterns are clearly inconsistent with the data, researchers continue to ask questions about the role of race in politics, political preference, and political discourse. For example, while many look at Obama's strong support among Whites as evidence of a "post-racial" society, there is a great deal of evidence that suggests we still have much work to do where race is concerned. In his observations on the 2008 election, Tim Wise (2009) suggests that the election of Obama could be explained within the context of a newer system of American racism in which Whites are able to continue to see the larger Black community through the prism of old racial stereotypes or hard racial framing, yet make room for individuals like Obama whom they deem "different" or "exceptional" (see also Harris, Essay 23). Wise's argument supports the notion that racism has transformed from old stereotypes into *symbolic racism,* which "represents a form of resistance to change in the status quo based on moral feelings that Blacks violate such traditional American values as individualism, and self-reliance, the work ethic, obedience and discipline" (Kinder & Sears, 1981, p. 416). According to Donald R. Kinder and David O. Sears, symbolic racists accept the basic concept of racial equality but discriminate against Blacks who they believe they are not "good Americans" and therefore not deserving of equality. In fact, there were several instances in which Obama's patriotism and Americanism were questioned, raising the issue of whether he was "American" enough to be president. Examples of this critique include questioning whether he wore an American flag pin on his lapel to pointing out *Hussein* as his unique middle name.

However, the presence of symbolic racism in both elections didn't preclude the presence of "old fashioned," that is, overt racism. Spencer Piston (2010) finds that old stereotypes continue to play a role in American politics, something not captured in previous studies because of their limitation. According to Piston,

Some studies ask respondents to evaluate fictitious candidates, a strategy that allows tight control over candidate characteristics but may lead to results that do not generalize to the real world. Others do not measure racial attitudes, making it impossible to tie prejudice directly to voter choice. Others that do measure racial attitudes often ask respondents to report those attitudes to an interviewer, despite the fact that racial prejudice is often underreported due to social desirability pressures [see earlier discussion on "The Bradley Effect"]. Finally, almost no studies analyze a national sample of White Americans. (p. 433)

By using the American National Election Studies (ANES) data set, Piston was able to overcome some of these limitations due to the design of the survey and subsequently found that overt, old-fashioned racism did play a role in the 2008 election (and probably the 2012 election as well). ANES survey respondents were allowed to enter all of their responses to racial stereotype questions into a computer, thus potentially eliminating the social desirability factor. In addition, the study analyzed a nationally representative sample of White voters who evaluated real-life candidates and made use of a self-administered measure of racial stereotypes. This more nuanced method allowed for greater reliability in the respondents' answers about racial stereotypes in today's society. Focusing on the role of racial prejudice in White voters' evaluation of Obama as compared to past Democratic presidential candidates and current prominent Democrats, Piston (2010) found that Obama's race hurt him more than his party affiliation or his platform with White voters. As such, his campaign was negatively influenced by racial prejudice. Moreover, at least 45% of the sample of White respondents rated Blacks as lazier than Whites and at least 39% rated Blacks as less intelligent than Whites. This data indicate that even with his significant backing from White voters, Obama's race did appear to trigger racist attitudes among some White voters.

Research from Redlawsk, Tolbert, and Franko (2010) offers similar insight into the presence of latent racial attitudes among White voters, particularly by party affiliation. Thirty-three percent of White respondents appeared to be troubled by Barack Obama becoming the first Black president. More importantly, there appeared to be partisan bias as 31% of Republicans and 34% of Independents were far more troubled by the prospect than a miniscule percentage of Democrats. In these ways, while we have elected and reelected a Black president, the significance of race remains.

Conclusion

Since the election of Barack Obama, America has seemed to become even more racially polarized. For instance, Tea Party rallies in 2009 included racially charged signs and banners that read, "Somewhere in Kenya, a village has lost its idiot," or that superimposed President Obama's face onto an image of a monkey. In addition, "birtherism," or the idea that Obama was not born in America and therefore was ineligible for the presidency, has also flourished with backers as high profile as business mogul Donald Trump.

Initially, Obama was able to unite a multiracial and multigenerational voting coalition, but by 2012, there were signs of some of his key constituencies breaking, even among staunch voting blocs like Blacks. According to Zoll (2012), there was growing unrest among Black voters in the 2012 presidential election, like Black ministers who disagreed with President Obama's stance on same-sex marriage. Reverend Jamal-Harrison Bryant states that, "This is the first time in black church history that I'm aware of that black pastors have encouraged their parishioners not to vote." Bryant, who opposes gay marriage, said that the president's position the issue was at the heart of the problem (Zoll, 2012). In addition, issues of high unemployment and joblessness in Black communities led Black political commentators like Tavis Smiley and Black scholars like Cornel West to speculate on Obama's remaining support among Blacks. These discussions again cast doubt on the notion of Blacks as a monolithic voter bloc who blindly supported Obama.

Despite the challenges and difficulties of the 2008 election, his first term in office, and a fairly contentious 2012 campaign, Barack Obama was successfully reelected. Yet, his rocky journey from candidate to two-term president reveals the complicated intersection of race and politics in America and the effects of identity on political behavior. Ultimately, Obama managed to build a unique coalition of supporters that transcended racial, socioeconomic status, gender, and generational boundaries. Therefore, his election in 2008 and reelection in 2012 cannot be explained by overwhelming support from Blacks, first because Blacks voting Democratic had long since been established and secondly, because Black support was not in and of itself sufficient to win the election. The elections can be explained as case studies in grassroots organizing, outreach and education efforts, and candidate and party mobilization strategies, as well as how to build a diverse coalition that is reflective of the American electorate. The Republican Party's candidates' inability to appeal to a broader demographic of voters in both the 2008 and 2012 presidential elections speaks to differences in party ideology and issues between the Democratic and Republican parties that result in a widening gap of minority support between the two parties. Thus, the success of Obama extends beyond race to issues and policies that reflect the voters that support him and the Democratic party.

Suggested Additional Resources

Novkov, J. (2008). Rethinking race in American politics. *Political Research Quarterly, 61*(4), 649–650.

Orbe, M. P. (2011). *Communication realities in a "post-racial" society: What the U.S. public really thinks about Barack Obama.* Lanham, MD: Lexington Books.

Simba, M. (2009). The Obama campaign 2008: A historical overview. *The Western Journal of Black Studies, 33*(3), 186–191.

Wingfield, A. H., & Feagin, J. R. (2009). *Yes we can: White racial framing and the 2008 presidential election.* New York, NY: Routledge.

Questions for Further Discussion

1. Do you think one can be racist and still vote for a Black candidate? Why or why not?

2. Do you think people join political parties based on race? Why or why not?

3. Discuss ways in which you think candidate Barack Obama was able to transcend race in the 2008 and 2012 elections.

Reaching Beyond the Color Line

1. If you are a White student, have you ever voted for a candidate of a different race? If so, what were the factors that influenced your decision? If not, explain what factors resulted in the decision.

2. Conduct an informal survey of 10 of your close friends and family members and ask them if they have ever voted for a candidate not of their same race and why.

3. If you are a student of color, assess how much you know about Barack Obama's racial heritage? Do you think your generation promotes post-racial politics? How could we achieve a post-racial society, to the extent that it is possible?

4. Have racial stereotypes ever played a role in your evaluation of a candidate? Discuss the types of stereotypes that come to mind.

References

"African Americans for Obama" launched by president's campaign to rally black voters (Video). (2012, February 1). *Huffingon Post*. Retrieved from http://www.huffington-post.com/2012/01/31/obama-campaign-unveils-la_n_1245395.html

Balz, D., & Cohen, J. (2007). Blacks shift to Obama, poll finds. *Washington Post*. Retrieved from http://www.washingtonpost.com/wp-dyn/content/article/2007/02/27/AR2007022701030.html

Berman, J. (2008, October 14). Will the Bradley effect be Obama's downfall? *ABC News*. Retrieved from http://abcnews.go.com/blogs/headlines/2008/10/will-the-bradle

CNNPolitics. (2008a, November 4). *Exit polls: Obama wins big among young, minority voters*. Retrieved from http://articles.cnn.com/2008-11-04/politics/exit.polls_1_exit-polls-obama-camp-john-mccain?_s=PM:POLITICS

CNNPolitics. (2008b). *Presidential national exit poll*. Retrieved from http://www.cnn.com/ELECTION/2008/results/polls/#USP00p1

CNNPolitics. (2012). *President full results*. Retrieved from http://www.cnn.com/election/2012/results/race/president

Dimock, M. (2007). *Black enthusiasm for Clinton and Obama leaves little room for Edwards*. Pew Research Center. Retrieved from http://www.pewresearch.org/2007/08/30/Black-enthusiasm-for-clinton-and-obama-leaves-little-room-for-edwards

Keeter, S., & Samaranayake, N. (2007). Can you trust what polls say about Obama's electoral prospects? Two important trends suggest Americans may now be ready to elect an African American president. *Pew Research Center*. Retrieved from http://pewresearch.org/pubs/408/can-you-trust-what-polls-say-about-obamas-electoral-prospects

Kinder, D. R., & Sears, D. O. (1981). Prejudice and politics: Symbolic racism versus racial threats to the good life. *Journal of Personality and Social Psychology, 40*(3), 414–431.

Kruse, R. (2009). The geographical imagination of Barack Obama: Representing race and space in America. *Southeastern Geographer, 49*(3), 221–239.

Kuhn, D. (2008). Exit polls: How Obama won. *POLITCO.com*. Retrieved from http://www.politico.com/news/stories/1108/15297.html

Lopez, M., & Taylor, P. (2009). Dissecting the 2008 electorate: Most diverse in U.S. history. *Pew Research Center.* Retrieved from http://pewresearch.org/assets/pdf/dissecting-2008-electorate.pdf

Newport. F. (2008, June 9). Most say race will not be a factor in their presidential vote. *Gallup.* Retrieved from http://www.gallup.com/poll/107770/Most-Say-Race-Will-Factor-Their-Presidential-Vote.aspx

Philpot, T., Shaw, D., & McGowen, E. (2009). Winning the race: Black voter turnout in the 2008 presidential election. *Public Opinion Quarterly, 73*(5), 995–1022.

Piston, S. (2010). How explicit racial prejudice hurt Obama in the 2008 election. *Political Behavior, 32*(4), 431–451.

Redlawsk, D. P., Tolbert, C., & Franko, W. (2010). Voters, emotions, and race in 2008: Obama as the first Black president. *Political Research Quarterly, 63*(4), 875–889.

Scocca, T. (2012). Eighty-eight percent of Romney voters were White. *Slate.* Retrieved from http://www.slate.com/articles/news_and_politics/scocca/2012/11/mitt_romney_white_voters_the_gop_candidate_s_race_based_monochromatic_campaign.html

Simba, M. (2009). The Obama campaign 2008: A historical overview. *The Western Journal of Black Studies, 33*(3), 186–191.

Taylor, P. (2012). *The growing electoral clout of Blacks is driven by turnout, not demographics.* Retrieved from http://www.pewsocialtrends.org/2012/12/26/the-growing-electoral-clout-of-Blacks-is-driven-by-turnout-not-demographics

Touré. (2012, October 19). *Viewpoint: Will Blacks vote for Obama "because he's Black"?* Retrieved from http://ideas.time.com/2012/10/19/viewpoint-will-Blacks-vote-for-obama-because-hes-Black/#ixzz2LZ0ru9yw

Williams, J. (2007, November 30). Obama's color line. *New York Times.* Retrieved from http://www.nytimes.com/2007/11/30/opinion/30williams.html

Wingfield, A. H., & Feagin, J. R. (2009). *Yes we can: White racial framing and the 2008 presidential election.* New York, NY: Routledge.

Wise, T. (2009). *Between Barack and a hard place: Racism and White denial in the age of Obama.* San Francisco, CA: City Light Books.

Zoll, R. (2012, September 16). Some Black clergy tell flock to skip vote. *Newsday.* Retrieved from http://www.newsday.com/news/nation/some-black-clergy-tell-flock-to-skip-vote-1.4008706

"We Don't Have to Listen to Al Sharpton Anymore"

Obama's Election and Triumphalist Media Narratives of Post-Racial America[1]

Enid Logan

University of Minnesota

Enid Logan is an associate professor of sociology at the University of Minnesota. She writes on race, gender, electoral politics, and the body, focusing on the experiences of people of African descent in the United States and in Latin America.

In November 2008, Barack Obama was elected to his first term as president of the United States. In the weeks following the 2008 election, as in the months that preceded it, numerous social observers from across the ideological spectrum offered commentary concerning the cultural, social, and political significance of the Obama phenomenon. While the voices were not monolithic, a sort of consensus

---

[1] A previous version of this essay was published as Chapter 2 of Logan's 2011 book, *At This Defining Moment: Barack Obama's Presidential Candidacy and the New Politics of Race*, New York University Press.

emerged in the public sphere. From the pages of major newspapers, news magazines, and political blogs, the pundits spoke, triumphantly, of the "major transformation" that had taken place in the life of the nation. With Obama's win, the *Wall Street Journal* and the *Boston Globe* claimed, the old politics of race, focusing on Black grievance, victimhood, and protest were vanquished, leaving in their place newer, more effective ways of getting things done. MSNBC and *Forbes Magazine* stated that Obama's success demonstrated that if racism was not dead, surely it was on its way out. And the *Washington Post, New York Times,* and *Black Enterprise Magazine* declared boldly that while the election held many lessons for the country as a whole, the ones it offered to Blacks were among the most important: it was time to stop complaining about racism and take full responsibility for their own lives.

The week after Obama's 2008 win, Black journalist Juan Williams declared in the *Wall Street Journal* that "the idea of black politics now tilts away from leadership based on voicing grievance, and identity politics based on victimization and anger." As Williams and others triumphantly slammed the door on the "old black politics," the pundits displayed special zeal in shoving the "old black politicians" out of the door with them. Obama's ascent was repeatedly cast as the final verdict on the tactics and careers of Jesse Jackson and Al Sharpton, whom many in the pundit class consistently discussed in ways that betrayed their disgust and irritation. In a 2007 *National Journal Magazine* article, one writer triumphantly proclaimed that with Obama's rise, America could "relegate to the dustbin of history the snake-oil salesmen who have been anointed by the media as the leaders of black America, even as they have used their prominence to poison race relations while in many cases living high on the hog" (Taylor, 2007).

Civil rights leaders and others who explicitly addressed the issue of racism were widely characterized as "race-baiters" and "agitators." Race, we were told, had hardly factored into the election at all, and Whites, through their support for Obama, had truly proven themselves to be color-blind. Essentially, race had been revealed to be a problem of people of color. Moreover, Obama's success was said to especially prove that affirmative action was unfair, and that Blacks who were struggling to make it were largely to blame for their own problems.

These types of interpretations of the significance of Barack Obama's win found in major American press outlets were strongly undergirded by the ideology of color-blind individualism. Sociologists have identified color-blind individualism as the dominant racial ideology of the post-civil rights era (Ansell, 2006; Bonilla-Silva, 2010; Brown, Carnoy, Currie, & Duster, 2003; Gallagher, 2003; Guinier & Torres, 2002; Winant, 2001). The central axiom of color-blind individualism is that we have already achieved an essentially color-blind society. While most Whites hold that they and others like them simply do not see race, people of color are understood to be irrationally preoccupied with color. In addition, acts of discrimination against people of color are viewed as infrequent, unlikely, and overreported. Persistent racial inequality, on the other hand, is viewed as natural and inevitable or explained as being due to the cultural deficiencies of people of color. Blacks, in particular, are called to "get over their victim mentalities," stop looking for increasingly rare instances of racism, and pull themselves up by their own bootstraps.

The danger of this ideology is that it works in many ways to hinder the achievement of racial justice. It demands a blindness to the historically accumulated advantages that

Whites receive in this society, as well as to the covert, routine mechanisms of discrimination that are in place today. It naturalizes racial inequality and allows strong anti-Black views to flourish under the cover of supposed race-blindness. Increasingly, this perspective positions Whites either as exempt from racial matters or as victims of "reverse racism." Furthermore, under this perspective, the achievement of abstract equality before the law, or "race neutrality," entirely supplants the goal of substantive equality. Thus, efforts to achieve parity in education or employment, for example, are characterized as illegitimate, anti-American, and unfair to Whites (Ansell, 2006; Bonilla-Silva, 2010; Gallagher, 2003; Lewis, 2001; Powell, 2009; see also Moore, Essay 20).

In this essay, I identify and critically evaluate the predominant narrative interpretation of the meaning of Obama's victory, which I call "the triumphalist narrative of post-race America." The central claim of this narrative was that with the election of Barack Obama, the United States had effectively overcome the scourge of racism. Whereas before the American public had "lesser" examples of Black success that suggested that racism was on its way out (e.g., Oprah Winfrey, Michael Jordan, Will Smith, and Tiger Woods), having a Black man in the White House signaled to many that racism was irrefutably dead. Post-race triumphalism thus goes significantly beyond the racial color-blindness discussed in the work of scholars such as Bonilla-Silva (2010), Gallagher (2003), Brown et al. (2003), and Guinier and Torres (2003). For many commentators in the American media, Obama was as a definitive, living embodiment of the end of racism in the United States, and therefore became the lightning rod for this type of discourse.

There are many reasons to be wary of post-race triumphalism however. A careful analysis reveals that this ostensibly celebratory narrative encodes a series of deeply problematic assumptions about Black Americans, the course of American history, and the roots of social inequality. Its assertion that the nation had been proven to be officially color-blind ignored the crucial, if complicated role race played in the 2008 presidential race. Most fundamentally, this narrative strongly supported the conservative, color-blind individualist perspective on race—a perspective that masks and defends entrenched racial inequality, while paradoxically claiming to champion racial justice.

The present essay draws upon several hundred news articles appearing in major newspapers, magazines, widely read political blogs, and other large media outlets in the months immediately before and after the 2008 election. The objects of my analysis, therefore, are the interpretative frames pertaining to the election found in the American media, a powerful means of socialization, particularly regarding race. It is vital that scholars and students alike critically engage these discourses, because the interpretations of Obama's victory that they encapsulate are implicated in the ways in which the meaning of race in American society is being renegotiated (see also Thornhill, Essay 5).

The Role of Color-Blind Racial Ideology in the 2008 Presidential Race

Three interrelated claims formed the cornerstones of the triumphalist narrative of post-race America. Each is explained in detail below along with a critical analysis.

A Nation Redeemed

The first claim of the triumphalist narrative was that Obama's victory redeemed the United States by proving that we were truly blind to color. A nearly universal claim of the pundit class was that Obama's victory stood as an affirmation of our most cherished national ideals and demonstrated the greatness of the nation. In the *Wall Street Journal*, for example, Black conservative Shelby Steele described the win as "documentation of the moral evolution we have gone through in the past 40 years" (Weisman & Meckler, 2008). Pundits especially emphasized Obama's purported power to redeem the United States in the eyes of the world. Whereas the "disgraceful" years of the Bush administration had led international leaders to regard the United States with condescension and scorn, our selection of Obama was said to have led to renewed appreciation. As a writer in the *Los Angeles Times* declared on November 5, "If the U.S. can overcome its racial past, it gives hope to other democracies as well" (Cain, 2008).

Despite claims like these that Obama's victory redeemed the nation by proving us to be truly blind to race, it is clear that the election was thoroughly saturated with racial meaning. For example, many of the attacks on the candidate relied upon veiled or explicit references to race (Wingfield & Feagin, 2010). But even more importantly, I submit, Obama's *appeal* to many voters was linked to his color as well. It was, after all, largely *from* his Blackness and *through* his Blackness that Obama was believed capable of redeeming the nation. Though Hillary Clinton's bid for the presidency was equally historic, there was, from the beginning, a presumption that an Obama presidency would be somehow more significant and more transformative for the nation. As Benjamin Wallace-Wells wrote in a November 2006 *Washington Post* article, "There is the sense that, by electing a female president, the nation would be meeting a standard set by other liberal democracies; the election of a black man, by contrast, would be a particularly American achievement, an affirmation of American ideals and a celebration of American circumstances."

In addition, Obama's attempt to portray himself as the embodiment of hope and change during the Democratic primary was astoundingly successful, despite the fact that his policies differed very little from those of his opponent. Obama's tremendous appeal to many voters stemmed in part from his personal charm and relative youth. But it was also certainly due to his race. To quote Black conservative Shelby Steele (2008) in the *LA Times*,

> Obama's special charisma . . . always came much more from the racial idealism he embodied than from his political ideas. In fact, this was his only true political originality. . . . This worked politically for Obama because it tapped into a deep longing in American life—the longing on the part of whites to escape the stigma of racism.

Post-Civil Rights and Nearly Post-Race

The second pillar of the triumphalist narrative was the claim that we had officially solved the problem of race. Obama's ascent was especially said to prove that racism in the United States was no longer systematic or institutionalized. In the *Chicago Tribune*, for example, liberal Black columnist Clarence Page (2008) stated, "It's hard to argue that our society is irredeemably racist when our multiracial electorate just elected a man with African roots and an Arabic-sounding name to be commander-in-chief." Still others claimed that with the election, the United States had solved the problem of race entirely. According to columnist Phillip Morris (2008), on November 4, "the nation unburdened itself of the albatross of race" and "completed its evolution into a racial meritocracy." And in the *Philadelphia Daily News,* writer Stu Bykofsky (2008) declared that with Obama's victory, "America got the race monkey off its back."

Such claims warrant careful interrogation, for while Obama's victory was an important milestone, a great deal of sociological research has revealed just how far we are from achieving a society that is racially just. We can begin by looking at the criminal justice system. Although Blacks comprise just 12.5% of the general population, they are nearly half of those in prison, and 42% of those on death row (Snell, 2010; see also Doude, Essay 19). In our supposedly race-blind society, White felons are more likely to be called back for a job interview than Blacks with no criminal record (Pager, 2003). Persistent residential segregation means that Blacks across the socioeconomic spectrum are far more likely to live in areas of super concentrated poverty, thus exposing them to higher levels of violence, social isolation, and chronic unemployment (Massey, 2000). Recent research has further shown that the extension of subprime loans to low-income borrowers of color in the 1990s made these homeowners especially vulnerable to foreclosure and increased the rate of residential segregation in many areas (Bond & Williams, 2007).

Inequality in the area of public education is particularly glaring. In the last decade and a half, courts around the country have reversed integration orders from the 1960s and 1970s, sending Black and Latino students back to schools that are 90% and above non-White (Boger & Orfield, 2005). Such high indices of segregation make it likely that the funding received in majority White and majority non-White school districts will continue to be vastly unequal, due to the greater political and economic power of White parents compared to parents of color (Kozol, 2005). History has shown us that "separate" is inherently unequal; the effects today are devastating (see also Meanwell, Patel, & McClure, Essay 13). In certain major American cities, fewer than 1 in 3 Black males graduates from high school and most Black male high school dropouts are eventually incarcerated (Edelman, Holzer, & Offner, 2006; Schott Foundation, 2008).

Sociologists have determined that one of the most important explanations for the persistence of racial inequality is the racial wealth gap (Oliver & Shapiro, 2006). The median net worth of the average White family in the United States is currently estimated to be *22 times* that of the average Black family (Luhby, 2012). The ideology of racial color-blindness implies that the wealth gap must be due to racial differences in drive and initiative—that is, Whites have more because they have worked harder. But a review of the historical record reveals that the wealth gap was created by generations of government programs and other policies that systematically favored Whites (Lui, Robles, Leondar-Wright, Brewer, & Adamson, 2006; see also Ioanide, Essay 6, & Moore, Essay 20). It has also been shown that racial differences in wealth have a substantial impact on other dimensions of racial inequality, including the likelihood of employment, years of education completed, marital stability, and out-of-wedlock births. Thus, some scholars argue that unless there is a leveling of the mechanisms of wealth accumulation, it will be virtually impossible for Blacks to achieve parity with Whites (Conley, 2010).

We must also keep in mind that the significance of race in America cannot be fully captured in statistics. Race pertains also to the domains of culture and ideas. In the recent election, pundits were obsessed with the question of race even before Obama officially declared his candidacy. Commentators asked: *Is Obama really Black? Is he Black enough? What kind of Black person is he?* (e.g., Coates, 2007; Crouch, 2006; Dickerson, 2007). Questions about Obama's racial identity were clearly embedded with a myriad of others. These included: *Will Obama make White Americans feel uncomfortable about race, or will he just let the issue go? Is he like or unlike "race baiters" and "agitators" like Al Sharpton and Jesse Jackson? Are we or are we not ready as a country to move beyond race? How did such a mild-mannered guy end up married to such an angry, bitter Black woman? Just how patriotic is Obama? Is he in fact, American at all?* Race may have mattered in the election in ways that were surprising, more complicated, or less predictable than we may have imagined, but to say that it mattered not at all is manifestly false.

We've Done Our Part, Black America, Now It's Up to You

The third aspect of the post-race triumphalist narrative that I highlight here concerns the meaning of the election for Black people. Essentially, the narrative claimed that all it would take for Blacks to be fully integrated into the American mainstream was a solid work ethic and a willingness to stop blaming Whites for all their problems. While different observers claimed that Obama's victory offered hope to Blacks, one argument forwarded by the press resonated above all: A Black president meant that the days of complaining about White racism were over. It was time for Blacks to give up their crippling sense of victimhood and claim full responsibility for their own lives.

The personal responsibility theme was originally introduced into the discussion by the candidate himself. During the 21 months of his campaign, Obama garnered both praise and scorn for repeatedly calling upon "Ray Ray," "Cousin Pookie" (in his own words), and other mythical low-income Black males to get up off the couch, go vote, and be responsible fathers to their children (e.g., Walsh, 2008). Black and White pundits alike seized upon this message with relish. A week after the election, retired Black columnist William Raspberry (a 40-year veteran of the *Washington Post*) wrote that Blacks must start to "see life as a series of problems and possibilities" rather than "just a list of grievances" (Raspberry, 2008). And conservative writer Stuart Taylor (2007) claimed that Obama's success "should tell black children everywhere that they, too, can succeed, and they do not need handouts or reparations."

In evaluating the personal responsibility argument, it is vital to note that Barack Obama was *not* just "any" Black man or woman. First, he was a Black man almost unlike any other—possessing a series of elite socioeconomic characteristics. Obama entered the race with educational qualifications that were far beyond the reach of most Americans, Black or non-Black alike. As repeatedly emphasized during the campaign, he came to politics with an Ivy League education, having served as editor of the *Harvard Law Review*, and later, as a law professor at the University of Chicago.

Secondly, he possesses an atypically "Black" personal biography. As the son of an East African immigrant, he had no Black ancestral ties to the histories of slavery or segregation in this country. Critical observers claimed from early in the race that Obama's appeal to Whites stemmed in large part from the fact that his biography allowed them to sidestep or ignore the realities of our racial history. As MSNBC commentator Chris Matthews declared in January 2007, "No history of Jim Crow, no history of anger, no history of slavery. . . . All the bad stuff in our history ain't there with this guy" (P. Williams, 2007). This particular point of view was one that Obama himself reinforced. From his 2004 speech at the Democratic National Convention forward, Obama repeatedly declared that "only in America is my story possible." Thus, through Obama, the slave was transformed into a voluntary migrant and notably, one who had achieved the American dream.

Finally, Obama had a "mainstream" (i.e., Whitened) physical appearance. Consider Obama's *physical* presentation of Blackness as a light-skinned, biracial man. Numerous studies of "colorism" have found that light skin has long offered myriad advantages to those socially categorized as Black in the United States (Hochschild & Weaver, 2007; Keith & Herring, 1991). Obama's appearance thus offered him a presumption of intelligence, trustworthiness, attractiveness, and safety, not available to the majority of Blacks, whose skin color, hair texture, and facial features make them more "typically" and problematically Black.

I do not wish to imply in any way that Obama is "not really Black" or less "authentically" Black than are other Black Americans. But it must be noted that his experiences and background made him far from the "average" Black man, and thus mean that it is profoundly illogical to argue that his success proves that the gateways of opportunity are fully open to all Black Americans.

Conclusion

While the arguments detailed in the media's triumphalist narrative are highly reductive, they have a certain appeal. After November 4, 2008, there was in this country a deep desire to celebrate Obama's victory, to make sense of it, and to take stock of where we were as a nation. In this context, the story that the media pundits offered—that the United States was still a land of opportunity, and that Blacks who worked hard could sail to the highest of heights—was a powerful one. The danger of this narrative, however, is that while it was superficially cloaked in the language of triumph and possibility, it was also firmly grounded in notions of White racial innocence and Black cultural pathology. Furthermore, though it utterly failed to grasp the complex, multidimensional nature of the social construct of race, this narrative is nevertheless poised to become the new common sense about race in the United States today.

The pundits hailed the Age of Obama as the dawn of a new era in racial politics, and as evidence of the nation's definitive triumph over the problem of race. But far from proving the nation to be "beyond" the issue of race, the 2008 presidential election was thoroughly saturated with racial meaning. Furthermore, the supposition that the United States has largely solved its racial problems may be disproven by a consideration of the deep and in many cases widening indices of racial inequality. And though there are those that assert that Obama's story proves that the failure of poor Blacks to rise from the bottom of the socioeconomic hierarchy is best explained by their cultural deficiencies, it was the exceptional, atypical, "post-racial" nature of Obama's Blackness that was crucial to his all-American success.

The outcome of the 2008 presidential election, then, in no way proves that we are a nation that is beyond race. An irony of the election of our first Black president is that the narrative forwarded in celebration of his victory may serve in fact to "stall transformation of the racial order in the direction of greater equality" (*Ansell, 2006,* p. 333). But we do find ourselves in a moment of possibility. After several years of race talk accompanying Obama's meteoric ascent, hegemonic conceptions of the ways that race operates in this society may be in a period of relative flux and renegotiation. Just how the nation's racial history will unfold from here forward, however, remains to be seen.

Suggested Additional Resources

Logan, E. (2011). *At this defining moment: Barack Obama's presidential candidacy and the new politics of race.* New York, NY: New York University Press.

See also these opinion pieces on Obama and racial identity, most of which are available online:

Beinart, P. (2007, February 5). Black like me: Why White people like Barack Obama. *The New Republic.*

Chang, R. (2009–2010). Asian Americans and the road to the White House: Musings on being invisible. *Asian American Law Journal, 16,* 205–213.

Coates, T. P. (2008, May 1). A deeper black. *The Nation.*

Crouch, S. (2006, November 2). Not Black like me. *New York Daily News.*

Graves, E. G., Sr. (2008). No more excuses. *Black Enterprise.*

Gray, K. A. (2008, July 11). Why does Barack Obama hate my family? Vilifying Black men to win favor with The Man. *Counterpunch.*

Harris, P. (2008, August 10). Young, gifted, Black . . . and leading America. *UK Observer.*

Kamiya, G. (2008, February 26). It's OK to vote for Obama because he's Black. *Salon.*

Lovato, R. (2008, January 22). Everyone's an expert on the Latino vote, except Latinos. *Huffington Post.*

Luqman, A. (2007, July 6). Obama's tightrope. *Washington Post.*

Obama, B. (2008, March 18). A more perfect union. *Organizing for America.*

Samuel, T. (2008, April 25). On the 2008 primary and Black anger. *The American Prospect.*

Serwer, A. (2008, December 5). He's Black get over it. *The American Prospect.*

Steele, S. (2008, November 5). Obama's post-racial promise. *Los Angeles Times.*

Wallace-Wells, B. (2006, November 12). Is America too racist for Barack? Too sexist for Hillary? *Washington Post.*

Williams, J. (2008, November 10). What Obama's victory means for racial politics. *Wall Street Journal.*

Questions for Further Discussion

1. Do you feel that the election of the first woman president would have been equally as significant as the election of the first Black president? Why or why not?

2. What do you make of the argument that Obama was able to win the election because he was an "exceptional" Black man? Which, if any, of the aspects of his identity that the author highlights do you think were the most important—his physical appearance, his Black immigrant background, or his elite education?

3. The author writes that Obama's win does *not* mean that the United States has solved the problem of race. But what, then, does it mean? What, to you, was the significance of the victory?

Reaching Beyond the Color Line

1. Race was again an important issue in the 2012 presidential election. But much of the coverage this time focused on Black Republican presidential nominee Herman Cain. How did race figure into discussions of Cain's candidacy? What kinds of parallels and distinctions were drawn between Cain and Obama? How do you think that race will factor into the 2016 presidential election, as the Republican Party seeks to appeal to a broader base of voters? Identify and analyze 5 to 7 articles discussing these issues. Also see Logan's essay, "Let Herman Be Herman: Republican Presidential Candidate Herman Cain and the Utility of Blackness for the Political Right" for some ideas.[2]

References

Boger, J. C., & Orfield, G. (2005). *School resegregation: Must the South turn back?* Chapel Hill: University of North Carolina Press.

Bond, C., & Williams, R. (2007). Residential segregation and the transformation of home mortgage lending. *Social Forces, 86*(2), 671–698.

Bonilla-Silva, E. (2010). *Racism without racists: Color-blind racism and the persistence of racial inequality in the United States* (3rd ed.). Lanham, MD: Rowman & Littlefield.

---

[2] As found at http://thesocietypages.org/specials/herman-cain.

Brown, M. K., Carnoy, M., Currie, E., & Duster, T. (2003). *Whitewashing race: The myth of a color-blind society*. Berkeley: University of California Press.

Bykofsky, S. (2008, November 6). My first post-racial column: America is on the ascent. *Philadelphia Daily News*. Retrieved from http://articles.philly.com/2008-11-06/news/24992437_1_post-racial-discrimination-bad-behavior

Cain, B. (2008, November 5). How long will the GOP be in the cold? (What Obama's win means for politics and America). *Los Angeles Times*. Retrieved from http://www.latimes.com/news/opinion/la-oew-schnur-cain5-2008nov05,0,7982924.story#ixzz2rTWyLsQt

Coates, T. P. (2007, April 13). Is Obama Black enough? *Time*. Retrieved from http://www.time.com/time/nation/article/0,8599,1584736,00.html

Conley, D. (2010). *Being Black, living in the red: Race, wealth, and social policy in America* (10th anniv. ed.). Berkeley: University of California Press.

Crouch, S. (2006, November 2). What Obama isn't: Black like me on race. *New York Daily News*. Retrieved from http://www.nydailynews.com/archives/opinions/obama-isn-black-race-article-1.585922

Dickerson, D. (2007, January 22). Colorblind: Barack Obama would be the great Black hope in the next presidential race—if he were actually Black. *Salon.com*. Retrieved from http://www.salon.com/news/opinion/feature/2007/01/22/obama

Edelman, P., Holzer, H. J., & Offner, P. (2006). *Reconnecting disadvantaged young men*. Washington, DC: Urban Institute Press.

Gallagher, C. A. (2003). Colorblind privilege: The social and political functions of erasing the color line in post-race America. *Race, Gender and Class, 10*, 22–37.

Guinier, L., & Torres, G. (2003). *The miner's canary: Enlisting race, resisting power, transforming democracy*. Cambridge, MA: Harvard University Press.

Hochschild, J., & Weaver, V. (2007). The skin color paradox and the American racial order. *Social Forces, 86*, 643–670.

Keith, V. M., & Herring, C. (1991). Skin tone and stratification in the Black community. *American Journal of Sociology, 97*(3), 760–778.

Kozol, J. (2005). *The shame of the nation: The restoration of apartheid schooling in America*. New York, NY: Crown.

Lewis, A. (2001). There is no "race" in the schoolyard: Color-blind ideology in an almost all-White school. *American Educational Research Journal, 28*(4), 781–811.

Logan, E. (2011). *"At this defining moment": Barack Obama's Presidential candidacy and the new politics of race*. New York: New York University Press.

Luhby, T. (2012, June 21). *Worsening wealth inequality by race*. CNN Money. Retrieved from http://money.cnn.com/2012/06/21/news/economy/wealth-gap-race/index.htm

Lui, M., Robles, B., Leondar-Wright, B., Brewer, R., & Adamson, R. (2006). *The color of wealth: The story behind the U.S. racial wealth divide*. New York, NY: New Press.

Massey, D. (2000). Residential segregation and neighborhood conditions in U.S. metropolitan areas. In N. Smelser, W. J. Wilson, & F. Mitchell (Eds.), *America becoming: Racial trends and their consequences* (pp. 391–434). Washington, DC: National Academies Press.

Morris, P. (2008, November 5). America begins its journey into a post-racial era. *Cleveland Plain Dealer*. Retrieved from http://www.cleveland.com/morris/index.ssf/2008/11/phillip_morris_america_begins.html

Oliver, M., & Shapiro, T. (2006). *Black wealth/White wealth: A new perspective on racial inequality*. New York, NY: Routledge.

Page, C. (2008, November 9). Jackson's eloquent tears. *Chicago Tribune*. Retrieved from http://articles.chicagotribune.com/2008-11-09/news/0811080277_1_election-night-barack-obama-exit-polls

Pager, D. (2003). The mark of a criminal record. *American Journal of Sociology, 108*, 937–975.

Powell, J. (2009). Post-racialism or targeted universalism? *Denver University Law Review, 86*(1), 785–806.

Raspberry, W. (2008, November 11). A path beyond grievance. *Washington Post*. Retrieved from http://www.washingtonpost.com/wp-dyn/content/article/2008/11/10/AR2008111001544.html

Schott Foundation for Public Education. (2008). *Given half a chance. The Schott 50 state report on public education and Black males*. Retrieved from http://www.blackboysreport.org

Snell, T. (2010). *Table 5: Demographic characteristics of prisoners under sentence of death, 2008. Capital Punishment, 2008- Statistical Tables*. U.S. Department of Justice Bureau of Justice Statistics. Retrieved from http://bjs.ojp.usdoj.gov/content/pub/pdf/cp08st.pdf

Steele, S. (2008, November 5). Obama's post-racial promise. *Los Angeles Times*. Retrieved from http://articles.latimes.com/2008/nov/05/opinion/oe-steele5

Taylor, S., Jr. (2007, February 3). The great Black-White hope. *The Atlantic*. Retrieved from http://www.theatlantic.com/magazine/archive/2007/02/the-great-black-white-hope/5647

Wallace-Wells, B. (2006, November 12). Is America too racist for Barack? Too sexist for Hillary? *Washington Post*. Retrieved from http://www.washingtonpost.com/wp-dyn/content/article/2006/11/10/AR2006111001387.html

Walsh, J. (2008, June 16). Obama on Father's Day: A tough, moving speech about absent fathers, including his own. *Salon.com*. Retrieved from http://www.salon.com/news/opinion/joan_walsh/feature/2008/06/16/obama_fathers_day

Weisman, J., & Meckler, L. (2008, November 6). Obama sweeps to historic victory: Nation elects its first African-American president amid record turnout; turmoil in economy dominates voters' concerns. *Wall Street Journal*. Retrieved from http://online.wsj.com/article/NA_WSJ_PUB:SB122581133077197035.html

Williams, P. (2007, March 5). L'étranger. *The Nation*. Retrieved from http://www.thenation.com/issue/march-5-2007

Winant, H. (2001). *The world is a ghetto: Race and democracy since World War II*. New York, NY: Basic Books.

Wingfield, A. H., & Feagin, J. R. (2010). *Yes we can? White racial framing and the 2008 presidential campaign*. New York, NY: Routledge.

"We Need to Take Care of 'Real Americans' First"

Historical and Contemporary Definitions of Citizenship

Kara Cebulko

Providence College

Kara Cebulko is an assistant professor of sociology and global studies at Providence College. Her current research focuses on legal status and the experiences of children of Brazilian immigrants in the United States. She teaches courses on immigration and global studies. Her book, *Documented, Undocumented and Something Else: The Incorporation of Children of Brazilian Immigrants*, was published in 2013 by LFB Scholarly.

Since 2001, anti-immigration laws have increased around the country. These laws capitalize on fears that we must protect "real Americans" from an "immigrant invasion," fears that are at least in part, constructed through media and public discourse (see Chavez, 2008).[1] But who, exactly, are "real" Americans

---

[1] The most explicit and vitriol rhetoric of protecting "real Americans" from immigrants appears in the comments' sections of online news articles and anti-immigrant websites. But the discourse is also present in mainstream media. In 2006, Patrick Buchanan, a one-time presidential candidate and analyst for MCNBC, expressed his alarm at the "invasion" of immigrants. His *New York Times* bestseller, *State of Emergency: The Third World Invasion and Conquest of America,* laments that immigration will ensure that White Europeans will become minority in the United States. See Chavez (2008) for a full discussion on the construction of the present-day Latino Threat Narrative in the media and public discourse.

and who aren't? As we will see, defining *who is, who can be, and who should be* an American—has been a reoccurring theme throughout American history (Daniels, 1998; Hing, 2004; Ngai, 2004). Because members of a nation-state cannot possibly know everyone in their national community, the nation-state is an "imagined community" (Anderson, 1991). Importantly, this "imagined community"—the collective vision of who we are—shapes (and is shaped by) immigration policies that decide entry and removal, access to citizenship and rights, and ultimately, the composition of the American community (Zolberg, 2006). Throughout history, race, ethnicity, and religion have played a large role in this collective vision of who we are and our immigration policies.

"Illegal Aliens," Presidents, and "Real Americans"

Posing for a photo op in 2007, then-leading Democratic candidate for President Hillary Rodham Clinton, held up a T-shirt that read, "Legalize the Irish!" Four years later, on April 27, 2011, the White House released the long form of President Barack Hussein Obama's birth certificate, despite the fact that rumors claiming he was not a U.S.-born citizen had long been discredited. Yet, the "birther" rumors, and the claims that President Obama is not a "real American" persist today.

What do these two seemingly different events have in common? Together, they say a lot about the roles that race, ethnicity, and religion play in the collective vision of who we are as a nation. The contrast is striking. On the one hand, an influential politician, Hillary Clinton poses for a photo op with "illegal aliens"—persons who exist at the outer most edge of American society—calling for their formal, legal inclusion into the national community.[2] Notably, there was no media or political firestorm denouncing her photo op with the *White, Irish,* "illegal aliens." On the other hand, the President of the United States continues to face allegations that he is not, in fact, a "real American." The irony, of course, is that the President's own biography seems to be the quintessential American immigrant success story: the son of an immigrant who worked hard, overcame obstacles, and became one of the most powerful men in the world. But of course, President Obama is not the son of an Irish man. He is the son of a Kenyan man. Moreover, his middle name is *Hussein.* Thus, in the eyes of some, he could not possibly be an American, even if he is the president of the United States. It is hard to imagine these stories playing out in similar fashion had the "illegal aliens" been Mexican rather than Irish and President Obama been White rather than Black with a Muslim middle name. Together, these two examples remind us that despite the diversity in contemporary America and the racial progress we have made, the collective vision of who we are (and who we should be) remains one of a White, Christian nation.

---

[2] *Illegal immigrant* and *illegal alien* are dehumanizing terms. Indeed, no human being is "illegal." Illegality is not an inherent condition of a person, it is produced by immigration laws—laws that change in each historical time period, reflecting the sociopolitical context of the time (De Genova, 2002; Ngai, 2004). Furthermore *illegality* suggests criminality. Being in the United States without documents, however, is a civil—not a criminal—offense.

The stories we tell about our nation's past and specifically, stories of voluntary, White European immigrants, also reflect this collective vision of ourselves (Chomsky, 2004). After all, largely excluded in the White European immigrant narrative are the experiences of people of color, experiences that often include forced migration, enslavement, or exclusion. The narrative also obscures the ways in which Whiteness has always provided advantages in access to entry, to citizenship, and to the full rights and privileges of citizenship. Moreover, it serves as a false and unattainable measuring stick against which today's immigrants, who largely hail from Latin America and Asia, are compared. Thus, it is important to debunk the White European immigrant narrative. When we do, we can see the ways in which becoming an American largely included "becoming White" and was aided by laws, public policy, government programs, unions, self-distancing by immigrants themselves, and by a time of economic expansion and decreased migration from Europe. But the question remains: Is Whiteness still key to becoming an American? Not only in regard to the law, but in the eyes of the public?

The Stories We Tell: The Great (White) Immigrant Narrative and the Immigrant Threats of Today

Look, I'm the son of an Italian immigrant. I think immigration is one of the great things that has made this country the dynamic country that it continues to be. . . . And so we should not have a debate talking about how we don't want people to come to this country, but we want them to come like my grandfather and my father came here. They made sacrifices. They came in the 1920's. There were no promises. There were no government benefits.

–Former senator Rick Santorum, R-PA, September 2011,
Republican Primary Presidential Debate

The story that many Americans, especially White Americans, tell resembles the story Senator Rick Santorum told (above) during a 2011 debate. It is a story that contrasts a nostalgic, romanticized immigrant past with a threatening story of an immigrant present. Thus, on one hand, many Americans celebrate the stories of past European immigrants who, according to the narrative, came to the United States "legally," pulled themselves up by their own bootstraps, and were quick to culturally and structurally assimilate—learning English, quickly adopting norms, beliefs, and values of American society, and ultimately, achieving the American dream. But on the other hand, these same Americans fear that today's immigrants, mostly immigrants of color, are poor "invaders/aliens" who migrate "illegally," refuse to assimilate, take jobs and resources away from "real" Americans, and ultimately threaten our national identity as a (White) Anglo-Saxon Christian nation (Huntington, 2004a, 2004b). Yet, as we will see, the United States has a history of viewing immigrants as threats and seeking restrictions on their migration and citizenship.

A History of Restriction and Exclusion of the "Other"

While many Americans assume that that United States has always welcomed immigrants as long as they work hard and assimilate, the reality is that from the colonial era to the present day, some nativist groups have pushed for restrictive and exclusionary laws and policies to protect "real Americans" from "threatening Others." At the heart of these historical and present-day fears lies the belief that America's national identity as a White, Anglo-Saxon, and Christian (Protestant) nation is in peril. For example, political scientist Samuel Huntington (2004a) argued that "the persistent inflow of Hispanic immigrants threatens to divide the United States into two peoples, two cultures, and two languages" since Latino immigrants are "rejecting the Anglo-Protestant values that built the American dream." Momentarily setting aside the claim that Latino immigrants are failing to assimilate, Huntington's fears are remarkable for their similarity to Benjamin Franklin's fears in 1751:

> Why Should Pennsylvania, founded by the English, become a Colony of Aliens, who will be so numerous as to Germanize us instead of our Anglicizing them, and will never adopt our Language or Customs, any more than they can acquire our Complexion. (as cited in Daniels, 1998, p. 38)

Germans then, Latinos now. The message is clear in both examples. Germans and Latinos are too numerous, incapable of assimilating (i.e., "will never adopt our Language or Customs"), and threaten America's Anglo-Protestant culture. Today, of course, the threat of Germans to America's national identity seems absurd. But in the eyes of many in 1751, the German threat was real, as was the Irish Catholic threat and the subsequent Italian threat. In all cases, these groups were seen as too numerous, incapable of assimilating, and as taking jobs from "real Americans." The hostility also led to restrictive immigration laws, such as the literacy law of 1917 and the National Origins Quota laws in the 1920s, which aimed to reduce the migration of Southern and Eastern Europeans (Hing, 2004).

The hostility and restrictions European groups faced were harsh, but paled in comparison to the exclusion, conquest, and extermination faced by Asians, Mexicans, other Latin Americans, Blacks, and Native Americans. Although the founding fathers wrote "All Men are Created Equal," the first Congress in 1790 limited citizenship through naturalization to "free White persons" of good moral character who had been in the United States for two years.[3] For persons who were of color and born in the United States, their access to citizenship depended on individual state laws (Daniels, 1998). Thus, although some White ethnic groups were subjected to xenophobic restriction laws, most who did arrive were allowed to become citizens through a relatively easy naturalization process (Ngai, 2004).[4]

---

[3] Citizenship in the United States is granted in three ways: (1) through birth on U.S. soil, (2) through naturalization—the process by which foreign nationals become citizens after meeting certain requirements, or (3) being born to U.S. parents abroad.

[4] For most of the 19th century, 5 years of residence and no criminal record were required for citizenship (Ngai, 2004). It was not until 1906 that English language ability was required for naturalization.

With citizenship, White ethnics gained access to other opportunities in achieving the American dream. In contrast, many (indeed, most) Blacks and Native Americans were enslaved, exterminated, pushed on to reservations, and later, (once granted citizenship) subjected to years of formal segregation and institutional discrimination. Meanwhile, xenophobia and racism led to laws that excluded Asian immigration altogether (on the grounds that they were "racially ineligible for citizenship") and relegated Mexican Americans to second-class citizenship in the American Southwest, the land that was their original homeland.

Racial requirements for citizenship were not fully lifted until 1952. But if Whiteness was so important for citizenship, *who* exactly was White? Whiteness, like all racial categories, was constructed over time, including through laws. The Johnson-Reed Act of 1924 and the Supreme Court Decisions of *Takao-Ozawa v. United States* (1922) and *United States v. Bhagat Singh Thind* (1923) were particularly instrumental in setting the legal boundaries of Whiteness (Ngai, 2004). Following on the heels of previous restriction and exclusion laws, the Johnson-Reed Act of 1924 sought to restrict Southern and Eastern European migration (on the grounds that they were inferior to Northern and Western Europeans) and ban all Asian migration (on the grounds that Asians were racially ineligible for citizenship). Ironically, while the law was discriminatory and reduced Southern and Eastern European migration, it also helped these very groups over time, as the law placed boundaries around Whiteness, boundaries that included them (Ngai, 2004).

The Supreme Court also played a large role in setting the legal boundaries of Whiteness. In 1922, in *Takao-Ozawa v. US*, Takao-Ozawa, a Japanese man, argued that the Japanese should be eligible for citizenship under the Naturalization Act of 1906—which limited citizenship to Whites and Blacks—because the Japanese were highly assimilable and that their "dominant strains are 'White persons,' speaking an Aryan tongue and having Caucasian root stock" (Ngai, 2004, p. 44). The Supreme Court ruled, however, that the Japanese were of the Mongolian race, not the "Caucasian" race. Thus, the Japanese were not White and ineligible for citizenship. Just months later, however, the Supreme Court reversed its own logic of using science as the basis of deciding Whiteness. In *U.S. v. Bhagat Singh Thind* (1923), Thind, a U.S. army veteran and Indian immigrant, used scientific evidence to claim that Indians were part of the Aryan race and thus, should be eligible for citizenship. But now, according to the Supreme Court, "Whiteness" was not based in science, but in what "the common man" said Whiteness was (Ngai, 2004).

Thus, the "law establishe[d] Whiteness as American identity" (Carbado, 2005, p. 637) and had very real effects on who became Americans and who had access to social and civil rights. Between 1907 and 1924, approximately 1.5 million immigrants became citizens, most all of whom were European immigrants (Ngai, 2004). Meanwhile, no amount of assimilation through socialization—adopting American customs and values—was enough to make Asians real Americans. "Real Americans" were those who not only adopted American values, but who could "become White" (Ngai, 2004). Without citizenship, Asians were denied other rights, including land ownership in most states (Hing, 2004; Ngai, 2004).

If Asians were deemed non-White, what about Mexicans? Per terms of the Treaty of Guadalupe Hidalgo in 1848, which ended the Mexican–American War, Mexico gave up the land that is now the American Southwest. Mexicans who remained on the land were allowed to become U.S. citizens. Since citizenship was restricted to "Whites," Mexican Americans were technically considered "White." But while legally White and legally citizens, Mexican Americans were "socially non-White" and the American public treated them as second-class citizens in their schools and communities—treatment akin to what Blacks experienced under Jim Crow segregation (Donato & Hanson, 2012).

The Historical "Rules" of Migration and the Production of Illegality

Some Americans state that they are not against immigration, just "illegal" immigration. This assertion is often accompanied by the claim that their ancestors came "legally" and thus, new immigrants should "play by the rules like my ancestors did." As Chomsky (2007) argues, this claim is "one of the most oft-repeated–and most puzzling comments" in the immigration debate (p. 53). It is puzzling and problematic for a number of reasons. First, as previously detailed, historically, the "rules" for migration have generally favored Europeans over other groups. Furthermore, the rules have changed over time. Thus, many White ethnics' ancestors would not be eligible to migrate under today's restrictions, which generally require family or employer sponsorships for migration (Immigration Policy Center, 2008). During the Open Door Era of Immigration, from 1776 until the late 1800s, there was no "line" for Europeans "to get in" because there generally were no restrictions on any migration (Bernard, 1998). When restrictions did emerge, Europeans continued to fare better than other groups. In contrast, today's restrictions on entry mean that there are few legal channels for entry, thus, there is no "line" for many immigrants around the world (Immigration Policy Center, 2008).

Second, this claim is problematic because it ignores the fact that some Europeans entered or stayed in the country "illegally" (and continue to do so). Restrictions on entry reduced but did not stop the flows of Southern and Eastern Europeans. Rather, the new laws made previously legal acts (i.e., migration) illegal or changed the route they took to come to America. But the sheer numbers of "illegal" Europeans never grew as large as the number of Mexicans. The question is, *why?* Part of the answer lies in policies that allowed Europeans to circumvent restriction laws *and* the selective application of (1) legalization policies and (2) enforcement policies.

Following the quota laws of 1921 and 1924 that restricted Southern and Eastern Europeans' entry at sea ports, thousands started arriving illegally into the United States through Canada and, especially, Mexico. It was their unlawful entry (and the unlawful entry of the Chinese), not the migration of Mexicans, that prompted the U.S. government to start heavy patrolling of its land borders and increasing deportation efforts. By the late 1920s, the flow of "illegal" Europeans had already declined. While enforcement policies (including the threat of deportation) may have deterred some migration, many Europeans actually circumvented the national origins restrictions through a different legal route: They migrated to Canada, and after 5 years of living in Canada, they were legally allowed to migrate to the United

States. Once in the United States, they could easily become U.S. citizens and then, legally apply to bring relatives into the United States as nonquota immigrants (Ngai, 2004).

Furthermore, Europeans benefited disproportionately from discretionary policies, which allowed certain "illegal" immigrants to legalize their status. Between 1925 and 1965, through various administrative policies and discretions, approximately 200,000 undocumented Europeans successfully adjusted their legal status (Ngai, 2004). The discourse painted White Europeans as "deserving" and as "good persons" whose lives should not be ruined for *minor* mistakes. These administrative policies and discretions, however, rarely benefited Mexicans, who were seen as poor criminals and who were racialized as "other" lying outside the "real American" community. Under this racialized construction, Mexicans became the main targets of enforcement policies (De Genova & Ramos-Zayas, 2003; Hing, 2004; Ngai 2004). Moreover, it was not just unauthorized Mexicans targeted for removal, but also lawfully present Mexicans and Mexican Americans. After the stock market crash of 1929, nativist alarm called for programs that encouraged Mexican and Mexican Americans, often through scare tactics, to return to Mexico. According to the U.S. Department of Labor, over 15 months, more than two million persons of Mexican descent returned to Mexico (Hing, 2004). While Mexicans were welcomed as laborers during economic booms (by some), they were never welcomed as persons, citizens, or as "real Americans."

Today, it is not just Mexicans, but all Latinos who are lumped together as "the threat" to American national identity (Chavez, 2008) and are the main targets of enforcement. Although the Department of Homeland Security emphasizes national security in the wake of 9/11 (implying a focus on counterterrorism), very few persons from countries the government associates with terrorism are deported. Instead, Afro-Caribbean drug peddlers (who, often, are lawful permanent residents) and Latino undocumented workers are disproportionately targeted (through racial profiling) for detention and deportation (Golash-Boza, 2012).

Immigrants, Past and Present, and Assimilation

Many Americans also assert that unlike previous waves of immigrants, today's immigrants do not want to assimilate. As Pat Buchanan (2002) says,

> Unlike the immigrants of old, who bade farewell forever to their native lands when they boarded the ship, for Mexicans, the mother country is right next door. Millions have no desire to learn English or to become citizens. America is not their home: Mexico is; and they wish to remain proud Mexicans. They come here to work. Rather than assimilate, they create Little Tijuanas in U.S. cities. With their own radio and TV stations, newspapers, films, and magazines, the Mexican Americans are creating an Hispanic culture separate and apart from America's larger culture. (pp. 125–126)

Thus, for Buchanan and many other Americans, the assertion that today's immigrants, unlike past immigrants, do not assimilate means that they refuse to learn

English, do not adopt American culture, and have no desire to become American citizens. Instead, they retain their own culture, live among themselves, and only come "to work" or "to take advantage of us" as one White woman told Lillian Rubin (1994) during the course of her research.

There are a few problems, however, with this contrasting assimilation narrative. First, it is simply not the case that past immigrants who came to the United States "bade farewell forever" to their homelands. In fact, some Europeans could be characterized as "Birds of Passage" (Piore, 1979), never intending to settle in the United States. Rather, they hoped to make money and to return to their homelands. An estimated 20% to 30% of Italian men who immigrated to the United States eventually returned permanently to Italy (Mintz & McNeil, 2012). Furthermore, the reality is that assimilation—becoming more culturally, linguistically, socially and socioeconomically integrated into the host society—rarely took place within one generation for past waves of European immigrants (Alba & Nee, 2003). For example, the language shift to English usually occurred over the course of three generations rather than within one generation (Veltman, 1983).

Scholarship suggests, however, that descendants of European immigrants did assimilate (Alba & Nee, 2003). But what is the story of more recent immigrants and their children? Contrary to claims that they are not learning English, scholarship suggests that children of immigrants, including all Asian and Latino ethnic groups, have shifted to English (Portes & Rumbaut, 2001; Tran, 2010). Importantly, however, learning English and speaking another language are not mutually exclusive and bilingualism may be advantageous not only for immigrant children, but in an increasingly globalized world (Portes & Rumbaut, 2001; Tran, 2010).

The question of assimilation may, perhaps, best be stated not as whether today's immigrant children *will* assimilate, but *to which segment of society* they will assimilate (Portes & Rumbaut, 2001; Portes & Zhou, 1993). According to segmented assimilation framework, factors in the contexts of exit and reception, including race, will shape specific integration patterns. While some immigrants may experience upward assimilation (and assimilate to the White mainstream), others might experience downward assimilation (as they assimilate to stigmatized groups of color and experience systematic disadvantages). Still, other immigrants may experience mostly upward assimilation through *selective acculturation,* or by selectively combining norms and values of both the dominant society and the immigrant community. Some research, however, finds little evidence of downward assimilation (Kasinitz, Mollenkopf, Waters, & Holdaway, 2008; Smith, 2003; Waldinger & Feliciano, 2004). For example, drawing on a large study of second-generation immigrants in adulthood in New York City, Kasinitz et al. (2008) find that most immigrant children, when compared to their native-born peers of the same race (rather than Whites), are doing quite well, having higher levels of education and labor force participation. Furthermore, they have had success by joining the mainstream economy rather than immigrant economic niches.

Achieving the American Dream:
Structural Opportunities and the Bootstrap Myth

Another repeated claim by many White Americans is that their ancestors, unlike today's immigrants, "never asked for government handouts" and instead, achieved upward mobility through their hard work alone. Yet, importantly, Whiteness not only provided advantages in entry and access to citizenship, it was a privileged status that allowed European ethnics access to opportunities, including government programs denied to non-Whites. Historians have shown that upward mobility for European ethnics was rarely achieved by hard work alone (Brodkin, 1998; Ignatiev, 1995; Roediger, 1991, 2005). Whiteness provided access to all sorts of social citizenship benefits, including union membership (which helped achieve safer working conditions and better wages); Social Security benefits (which initially excluded agricultural and domestic service workers—sectors that were overwhelmingly Black and Mexican); GI bills that helped subsidize the cost of higher education; and federal loans for housing, which subsidized Whites in home ownership and accumulation of wealth. Furthermore, Southern and Eastern European immigrants often distanced themselves from stigmatized people of color as they pursued new opportunities—opportunities only available because they were classified as racially White (Roediger, 2005; see also Ioanide, Essay 6, & Moore, Essay 20).

Conclusion

Today's anti-immigrant policies and rhetoric about protecting real Americans are nothing new. Both the rhetoric and the policies reflect—and hope to maintain—a vision of the United States as an "imagined community" (Anderson, 1983/1991) of White Anglo-Saxon Americans. The difference today, however, is that the policies and rhetoric are rarely explicitly racist. For example, Arizona's controversial Senate Bill 1070, passed in 2010, requires police to check the papers of persons they have a "reasonable suspicion" of being present unlawfully. But what visible indicators exist of "illegality"? As critics point out, this law necessarily encourages racial profiling. Whites are rarely suspected of being foreigners, let alone "illegal aliens."

What lies at the heart of anti-immigrant policies? A failure to assimilate seems unlikely. Undocumented youth who came to the United States as children often cite their assimilation to American society as evidence of their deservingness of being granted American citizenship. Yet, at the time of this writing, Congress continues to deny them a pathway to citizenship. The claim that immigrants "break our laws" also seems insufficient, particularly when Americans break laws all the time. Furthermore, when we examine the past and present laws that created high numbers of undocumented populations among some populations, but not others, we can raise the question of whether these laws are or were just. Additionally, "illegality" does not explain why Latino and (lawfully present) Black immigrants are disproportionately targeted in deportation and detention policies. According to Douglas S. Massey (1995), the "real nature of the anti-immigrant reaction among non-Hispanic Whites" is "a fear of cultural change and a deep seated worry that European Americans will be displaced from their dominant position in American life" (p. 632). Eduardo Bonilla-Silva (2004), argues, however, that Whites are not being displaced. While he claims that the United States is moving from a biracial order to a triracial order, Whites—including some immigrants who can be considered "White"—will remain on top of the racial hierarchy. Thus, Whiteness continues to be constructed and to be important in gaining the full benefits of citizenship and belonging.

Suggested Additional Resources

Hing, B. O. (2004). *Defining America through immigration policy.* Philadelphia, PA: Temple University Press.

Ngai, M. M. (2004). *Impossible subjects: Illegal aliens and the making of modern America.* Princeton, NJ: Princeton University Press.

Portes, A., & Zhou, M. (1993, November). The new second generation: Segmented assimilation and its variants. *Annals of the American Academy of Political and Social Science, 530,* 74–96.

Roediger, D. (2005). *Working toward Whiteness: How America's immigrants became White: The strange journey from Ellis Island to the suburbs.* New York, NY: Basic Books.

Questions for Further Discussion

1. What does it mean to be *an American*? What do you think of when you imagine a *quintessential American*? What does it mean to be a *citizen*? In what ways are—or should—these concepts be related to one another?

2. How has race, historically, played a role in defining who is—and who can become—an American? Did any of these past events surprise you? Why?

3. How might the collective vision of "who we are" help explain our response to tragedy? Consider the following: in the summer of 2012, two tragedies happened within a few weeks of each other. In the first case, a White man opened fire in a movie theater in Aurora, Colorado, killing 12 persons and injuring 56. In the second tragedy, a White supremacist went into a Sikh Temple and murdered six persons. In comparison to the Aurora shooting, very little public attention was paid to the Sikh temple shooting. Why is that? Could we imagine such little attention being paid to the second tragedy if it involved a person of color or non-Christian background walking into a White Christian church? Or, consider gun violence and the death of children. In December 2012, a gunman opened fire on an elementary school in Newtown, Connecticut, killing 27 persons, mostly young, White children. It was a horrific mass murder. Yet, young children, especially

children of color, die every night in many of our nation's cities. There were approximately 500 murders in Chicago around the same time, many more deaths than in the Newtown tragedy. Yet, their deaths do not result in the same public media outcry. How do we make sense of these varying reactions from the public?

4. What are some potential viable solutions for the issues discussed in this chapter?

Reaching Beyond the Color Line

1. Read the essay, "My Life as an Undocumented Immigrant," by Jose Antonio Vargas. http://www.nytimes.com/2011/06/26/magazine/my-life-as-an-undocumented-immigrant.html?ref=magazine&pagewanted=all. After reading this essay, reflect on the following: What does it mean to be an American? In what ways does Vargas's story both challenge and reinforce our ideas of what a real American is?

2. We are often surprised when we examine the ways in which Irish, Italians, and others were depicted in popular media throughout history. Do your own research. Go to the Internet and find old political cartoons and media depictions of the Irish and Italians throughout history. Analyze them. What do these images and cartoons convey about conceptions of race, citizenship, and the possibilities to become American?

3. After collecting political cartoons depicting Italian and Irish immigrants, collect some contemporary images and cartoons of Latinos and undocumented immigrants. What do these images and cartoons convey about conceptions of race, citizenship, and the possibilities of these groups to become American? Compare and contrast the depictions and messages they convey.

References

Alba, R., & Nee, V. (2003). *Remaking the American mainstream: Assimilation and contemporary immigration.* Cambridge, MA: Harvard University Press.

Anderson, B. (1991). *Imagined communities: Reflections on the origin and spread of nationalism.* London, UK: New Left Books. (Original work published 1983)

Bernard, W. S. (1998). Immigration: History of U.S. policy. In D. Jacobson (Ed.), *The immigration reader: America in a multi-disciplinary perspective* (pp. 48–71). Malden, MA: Blackwell.

Bonilla-Silva. E. (2004). From bi-racial to tri-racial: Towards a new system of racial stratification in the USA. *Ethnic and Racial Studies, 27*(6), 931–950.

Brodkin, K. (1998). *How Jews became White folks: And what that says about race in America.* New Brunswick, NJ: Rutgers University Press.

Buchanan, P. J. (2002). *The death of the West: How dying populations and immigrant invasions imperil our country and civilization.* New York, NY: St. Martin's Press.

Buchanan, P. J. (2006). *State of emergency: The third world invasion and conquest of America*. New York, NY: St Martin's Press.

Carbado, D. W. (2005). Racial naturalization. *American Quarterly, 57*(3), 633–658.

Chavez, L. R. (2008). *The Latino threat: Constructing immigrants, citizens, and the nation*. Stanford, CA: Stanford University Press.

Chomsky, A. (2007). *They take our jobs! And 20 other myths about immigration*. Boston, MA: Beacon Press.

Daniels, R. (1998). What is an American? Ethnicity, race, the Constitution and the immigrant in early American history. In. D. Jacobson (Ed.), *The immigration reader: America in a multi-disciplinary perspective* (pp. 29–47). Malden, MA: Blackwell.

De Genova, N. P. (2002). Migrant "illegality" and deportability in everyday life. *Annual Review of Anthropology, 31*, 419–447.

De Genova, N. P., & Ramos-Zayas, A. Y. (2003). *Latino crossings: Mexicans, Puerto Ricans, and the politics of race and citizenship*. New York, NY: Routledge.

Donato, R., & Hanson, J. S. (2012). Legally White, socially "Mexican": The politics of de jure and de facto school segregation in the American Southwest. *Harvard Educational Review, 82*(2), 202–225.

Golash-Boza, T. M. (2012). *Immigration nation: Raids, detentions, and deportations in post-9/11 America*. Boulder, CO: Paradigm.

Hing, B. O. (2004). *Defining America through immigration policy*. Philadelphia, PA: Temple University Press.

Huntington, S. P. (2004a). The Hispanic challenge. *Foreign Policy*. Retrieved on from http://www.foreignpolicy.com/articles/2004/03/01/the_hispanic_challenge

Huntington, S. P. (2004b). *Who are we? The challenges to America's national identity*. New York, NY: Simon & Schuster.

Ignatiev, N. (1995). *How the Irish became White*. New York, NY: Routledge.

Immigration Policy Center. (2008). *Deromanticizing our immigrant past: Why claiming "my family came legally" is often a myth*. Retrieved from http://www.immigrationpolicy.org/just-facts/de-romanticizing-our-immigrant-past-why-claiming-my-family-came-legally-often-myth

Kasinitz, P., Mollenkopf, J. H., Waters, M. C., & Holdaway, J. (2008). *Inheriting the city: The children of immigrants come of age*. New York, NY: Russell Sage Foundation.

Massey, D. S. (1995). The new immigration and ethnicity in the United States. *Population and Development Review, 21*(3), 631–652.

Mintz, S., & McNeil, S. (2012). Italian immigration. *Digital History*. Retrieved from http://www.digitalhistory.uh.edu/historyonline/italian_immigration.cfm

Ngai, M. M. (2004). *Impossible subjects: Illegal aliens and the making of modern America*. Princeton, NJ: Princeton University Press.

Piore, M. (1979). *Birds of passage: Migrant labor and industrial societies*. Cambridge, UK: Cambridge University Press.

Portes, A., & Rumbaut, R. G. (2001). *Legacies: Stories of the immigrant second generation*. Berkeley: University of California Press.

Portes, A., & Zhou, M. (1993, November). The new second generation: Segmented assimilation and its variants. *Annals of the American Academy of Political and Social Science, 530*, 74–96.

Roediger, D. (1991). *The wages of Whiteness*. New York, NY: Verso.

Roediger, D. (2005). *Working toward Whiteness: How America's immigrants became White: The strange journey from Ellis Island to the suburbs*. New York, NY: Basic Books.

Rubin, L. (1994). *Families on the fault line: America's working class speaks about the family, the economy, race and ethnicity*. New York, NY: HarperCollins.

Smith, J. (2003). Assimilation across the Latino generation. *American Economic Review, 93*, 315–319.

Takao Ozawa v. United States, 260 U.S. 178 (1922).

Tran, V. (2010). English gain vs. Spanish loss? Language assimilation among second-generation Latinos in young adulthood. *Social Forces, 89*(1), 257–284.

United States v. Bhagat Singh Thind, 261 U.S. 204 (1923).

Veltman, C. (1983). *Language shift in the United States.* The Hague: Walter De Gruyter.

Waldinger, R., & Feliciano, C. (2004). Will the second generation experience "downward assimilation"? Segmented assimilation reassessed. *Ethnic and Racial Studies, 27,* 376–402.

Zolberg, A. (2006). *A nation by design: Immigration policy in the fashioning of America.* New York, NY: Russell Sage Foundation.

"If Black People Aren't Criminals, Then Why Are So Many of Them in Prison?"

Confronting Racial Biases in Perceptions of Crime and Criminals

Sara Buck Doude
Georgia College

Sara Buck Doude is an associate professor of criminal justice at Georgia College. Her scholarship focuses on radical criminological theory, gender and racial biases within criminal justice, and interpersonal violence within marginalized groups. Her work has appeared in the *Encyclopedia of Theoretical Criminology* (2005). Her forthcoming work focuses on perceptions of rape based on the sexuality of the victim and offender.

When discussing race in relation to crime, students often focus on a few observations to support their idea that racism ended with the civil rights movement and that therefore the criminal justice system is without racial bias. Each semester, I ask criminology students to anonymously write down their picture of the typical criminal. Responses vary. Often, recently publicized crime stories come to mind like the 2012 mass shootings at the *Dark Knight Rising* viewing in Colorado or the Sandy Hook Elementary School tragedy in Connecticut. However, the general picture of a criminal is a young Black male who, in the process of drug dealing or gang banging, commits murder via drive-by shooting. Recent examples from this assignment reveal students' perceptions are veiled in stereotypes associated with Black males. For example, one student writes, "hooded male with baggy clothes." Another student writes, "thugs," while another writes, "Black male, sweatpants, and hoodie" (for further discussion on race and perception, see Ray, Essay 7). Although this is anecdotal evidence, I have experienced these types of responses over the course of many years of teaching criminology.

Generally, students do not recognize racial disparities in those arrested and convicted of crimes until it is pointed out through this assignment. They may recognize this perception subconsciously but do not acknowledge it until they have to write or verbalize their picture of the typical criminal. When and if they do recognize such disparities, they argue that it isn't due to racism, because the justice system is color-blind and racism isn't as bad today as it was in the past. As Rose M. Brewer and Nancy A. Heitzeg (2012b) argue, for many, "the issue then is crime, not race, and certainly not racism" (p. 383). Thus, many look at the "personal responsibility" involved in those who commit crime, rather than a racially biased justice system. Others make group-based arguments, but about the culture of the perceived criminals and not about the system; that it just so happens that certain groups of people (specifically Black males) are crime prone, have bad values, and choose to commit crimes. The possibility that racism is institutionalized in the justice system is met with deep hostility. If students consider such a fact, they propose that there may be racist individuals among those enforcing laws, but the legal system itself is not a racist entity. Student responses to these questions are a reflection of social perceptions of crime and criminals, and research reveals that this is not a recent phenomenon. The stereotype of the Black criminal prevails in American history and popular culture, and perhaps most recently, a possible contributing factor in the 2012 shooting death of unarmed teenager, Trayvon Martin (a 17-year-old Black boy), by George Zimmerman (a White Hispanic man) in which Zimmerman was found not guilty of second degree murder and manslaughter.

According to Katheryn K. Russell (1996), "'race and crime' is almost always a negative referent for 'Blacks and crime'" (p. 595). Analysis of race and crime coverage in media has been extensively studied (e.g., Feagin, 2000; Loury, 2008; Rome, 2006; Tonry, 1995; Western, 2006). Britto and Dabney's (2010) analysis of three political talk shows on cable television reveal that people of color were presented as offenders nearly 10 times more frequently than they were presented as victims and were 7.5 times more likely to be shown as evil as compared to Whites (pp. 210–211). However, when White violent offenders are presented like mass shooters who are predominately White males, they are presented as mentally ill and coming from good families and neighborhoods (see, for example, media coverage regarding the *Dark Night Rising* and Sandy Hook shooters). Meanwhile, people of color, specifically Black Americans who commit crimes, are presented as having bad values and no role models, as coming from bad families, and as living in bad neighborhoods (read: urban inner city). These portrayals heighten fear of crime in neighborhoods with higher proportions of non-Whites and those who perceive that Blacks or Latinos live nearby (Chiricos, McEntire, & Gertz, 2001). These messages are absorbed by the public through the media, which has a horrid history of portraying the typical criminal as a person of color (more specifically, a Black man) with White female victims—a stereotypical portrayal that is not consistent with offending and victimization data (Britto & Dabney, 2010).

Incarceration data also support this perception of the Black criminal. State prisons house disproportionately poor, uneducated, Black men (Loury, 2008; Western, 2006). Approximately two thirds of all inmates are serving time for drug and property offenses, while one third are serving time for violent crimes (Loury, 2008). When analyzing the ratios of incarceration, Black men are imprisoned at seven times the rate of White men and Black women are imprisoned at three times the rate of White women (Guerino, Harrison, & Sabol, 2012).

This increasingly punitive response is based on the perception of the Black criminal. This perception is reflected in statistics from the Federal Bureau of Investigation's (FBI) Uniform Crime Report (UCR) where Blacks are overrepresented in crime statistics. While Whites comprise 78.1% of the U.S. population and are underrepresented in arrest and incarceration data, Blacks comprise 13.1% of the U.S. population and are overrepresented in arrest and incarceration data (FBI, 2011; U.S. Census, 2010). In 2011, 59.4% of all persons arrested for violent crime were White and 38.4% were Black (FBI, 2011). Of those arrested, 47% of Whites were charged with a crime, whereas 53.4% of Blacks were charged (FBI, 2011). In nearly all categories of crime recorded by the UCR, Blacks are overrepresented as per their population, with the exception of gambling (FBI, 2011).

How should we interpret the overrepresentation of Blacks in crime statistics? As Loury (2008) argues, "the nation's social policy—intimately connected with public rhetoric about responsibility, dependency, social hygiene, and the reclamation of public order—can be fully grasped only when viewed against the backdrop of America's often ugly and violent racial history" (p. 11).

Fear of the Black Male

Throughout American history, the behavior of Black men has been strictly policed through both formal (e.g., the criminal justice system) and informal (e.g., vigilantism) social control and for the purposes of maintaining a White patriarchal society. We can see this most specifically when we look at the crime of rape. As Susan Brownmiller (1975) states, "The White man has used the rape of 'his' women as an excuse to act against Black men" (p. 255). Prior to the mid-1900s, in cases of rape when the offender was Black and the victim was White, White male juries and judges assumed that a White woman would not consent to sexual relations with a Black man (Allison & Wrightsman, 1993; Estrich, 1987). Ample historical evidence has shown, however, that rapes of White women committed by Black men were very rare and often fabricated by Whites as an excuse to lynch a Black man, where this "explanation" was frequently retroactively applied *after* the alleged assailant had already faced a horrific death at the hands of White mobs (Chasteen, 1998). Lynchable offenses related to rape included "whistling at a White woman, entering a White woman's home or talking 'inappropriately' around White women" (p. 30).

Historically, Black men were more likely to serve a heavier sentence for rape, which is still the case today. In addition, Black men were more likely than White men to be executed by the state or lynched if they raped a White woman or were merely suspected of doing so. Punishment during the colonial South was especially harsh. In Virginia, the punishment for a slave raping a White woman was dismemberment. Indeed, a Black man raping a White woman was perceived as the "ultimate purpose of the slaves' revenge" (Brownmiller, 1975, p. 237), where Black men were perceived as being determined to get back at White men for a variety of injustices by raping "their" White women (see also Chasteen, 1998). After slavery, the lynching of Black men increased as Whites sought new ways to police the behavior of Black men in the absence of institutionalized slavery.

Black men have felt the brunt of the vigilante justice system as well as the criminal justice system throughout the history of the United States; at many points in history, these two systems were one and the same. The perception of the criminality of the Black male still prevails with the stereotype of the Black rapist and has subsequently transformed into the Black criminal or drug dealer. This perception has been accepted by governmental agencies and the public, specifically the White public.

The Evolution of the Stereotype of the Black Criminal

From the fear of the Black rapist, the stereotype of the Black criminal as a drug dealer or a violent criminal has evolved. It has yet to be determined as a cause or an effect in relation to racial profiling and racial hoaxes, although correlations exist. Racial profiling is the use of race in conjunction with the profile of criminal suspect. It encompasses many activities such as "Driving While Black," wherein drivers are stopped because of their race and not because of illegal activity. The term *racial profiling* didn't become a part of lexicon until 1994, when minority drivers were subject to a disproportionate number of stops, searches, and arrest along the New Jersey Turnpike (Withrow & Dailey, 2012). Stopping someone exclusively based on race is discrimination, yet it is often difficult to ascertain if race is the determinant for a traffic stop. In order for a stop or arrest to be legal, race must be one of several descriptors of an individual suspect. Race and other factors constitute "reasonable suspicion," which is cause for a lawful stop (Walker, Spohn, & DeLone, 2007; Withrow & Dailey, 2012). That is, if a tall young Black man committed robbery in a red T-shirt and drove away in a red car, stopping all Black men not fitting that description in the area would be illegal according to the U.S. Supreme Court (Withrow & Daily, 2012).

Racial profiling has primarily occurred in the context of the War on Drugs, which has come to be interpreted as a war on Black Americans (Tomaskovic-Devey & Warren, 2009; Withrow & Dailey, 2012). Tomaskovic-Devey and Warren

(2009) describe the DEA's Operation Pipeline, which began in 1984. Officers were trained to recognize profiles of drug couriers, which included drivers who didn't "fit" their cars (i.e., drivers in cars that appear to be above their economic means), drivers with dark skin, drivers who wear gold jewelry, and drivers belonging to racial groups involved in the drug trade. Thus, racial profiling became a practice endorsed by the federal government. Further, the Department of Justice has insisted that racial profiling is a more effective strategy to control crime than random stops (Tomaskovic-Devy & Warren, 2009). Withrow and Dailey (2012) elaborate on this practice along the New Jersey Turnpike: "[M]ore than 250 troopers are assigned to patrol this stretch of highway. Most of them . . . are heavily influenced by intelligence reports of the U.S. Drug Enforcement Agency indicating the increased probability that racial and ethnic minorities are drug couriers" (pp. 134–135). This profile is a contributor to the overrepresentation of Black men in state and federal prison systems for drug related crimes. Indeed, Tonry (1995) argues that "urban Black Americans have borne the brunt of the War on Drugs" and "the recent Blackening of America's prison population is the product of malign neglect of the war's effects on Black Americans" (p. 105).

Allegations of racial profiling have led to lawsuits involving traffic stops in the states of New Jersey and Maryland (Walker et al., 2007; Withrow & Dailey, 2012). More recently, research from Philadelphia and New York City law enforcement agencies finds that people of color are stopped and frisked at far higher rates than Whites (Buettner & Glaberson, 2012). Stop-and-frisks, or *Terry stops,* occur when a police officer stops and detains an individual for a short period of time. Stops are based on reasonable suspicion and officers are required to articulate the suspicion for said search, or the suspicion that someone is breaking the law, has likely committed a crime, or is in the process of committing a crime (Withrow & Dailey, 2012; again see Ray, Essay 7). Police are required to have reasonable suspicion that a person is about to or has just committed a penal code violation before stopping that person (Goldstein, 2012). However, what constitutes reasonable suspicion is highly subjective and not an objective decision, which causes much disagreement in the courts.

The New York Police Department's (NYPD) stop-and-frisk policy led to 685,724 stops in 2011, in which people of color represented over 80% of those stops, despite the fact that they represent about half of the New York City population. Only 1.9% of those stops resulted in a weapon confiscation and Whites were more likely to possess a weapon. Young people of color experienced over 40% of the stops despite only being 4.7% of the city's population. Shockingly, young Black men were stopped 168,124 times, which exceeds the population of 158,406 young Black men in the city (Baker, 2012). Some were likely stopped more than once.

In the August 2013 ruling on the constitutionality of the policy, U.S. District Court Judge Shira A. Scheindlin asserted that the policy is unconstitutional and in violation of protections provided by the Fourth and Fourteenth Amendments[1].

---

[1] The order also freezes the stop-and-frisk cases until further appellate rulings. However, New York City challenged the ruling under former mayor Michael Bloomberg. Newly elected mayor Bill de Blasio hasn't yet dropped the city's challenge to Scheindlin's ruling.

Coining the term *indirect racial profiling*, she explained how the department's reliance on data indicating that Black men committed a disproportionate amount of crime amounted to a constitutional violation (Goldstein, 2013). Her decision was partially based on a commander's testimony on the "right people" to stop in which he was specifically referring to people of color. The NYPD defended this policy by asserting that specific people (read: people of color) were committing violent crimes in specific neighborhoods and needed additional police scrutiny. The police commissioner allegedly stated that young Black and Latino men were the focus of the stops because the commissioner "wanted to instill fear in them, [that] every time they leave their home, they could be stopped by the police" (Goldstein, 2013). In these ways, the disparate stop-and-frisk statistics reflect a long history of demonizing Black men in particular, instilling fear in them, and in general, reinforcing a racist, White patriarchal system.

Racial profiling and a history of racial discrimination in the criminal justice system are also precipitating factors for racial hoaxes. A *racial hoax* is the accusation that a person of color committed a crime—usually murder, rape, or assault—when in fact the crime was committed by those making the accusation, usually a White person. The Black male criminal stereotype is thus used as a method to hide the crime (Russell, 2009), usually a violent crime. Examples of racial hoaxes include Susan Smith's 1994 claim that a Black male carjacked her and fled with her two children when in fact she had killed her two children (also referenced by Tatum, Essay 2). In a more recent example, during the 2008 presidential election, a White female student accused an Obama supporter of carving a *B* for Barack into her face because she was a McCain supporter. It was later discovered that she had done the carving herself (Russell, 2009). These hoaxes are ultimately believable because Americans' perceptions of crime include the criminal as having a Black face. The consequences of this perception contribute to higher arrest rates and overrepresentation of Black men in the correctional system.

Race and Incarceration

Through examining the number of Black males under correctional supervision, we see another indicator of racial biases in the criminal justice system: their overrepresentation in jail and prison populations. This is often the result of compounding racial biases throughout the whole criminal justice process—arrest, courts, adjudication, and corrections (Brewer & Heitzeg, 2012a, 2012b; Walker et al., 2008). It is also the result of the idea of neutral application of law, which presumes White innocence and ignores the cultural context in which people of color live, a context shaped by America's racially charged past (Loury, 2008; Ross, 1996).

Essentially, Black Americans now experience "the new plantation—in the prison industrial complex" (Brewer & Heitzeg, 2012b, p. 380) where they are victimized by the unequal protection of law, greater police surveillance, and ultimately greater rates of incarceration. After incarceration, they often become inmate labor (which closely aligns with slave labor) within the confines of the penitentiary and are thoroughly under the control of the state (Alexander, 2010; Davis, 2003). Inmate labor has been utilized throughout the 20th century through the inmate lease system (Blackmon, 2008). Throughout the early 20th century, the inmate lease system (which was primarily composed of Blacks) was utilized to build mines in Birmingham, Alabama, and pave the streets in Atlanta, Georgia (Blackmon, 2008). These inmates had often been charged with crimes specifically created to target Blacks like "carrying a weapon, riding on empty freight train cars, or violation of racial etiquette such as speaking loudly in the presence of white women" (p. 67). Douglas Blackmon (2008) asserts that throughout the late 1860s and 1870s, "every southern state enacted an array of interlocking law essentially intended to criminalize Black life" (p. 53). The inmate lease system still exists and is currently utilized by several companies such as Wal-Mart, Hewlett-Packard, McDonald's, BP Oil, Chevron, Bank of America, AT&T, and IBM, among others (Fraser & Freeman, 2012; Thompson, 2012). This labor is cheap and inmates are paid very little; federal inmates are paid $0.12 to $1.15 per hour, while state inmates are paid $0.13 to $0.32. Some states compensate inmates by decreasing the length of their sentence (Thomson, 2012). In addition, child support and victim compensation are frequently deducted from federal inmates' wages. According to Fraser and Freeman (2012), "the caste nature of the South's convict lease system should remind us of the unbalanced racial profile of America's bloated prison population today" (p. 96).

While "national security" and "crime control" are often given as reasons for the mass imprisonment of Blacks (Brewer & Heitzeg, 2012a, 2012b), incarceration actually functions as a way to segregate Blacks from the rest of American society. Brewer and Heitzeg (2012a, 2012b) and Western (2006) argue that a variety of factors contribute to the overrepresentation of people of color in corrections. Specifically, the political economy of the correctional industry, which includes the prison construction boom and development of private prisons as well as economic decline and fewer low-skilled jobs have contributed to harsher sentences. Policies such as "three strikes" laws, "truth in sentencing" laws as opposed to indeterminate sentencing, the end of rehabilitation as a correctional philosophy, the incarceration for nonviolent crimes as a result of the War on Drugs, and a general increase in the use of incarceration in response to criminal behavior are all contributing factors to the number of people of color under correctional supervision. These factors have led to an attitude of resignation on behalf of young men of color toward the criminal justice system given the oppressive realities listed above: "For many young males, especially African Americans and Hispanics, the threat of going to prison or jail is not a threat at all but rather an expected or accepted part or life" (Irwin & Austin, 1997, p. 156, as cited in Western, 2006).

Conclusion

As Loury (2008) states, "crime and punishment has a color in America" (p. 22). Americans' conceptualization of the rapist, drug dealer, and general criminal have more often than not involved people of color and specifically, Black males. This conceptualization is representative of a long history of racial biases prevalent within American society and is well reflected in our justice system—from arrest rates to corrections to the death penalty. How do we rid ourselves of this harmful ideal? Evidence is prevalent that racial biases begin before stop-and-frisk stops and traffic stops. If race is part of the American perception of crime, then it is no wonder that it is a consideration in the first stage of the criminal justice process (e.g., a stop), which can only mean that it is compounded toward the end of the criminal justice process (e.g., corrections and imprisonment). In the end, Loury (2008) raises some key questions:

> Who is to blame for the domestic maladies that beset us? We have constructed a national narrative. We have created scapegoats, indulged our need to feel virtuous, and assuage our fears. We have met the enemy and the enemy is them. Incarceration keeps them away from us. (p. 25)

Essentially, as Loury indicates, public safety has come to mean keeping the public (presumably, the White public) "safe" from people of color.

Suggested Additional Resources

Alexander, M. (2010). *The new Jim Crow: Mass incarceration in the age of color blindness.* New York, NY: The New Press.

Blackmon, D. A. (2008). *Slavery by another name: The re-enslavement of Black Americans from the Civil War to World War II.* New York, NY: Random House.

Feagin, J. R. (2000). *Racist America: Roots, current realities, and future reparations.* New York, NY: Routledge.

Irwin, J., & Austin, J. (1997). *It's about time: America's imprisonment binge* (2nd ed.). Belmont, CA: Wadsworth.

Loury, G. C. (2008). *Race, incarceration, and American values.* Cambridge, MA: Boston Review.

Parsons-Pollard, N. (2011). *Disproportionate minority contact: Current issues and policies.* Durham, NC: Carolina Academic Press.

Rios, V. (2011). *Punished: Policing the lives of Black and Latino boys.* New York, NY: New York University Press.

Tonry, M. (1995). *Malign neglect: Race, crime, and punishment in America.* New York, NY: Oxford University Press.

Western, B. (2006). *Punishment and inequality in America.* New York, NY: Russell Sage Foundation.

Websites

Blackmon, D. A., Allan, C. (Executive Producers), & Pollard, S. (Director). (2012). *Slavery by another name* [Documentary]. United States: Public Broadcasting Service. Retrieved from http://www.pbs.org/tpt/slavery-by-another-name/watch

CBS News. (2012). *"Stop and frisk": Fighting crime or racial profiling?* Retrieved from http://youtube/sVaD0Aljx0k

Federal Bureau of Investigation. (2011). *Uniform crime reports: Hate crime statistics.* Retrieved from http://www.fbi.gov/about-us/cjis/ucr/ucr-publications#Hate

N.Y. region: Stop and frisk in Brownsville, Brooklyn. (2010). *New York Times.* nytimes.com. Retrieved from http://youtube/iW8ZXrps9ys

Reuters TV. (2012). *Stories of "stop and frisk"—Reuters Investigates.* Retrieved from http://youtube/rsrvRSxP1a8

Western, B. (2012). Academic articles on the social impact of incarceration. Retrieved from http://scholar.harvard.edu/brucewestern/publications/term/3695

Questions for Further Discussion

1. Is arrest and incarceration data a reflection of true and actual amounts of crime? Why or why not? What do you believe official crime data tell us about the nature of crime in America? How would you explain the overrepresentation of people of color at all stages of the criminal justice system?

2. According to the essay, how has the history of America contributed to the Black criminal stereotype? Is the criminal stereotype applied to other groups? (How) is the stereotype of the Black rapist still prevalent in current American society? Why were White women seen as entities to be protected? Are White women still portrayed this way in regard to crime?

Reaching Beyond the Color Line

1. Select a popular television crime show or procedural (e.g., *Law & Order*, *CSI, Criminal Minds*). Conduct a content analysis of four to six episodes. Is the Black criminal stereotype prevalent? If yes, what are the crimes portrayed? Who are the victims?

2. As a class, construct a survey instrument about perceptions of the police. Gather data from a representative sample of the student body at your college and compare the findings across racial and ethnic groups.

References

Alexander, M. (2010). *The new Jim Crow: Mass incarceration in the age of colorblindness.* New York, NY: The New Press.

Allison, J. A., & Wrightsman, L. S. (1993). *Rape: The misunderstood crime.* Newbury Park, CA: Sage.

Baker, A. (2012, May, 12). New York Police release data showing rise in number of stops on streets. *New York Times.* Retrieved from http://www.nytimes.com/2012/05/13/nyregion/new-york-police-data-shows-increase-in-stop-and-frisks.html?_r=0

Blackmon, D. A. (2008). *Slavery by another name: The re-enslavement of Black Americans from the Civil War to World War II.* New York, NY: Doubleday.

Brewer, R. M., & Heitzeg, N. A. (2012a). The racialization of crime and punishment: Criminal justice, color-blind racism and the political economy of the prison industrial complex. *American Behavioral Scientist, 51,* 625–644.

Brewer, R. M., & Heitzeg, N. A. (2012b). The racialization of crime and punishment: Criminal justice, color-blind racism and the political economy of the prison industrial complex. In H. T. Greene & S. L. Gabbidon (Eds.), *Race and crime: A text/reader* (pp. 380–388). Thousand Oaks, CA: Sage.

Britto, S., & Dabney, D. A. (2010). "Fair and balanced?" Justice issues on political talk shows. *American Journal of Criminal Justice, 35*(4), 198–218.

Brownmiller, S. (1975). *Against our will: Men, women, and rape.* New York, NY: Fawcett Columbine.

Buettner, R., & Glaberson, W. (2012, July 10). Courts putting stop-and-frisk policy on trial. *New York Times.* Retrieved from http://www.nytimes.com/2012/07/11/nyregion/courts-putting-stop-and-frisk-policy-on-trial.html

Chasteen, A. L. (1998). *Rape narratives in the United States: Feminism, culture and the construction of rape as a social problem* (Doctoral dissertation). Retrieved from ProQuest Digital Dissertations database. (Publication No. AAT 9825180)

Chiricos, T. G., McEntire, R., & Gertz, M. (2001). Perceived racial and ethnic composition of neighborhood and perceived risk of crime. *Social Problems, 48*(3), 322–340.

Davis, A. Y. (2003). *Are prisons obsolete?* New York, NY: Seven Stories Press.

Estrich, S. (1987). *Real rape: How the legal system victimizes women who say no.* Cambridge, MA: Harvard University Press.

Feagin, J. R. (2000). *Racist America: Roots, current realities, and future reparations.* New York, NY: Routledge.

Federal Bureau of Investigation's Uniform Crime Reports. (2011). *Crime in the United States.* Retrieved from http://www.fbi.gov/about-us/cjis/ucr/crime-in-the-u.s/2011/crime-in-the-u.s.-2011

Fraser, S., & Freeman, J. B. (2012). In the rearview mirror. *New Labor Forum, 21*(3), 94–98. doi:10.4179/NFL.213.0000014

Goldstein, J. (2012, September 25). Prosecutor deals blow to stop-and-frisk tactic. *New York Times.* Retrieved from http://www.nytimes.com/2012/09/26/nyregion/in-the-bronx-resistance-to-prosecuting-stop-and-frisk-arrests.html

Goldstein, J. (2013, August 14). Police dept.'s focus on race is at core of ruling against stop-and-frisk tactic. *New York Times.* Retrieved from http://www.nytimes.com/2013/08/15/nyregion/racial-focus-by-police-is-at-core-of-judges-stop-and-frisk-ruling.html

Guerino, P., Harrison, P. M., & Sabol, W. J. (2012). *Prisoners in 2010.* (NCJ 236096). U.S. Department of Justice, Office of Justice Programs, Bureau of Justice Statistics. Retrieved from http://www.bjs.gov/content/pub/pdf/p10.pdf

Irwin, J., & Austin, J. (1997). *It's about time: America's imprisonment binge* (2nd ed.). Belmont, CA: Wadsworth.

Loury, G. C. (2008). *Race, incarceration, and American values.* Cambridge, MA: Boston Review.

Rome, D. M. (2006). The social construction of the African American criminal stereotype. In M. Zatz, C. Mann, & N. Rodriguez (Eds.), *Images of color: Images of crime* (3rd ed.). Los Angeles, CA: Roxbury.

Ross, T. R. (1996). *Just stories: How the law embodies racism and bias.* Boston, MA: Beacon Press.

Russell, K. K. (1996). The racial hoax as crime: The law as affirmation. *Indiana Law Journal, 71*(3), 594–621.

Russell, K. K. (2009, June 8). Racial hoaxes: Black men and imaginary crimes [Radio series program]. In M. Martin, *Tell Me More.* Washington, DC: National Public Radio. Retrieved from http://www.npr.org/templates/story/story.php?storyId=105096024

Thompson, H. (2012). The prison industrial complex. *New Labor Forum, 21*(3), 38–47. doi:10.4179/NFL.213.0000006

Tomaskovic-Devey, D., & Warren, P. (2009). Explaining and eliminating racial profiling. *Social Contexts.* Retrieved from http://contexts.org/articles/spring-2009/explaining-and-eliminating-racial-profiling

Tonry, M. (1995). *Malign neglect: Race, crime, and punishment in America.* New York, NY: Oxford University Press.

U.S. Census. (2010). Retrieved from http://www.census.gov/2010census

Walker, S., Spohn, C., & DeLone, M. (2007). *The color of justice: Race, ethnicity, and crime in America* (4th ed.). Belmont, CA: Thompson Wadsworth.

Western, B. (2006). *Punishment and inequality in America.* New York, NY: Russell Sage Foundation.

Withrow, B. L., & Dailey, J. D. (2012). Racial profiling litigation: Current status and emerging controversies. *Journal of Contemporary Criminal Justice, 28*(2) 122–145.

"Now All the Good Jobs Go to Them!"

Affirmative Action in the Labor Market

Wendy Leo Moore

Texas A&M University

Wendy Leo Moore is an associate professor of sociology at Texas A&M University, and the author of the award winning 2007 book *Reproducing Racism: White Space, Elite Law Schools, and Racial Inequality*, published by Rowman & Littlefield. Her research focuses on the intersections of race and law.

In September of 1965, President Lyndon B. Johnson signed Executive Order 11246, prohibiting discrimination on the basis of race, color, religion, sex, or national origin in federal public contracts. This executive order, in addition to prohibiting discrimination, called for federal contractors to "take affirmative action to ensure that applicants are employed, and that employees are treated during employment, without regard to race, color, sex or national origin." The innocuous command of EO 11246, to act affirmatively to ensure people are treated equally, contrasts sharply with contemporary rhetoric concerning affirmative action. These two words have come to signify conflicting meanings concerning U.S. democracy and racial inequality; the mere mention of the term *affirmative action* can lead to heated and emotional debates including assertions of "unfair race based privilege" or "reverse discrimination" (see Curry, 1996; Pierce, 2012).

By the 1990s, the discourse surrounding affirmative action had shifted from one about discrimination and equality, to one about White innocence and injury resulting from the hiring of unqualified people of color. Pierce (2012) notes that throughout the 1990s, media stories slanted against affirmative action were much more common than stories in support of affirmative action—as many as 3:1 tilted against affirmative action (p. 35). In January of 1994, the topic of affirmative action made the cover story of *Business Week* where the issue was titled, "White, Male and Worried," and the July 1995 *Newsweek* cover read "Race and Rage" (Pierce, 2012, p. 27). The discursive framing of affirmative action had shifted dramatically from the frame constructed by President Johnson in 1965. The sentiment is summed up by a 2011 blogger on worldinconversation.org who responded to a question about opinions of affirmative action by saying, "I don't agree with hiring someone who may or may not be less qualified than someone else just because their race needs to be represented better"[1] (see also Bonilla-Silva, 2009; Moore, 2008). In order to understand this debate and also the context of President Johnson's command for affirmative action, it is necessary to journey into the history of race and government action.

Where the Story Begins:
A Legacy of Affirmative Action for Whites

Most of the informed public is aware of the history of racialized slavery in the United States, the institution through which Blackness became a justification for the enslavement of people of African descent (see Harris, 1993). During the centuries of slavery in this country, race and class converged, as people of color were prohibited from access to resources such as education, property, and political rights. As Cheryl Harris (1993) suggests, the economic interests of Whites were so integral to the law and politics of the United States that Whiteness itself was valued by the government like a form of property. Initially, this occurred through explicit legal and political policies concerning who had the right to own property (Whites), who did not (American Indians), and who became the object of property (Blacks). However, for at least 100 years after the end of slavery, U.S. law and social policy continued to overtly and explicitly privilege the economic interests of Whites, perpetuating the material value of Whiteness.

The end of racialized slavery did not mean the end of systematic racial oppression. After the Civil War, Southern states immediately enacted laws, such as those making vagrancy or joblessness a crime, which forced Blacks back into exploitative economic relations (DuBois, 2001; Woodward, 2002). A new economic system, based upon tenant farming, sharecropping, and a convict-lease system, combined with legally mandated segregation, supported by the Supreme Court in the 1896 case of *Plessy v. Ferguson,* resulted in a racial order that was not meaningfully different from slavery (Woodward, 2002). Within this social and historical context

---

[1] *What is your opinion of affirmative action and has the lecture had an effect on you?-119 Blog.* (2011, February 23). In World Conversation Project. Retrieved June 9, 2012, from http://www .worldinconversation.org/2011/02/23/what-is-your-opinion-of-affirmative-action-and-has-the-lecture-had-an-effect-on-you-119-blog/.

begins the real story of a legacy of affirmative action *for Whites*; that is, affirmative government action taken to protect and stabilize the economic conditions of White people during times of economic disruption.

At the end of the 1920s, the world experienced a severe economic depression. Millions of Americans were thrown into joblessness and poverty. The widespread suffering caused by the Great Depression led to support for massive government intervention. In the 1930s, President Franklin D. Roosevelt proposed and signed into law a series of legislative initiatives designed to ease economic suffering. Roosevelt's New Deal legislation created federally funded unemployment insurance, public assistance for the poor, old age pensions, work relief for the unemployed, and injected federal funds into severely depressed local economies (Takaki, 2008). These programs were the most extensive government economic aid interventions in the history of the United States and they helped to end the severe economic depression. Yet, to secure the Southern votes necessary to enact the New Deal legislation, Southern states required that terms be implemented to ensure that these policies would not disrupt the racial status quo of Jim Crow (Katznelson, 2005).

Three mechanisms allowed Whites to benefit from government economic assistance while Blacks were excluded (Katznelson, 2005, pp. 22–23). First, work-related policies like unemployment and social security were constructed to leave out as many Blacks as possible through racially coded definitions of work. New Deal employment-related policies excluded individuals employed in farm-related or domestic-labor jobs. Nationwide, in the 1930s, 60% of Blacks were employed in these sectors; in the South, that figure was 75%. Thus, the vast majority of Black workers were excluded from all the federal employment assistance programs. The second mechanism that functioned to exclude Blacks from federal benefits was the placement of the administration of federal funds in the hands of local officials. In the South, this resulted in widespread racial discrimination in the implementation of these programs and the enactment of explicitly racist policies at the local level; the level of poverty required to qualify for financial aid was set much lower for Blacks than for Whites (see Katznelson, 2005, p. 37). And finally, Southern House and Senate members resoundingly rejected the attachment of anti-discrimination provisions to the legislation. The lack of anti-discrimination measures in the New Deal bills facilitated Southern states' segregation and racist policies with regard to the administration of federal aid programs, leaving no recourse for Blacks denied federal assistance by local administrators.

The New Deal "combined unprecedented [levels of government] assistantship with racist policies," the result of which was a program of affirmative government action created to end economic suffering largely for Whites only (Katznelson, 2005, p. 29). But the New Deal policies were not the end of affirmative action for Whites. During and after World War II, economic shifts led to more government actions to stabilize the economy. When the United States entered World War II, there was an immediate need for military to fight in the war effort. Many White men left their jobs to join the military (or were drafted), which resulted in a shortage of workers in Northern industrial jobs. Blacks faced widespread discrimination in the military, either through complete exclusion from service, or when they were allowed to serve, exclusion from advanced military training programs necessary for skilled positions (Katznelson, 2005; Takaki, 2008). By contrast, employers with labor shortages engaged in a campaign to recruit Black workers to take positions from which Blacks had previously been excluded. These new job opportunities, on the one hand, and the desire to escape the racist violence of the South on the other, facilitated an unprecedented migration of Blacks from the rural South to the urban North (Massey & Denton, 1993). Unfortunately, however, these jobs were not permanent. At the end of World War II, many Blacks lost the jobs they had been recruited for when White men returned from military service.

At the same time, a widespread housing shortage and desire to ensure postwar economic stability lead the federal government, at the end of World War II, to enact the Selective Service Readjustment Act, widely known as the G.I. Bill. The G.I. Bill assisted veterans with buying homes, attending college, getting loans to start up small businesses, and finding skill-appropriate jobs. Many young veterans, most of them White, utilized these government services and as a result were able to move into the middle class (Katznelson, 2005; Massey & Denton, 1993). As well, the G.I. Bill, in combination with the construction of the Federal Housing Authority, which provided government subsidies enabling Americans to secure loans to purchase homes without huge down payments, facilitated a boom in home ownership, the result of which was the largest swelling of the middle class in U.S. history (Massey & Denton, 1993). However, repeating a history of White economic advantage, the boom in the middle class occurred disproportionately for Whites. The majority of Blacks were shut out through explicit discrimination in the implementation of the G.I. Bill, which like the New Deal programs took place at the local level, as well as through policies of discriminatory lending and racial segregation.

Black veterans wishing to access the education assistance of the G.I. Bill found that there were not enough spaces for them in Black educational institutions, but they were excluded from White institutions in the South completely, and Northern schools only allowed a small number of non-White applicants each year. In 1947, 20,000 Black veterans eligible for G.I. Bill education assistance could not find schools to attend because Black colleges and vocational schools were filled (Katznelson, 2005, p. 133). Blacks, veterans, and nonveterans wishing to purchase homes were excluded in two ways. First, many Blacks faced explicit discrimination from local administrators of the G.I. Bill, as well as from banks, so they were not able to secure loans to purchase homes. Second, residential segregation and lending policies often meant that even those who could qualify for loans could not find neighborhoods where they could purchase homes. White neighborhoods were off limits to Blacks through legal instruments like racially restrictive covenants and government policies that favored segregation, so they could not secure loans for houses in these White neighborhoods (Massey & Denton, 1993). Black neighborhoods were in a state of economic crisis—resulting mainly from the massive loss of employment that occurred as Blacks were displaced from jobs they had been recruited for when White men returned from military service. The result of the poverty and economic instability in these neighborhoods meant that banks could "red line" Black neighborhoods, which literally meant that these neighborhoods had red lines across them on maps, signifying they were ineligible for federally secured housing loans (Massey & Denton, 1993).

Katznelson (2005) notes, "there was no greater instrument for widening an already huge racial gap than the G.I. Bill" (p. 121). The reason for the widening economic gap was not just racial discrimination against Blacks, which was nothing new, but instead was a result of the widespread *upward mobility* of huge numbers of Whites resulting from affirmative government actions to facilitate their economic security and growth. Thus, affirmative government actions resulted in the racially unjust enrichment of Whites and corresponding unjust impoverishment of Blacks (see Feagin, 2010, p. 10).

It was within this context on June 4, 1965, only months before President Johnson issued Executive Order 11246, that he called for affirmative government action to create equality in his speech "To Fulfill These Rights" at Howard University. Acknowledging the connection between racial inequality and government action, Johnson said

You do not take a person who, for years, has been hobbled by chains and liberate him, bring him up to the starting line of a race and then say, "you are free to compete with all the others," and still justly believe that you have been completely fair . . . [E]qual opportunity is essential, but not enough, not enough. Men and women of all races are born with the same range of abilities. But ability is not just the product of birth. Ability is stretched or stunted by the family that you live with, and the neighborhood you live in—by the school you go to and the poverty or the richness of your surroundings.

The U.S. government, which had for centuries acted affirmatively to create economic stability and prosperity for Whites, would now have to act not merely passively by no longer permitting racial discrimination, but affirmatively again to correct the structural racial inequalities resulting from centuries of racial discrimination.

Affirmative Inaction: The Policy That Wasn't

Although President Johnson articulated a government obligation to take affirmative steps beyond just ending discrimination to create economic security for Blacks, Johnson's view of affirmative action never came to pass. There occurred a political backlash against affirmative action, one that has been virulent and pervasive throughout the decades since Johnson's speech. Rhetorical assertions of the supposed unfairness of unqualified minorities gaining access to jobs that should go to Whites as a result of quotas, as illustrated in the introduction to this chapter, guided that backlash into a frenzied attack on the idea of affirmative action (Pierce, 2012). What is particularly confounding about this anti-affirmative action sentiment is that U.S. law does not permit quotas as part of affirmative action programs. In fact, the language of Title VII of the 1964 Civil Rights Act that prohibited racial discrimination in employment also explicitly prohibits quota-type systems. Section 703 (j), titled, "Preferential treatment not to be granted on account of existing number or percentage imbalance" specifies that

[n]othing contained in [this subchapter on non-discrimination in employment] shall be interpreted to require any employer . . . to grant preferential treatment to any individual or to any group because of the race, color, religion, sex, or national origin of such individual or group on account of an imbalance which may exist with respect to the total number or percentage . . . employed by any employer.

Moreover, in 1978, the U.S. Supreme Court ruled definitively on the issue of quotas in the case of *The Regents of the University of California v. Bakke*, outlawing quota systems, even as a remedy for historical discrimination, in higher education admissions (Greene, 1989).

Rigid quotas were never legal and there was never an intention to create a system of affirmative action employing such a method. What affirmative action was, then, was a system of laws and policies designed to allow educational institutions and businesses to take into consideration the social consequences of racial inequality when making decisions about *equally* qualified candidates in school admissions and employment. Affirmative action occurred in two ways in employment. First, private (nongovernment) employers were legally able to enact *voluntary* affirmative action programs as part of a program to increase their numbers of underrepresented groups, including racial minorities (see Greene, 1989; Pierce, 2012; Reskin, 1998). The types of voluntary affirmative action programs employers could enact ranged from advertising in news outlets catering to people of color, to recruiting from schools that are predominantly of color, to giving preference to an *equally qualified* candidate for hire or promotion because the person was a member of a group underrepresented in the institution (Greene, 1989). Note, however, that when private businesses chose to implement voluntary affirmative action plans that include giving preference to underrepresented groups in hiring and promotion decisions, they must take on the heavy burden of documenting that their business does in fact have an underrepresentation (this must include statistical demonstration), and that their race-conscious employment decisions are based only upon otherwise equally qualified candidates, and will only remain until the underrepresentation is remedied (Greene, 1989). The burden of this requirement is one reason that many businesses do not implement this form of affirmative action (as opposed to purely recruiting programs).

The second labor market arena in which affirmative action based programs take place is in federal contract compliance. Federal agencies and employers who hold federal contracts in excess of $50,000 must demonstrate that they are "affirmative action compliant," which means that they are taking positive steps to increase racial equality in their organization (Greene, 1989; Pierce, 2012). To be compliant with this regulation, businesses must illustrate that they are making a "good faith" effort to recruit underrepresented minorities (they need not actually recruit underrepresented minorities, only show a good faith effort). Although President Johnson conceived of an affirmative action program that would set aside a percentage of government contracts (10% to be exact) for qualified minority-owned businesses (businesses whose ownership was at least 50% racial minorities), the U.S. Supreme Court rejected that program as unconstitutional, first prohibiting state government set-asides in the 1989 *City of Richmond v. J. A. Croson Co.* case, then in federal contract set-asides in the 1995 *Adarand Constructors, Inc. v. Peña* case. Thus, even this limited attempt at redistribution of government resources to remedy racial inequalities was declared unconstitutional.

There is one other area of government policy that has sometimes mistakenly been considered affirmative action; it is not actually affirmative action at all, but anti-discrimination enforcement. The enactment of the civil rights legislation of the 1960s, which prohibited discrimination on the basis of race in U.S. institutions and organizations such as education and employment, was met with resistance, particularly in the South. For example, in 1972 the Alabama Department of Public Safety was held to have engaged in "egregious discrimination" by systematically excluding Blacks from employment and promotion among state troopers. After the initial finding of discrimination, the Department failed to enact remedies to correct the discrimination, particularly in the promotion of Black employees. As a result, in 1981 the court ordered that the department promote one Black trooper for every White trooper promoted until the systematic discrimination was remedied (see *United States v. Paradise, 1987*). Court orders like this one may be a source for the myth that affirmative action meant quotas and "reverse discrimination"; yet these remedies were not affirmative action, but punitive court-ordered sanctions for failing to comply with anti-discrimination laws.

Racial inequality continues to organize United States society today, as it did before the civil rights movement. The inequalities in wealth resulting from the housing boom experienced by Whites post-World War II, which largely excluded people of color, has left us with extreme and pervasive racial inequalities in wealth (Massey & Denton, 1993; Oliver & Shapiro, 2006). In 2007, the census reported that the median net worth (total assets minus total debt) of White, non-Hispanic families was $170,400, whereas the median wealth of non-White and Hispanic families was $27,800.[2] These figures, because they compare Whites to all non-Whites, obscure the disparities between White and Black families; the Pew Research Center reported that in 2009, White family wealth had declined (possibly due to the housing crisis) to a median of $113,149, but median family wealth for Blacks in 2009 was only $5,677.[3] This difference in wealth, as Melvin Oliver and Thomas Shapiro (2006) explain, means differential access to equity, which may be used for such things as collateral for education or small business loans, and a cushion during times of economic recession. Blacks and other people of color do not have the same access to these resources as Whites and this is largely the structural result of wealth disparities solidified post-World War II.

Wealth inequality is distinct from inequality in income and employment. In 2009, 11.3% of Black families made less than $10,000 per year, compared to 4.2% of White families. On the opposite end of the spectrum, among families that made between $100,000 and $149,999 per year, 15.7% of White families were represented and only 8.1% of Black families (U.S. Bureau of Labor Statistics, 2011).

---

[2] See http://www.census.gov/compendia/statab/2012/tables/12s0720.pdf.

[3] See http://pewresearch.org/pubs/2069/housing-bubble-subprime-mortgages-hispanics-blacks-household-wealth-disparity.

This can be partially explained by the fact that Blacks remain overrepresented in unskilled labor. As Bonilla-Silva (2013) notes, in managerial and professional occupations you find, "35.43 percent of white males and 40.64 percent of white females, compared to 21.65 percent of black males and 31 percent of black females" (p. 55). Whereas in service-related occupations, we find, "20.23 percent of black males and 26.39 percent of black females compared to 10.85 percent of white males and 17.03 percent of white females" (Bonilla-Silva, 2013, pp. 55–56). Although much of this inequality can be linked to inequalities in education, researchers also continue to find persistent patterns of racial discrimination in employment (see, for example, Bendick, Jackson, Reinoso, & Hodges, 1991; Pager, 2003; see also Hughey, Essay 3).

Thus, affirmative action—as a policy originated to remedy the unjust enrichment of Whites and unjust impoverishment of people of color resulting from years of government sponsored racial discrimination—has widely failed. Although exceptional individual Blacks and other Americans of color have probably benefitted from affirmative action programs (and it is hard to know what portion of the benefit is a result of nondiscrimination, as opposed to true affirmative action programs), these programs have failed to change the inequalities in the racial social structure. Moreover, a 1995 study conducted by the U.S. Department of Labor revealed that of the 300 cases filed by Whites against employers for so-called "reverse discrimination," only *six* cases were found to have been unlawfully based upon race. The rest of the cases involved erroneous assumptions, on the part of Whites who did not receive jobs or promotions, that affirmative action was used to give less qualified minorities the position (Pierce, 2012, p. 39). Thus, much of the vehement criticism and debate concerning "reverse discrimination" and preferences for undeserving or unqualified minorities are simply factually inaccurate.

White Racial Framing: Turning the Myth of Reverse Discrimination on Its Head

Given that quotas, as well as all allocation programs that consider racial demographics in any meaningful way, have been declared illegal, it is curious that the rhetoric of quotas and reverse racism persists. Even more curious is the continued persistence of heated and emotional debates concerning affirmative action in the face of its clear failure to affect structural racial inequality. Sociologist Jennifer L. Pierce (2012) notes that the notion of reverse discrimination against victimized Whites became part of a dominant narrative in the post-civil rights era, and thus became a "broader cultural memory" (p. 3). The cultural memory of the victimization of Whites by affirmative action supplanted our memory of a legacy of affirmative government action *for* Whites, and President Johnson's comment that equal opportunity was not enough to remedy the resulting racial inequality. Because of that shift in cultural memory, Whites massively rejected and resisted affirmative action (as well as anti-discrimination laws), and the result has been that affirmative action has been a bust as a policy.

This process is an example of what Joe R. Feagin (2009) has called "White racial framing." The *White racial frame* can be defined as "an organized set of racialized ideas, emotions, and inclinations, as well as recurring or habitual discriminatory actions, that are consciously or unconsciously expressed in, and constitutive of, the routine operation and racist institutions of US society" (Feagin, 2006, p. 23). This frame facilitates the development of a cultural memory of (false) White victimization and the collective forgetting of a legacy of (true) racial advantage for Whites and oppression of people of color. If we were to reject the White racial frame and reframe the debate about affirmative action in the context of the structural reality that President Johnson emphasized in his Howard speech, we could create a new and more accurate argument concerning affirmative action: Racially conscious affirmative action is *necessary* for democracy and the assessment of individuals based solely upon their merit. Historical and current racial conditions provide Whites with unfair advantages in the form of access to resources that have been denied to people of color. In order to prevent Whites from feeling inferior because their successes are not based upon merit alone, but instead stem from unearned privilege, we must institute affirmative action programs that correct for structural racial differences and racial oppression. This will result in a better system of evaluation of the talents and contributions of all individuals based upon their relative access to resources.

Suggested Additional Resources

Feagin, J. R. (2006). *The White racial frame.* New York, NY: Routledge.

McIntosh, P. (2003). White privilege: Unpacking the invisible knapsack. In S. Plous (Ed.), *Understanding prejudice and discrimination* (pp. 191–196). New York, NY: McGraw-Hill.

Pierce, J. (2012). *Racing for innocence: Whiteness, gender, and the backlash against affirmative action.* Stanford, CA: Stanford University Press.

Reskin, B. (1998). *The realities of affirmative action in employment.* Washington, DC: American Sociological Association.

Wise, T. (2005). *Affirmative action: Racial preference in Black and White.* New York, NY: Routledge.

Websites

African American Policy Forum: http://www.youtube.com/watch?v=eBb5TgOXgNY

American Association for Affirmative Action: http://www.affirmativeaction.org

American Civil Liberties Union: http://www.aclu.org/racial-justice/affirmative-action

Americans for a Fair Chance: http://www.civilrights.org/equal-opportunity/fact-sheets/fact_sheet_packet.pdf

U.S. Department of Labor: http://www.dol.gov/ofccp/regs/compliance/aa.htm

Questions for Further Discussion

1. Watch the YouTube video titled, "The Unequal Opportunity Race," created by the African American Policy Forum (http://www.youtube.com/watch?v=eBb5TgOXgNY); discuss the elements of structural racism visually

presented in the video and the discussions about material inequality presented in this chapter. What role, if any, should government play in the dismantling of racial inequality? Does it matter that government policies facilitated the creation of racial inequality?

2. What do you think of the counterframe presented at the end of this chapter? Would merit be more accurately evaluated if we considered people's accomplishments in relation to their access to differential resources?

3. Given that quotas and the hiring of unqualified people of color over more qualified Whites is not legal affirmative action, why do you think the myth of quotas has had such staying power?

4. How do you think the current myths about affirmative action affect the experiences of people of color in institutions (employment and education) who are presumed to be there as a result of affirmative action and not their qualifications?

5. In a democracy, what is the relevance of racial inequality, or conversely does a democracy require a commitment to some level of racial equality?

Reaching Beyond the Color Line

1. Imagine that you are the chief human resources officer for a major company in a diverse city and your board has asked you to develop a diversity plan to ensure that the company is truly providing equal opportunities to the community in which it is located. Using the materials you've learned from this reading, develop a diversity plan for the company that considers the following:

- Recruiting (i.e., Where will you advertise for your hires or go to locate your workforce?)
- Hiring (i.e., How will individual applicants be evaluated in the hiring process?)
- Retention (i.e., What kinds of steps might you take to ensure that people from different backgrounds feel welcome in your company?)
- Promotion (i.e., What kinds of trainings or opportunities for promotion will you implement so that people from diverse backgrounds will rise to positions of experience and power?)

References

Adarand Constructors, Inc. v. Pena, 515 U.S. 200 (1995).

Bendick, M., Jackson, C. W., Reinoso, V. A., & Hodges, L. E. (1991). Discrimination against Latino job applicants: A controlled experiment. *Human Resource Management, 30*(4), 469–484.

Bonilla-Silva, E. (2009). *Racism without racists* (3rd ed.). Lanham, MD: Rowman & Littlefield.

Bonilla-Silva, E. (2013). *Racism without racists* (4th ed.). Lanham, MD: Rowman & Littlefield.

City of Richmond v. J. A. Croson Co., 488 U.S. 469 (1989).

Curry, G (Ed.). (1996). *The affirmative action debate.* Reading, MA: Addison-Wesley.

Du Bois, W. E. B. (2001). The spawn of slavery: The convict lease system in the South. In S. Gabbidon, H. Greene, & V. Young (Eds.), *African American classics criminology and criminal justice* (pp. 83–88). Thousand Oaks, CA: Sage.

Feagin, J. R. (2006). *The White racial frame.* New York, NY: Routledge.

Feagin, J. R. (2010). *Racist America* (2nd ed.). New York, NY: Routledge.

Greene, K. (1989). *Affirmative action and principles of justice.* New York, NY: Greenwood Press.

Harris, C. (1993). Whiteness as property. *Harvard Law Review, 106*(8), 1709–1795.

Johnson, L. B. (1965, June 4). *To fulfill these rights.* Speech at Howard University, Washington, DC. Retrieved from http://www.lbjlib.utexas.edu/johnson/archives.hom/speeches .hom/650604.asp

Katznelson, I. (2005). *When affirmative action was White: An untold history of racial inequality in twentieth-century America.* New York, NY: W. W. Norton.

Massey, D., & Denton, N. (1993). *American apartheid: Segregation and the making of the underclass.* Cambridge, MA: Harvard University Press.

Moore, W. L. (2008). *Reproducing racism: White space, elite law schools and racial inequality.* Lanham, MD: Rowman & Littlefield.

Oliver, M., & Shapiro, T. (2006). *Black wealth/White wealth: A new perspective on racial inequality.* New York, NY: Routledge.

Pager, D. (2003). The mark of a criminal record. *American Journal of Sociology, 108,* 937–975.

Pierce, J. L. (2012). *Racing for innocence: Whiteness, gender, and the backlash against affirmative action.* Stanford, CA: Stanford University Press.

Plessy v. Ferguson, 163 U.S. 537 (1896).

Reskin, B. (1998). *The realities of affirmative action in employment.* Washington, DC: American Sociological Association.

Takaki, R. (2008). *A different mirror* (Rev. ed.). New York, NY: Bay Back Books.

The Regents of the University of California v. Bakke, 438 U.S. 265 (1978).

United States v. Paradise, 480 U.S. 149 (1987).

U.S. Bureau of Labor Statistics. (2011, August). *Labor force characteristics by race and ethnicity, 2010.* Washington, DC: U.S. Department of Labor, Bureau of Labor Statistics. Retrieved from http://www.bls.gov/cps/cpsrace2010.pdf

Woodward, C. V. (2002). *The strange career of Jim Crow.* New York, NY: Oxford University Press.

PART IV

Race in Everyday Interactions

"Native American/ Indian, Asian/Oriental, Latino/Hispanic . . . Who Cares?"

Language and the Power of Self-Definition

Bradley Koch
Georgia College

Bradley Koch is an assistant professor of sociology and the chair of the Institutional Review Board (IRB) at Georgia College. His blog can be found at http://socingoutloud .blogspot.com. He teaches courses on the sociology of religion, research methods, and social problems. His research interests include religion, sexuality, higher education, and teaching and learning.

Students are often intimidated when it comes to discussing race in a public setting like a classroom. Discussions of race appear to them like minefields, wrought with unseen danger, with the potential to maim and disfigure. Because of what seem like the vagaries of usage, many students assume that they should avoid certain words simply out of a sense of political correctness. To be "politically correct" is to avoid offense and the semblance of injury or ill intent. The problem with both the practice of political correctness and the framing of this issue in terms of political correctness is that it ignores the structural nature of racism and the subtleties of individual racism.

One place where we see the notion of political correctness muddying the waters is with the avoidance of racial terms that are not racist at all. As a hypercorrection, people often avoid terms like *Mexican, Jew, Puerto Rican*, and even *Black*, assuming that it is the terms that are negative. There is a great irony here, however, because when we extend a politically correct prohibition to words that are not in and of themselves socially or psychologically damaging like *Mexican, Jew*, or *Puerto Rican*, we unintentionally stigmatize the identity of those who should otherwise proudly embrace those identities. In these ways, language and terminology are important and carry social meanings that merit attention.

Race and the Importance of Language

When most students think of racism, they imagine overt individual racism. They think of a White man in a robe burning a cross or a storeowner who refuses to serve Black customers. The good news is that the civil rights movement has been largely successful in reducing this kind of racism. However, there has been less success in convincing people that racism also exists in the invisible patterns of our social behavior and in the often-unconscious biases that are difficult to recognize.

Sociologists recognize that people create and transmit meaning through language. Because of that, words can have great power. The meaning and intent behind the use of racial pejoratives like the N-word is to denigrate a racial group and, in the case of the N-word, has been the intent of the word since its coining (Asim, 2007; see also Harkness, Essay 22). It is not, however, only about pejoratives. Many terms that are not inherently offensive and are not leveled intentionally as a way to demean and dehumanize nonetheless perpetuate differences in the historical and lingering advantages, power, and privilege between different racial and ethnic groups. Sociologically, the greater concern is the inequality. We are worried about how the biases inherent in language reinforce unequal outcomes by race. The way we all write, talk, and ultimately think about who we are—and who "they" are—influences these outcomes.

One way to think about the importance of language is to engage the language of identity as reflected in the question: "What are you?" It is hard to imagine a less couth question, and yet, it strikes at the heart of two issues: What is one's identity and who gets to decide? There is tremendous power embedded in the process of definition. Historically, colonization has left some telling scars. As world powers began dominating other peoples, they regularly imposed their own labels on them. Take, for example, the original human inhabitants of the Americas. We continue to call many of these peoples *Indians* after Christopher Columbus's lifelong and mistaken belief that he had made it to India. Despite its inaccuracy, the term has stuck. As time has passed and overt imperial domination has largely waned (replaced by a system of global capitalism), many racial and ethnic groups have attempted to shed historically subjugating *exonyms*, or terms for a group created by an outside dominant group, for *endonyms* or terms for a group created by the group members themselves.

Latino, for example, is an endonym, the name that those to whom the term refers use for themselves. *Hispanic* (literally "Spanish-speaking"), on the other hand, is an exonym, a name outsiders impose on those to whom the term refers. After all, one's language is not a designation that would help those who already know they speak the same language. Interestingly, Pew Research from 2012 indicates that most Hispanics/Latinos (51%) surveyed prefer their family's country of origin as a descriptor of their ethnicity, meaning they preferred not to use panethnic terms like *Hispanic* or *Latino* and instead identified as *Mexican, Cuban,* or *Dominican,* for example. Only about one quarter (24%) said they used *Hispanic* or *Latino* most often to describe their identity (Taylor, Lopez, Martínez, & Velasco, 2012). Regarding the terms *Hispanic* or *Latino,* most (51%) had no preference for either term, but when a preference was indicated, *Hispanic* was preferred over *Latino* (33% vs. 14% respectively). This shows some preference for exonyms, perhaps because they tend to have been present in the culture longer than some endonyms and also tend to be terms (historically) used on government documents.

Oriental—literally meaning "of the east"—is an exonym, too. It begs the question, East of what? *Oriental* only makes sense from the perspective of those in the West. The perspective and ascription of the terms matters. In fact, one way to make sense of racial or ethnic categories is as "ascribed statuses." Ascribed statuses are social positions that others impose on individuals irrespective of the individual's wishes (Linton, 1936). All exonyms are ascribed statuses. Inasmuch as there is widespread cultural acceptance of the term, exonyms carry with them a reminder of the social and political power that the subjugating group wields over the oppressed group. In these terms, it is not difficult to see why groups would be anxious to shed their exonyms and replace them with endonyms. First, such substitutions challenge the historically oppressive social relationships between groups, and second, the individual-level sense of agency that comes from self-definition can increase self-esteem and reduce anxiety (Cahill, 1986).

Changes in Racial Language

As a way to orient yourself to this social process, it is useful to think about how racial terminology has shifted over time as the concepts of race and ethnicity have shifted. One great new tool with which to see this is Google Ngrams. The Ngram tool draws from Google's growing collection of digitized books (Michel et al., 2011). By searching a word or series of words, Ngram will chart the frequency of those words as they show up in books over time. It is not a perfect tool in that it limits analysis to content that elites have created for themselves, it cannot differentiate between critical and noncritical usages, and it cannot control for any other independent factors, making Ngrams of limited use for rigorous scholarship. They can, nonetheless, point to larger historical trends in usage in ways that can be informative.[1]

---

[1] I use the full English corpus of terms with a smoothing of 3 years for all Ngrams below.

I begin by comparing the terms *American Indian* and *Native American* (Figure 21.1). I use *American Indian* instead of just *Indian* to avoid any confusion over Asian Indians. (Years below in curly brackets (braces) represent the first recorded use of the term and come from Harper [2001].)

While both terms are relatively scarce until the early 1900s, *Native American* {1956}, which had been the less frequent term, overtakes *American Indian* {1553?} around 1992, signaling a significant victory for Native Americans in their ability to self-define. While the term is still of European origin, it at least is not a coinage of an unapologetic conqueror.

The tough thing, of course, with *Asian* {late-1300s} and *Oriental* {1701} is that they can just as easily refer to inanimate objects (e.g., rugs) as they can human beings. Still, *Asian American* is slowly replacing *Oriental* (Figure 21.2). Interestingly, though, more than three quarters (76%) of Asian Americans do not often describe themselves with the terms *Asian* or *Asian American*; instead, most (62%) prefer to use their country of origin to define themselves, for example, Chinese (Pew, 2012). In fact, the ability of the dominant group (e.g., Whites) to impose terms like *Asian* on a set of heterogeneous ethnic groups obscures diversity and thus further reifies the power of the dominant group.

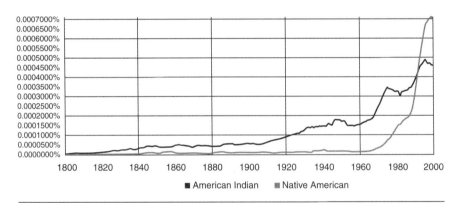

Figure 21.1 *American Indian* Versus *Native American* Ngram

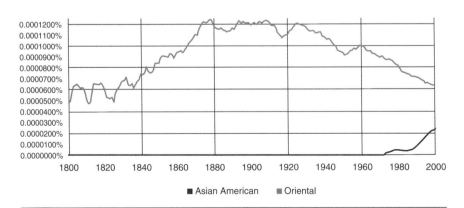

Figure 21.2 *Asian American* Versus *Oriental* Ngram

Use of both *Latino* {1946} and the corresponding *Hispanic* {c.1972} spike in the 1970s and 1980s (Figure 21.3). What most of us assume are neologisms are often the older of the two terms. *Latino* for example is older than *Hispanic*, and increasingly, many academics and progressives view *Latina* and *Latino* as more appropriate. As with Asian Americans, people of these ethnicities are questioning the use of many of these terms, though, and even the very existence of an all-encompassing ethnicity. As stated above, most prefer nationalistic labels (e.g., *Mexican*) to either *Hispanic* or *Latino*, and more than two thirds (69%) believe that the latter two terms represent multiple cultures (Taylor et al., 2012). Adding a further level of complexity, many use the term *Latin@* (see Delgado, 2010) so as not to normalize the masculine and devalue the feminine.

I do not show the Ngrams for the terms related to the "Black" racial category here, but they still deserve our attention as they are important in and of themselves and as they are illustrative of the other terms we have addressed above. (Notably, it is nearly impossible to compare "Black" {1620s} to these other terms because it has several definitions pertaining to the color that are unrelated to race.)

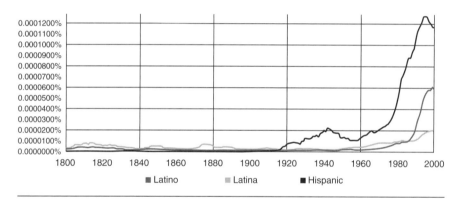

Figure 21.3   *Latino/a* Versus *Hispanic* Ngram

When we look at Ngrams comparing terms used for Black Americans, three things are apparent. First, use of both the N-word {1786} and *Negro* {1550s} peak during the Civil War and at the tail end of the civil rights movement; however, *Negro* has until recently dwarfed all other terms. However, *Negro* is certainly out of date and is considered offensive by some. Certainly, the deliberate use of outdated terms is one way to signal intentional insult. Imagine a White speaker emphatically using *Negro* when we could assume he is aware of the alternative and generally accepted terms like *Black*. Though older speakers may have been socialized to use now-bygone terms, even the most aged of speakers are likely today to be aware of such changes in convention and breaks with convention carry symbolic power. Second, use of the N-word has remained surprisingly high from the mid-1800s on (Figure 21.4). Finally, we can see that *African American* {1969} developed only quite recently, while *Afro American* {1853} has always been rare (Figure 21.5).

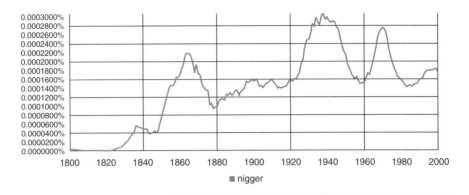

Figure 21.4 *Nigger* Ngram

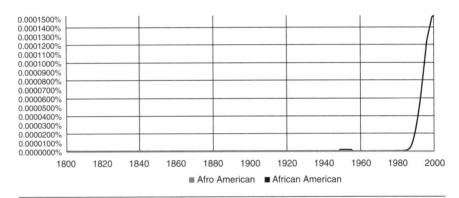

Figure 21.5 *Afro American* Versus *African American* Ngram

Students often are not aware that most generally consider *Colored people* {1610s} an offensive term and prefer *people of color* {?}. Admittedly, it is an odd distinction. Unlike other terms that are preferred over alternatives because they are endonyms (e.g., *Native American* vs. *Indian*), there does not seem to be an obvious reason to favor *of color* over *Colored* aside from convention. It may be that *Colored* serves as a reminder for many of the language and hatred of the segregated South, but its semblance to *of color* makes the distinction confusing for some. The related Ngrams are below in Figures 21.6 and 21.7.

Colored starts to fall out of favor around 1970 and *of color* replaces it beginning around 1988 to 1989. Initially, though, *of color* declined with *Colored*. It was only later that it gained acceptance and became a replacement. While *of color* solves some problems when trying to reference those who are not White (as if white were the absence of color), it is relatively imprecise. I encourage students to say and write *Black* when they mean Black. If they mean "those who are not White," "non-White" is sometimes permissible. (This distinction is related to the common practice in quantitative sociological analysis to dichotomize race to Black/non-Black or White/non-White because of limitations of many datasets or for ease of interpretation.)

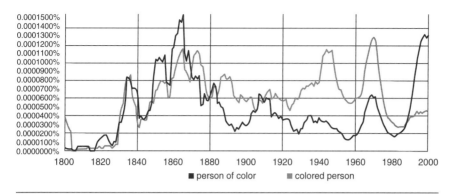

Figure 21.6 *Person of Color* Versus *Colored Person* Ngram

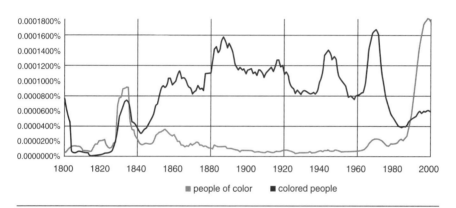

Figure 21.7 *People of Color* Versus *Colored People* Ngram

Even this, however, is problematic as it normalizes Whiteness while othering all other identities. Whenever possible, specificity is preferred.

The confusion over these terms is not isolated to people of color. Students are equally confused about how to refer to Whites. Many will use the term *Caucasian* {1807}. It has a ring of intellectualism so students will use it to appear more erudite. The term, however, comes from a misunderstanding about race that began in 1795 when the German anthropologist Johann Blumenbach (1865) theorized that the ancestral homeland of White Europeans was in the Caucasus Mountain region of what is today the border between Russia and Georgia. While scientists discredited the theory long ago, use of the term has persisted. *White* {c.1600} is a better term.

Language as a Form of "Othering"

Many of us who are instructors worry about what some of our less-than-tactful students might say in classroom discussions about contentious issues like those that sociology is wont to address, but we often worry about the wrong kind of tactlessness.

Fears about egregious and inappropriate use of the N-word are largely hollow. What should be of far greater concern is language that is much more subtle and, thus, much more dangerous. It usually goes something along the lines, "Professor, why are *they* [meaning Blacks] so much more likely to be poor?" Because students are not accustomed to openly discussing topics such as race that are largely taboo in American culture, they do not think critically about the vocabulary that they employ. Too often, it becomes "we" versus "they." Students rarely do this in an intentionally malicious manner, however. As in the example above, it is often an honest attempt at understanding or benevolence (albeit condescendingly); however, the employment of this kind of language can be alienating to the *theys* in the class and is an insidious route by which racism is reified. Along with we/they–us/them dichotomies, students are often prone to statements such as "you people" or "*the* Blacks." The inclusion of pronouns or articles has the unintended effect of distancing the speaker from the subject, further exacerbating racism.

Talking About Talking About Race

It is one thing to read and think about these racial terms and quite another to take the understanding and apply it in one's life. Most people loathe confrontation, especially with people whom they love and respect. It often happens that a friend or family member will unwittingly say something quite hateful or ignorant, and quite regularly, classmates—and at times even faculty—will speak in ways that may give one pause. While sociologists are trained to spot these instances, they are often much less obvious to others. As I half-jokingly tell my students, any sentence that begins, "I'm not a racist, but . . ." (or less frequently, "Not to sound like a racist, but . . .") almost invariably is followed by a blatantly racist statement. If we were quick enough, we might try to catch these folks after the *but* and ask if what they were about to say in any way is in conflict with what they just said. In effect, it would be wonderful to be able kindly to make salient people's cognitive dissonance. Alas, even the most motivated among us rarely do this. More often than not, we avoid the confrontation altogether, typically hoping that the conversation will change topic as quickly as possible. In many ways, this is an abdication of our civic duty to confront such ignorance. It is all too easy to rationalize such interactions, arguing that we do better in the long run to model appropriate speaking and thinking instead of risking the wholesale dismissal of our ideas and expertise. It takes both confidence and a soft touch to deal with this topic.

    I hope, along with my fellow authors and the editors of this volume, if you had begun with any reticence about learning about race and the problems that come along with it, that you are a bit more confident about the topic. Even if this is the case, though, you likely still have some reservations about how to discuss such topics with others, particularly family, friends, and other loved ones who use outmoded language and hold damaging beliefs. Here are two important tips. First, if and when you take on these conversations, it is important to be prepared for others to be dismissive. Do not take it personally. Dismissiveness is a reaction prompted by misunderstanding and unrecognized privilege. Open, respectful dialogue is the only way to overcome that misunderstanding. Second, even when one follows the above advice, not every battle needs to be fought. As much as you might lament it, you cannot change the world in a day, and you are not even likely to rearrange a person's thinking and speaking in an afternoon. Be selective in your critiques and keep your goals long and broad.

Conclusion

Racial and ethnic dynamics change over time, which means the language used to refer to the dynamics also changes over time. The meanings inherent to the terminology around race and ethnicity are about power and dominance. By fighting to replace ascribed exonyms with endonyms, groups have correspondingly challenged the structural oppression the terms themselves have reflected. By contextualizing public discussions about the proper use of language when identifying racial and ethnic groups, we help recognize and, ultimately, critically engage the historical legacy of colonialism and racism and discard the misguided belief that it is all a matter of being politically correct.

As is often the case, new understanding often leads to more questions than answers. If as the reader you have reached the end of this essay and are unsatisfied by the absence of simple, straightforward answers, I would hope that you recognize, first, that you are not alone and that, second, the confusing language around race and ethnicity is a symptom of both the messy and lamentable history of the topic and the complexity of social interaction. It is only by engaging in this topic that we can move together toward a more equitable future.

Suggested Additional Resources

Google. (2012). Google books Ngram viewer. Retrieved from http://books.google.com/ngrams

Pew Social & Demographic Trends. (2012). The rise of Asian Americans. *Pew Research Center*. Retrieved from http://www.pewsocialtrends.org/asianamericans

Taylor, P., Lopez, M. H., Martínez, J. H., & Velasco, G. (2012). When labels don't fit: Hispanics and their views of identity. *Pew Hispanic Center*. Retrieved from http://www.pewhispanic.org/2012/04/04/when-labels-dont-fit-hispanics-and-their-views-of-identity

Questions for Further Discussion

1. What fears do you have about using or hearing inappropriate language regarding race? What prior experiences do you have with these issues? How does this illustrate the complex and "messy" nature of race and identity that the author discusses in his essay?

2. Can you identify currently acceptable racial or ethnic terms not mentioned above that you believe still reflect historic and ongoing oppression?

Reaching Beyond the Color Line

1. Make your own Ngrams. Choose a race or ethnicity with different labels (e.g., *African American* and *Negro* [or *negro*]), and go to the Ngram website to investigate the changes in the use of these terms over time.

2. In small groups, role-play a situation in which someone uses inappropriate or outdated racial terminology. Stage a mock intervention in which group members attempt to correct the lone member's thinking and speech.

3. Interview older members of your own families about their ethnic and racial identities. What terms do they use? What terms do they prefer? How have the terms that others have used about them changed over their lifetimes?

4. Ask people in the course of everyday interactions what terms they prefer. Devise other ways to determine what terms your peers use and prefer.

References

Asim, J. (2007). *The N word: Who can say it, who shouldn't, and why.* New York, NY: Houghton Mifflin.

Blumenbach, J. (1865). *The anthropological treatises of Johann Friedrich Blumenbach* [1775–1833]. London, UK: The Anthropological Society.

Cahill, S. E. (1986). Language practices and self definition: The case of gender identity acquisition. *The Sociological Quarterly, 27*(3), 295–311.

Delgado, D. (2010). Middle-class Latin@ identity: Building a theoretical and conceptual framework. *Sociology Compass, 4*(11), 947–964.

Harper, D. (2001). *Online etymology dictionary.* Retrieved June 27, 2012, from http://www.etymonline.com

Linton, R. (1936). *The study of man: An introduction.* New York, NY: Appleton-Century-Crofts.

Michel, J.-B. Shen, Y. K, Aiden, A. P., Veres, A., Gray, M. K., Pickett, J. P., . . . Aiden, E. L. (2011). Quantitative analysis of culture using millions of digitized books. *Science, 331*(6014), 176–182.

Pew Social & Demographic Trends. (2012). The rise of Asian Americans. *Pew Research Center.* Retrieved from http://www.pewsocialtrends.org/asianamericans

Taylor, P., Lopez, M. H., Martínez, J. H., & Velasco, G. (2012). When labels don't fit: Hispanics and their views of identity. *Pew Hispanic Center.* Retrieved from http://www.pewhispanic.org/2012/04/04/when-labels-dont-fit-hispanics-and-their-views-of-identity

"Why Do They Get to Use the N-word But I Can't?"

Privilege, Power, and the Politics of Language

Geoff Harkness

Grinnell College

Geoff Harkness is a visiting assistant professor of sociology at Grinnell College. His scholarship focuses on the interactive practices of youth cultures, and the role of stratification in shaping the content and character of youth culture and identity. His research on hip-hop has been published in *Poetics, Cultural Sociology, American Behavioral Scientist, Journal of Popular Music Studies, Journal of Workplace Rights,* and *Contexts*. His forthcoming book, *Chicago Hustle and Flow,* is an ethnography that examines street gangs and rap music through the lens of social class.

Nigger may be the most controversial word in the history of the English language, capable of provoking everything from outrage to violence when uttered by the "wrong" person or in the wrong context. In 2010, conservative talk-radio host Dr. Laura Schlessinger shocked listeners by using the term repeatedly during an on-air rant. "Black guys use it all the time," Schlessinger declared during the tirade. "Turn on HBO and listen to a Black comic, and all you hear is nigger, nigger, nigger. I don't get it. If anybody without enough melanin says it, it's a horrible thing. But when Black people say it, it's affectionate. It's very confusing." Schlessinger issued a public apology the following day but announced her retirement from nationally syndicated radio a week later. (She eventually moved to a satellite channel.)

The outcry over Schlessinger's liberal use of the N-word was partially attributable to the word's history as a racist term: It dates to at least the 17th century, when it was applied to slaves as an insult (Asim, 2007). Schlessinger's initial defense, however, echoed the same question raised by many White students today: Isn't it unfair that Whites are prohibited from saying a word that Blacks are allowed to use without prohibition? After all, Black comedian Chris Rock went from bit player to superstar after declaring during a 1996 comedy routine that he "hated niggas" and hoped to join the Ku Klux Klan. A decade later, actor Michael Richards instantly torpedoed his career after screaming the N-word at a group of Black hecklers during a standup comedy appearance. Is there a double standard here, based on race? And what do we make of Paula Deen, the White Southern restaurateur and celebrity chef who lost numerous endorsement deals after she testified during a 2013 court case that "of course" she had used the N-word? In defending herself during a *Today Show* interview, Deen swore that her use of the term did not mean that she was racist, arguing: "It's very distressing to me to go into my kitchens and I hear what these young people are calling each other. . . . These young people are gonna have to take control and start showing respect for each other and not throwing that word at each other."

Deen's and Schlessinger's "analyses" are shortsighted at best and represent a denial of the word's rooting in our troubled racial history. For many Blacks and non-Blacks alike, the word is a powerful symbol of the history of anti-Black oppression in the United States. On its own, it has come to represent the virulent and violent institutions of slavery, Jim Crow, and a post-Jim Crow era marked by varied forms of institutional racism. Certainly, the term has been applied to enslaved Africans, to men and women lynched during legalized segregation, and is *still* applied toward Blacks in a negative fashion. For example, in August 2013, a famed statue of Black baseball legend Jackie Robinson was vandalized in Brooklyn, New York, including the words "die nigger," scrawled in black marker. In October 2013, self-proclaimed White supremacist Kynan Dutton disrupted a town council meeting in Leith, North Dakota, ranting about what he perceived to be a lack of civil rights for White people: "You treat me worse than a freakin' black man in the [19]60s . . . I'm not a nigger, I shouldn't be treated liked one." In May 2013, police arrested five White males for beating a Black man on the streets of Seattle. Because witnesses overheard the accused calling the victim "nigger" during the beating, the five were charged with a hate crime. Yet, a good deal of the controversy and confusion over the term arises from its frequent use in rap music.

A Bad Rap?

Frequent and varied use of the N-word in present-day rap music remains a common—albeit controversial—claim to authenticity. Some believe that the use of the word in rap music has stripped it of its original racist meaning; others assert that any use of the term should be forbidden. This debate is further complicated by overlapping and intertwined matters of race, social class, and gender, all of which impact one's "right" to say America's most controversial word.

Nigga, a derivation of the pejorative *nigger,* has become somewhat common-place, particularly in rap music, where it has been deployed with growing frequency. Even so-called "conscious" rappers say it frequently (Asim, 2007). Among the primary justifications for the widespread use of the N-word in rap music is that it has undergone what linguist Geneva Smitherman (1997) calls *semantic inversion,* or a process whereby people "take words and concepts from the [English] lexicon and either reverse their meanings or impose entirely different meanings" (p. 17). In this context, the N-word is no longer a racist term, but one whose original meaning is reversed to symbolize camaraderie or affection. When Kanye West rapped that he's got his "niggas in Paris" on a 2012 song of the same title, this was how it was intended and interpreted. In June 2012, however, White actress Gwyneth Paltrow caused a minor stir in Paris, France, when she attended a concert by West and Jay-Z and tweeted "Ni**as in paris for real." The Twitterverse instantly lit up with accusations of racism, while Paltrow defended herself by tweeting, "Hold up. It's the title of a song!" Thus, even in contexts where White use of the word is intended to signify the inverted use of the term, it can be interpreted as symbolizing its original racist meaning, which is important for Whites to understand when using the term. As historian Jeffrey O. G. Ogbar, author of *Hip-hop Revolution: The Culture and Politics of Rap* (2007) explains, "Black people have refused Whites' opportunity to partake in the term, whether they hope to use it affectionately or not . . . The Black intolerance for White use of the N-word clearly reflects the sensitivity of the word to Black people and the resilience of its power" (p. 67). Nevertheless, the N-word is routinely employed in rap music and other entertainment outlets, where its usage is further complicated by matters of gender and class.

Gender, Class, and the N-word

Musicologist Emmett Price (2006) points out that having exclusive right to the term in rap music places Blacks in a "subtle position of power" over other ethnoracial groups, especially Whites (p. 57). In this context, the N-word upends (however symbolically and temporarily) longstanding hierarchies of race by giving Blacks power and authority over Whites. This may help explain the appeal of rap music for Blacks, particularly young Black men, a historically marginalized group. Rap music is a space where this group is afforded a command and respect not found as easily in other realms of social life. Moreover, its usage by Black men is not only an effort to upend racial hierarchies, but it is also an attempt to reinforce masculinity and stake a claim to patriarchal power. Rap music often entails a hypermasculine performance, where the frequent usage of the N-word appears to play a key role in that performance. Even Black female MCs such as Eve, Foxy Brown, and Lil' Kim have employed the N-word frequently in their rhymes, typically as a means by which to accentuate both Blackness and masculinity. For example, on the posse track "The Illest" Jean Grae boasted that she would "fuck your girl like a nigga." In doing so, Grae made a claim to authenticity, equated here (as elsewhere in hip-hop culture) with both Blackness and maleness. Performance studies scholar Shanté Paradigm Smalls (2011) notes that Grae's lyrics are a declaration that she is "quite capable, because of her tremendous skill, of inserting herself into the position held for men" (p. 87).

White female rappers have also attempted to use the term, with very different response. In 2011, Kreayshawn, a White female MC from Oakland, tweeted, "WTF YOU WANT FROM A NIGGA?! *DMX VOICE*." The tweet caused an immediate media and online stir, and received a swift denunciation from Black male rapper Game, who blasted Kreayshawn on a track entitled, "Uncle Otis": "Lil' White bitch, better stay in your place/You call me a nigga, I'ma put the K in your face." Game told a reporter, "You can't be playing with that word, some people will take it serious. Especially coming from someone that's [not Black]. There's a lot of tragic history behind it" (J. Rodriguez, 2011). Taken at face value, Game problematized the term due to its racist history, rather than its use by a woman. "Uncle Otis," however, implied that White "bitches" had a position subordinate to men, and women who challenged male authority by using the N-word could be subjected to violence.

When asked about the kerfuffle, Kreayshawn responded that she never stated the N-word in her recorded music but occasionally did so when freestyling. In Oakland, she claimed, all racial groups routinely used the term, and that members of the lower classes should be allowed to do so. "That word is used in the low income community more than anything," she said. "I can see if I was some rich crazy trick and I was just saying this because it's hip-hop. No, I was raised around this. Me and my sisters were all raised around this. People call me that" (Gipson, 2011).

Communications scholar Kembrew McLeod links rap's emphasis on Black masculinity to "authenticity," or the socially constructed belief that something or someone is genuine, original, true, or pure. McLeod (1999) asserts that, "To its core community members, hip-hop remains strongly tied to Black cultural expression" and male dominance (p. 140). Thus, in rap music, Black masculinity denotes "keeping it real," while Whiteness and femininity are equated with artifice. According to McLeod, Black male rappers create verbal "rules" related to authenticity in order to preserve its "pure" core from co-option by outsiders, including Whites and women. Extending McLeod's theory to the N-word, the prohibition against White and female use of the term is a means by which Black men can protect rap music from White and/or female co-option by upholding the belief that authentic rap music is the exclusive domain of Black men. This strategy is complicated by the fact that rap music is also created and consumed by plenty of folks who do not fit the Black–White racial binary.

Beyond Black and White

Scholars of the N-word (Asim, 2007; Kennedy, 2003) tend to frame debates over its use as matters of Black versus White, but lots of rappers and rap-music fans who don't fit either ethnoracial category use the word. Concurrent with rap's rise in popularity, by the turn of the century "numerous non-Black communities began using the term, and it became prominent in the lyrics of top-selling artists. Asian

American, Latino, and numerous other non-Black practitioners and fans began to call one another by the term" (Price, 2006, p. 57). For example, Puerto Rican rapper Big Pun's posthumous 2000 CD, *Yeeeah Baby,* included a track called "Nigga Shit" that detailed his love for smoking pot, dealing drugs, getting drunk, going to jail, beating his children, "talkin' loud at flicks," and a host of additional Black "ghetto" stereotypes. Pun's appropriation of the N-word in the song could be viewed as a signifier of Black authenticity in a Black-dominated field: he portrayed himself as a "real nigga" with the pedigree to prove it. Backlash over the track was nonexistent and *Yeeeah Baby* sold more than half a million copies within months of its release. This raises an important question: If Black use of the term is considered acceptable and White use is forbidden, where do Latinos and other ethnoracial groups fit into the debate?

Ogbar (2007) points out that Latino rap acts such as Cypress Hill, Fat Joe, and Cuban Link have employed the N-word in their songs without censure, while artists such as Kid Frost avoided it. Ogbar believes that part of the reason for this is that Latinos who said the term generally had Caribbean lineage that afforded them a degree of leeway not enjoyed by rappers with Chicano roots. He argues that the division between Latinos of Caribbean and Chicano origin reveals

> (1) the historical, cultural, and social relationships between different Latino nationalities and African Americans and (2) African diasporic connections between people in the Caribbean and North America. Since the early twentieth century, Puerto Ricans and African Americans in New York City have had relatively close social relations in various cultural and political institutions from sports teams (professional and recreational), to residential areas, to musical groups, and to politics. (p. 48)

While it may be true that Puerto Ricans claim a unique relationship to Blacks that renders rappers from this group less scrutinized than Latino MCs of other ethnic backgrounds, studies of rap music (Harkness, 2008) find a conviction among Latino MCs of all ethnic backgrounds that these groups share historical, social, and cultural characteristics with Blacks in the United States, an opinion often echoed by Black rappers as well.

Still, even Puerto Rican artists find themselves under scrutiny when employing the N-word. For example, in Jennifer Lopez's 2001 remix of her song, "I'm Real," featuring rapper Ja Rule, she sang this lyric: "Now people screamin' what the deal with you and so and so/ I tell them niggas, mind their biz, but they don't hear me though." Lopez was lambasted across media outlets by Blacks (and others) who thought her usage of the word was inappropriate. In some part, the critique was due to the fact that she isn't considered Black despite her Puerto Rican roots and diasporic connections and despite the fact that she dated prominent rap mogul Diddy (a.k.a., Sean "Puffy" Combs). The outcry might also have been due to her status as a woman; where Big Pun and other Puerto Rican rappers have been given a "pass," she was not and her claim to power through usage of the word was firmly denied. The differences in these cases reiterate the complexities of the N-word's usage among other groups of color.

Use of the term among Asian rappers provides further illustration of the controversies surrounding the N-word. Race and ethnicity scholar Nitasha Tamar Sharma's (2010) study of South Asian American (or "desi") rappers finds that male desis frequently use the N-word in referring to themselves and their friends, "particularly when there [are] no Black people around" (p. 241). While Sharma's desi MCs decry White use of the term as racist, in their own use of the word they "emphasize their knowledge of context, respect for the music, and their position as non-White 'outsider' contributors" to rap music and hip-hop culture (p. 242). However, many Blacks might find desis' use of the word offensive, particularly in light of the ways in which (some) Asian American groups are positioned as "model minorities" and thus enjoy a social prestige often not accorded to Blacks (for further discussion, see Zhou, Essay 8). Yet the question remains: Should desis and any other non-Blacks be "allowed" to use the term?

In hip-hop culture—where Blackness is associated with authenticity and Whiteness with inauthenticity, and those who do not fit the Black–White racial binary fall somewhere in between—use of the N-word serves as a signifier of Blackness in a culture where Blackness is at the center of the status system. It also functions as a verbal means of distancing oneself from alleged White fakeness. Having the "right" to say the N-word is a claim to authenticity in a culture where "keeping it real" is paramount. Yet, the fact remains that non-Black usage of the word remains questionable at best, offensive at worst. Essentially, artistic license aside, language is a powerful conveyor of inequality, where the N-word remains historically and presently loaded with connotations of racism and inequality. Nevertheless, it is sometimes the "artistic license" aspect of the term that leads to its usage among non-Blacks, especially those in the rap industry. But race is not the only factor in whether or not an artist, group, or individual employs the term; among Blacks, class also factors into the word's usage.

Class Matters

As alluded to above in the Kreayshawn example, class clearly plays a role in usage of the N-word. Studies that frame its use as a simple matter of ethnoracial status overlook the crucial role of social class. While race is important, "more common, however, is the use of 'nigga' to describe a condition rather than skin color or culture. Above all, 'nigga' speaks to a collective identity shaped by class consciousness" (Kelley, 1996, p. 137). Despite popular perceptions to the contrary, in terms of sheer numbers, most poor people in the United States are White, and most Blacks are members of the middle or working classes. In part, this is due to the ongoing expansion of the Black middle class, a group that is increasing numerically and as a percentage of the Black population (Marsh, Darity, Cohen, Casper, & Salters, 2007, p. 20; Pattillo-McCoy, 1999). These structural changes have impacted culture within the Black community: There is a growing cultural divide between middle-class Blacks and those from lower and working classes. Cherise Harris and Nikki Khanna (2010) point out that, "Because of the conflation of race and class in America, middle-class culture is often understood as Whiteness and Blackness is understood as the behavior and experiences associated with the urban ghetto" (p. 644).

Within the Black middle class there is an emphasis on "academic excellence, conservative styles of hair and dress, proficiency in Standard English, and the values of sacrifice and delayed gratification" (Harris & Khanna, 2010, p. 653). Adopting such behaviors, however, does not come without penalty. Black people who do not dress, speak, act, and consume culture that symbolizes alleged Black low-income and working-class membership sometimes face accusations of selling out or being deemed inauthentically Black. As Harris and Khanna (2010) note, "Black middle-class respondents frequently describe rejection by other Blacks, often because of their lack of familiarity with Black lower-class culture that has in large part become the standard by which authentic Blackness is measured" (p. 652). From this perspective, Blacks who signal association with the upper and middle classes by refusing to say the N-word may be labeled inauthentic by low-income and working-class Blacks. Conversely, Blacks who signal association with the Black lower and working classes by saying the N-word may do so as a claim to authentic "hood" membership.

The perception that there are two "types" of Blacks, symbolized by linguistic differences associated with upper and lower class status, illustrates the increasing cultural, social, and economic disparities described by scholars of the Black middle class. Michael Eric Dyson (2005) writes of an *Afristocracy*, which he defines as "upper-middle-class Blacks and the Black elite who rain down fire and brimstone upon poor Blacks for their deviance and pathology, and for their lack of couth and culture" (p. xiii–xiv). He contrasts this with what he calls the *Ghettocracy*, which consists of the Black underclass and working poor. Dyson's Ghettocracy construct also includes celebrity rappers "whose values and habits are alleged to be negatively influenced by their poor origins" (p. xiv) and who romanticize a fabled (and fictional) Black ghetto in their music and lifestyles.

These issues are not limited to the Black population. Similar class-based differences have been found in studies of the growing Latino middle class. For example, G. Rodriguez (1996) finds that Latinos are often stereotyped in the mainstream media as gangbangers or irate political activists. As occurs in the Black population, middle-class Latinos are accused by their working-class and low-income counterparts of being sellouts, White wannabes, and cultural traitors: "Apparently, retaining one's 'authentic' Latino ethnicity requires remaining in place both socio-economically and geographically. Even the accomplished have often felt a need to feign 'street-wise' mannerisms and humble roots" (G. Rodriguez, 1996, p. 2).

These class-based divisions, disparities, and tensions are reflected in rap music, mirrored, for example, in the perceived split between the so-called "conscious" rap subgenre and gangsta rap, where the word is found more frequently. According to historian Robin Kelley (1996), the style and sound of gangsta rap, including its use of the N-word, is partially a Black underclass response to the Black middle class. Gangsta rappers "remind listeners that they are still second-class citizens— 'Niggaz'—whose collective lived experiences suggest that nothing has changed *for them* as opposed to the Black middle class. In fact, 'Nigga' is frequently employed to distinguish urban Black working-class males from the Black bourgeoisie" (p. 137).

Thus, in addition to its use as a linguistic divider between ethnoracial groups, the N-word is also deployed within ethnoracial groups to make class-based distinctions. From this point of view, the N-word is a discursive means of creating a space where, for example, working-class and low-income Blacks and Latinos have more power than their middle-class counterparts, thereby reversing social-class hierarchies found within ethnoracial categories. While scholars of rap music have spent considerable energy on matters of race and ethnicity, less attention has been afforded to social class, particularly within ethnoracial groups. Focusing on the intersection of ethnoracial status and social class offers a more complete understanding of present-day rap-music culture, including its varied use or nonuse of the N-word.

Some scholars believe that rap music serves as a sort of racial melting pot that disintegrates existing race-based tensions and allows for greater understanding between ethnoracial groups. For example, Pancho McFarland (2008) describes rap music as an "interethnic contact zone," a location where "young people of various ethnicities come together and exchange ideas, experiences, understandings, and analyses, resulting in profound changes in individuals and in the cultures of each group" (p. 173). Hip-hop scholar and author Bakari Kitwana (2005, p. xii) asserts that White assimilation into hip-hop culture marks "the dawning of a new reality of race in America."

The politics of language surrounding the N-word, however, serve as a potent reminder that ethnoracial and social class divisions have hardly disappeared. Debates over who has the "right" to say the N-word, or how using the term reflects upon those who chose to say it or not say it, illustrate how race, social class, and gender continue to be key means by which people remain divided. Nevertheless, what cannot be forgotten is the loaded history of the terms *nigger* or *nigga*, which is why they remain controversial in the first place.

Privilege, Power, and the N-word

While most of this essay focuses on the N-word and the varied ways in which some justify its use, it is important to consider arguments for why it shouldn't be used. As noted above, the N-word is, to say the least, racially loaded and embedded in a long, troubled, and violent history of anti-Black oppression. As such, while it is commonly used in the rap industry, some White rappers don't believe they have the right to use the term. Eminem, easily the world's most prominent and respected White MC, has never used the term publically or on a commercial recording, saying to a *Rolling Stone* reporter in 2000, "That word is not even in my vocabulary" (DeCurtis, 2000, p.18). When an early homemade recording of a teenage Eminem using the term in a derogatory manner surfaced a few years later, he immediately issued a public apology. What did Eminem understand that Paula Deen, Laura Schlessinger, and Kreayshawn didn't? Perhaps he understood that even as a prominent player in the Black-dominated rap industry, he was still a White man and given his White privilege, it was inappropriate for him to use even a derivation of a word that has been used to oppress Black people in systematic fashion. In a 2011 interview for the Southern Poverty Law Center's magazine, *Teaching Tolerance*, Neal A. Lester, dean of humanities and former chair of the English department at Arizona State University, argued

> We know that as early as the 17th century, "negro" evolved to "nigger" as intentionally derogatory, and it has never been able to shed that baggage since then—even when black people talk about appropriating and reappropriating it. The poison is still there. The word is inextricably linked with violence and brutality on black psyches and derogatory aspersions cast on black bodies. No degree of appropriating can rid it of that bloodsoaked history.

Lester, who in 2008 taught the first ever college-level course designed to explore the word *nigger*, went on to discuss how students in his classes admit to using the term:

> In their circles of white friends, some are so comfortable with the N-word because they've grown up on and been nourished by hip-hop. Much of the commercial hip-hop culture by black males uses the N-word as a staple. White youths, statistically the largest consumers of hip-hop, then feel that they can use the word among themselves with black and white peers. . . . But then I hear in that same discussion that many of the black youths are indeed offended by [whites using the N-word]. And if blacks and whites are together and a white person uses the word, many blacks are ready to fight. So this word comes laden with these complicated and contradictory emotional responses to it. It's very confusing to folks on the "outside," particularly when nobody has really talked about the history of the word in terms of American history, language, performance and identity.

While this discussion from Lester further illustrates the complexity of the term's usage, it also illustrates this unmistakable, simple truth: At its core, the word is freighted with a history of anti-Black racism and oppression that still resonates today. For these reasons, it cannot be casually used without consequence by Whites and other non-Blacks whose ancestors haven't been victimized by anti-Black oppression and who don't currently experience this kind of oppression. Moreover, as Lester (2011) indicates above, Black usage of the word as a method of reappropriation and reclamation may also be ineffective as "the poison is still there." In this manner and in other ways, the power reclaimed by Blacks' reappropriation of the term may be temporary and fleeting in a society still characterized by institutional racism and the continued systematic subjugation of Black Americans.

Suggested Additional Resources

Asim, J. (2007). *The n word: Who can say it, who shouldn't and why.* New York, NY: Houghton Mifflin.

Forman, M., & Neal, M. A. (Eds.). (2012). *That's the joint! The hip-hop studies reader* (2nd ed.). New York, NY: Routledge.

Harkness, G. (2008). Hip hop culture and America's most taboo word. *Contexts, 7*(3), 38–42.

Harrison, A. K. (2009). *Hip hop underground: The integrity and ethics of racial identification.* Philadelphia, PA: Temple University Press.

Jeffries, M. (2011). *Thug life: Race, gender, and the meaning of hip-hop.* Chicago, IL: The University of Chicago Press.

Kennedy, R. L. (1999–2000). Who can say "nigger"? And other considerations. *The Journal of Blacks in Higher Education, 26,* 86–96.

Lacy, K. (2007). *Blue-chip Black: Race, class, and status in the new Black middle class.* Berkeley: University of California Press.

Oware, M. (2014). (Un)conscious (popular) underground: Restricted cultural production and underground rap music. *Poetics* 42, 60-81.

Sharma, N. T. (2010). *Hip hop desis: South Asian Americans, Blackness, and a global race consciousness.* Durham, NC: Duke University Press.

Websites

- A conversation about the N-word between rapper KRS-ONE and comedian Paul Mooney titled "When the 'N' Word is Part of a Routine" can be found at http://www.npr.org/templates/story/story.php?storyId=6560171.
- Radio Capicu discusses and debates Latino use of the N-word in a show titled "Should Latinos Use the 'N' Word?": http://www.blogtalkradio.com/radiocapicu/2008/02/28/radio-capicu-should-latinos-use-the-N-word

Questions for Further Discussion

1. Is the N-word more or less acceptable when stated by certain people? If so, for whom is it more or less acceptable? What role do race, social class, and gender play in this?

2. Do people make too big of a deal over the N-word? Do you believe that it has lost its original racist meaning?

3. Is the "er" form of the N-word more offensive than the "ga" form? Why or why not? Is the N-word acceptable in the context of rap music and hip-hop culture? Why or why not?

4. Would you feel comfortable saying the N-word in any context? If not, under which contexts would you feel comfortable or uncomfortable saying it? What are your reasons for this?

5. How is the N-word different from or similar to other forms of "injurious speech," such as redneck, spic, chink, bitch, ho, gay, queer, and fag?

Reaching Beyond the Color Line

1. If you are a White student who says the N-word, think about when and how you use it. Do you say it publically and privately? Do you say it around people of color? Do you believe that there is a double standard for Whites

when it comes to White use of the N-word? If yes, why do you think this double standard exists?

2. If you are a Black student who uses the N-word or doesn't use the N-word, what are your reasons for this decision? What standards or rules should apply to Whites when it comes to the term? Should all Whites be "allowed" to say the word or just certain Whites? If only certain Whites should be allowed to say it, which ones and why? What about those who do not fit the Black-White racial binary?

3. If you are a non-White and non-Black student who uses or does not use the N-word, what is your justification for this? Do you believe that there are different standards applied to different ethnoracial groups, such as Latinos, Asians, Arabs, Native Americans and others, when it comes to the N-word? What are these standards and why do you think they exist?

References

Asim, J. (2007). *The n word: Who can say it, who shouldn't and why.* New York, NY: Houghton Mifflin.

DeCurtis A. (2000). Eminem responds: The rapper addresses his critics. *Rolling Stone, 846,* 18.

Dyson, M. E. (2005). *Is Bill Cosby Right? Or has the Black middle class lost its mind?* New York, NY: Basic Civitas Books.

Gipson, B. (2011, June 8). Kreayshawn on that million dollar (?) deal with Columbia/Sony, being a femcee and working with Lil B and Snoop Dogg. *OC Weekly.* Retrieved from http://blogs.ocweekly.com/heardmentality/2011/06/kreayshawn_on_being_a_femcee_w.php

Harkness, G. (2008). Hip hop culture and America's most taboo word. *Contexts, 7*(3), 38–42.

Harris, C. A., & Khanna, N. (2010). Black is, Black ain't: Biracials, middle-class Blacks, and the social construction of Blackness. *Sociological Spectrum, 30 (6),* 639–670.

Kelley, R. D. G. (1996). Kickin' reality, kickin' ballistics: Gangsta rap and postindustrial Los Angeles. In W. E. Perkins (Ed.), *Droppin' science: Critical essays on rap music and hip hop culture* (pp. 117–158). Philadelphia, PA: Temple University Press.

Kennedy, R. L. (2003). *Nigger: The strange career of a troublesome word.* New York, NY: Vintage.

Kitwana, B. (2005). *Why White kids love hip hop: Wankstas, wiggers, wannabes, and the new reality of race in America.* New York, NY: Basic Books.

Lester, N. (2011, Fall). Straight talk about the N-word. *Teaching Tolerance, 40.* Retrieved from http://www.tolerance.org/magazine/number-40-fall-2011/feature/straight-talk-about-N-word

Marsh, K., Darity, W. A., Cohen, P., Casper, L., & Salters, D. (2007). The emerging Black middle class: Single and living alone. *Social Forces, 86*(2), 1–28.

McFarland, P. (2008). Chicano hip-hop as interethnic contact zone. *Aztlán: A Journal of Chicano Studies, 33*(1), 173–183.

McLeod, K. (1999). Authenticity within hip-hop and other cultures threatened with assimilation. *Journal of Communication, 49*(4), 134–150.

Ogbar, J. O. G. (2007). *Hip-hop revolution: The culture and politics of rap.* Lawrence: University Press of Kansas.

Pattillo-McCoy, M. (1999). *Black picket fences: Privilege and peril among the Black middle class.* Chicago, IL: University of Chicago Press.

Price, E. (2006). *Hip hop culture*. Santa Barbara, CA: ABC-CLIO.

Rodriguez, G. (1996, October). *The emerging Latino middle class*. Malibu, CA: Pepperdine University Institute for Public Policy. Retrieved from http://publicpolicy.pepperdine .edu/davenport-institute/content/reports/latino.pdf

Rodriguez, J. (2011). Game says "Uncle Otis" is "just fun," not a Jay-Z Dis. *XXL* July 22. Retrieved from http://www.xxlmag.com/news/2011/07/game-says-"uncle-otis"-is-just-fun-not-a-jay-z-dis

Sharma, N. T. (2010). *Hip hop desis: South Asian Americans, Blackness, and a global race consciousness*. Durham, NC: Duke University Press.

Smalls, S. P. (2011). "The rain comes down": Jean Grae and hip hop heteronormativity. *American Behavioral Scientist, 55*(1), 86–95.

Smitherman, G. (1997). "The chain remain the same": Communicative practices in the hip hop nation. *Journal of Black Studies, 28*(1), 3–25.

"I'm Not Racist. Some of My Best Friends Are . . ."

The Shift From Being a "Friend" to Becoming an Ally

Cherise A. Harris
Connecticut College

Cherise A. Harris is an associate professor of sociology at Connecticut College. She specializes in race, class, and gender and teaches classes on the sociology of ethnic and race relations; the sociology of inequality; race, gender, and the mass media; and middle-class minorities. Her book, *The Cosby Cohort: Blessing and Burdens of Growing Up Black Middle Class*, was published in 2013. She has also published in *Teaching Sociology*, *Sociological Spectrum*, and *Journal of African American Studies*.

Of all the names White Americans could be called in American society, *racist* ranks as one of the worst. As psychology professor Beverly Daniel Tatum says in Essay 2 of this volume, "The word racist holds a lot of emotional power. For many White people, to be called racist is the ultimate insult." One of the reasons why the term is considered anathema by most Whites is because of the images it conjures up in the public imagination. For example, in Joe Feagin and Hernán Vera's book, *White Racism* (2000), one of their White respondents referred to Blacks a number of times as "apes" and admitted that her parents "always instilled in me that blacks aren't equal," but nevertheless maintained: "I don't consider myself racist . . . when I think of the word racist, I think of KKK, people in white robes burning black people on crosses and stuff, or I think of the Skinheads or some exaggerated form of racism" (pp. 215–216; see also Ashmore, 2009; Culp, 1993). Essentially, many Whites are reluctant to admit their racial prejudices and instead believe that "[R]acism does not exist among the people of goodwill in America, who include most Americans. Racism and white supremacy are relegated in our time to the David Dukes and the few white supremacists" (Culp, 1993, pp. 211–212; see also Feagin, 2010). As a result, we often don't recognize omnipresent forms of systemic and everyday racism when they appear because we have reduced our notions of racism to these narrow confines; so long as one doesn't participate in overtly racist speech or activities, or so long as one has good will (despite saying or doing something that is racially intolerant), that person cannot reasonably be considered a racist.

Yet, racism is often practiced by people of "good will" and in the contexts of both individual and institutional racism. Being a "mean" person or a "bad" or "evil" person isn't a requirement for being a racist or practicing racist behavior. Racists are often people who go to church, do charity work, love their families, and generally experience themselves and are experienced by others as "nice people." However, under particular circumstances, they are willing to participate in racist, discriminatory behavior. Writer Ta-Nehisi Coates gives an example of this in his *New York Times* op-ed piece, "The Good, Racist People" (2013):

> In modern America we believe racism to be the property of the uniquely villainous and morally deformed, the ideology of trolls, gorgons and orcs. We believe this even when we are actually being racist. In 1957, neighbors in Levittown, Pa., uniting under the flag of segregation, wrote: "As moral, religious and law-abiding citizens, we feel that we are unprejudiced and undiscriminating in our wish to keep our community a closed community." A half-century later, little [has] changed.

As Coates suggests in his recounting of the skirmishes over integrating Levittown, Pennsylvania (one of the now-iconic, post-World War II planned suburban communities), racism isn't limited to people many consider "evil" or "bad" like White supremacists but is also the practice of everyday Whites who consider themselves "good" people.

In an effort to avoid the stigma that accompanies the term *racist*, when Whites are accused of racism, a common refrain is, "I'm not racist!," which is frequently followed by another popular refrain: "Some of my best friends are [insert targeted group here, e.g., Black, Latino, Asian, Native American]!" Indeed, when public figures face accusations of racism, it's one of the first defenses they offer. For instance, when radio personality Don Imus was accused of being a racist after calling the Rutgers University's women's basketball team "nappy-headed ho's," his defense was, "I'm not a white man who doesn't know any African-Americans" (MSNBC, 2007). He went on to discuss his work with ill children and how he attends funerals for many of the children, not just the White ones. The "friends" defense was also used in the George Zimmerman case. After the White Hispanic man killed 17-year-old Trayvon Martin in his father's neighborhood because he looked suspicious, Zimmerman "family friend" Joe Oliver gave interviews vouching for Zimmerman by saying: "I'm a black male and all I know is that George has never given me any reason whatsoever to believe he has anything against people of color" (Trotta, 2012; see also MSNBC, 2012). Yet, when pushed, Oliver seemed to know few other details about Zimmerman's life (Agyeman-Fisher, 2012; Valbrun, 2012), thus ultimately casting doubt on their "friendship" and the extent to which he could vouch for Zimmerman's racial proclivities.

In a noteworthy application of the friends defense, in 2010, singer John Mayer caused an uproar when during an interview with *Playboy* magazine, he boasted about his Black friends (e.g., "Black people love me") and wondered aloud whether those relationships made him eligible for a "hood pass" or "nigger pass." He went on to make several additional racist and sexist statements, including describing his penis as having White supremacist tendencies because he doesn't seek out sexual relationships with Black women (Tannenbaum, 2012). Mayer was trounced in the media and subsequently lamented his arrogance while vowing to never say the "n-word" again (see Harkness, Essay 22 for further discussion of the "n-word").[1]

The friends defense has also been used by college students to excuse racist behavior. Leslie Houts Picca and Joe Feagin (2007) analyzed journals from 626 White students at over two dozen colleges and universities in several regions over a course of six to nine weeks. The diarists were asked to record their observations of everyday events in their lives that "exhibited racial issues, images, and understandings" (Feagin, 2010, p. 124). Hannah, one of their diarists, discussed going out with three other White friends, where her friend Dylan started telling racist jokes including referring to Black people as "porch monkeys" and joking that the most confusing day of the year in Harlem is Father's Day. Despite noting her own discomfort about his "jokes," Hannah firmly maintained, "My friend Dylan is not a racist person. He has more black friends than I do, that's why I was surprised he so freely said something like that. Dylan would never have said something like that around anyone who is a minority" (Picca & Feagin, 2007, pp. 17–18). In the minds of many Whites, social interactions with people of color frequently serve as proxy for racial tolerance and understanding. Yet, Hannah's account reflects two important points: (1) how easy it is for Whites like Dylan to have friends of color and still make racist statements, and (2) that a good deal of racist commentary from people who allegedly have friends of color happens in the social "backstage" or areas where only Whites are present and not on the "frontstage" where strangers or people from diverse racial backgrounds are present and might express disapproval (Feagin, 2010, p. 124; Picca & Feagin, 2007; see also Goffman, 1959). Moreover, that Dylan would make such racist comments about a group with whom he purportedly

---

[1] It should also be noted that the "I have friends" defense is not unique to those who express racial prejudice; it's also been used by people accused of homophobia. In April 2013, in response to NBA player Jason Collins coming out, Chris Broussard (ESPN host of "Outside the Lines") said that living an openly gay "lifestyle" is a "sin" and suggested that gays should "repent and ask for forgiveness." Nevertheless, he claimed, "I'm fine with homosexuals," and went on to insist that he has at least one gay friend (Bennett-Smith, 2013). Apparently, the "I have friends" defense is common among many who harbor prejudices toward disenfranchised groups.

has friendships means that we must also look at how Whites often overestimate or in other ways mischaracterize their friendships and relationships with people of color and the subsequent way in which they conflate these relationships with being an ally.

The "Friends" Defense Debunked

When we take a closer look at the "friends" defense and examine its merits, several issues arise. For one, research shows that Whites tend to exaggerate the depth of their friendships with people of color. In his book *Racism Without Racists* (2010), sociologist Eduardo Bonilla-Silva uses survey data from the Detroit Area Study (DAS) to investigate this phenomenon. The data set included 323 Whites, where 66 of these were randomly selected for in-depth interviews. Of the 66, a little more than a third ($n = 24$) claimed that they had Black friends whom they characterized as "good friends," "best friends," or friends with whom they "hung out." However, after probing a bit further, Bonilla-Silva (2010) found that the strength of these friendship ties was more tenuous than his respondents originally indicated. For example, White respondents tended to "otherize" their Black friends using distancing terms like "these people" or "them," and often didn't (or couldn't) identify them by their first name. Additionally, the contact with these friends proved very superficial and typically taking place in the context of sports, music, or the occasional friendly talk with a fellow student or coworker; all of these were characterized as "friendships." Yet, as Bonilla-Silva indicates, "Missing from these reports of friendship with blacks is evidence of trust, of the capacity of confiding, and of interactions with these friends beyond the place or situation of formal contact (classroom, assigned roommates, or job)" (p. 111). Finally, these "friendships" tended to evaporate after the class, rooming experience, band season, or job ended (Bonilla-Silva, 2010, p. 111). Thus, the friendships proved to be rather shallow and incomplete, which casts doubts on whether having "friends" of color can really be used to prove one doesn't have racial prejudices.

Moreover, even if one did have friendships with people of color, research shows that when the stakes of social interaction are even higher, the depths of racial prejudices emerge. *Social distance* is the level of intimacy a person is willing to accept in his or her relations with people of other social groups. Creator of the social distance scale, Emory Bogardus (1933), specified seven dimensions of social distance: (1) close kinship by marriage, (2) members of one's club or personal friends, (3) neighbors on one's street, (4) employed in one's occupation, (5) citizens in one's country, (6) visitors to one's country, and (7) would exclude from one's country (cited in Healey, 2012, p. 27). Frequently, racial prejudices surface the further one travels on the social distance scale. For example, while people might be accepting of a Latino person in their workplace (dimension 4) or living in their neighborhood (dimension 3), they may not be as accepting of a Latino person marrying into the family (dimension 1). In these ways, those who might present or view themselves as racially tolerant frequently show signs of prejudice as the contact in question becomes more intimate. In *Why Are All the Black Kids Sitting Together in the Cafeteria,* Beverly Daniel Tatum (1997) illustrates how this phenomenon is evident in the changing racial composition of children's birthday parties as children get older. Termed the "birthday party effect" (pp. 56–57), Tatum observes that in elementary school, birthday parties in multiracial communities reflect the area's diversity, but as children get older, parents' anxiety about puberty raises fears about interracial dating and causes birthday parties to become more racially homogeneous.

Indeed, attitudes toward interracial dating often expose hidden prejudices even among those who appear racially tolerant and open minded. Erica Chito Childs (2005) suggests that attitudes toward interracial dating and marriage serve as "a miner's canary, revealing problems of race that otherwise can remain hidden, especially to whites" (2005, p. 6; see also Bonilla-Silva, 2003; Khanna, Essay 11). Childs witnessed this firsthand in her own family. She married a Black man and noted that her sister and her family never expressed any opposition to her relationship and in fact, appeared supportive. However, when her sister's daughter wanted to attend the prom with a Black schoolmate she was dating, the sister and her husband refused to let him in the house, claiming he was "not right" for her (Childs, 2005, p. 4). Childs maintains, "It was clear to everyone, however, that skin color was the problem. To this day, my niece will tell you that her parents would never have accepted her with a black man" (p. 4). From this story, it seems that Childs' sister and brother-in-law were accepting of interracial dating in theory, but when it came to *their daughter* potentially becoming involved with a Black person, the stakes were much higher and hidden prejudices suddenly emerged. In these ways, Whites who are seemingly tolerant can simultaneously hold racist views that become evident when put to the test.

Perhaps most detrimental is when this type of discrimination occurs within the context of more formal spaces like the workplace. In this context, discrimination can be more than psychologically painful; it can lead to differential outcomes in hiring and promotion. For instance, legal scholar Jerome McCristal Culp Jr. (1993) offers several examples of how his family members have battled this type of discrimination. In one instance, he tells the story of a relative who worked in a state agency and finished first on the approved tests for a particular position but was still denied the position by her supervisors and instead offered another position with equal pay but less flexibility than the job for which she was applying. In another instance, he tells the story of how his uncle who served on a police force was at the top of the promotion list but was forced to take an additional test beyond those previously required of White candidates before he could become the first Black lieutenant on the force. As Culp explains about these examples, "In none of these situations were white people always evil or impolite to black people. Many of the supervisors thought they were true friends of my relatives, but they were willing to manipulate the situation to ignore the concerns of black people" (p. 241). While these instances may appear anecdotal, the presence of this kind of discrimination in the workplace has been well documented (Bertrand & Mullainathan, 2004; Cose, 1993; Feagin & Sikes, 1994; Pager & Shepherd, 2008). In these ways, White Americans who are experienced as otherwise "nice" and "friendly" people may discriminate if it is to their advantage. The failure to acknowledge these more covert forms of racism results in a worldview where many may believe that racism no longer exists and that America is a meritocracy where the playing field is level and anyone who works hard can be successful (Bonilla-Silva, 2010; Gallagher, 2004; McIntosh, 2007; see also Ioanide, Essay 6). In these ways, the subtler forms of racism that are more prevalent and more destructive go undetected and remain unchallenged.

To be sure, avoidance of racial topics and issues fits well within the current discourse on "post-racialism" where some argue that race doesn't matter or carries much less importance than in previous moments in American history (for a recent debate on the term *post-racial*, see National Public Radio, 2010; see also Bonilla-Silva, 2010, & Wise, 2009, 2010 for critical responses to the term). Use of this term became more frequent after the election of America's first Black president, Barack Obama. Social critics, political pundits, and academics alike asserted that his election wouldn't have been possible had the nation not been taking a gradual turn toward post-racialism.

However, voter data show that it is entirely possible to hold racist views and still vote for a Black president (Pettigrew, 2009). For example, in his article, "Racial Views Steer Some Away From Obama," Ron Fournier of the Associated Press (2008; also cited in Pettigrew, 2009) found that a third of White Democrats ascribed one or more negative adjectives (e.g., violent, complaining, lazy, irresponsible) to Blacks, yet 58% of them still supported Obama in the 2008 election. Moreover, as Thomas F. Pettigrew (2009) pointed out, "While Nebraska voters gave one of its electoral votes to Obama, they also passed by 58% to 42% a ban on race- and gender-based affirmative action. Previously voters in California, Michigan and Washington State had passed similar referenda, yet all three provided Obama wide winning margins in 2008" (p. 283). This evidence suggests that it is indeed possible to support and vote for a Black president and still harbor biases (see also Womack, Bridgeforth, & Beasley, Essay 16).

To some degree, Obama's victory has been based on a sense of "enlightened exceptionalism" (Wise, 2009), or a type of racism in which Whites show an affinity for "special" Black people whom they perceive as different from most Blacks. Citing journalistic and academic research on Obama's triumph, Bobo and Dawson (2009, p. 7) provide evidence of this:

> [O]ne *New York Times* story reported on racial prejudice as a possible influence even among young voters. It quoted a White student from the University of Kentucky as saying: "I don't have any problem with a black president. I think it would be fine, because a lot of things people stereotype black people with, I don't think Obama has any of them" (Dewan, 2008). In short, Obama had "escaped" or transcended the stereotype.

Enlightened exceptionalism also often occurs with friendships, where one accommodates certain specific individuals of color without modifying a wider set of attitudes about people of color as a whole. In these ways, it is possible to have friends of color and still be prejudiced toward that same group.

Likewise, it is also possible to express interest in or appreciation for aspects of a group of color's culture (e.g., music, food, language, etc.) without having a true awareness or understanding of the sociopolitical struggle that group faces. Critical race theorist Patricia Hill Collins (2009) refers to this phenomenon as "voyeurism," where the lives of people of color "are interesting for entertainment value" and the "privileged become voyeurs, passive onlookers who do not relate to the less powerful, but who are interested in seeing how the 'different' live" (p. 104). Prominent Black feminist scholar bell hooks (1992) refers to a similar phenomenon as "eating the Other," where some Whites believe that exposure to different peoples and cultures "will provide a greater, more intense pleasure than any that exists in the ordinary world of one's familiar racial group" (p. 24; see also Ott & Mack, 2010, p. 145). Many would point to the mass consumption of hip hop music and culture by middle-class Whites as examples of these phenomena.

Feminist and race bloggers have been calling attention recently to a comparable strain of racism also based on a type of cultural appropriation, called "hipster racism." Some define hipster racism as instances where college-educated Whites (many of whom live in gentrifying areas and claim to have friends of color) co-opt elements of various cultures that belong to people of color for the purposes of entertainment, like Native American articles of clothing or symbols or Asian cuisine (West, 2012). Others argue that it consists of expressing essentially racist ideas "under the guise of being urbane, witty (meaning 'ironic' nowadays), educated, liberal, and/or trendy" (Plaid, 2008; see also West, 2012). Passing familiarity with people of color or mass consumption of their cultures rarely serves as proxy for racial understanding and, in fact, frequently reflects a covert form of "Othering." For all of these reasons, it is important to begin to shift our discourse away from appreciating diverse cultures and having diverse friends as evidence of support for groups of color and instead move toward a definition of what it really means to be an *ally*.

From "Friends" to Allies

The aforementioned racial rationalizations in this essay are often the result of well-meaning Whites attempting to express support for and identification with people of color, albeit in a superficial way (Feagin, 2001). Typically, it's an attempt to present one's self as an ally to people of color. However, as Andrea Ayvazian (2009) says in her article, "Interrupting the Cycle of Oppression: The Role of Allies as Agents of Change," "An ally is a member of a dominant group in our society who works to dismantle any form of oppression from which she or he receives the benefit" (p. 612). She goes on to say that being an ally means taking personal responsibility for the changes necessary in society and not ignoring or leaving others to deal with it: "Allied behavior is intentional, overt, consistent activity that challenges prevailing patterns of oppression, makes privileges that are so often invisible visible, and facilitates the empowerment of persons targeted by oppression" (p. 612; see also the definition of an *advocate* in Welp, 2009). Paul

Kivel (2012) adds that there is no one way to be an ally as each of us have different relationships to social organizations, political process, and economic structures. Nevertheless, being a racial ally is "an ongoing strategic process in which we look at our personal and social resources, evaluate the environment we have helped to create and decide what needs to be done" (p. 157). Furthermore, allies act on the basis of ethical commitments to a sense of justice and fairness, regardless of friendship.

Feagin and Vera's research on anti-racist Whites lends further insight into the behavior of allies. Anti-racist Whites, in particular, actively seek out interactions with people in other racial/ethnic groups and have cultivated *close* (emphasis added) friendships across the color line (Feagin & Vera, 2012). Moreover, they tend to be Whites who are most aware of their own racism and the racism of others, and while they aren't certain they can really understand the experiences of people of color, they make an honest attempt. For many, they come to recognize their own racism after a critical event or experience. In Feagin and Vera's, "Confronting One's Own Racism" (2012), this happened for a White teacher when she noticed she gave support and attention to Latino toddlers, but not the Black toddlers where she once worked. Once she realized her prejudice toward the Black toddlers, she then made a very deliberate, concerted effort to interact equally with all of the toddlers, but noted: "I had to *make myself* do it . . . it wasn't easy to do, [but] once I knew that I was acting in a way that was prejudiced, I had to work very hard to overcome that" (Feagin & Vera, 2012, p. 153). The authors find that this is a common quality among anti-racist Whites, where they go beyond empathy and understanding for what people of color have experienced to taking "proactive stances to confront their own internalized racism and the racist views and actions of other whites" (p. 154). Feagin and Vera further maintain (like Ayvazian above) that part of being an anti-racist is being willing to risk one's own privilege or resources on behalf of people of color, thus demonstrating "a strong commitment to a non-racist society" (2012, p. 154).

In order for Whites to be allies, they may need role models who can demonstrate what real allied behavior looks like so that they may enact similar behaviors and strategies. Essentially, the adage holds true: You cannot be what you cannot see. Ayvazian (2009) discusses how White allies have long played an integral role in social justice movements, like Laura Haviland who was a conductor on the Underground Railroad and helped enslaved Africans flee to Canada; Sarah and Angelina Grimké who were abolitionists that faced ridicule and abuse for their anti-slavery stance; and John Brown who was hanged after leading a rebellion against slavery in Harper's Ferry, West Virginia. The civil rights movement includes more examples of White allies, including Virginia Foster Durr who drove Black workers during the Montgomery Bus Boycott and along with her husband, attorney Clifford Durr and Rev. E. D. Nixon, bailed Rosa Parks out of jail; Rev. James Reeb, a Boston minister who was killed by segregationists during the voting rights march in Selma, Alabama; and Anne and Carl Braden who fought for desegregated schools and open housing and even bought a house for a Black couple in an all-White neighborhood in Kentucky, for which they had their windows shot out, their house bombed, and a cross burned in their yard.

More recent examples of White allies include Morris Dees who started the Southern Poverty Law Center and brings lawsuits designed to cripple White supremacist hate groups; Dr. Laurie Olsen who has spent decades working on projects designed to improve the treatment of immigrant students and protect the rights of Americans for whom English is a second language; and Dr. Peggy McIntosh who wrote the groundbreaking piece, "White Privilege and Male Privilege: A Personal Account of Coming to See Correspondences Through Work in Women's Studies" (1988) and consults with colleges and universities on creating multicultural and gender-fair curricula. The *actions* of these people are indicative of what it really means to be an ally and support people of color: to be willing to forego one's own privilege in the pursuit of social justice and to do so in the face of significant opposition.

In "Ten Things You Can Do to Improve Race Relations," racial inequality scholar Charles A. Gallagher (2012) offers that while ongoing and pervasive institutional racism may lead us to believe that there is nothing that can be done to improve race relations, "[a]t the individual, interpersonal, and community level you can engage in activities to promote equal opportunity while building bridges between people from different racial backgrounds" (p. 401). Among other things, Gallagher (p. 402) suggests

- respectfully engaging friends and family in what you learn in your race classes, including politely and nonjudgmentally asking them about the origins of their racial prejudices;
- stopping others from telling racist jokes;
- being introspective and honest enough to examine why you act or behave in a certain way toward someone of a different ethnic or racial group;
- stepping out of your comfort zone enough to involve yourself in places where you will be exposed to people of different racial and ethnic backgrounds; and
- being a positive role model to younger people in your life who look up to you and explain what it really means to live in a multiracial, multiethnic society.

Incorporating these kinds of attitudes, orientations, and strategies is often one of the first steps toward becoming an ally.

Being an ally is risky as it involves giving up one's own privileges and may also result in losing friends or relatives who aren't like minded. As a result, it may be difficult to enact or practice with a great deal of consistency (Ayvazian, 2009). The level of discomfort involved in understanding privilege can itself be enough to put off Whites who are considering becoming an ally. For example, for many White students who first begin to engage with a definition of racism that moves beyond the individual to the systemic, understanding dynamics of power and privilege can be quite difficult. They may feel a sense of embarrassment, guilt, compassion, or even obligation (see Hardiman, 2001; Tatum, 1997) toward people of color and may want to act out of empathy. When students of color are on the receiving end of this behavior, they may react with frustration toward yet another well-meaning White person who "doesn't *really* get it" (see Tatum, 1997) or in other ways exhibit what White students might perceive as a lack of proper appreciation. While this may cause White students to become angry at not being seen as an individual (Tatum, 1997) or as "one of the good ones," coming to terms with the challenges of social justice is part of the racial identity development process for Whites in a racialized society (Hardiman, 1994; Helms, 1990; Tatum, 1992). Furthermore, as Kivel (2012), another White ally, states in "How White People Can Serve as Allies to People of Color in the Struggle to End Racism," the point of being an ally isn't necessarily to curry favor with people of color: "We are not fighting racism so that people of color will trust us. Trust builds over time through our visible efforts to be allies and fight racism. Rather than trying to be safe and trustworthy, we need to be more active, less defensive, and put issues of trust aside" (p. 160). Thus, being a true ally requires some "unglamorous" work and often the help and support of like-minded others (Ayvazian, 2009; Kivel, 2012; Tatum, 1997; Welp, 2009).

Suggested Additional Resources

Bonilla-Silva, E. (2010). *Racism without racists: Colorblind racism and the persistence of inequality in America.* Lanham, MD: Rowman & Littlefield.

Doane, A. W., & Bonilla-Silva, E. (2003). *White out: The continuing significance of racism.* New York, NY: Routledge.

Feagin, J. R. (2010). *The White racial frame: Centuries of racial framing and counter-framing.* New York, NY: Routledge.

Tatum, B. D. (1997). *Why are all the Black kids sitting together in the cafeteria? And other conversations about race.* New York, NY: HarperCollins.

Wise, T. (2009). *Between Barack and a hard place: Racism and White denial in the age of Obama.* San Francisco, CA: City Lights Books.

Wise, T. (2010). *Colorblind: The rise of post-racial politics and the retreat from racial equity.* San Francisco, CA: City Lights Books.

Audio/Visual

Mulholland, L. (Director and Writer). (2013). *An ordinary hero.* United States: Taylor Street Films. Film documents the story of Joan Trumpauer Mulholland, a White anti-racist who spent months in prison during the Freedom Rides and fought alongside leaders in the civil rights movement.

Wah, L.M. (1994). *The color of fear.* United States: Stir Fry Productions. Film features a multiracial cast of men discussing the state of race relations and the challenges of allyship.

Websites

Alliance of White Anti-Racists Everywhere-Los Angeles (AWARE-LA):

http://www.awarela.org

The group's mission is "to work toward the abolition of the white supremacist system and all systems of supremacy through building communities of Radical White people in solidarity with people of color in the larger movement for racial, social, economic, and environmental justice."

Safehouse Progressive Alliance for Nonviolence:

http://www.safehousealliance.org/index.cfm

The website also offers extensive information on racism and anti-racism in their manual, *Tools for Liberation: Building a Multi-Ethnic, Inclusive & Antiracist Organization.*

Training for Change:

http://www.trainingforchange.org

The website provides activist training for groups standing up for justice, peace, and the environment through strategic nonviolence.

White Anti-Racism: Living the Legacy:

http://www.tolerance.org/supplement/white-anti-racism-living-legacy

From *Teaching Tolerance,* published by The Southern Poverty Law Center

White Men as Full Diversity Partners:

http://www.wmfdp.com

Questions for Further Discussion

1. Do you think it is possible to have friends of another race and still hold racist attitudes? Why or why not?

2. Do you think it is possible to oppose interracial dating and not have racist attitudes? Why or why not?

3. What aspects of other cultures have you embraced? Do you feel equally as comfortable with the group of people who consider that culture their own?

4. Often, in popular media, celebrities and artists co-opt parts of a racial or ethnic group's culture (e.g., Madonna, Gwen Stefani, Miley Cyrus). What do you think about the way celebrities like these co-opt Asian or Black culture, for example? Is this racist? Is it similar or different than the use of Native American culture in the naming of sports teams (e.g., Washington Redskins, Atlanta Braves, Cleveland Indians, Florida State Seminoles, etc.) like Eitzen and Baca Zinn discuss in Essay 10? Debate your classmates.

5. Consider Bogardus's scale. List the major racial and ethnic groups in America and apply them to each item. As you travel up the scale, how

do you feel about increased contact with a particular racial group? What do you make of your findings? Now, think about yourself as a parent and do the scale again. Would your level of comfort toward particular racial or ethnic groups change if they lived in your neighborhood and could play with your child or date your child when he or she becomes a teenager?

6. If you're still struggling with issues of race and racism, with what do you struggle? What are your hang-ups around this issue?

Reaching Beyond the Color Line

1. If you are a White student, think about the people of color whom you consider friends and examine the depth of your friendship. Do you know their last name? Do you know how many brothers or sisters they have? Do you know where they grew up? What is their experience of being a student of color on campus? Consider finding out the answers to these questions if you don't already know these answers.

2. If you are a student of color, think about the White people whom you consider friends and examine the depth of your friendship. How much do you know about them? How much do they know about you? Do you ever hold back on telling them things about your life? Why or why not? Do you feel that White people will ever be able to "get it"?

3. Given the information above on being an ally, what are you committed to do in order to promote greater social justice? And, what else do you need in order to move forward (e.g., greater education or knowledge, the support of like-minded others, etc.)?

References

Agyeman-Fisher, A. (2012, March 28). *Zimmerman's "Black friend" exposed as fraud.* NewsOne. Retrieved from http://newsone.com/1963015/joe-oliver-lawrence-o-donnell-last-call-interview

Ashmore, K. (2009). Is your world too White? A primer for Whites trying to deal with a racist society. In A. Ferber, C. M. Jimenez, A. O. Herrera, & D. R. Samuels (Eds.), *The matrix reader: Examining the dynamics of oppression and privilege* (pp. 638–642). New York, NY: McGraw-Hill.

Ayvazian, A. (2009). Interrupting the cycle of oppression: The role of allies as agents of change. In A. Ferber, C. M. Jimenez, A. O. Herrera, & D. R. Samuels (Eds.), *The matrix reader: Examining the dynamics of oppression and privilege* (pp. 612–616). New York, NY: McGraw-Hill.

Bennett-Smith, M. (2013, May 2). Chris Broussard, ESPN reporter, thinks Jason Collins, gays, can be "saved" if they "ask God for forgiveness." *The Huffington Post.* Retrieved from http://www.huffingtonpost.com/2013/05/02/chris-broussard-jason-collins-ask-forgiveness-gays_n_3202418.html

Bertrand, M., & Mullainathan, S. (2004). Are Emily and Greg more employable than Lakisha and Jamal? A field experiment on labor market discrimination. *American Economic Review, 94*(4), 991–1013.

Bobo, L. D., & Dawson, M. C. (2009). A change has come: Race, politics, and the path to the Obama presidency. *DuBois Review, 6*(1), 1–14.

Bogardus, E. (1933). A social distance scale. *Sociology and Social Research, 17,* 265–271.

Bonilla-Silva, E. (2003). *Racism without racists: Colorblind racism and the persistence of inequality in America.* Lanham, MD: Rowman & Littlefield.

Bonilla-Silva, E. (2010). *Racism without racists: Colorblind racism and the persistence of inequality in America.* Lanham, MD: Rowman & Littlefield.

Childs, E. C. (2005). *Navigating interracial borders: Black-White couples and their social worlds.* Piscataway, NJ: Rutgers University Press.

Coates, T. (2013, March 6). The good, racist people. *New York Times.* Retrieved from http://mobile.nytimes.com/2013/03/07/opinion/coates-the-good-racist-people.html

Collins, P. H. (2009). Toward a new vision: Race, class, and gender as categories of analysis and connection. In A. Ferber, C. M. Jimenez, A. O. Herrera, & D. R. Samuels (Eds.), *The matrix reader: Examining the dynamics of oppression and privilege* (pp. 97–108). New York, NY: McGraw-Hill.

Cose, E. (1993). *The rage of a privileged class: Why are middle-class Blacks angry? Why should America care?* New York, NY: HarperCollins.

Culp, J. M., Jr. (1993, Fall). Water buffalo and diversity: Naming names and reclaiming the racial discourse. *Connecticut Law Review, 26,* 209–263.

Dewan, S. (2008, October 15). The youth vote: In generation seen as colorblind, Black is yet a factor. *New York Times.* Retrieved from http://www.nytimes.com/2008/10/15/us/politics/15youth.html?_r=0

Feagin, J. R. (2001). *Racist America: Roots, current realities, and future reparations.* New York, NY: Routledge.

Feagin, J. R. (2010). *The White racial frame: Centuries of racial framing and counter-framing.* New York, NY: Routledge.

Feagin, J. R., & Sikes, M. P. (1994). *Living with racism: The Black middle-class experience.* Boston, MA: Beacon Press.

Feagin, J. R., & Vera, H. (2000). *White racism: The basics.* New York, NY: Routledge.

Feagin, J. R., & Vera, H. (2012). Confronting one's own racism. In P. S. Rothenberg (Ed.), *White privilege: Essential readings on the other side of racism* (pp. 151–155). New York, NY: Worth.

Fournier, R. (2008, September 20). Racial views steer some away from Obama. *Politico.com.* Retrieved from http://www.politico.com/news/stories/0908/13658.html

Gallagher, C. A. (2004). Color-blind privilege: The social and political functions of erasing the color line in post-race America. In C. A. Gallagher (Ed.), *Rethinking the color line: Readings in race and ethnicity* (pp. 575–588). New York, NY: McGraw-Hill.

Gallagher, C. A. (2012). Ten things you can do to improve race relations. In C. A. Gallagher (Ed.), *Rethinking the color line: Readings in race and ethnicity* (pp. 400–402). New York, NY: McGraw-Hill.

Goffman, E. (1959). *The presentation of self in everyday life.* New York, NY: Doubleday.

Hardiman, R. (1994). White racial identity development in the United States. In E. P. Salett & D. R. Koslow (Eds.), *Race, ethnicity and self: Identity in multicultural perspective* (chap. 6), Washington, DC: National MultiCultural Institute.

Hardiman, R. (2001). Reflections on White identity development theory. In C. L. Wijeyesinghe & B. W. Jackson III (Eds.), *New perspectives on racial identity development: A theoretical and practical anthology* (pp. 108–128). New York, NY: New York University Press.

Healey, J. F. (2012). *Diversity and society: Race, ethnicity, and gender.* Thousand Oaks, CA: Pine Forge.

Helms, J. E. (1990). Toward a model of White racial identity development. In J. E. Helms (Ed.), *Black and White racial identity: Theory, research and practice* (pp. 49–66). Westport, CT: Greenwood.

hooks, (1992). *Black looks: Race and representation.* Boston, MA: South End Press.

Kivel, P. (2012). How White people can serve as allies to people of color in the struggle to end racism. In P. S. Rothenberg (Ed.), *White privilege: Essential readings on the other side of racism* (pp. 157–165). New York, NY: Worth.

McIntosh, P. (2007). White privilege: Unpacking the invisible knapsack. In M. L. Andersen & P. H. Collins (Eds.), *Race, class, and gender: An anthology* (6th ed., pp. 99–104). Belmont, CA: Wadsworth.

MSNBC. (2007, April 9). Transcript: Imus puts remarks into context. *MSNBC.com.* Retrieved from http://www.msnbc.msn.com/id/18022596/ns/msnbc_tv-imus_on_msnbc

MSNBC. (2012, March 27). *Interview: The last word with Lawrence O'Donnell.* Retrieved from http://www.nbcnews.com/id/45755883/ns/msnbc-the_last_word/vp/46875482#46875482

National Public Radio. (2010, January 18). The "post-racial" conversation, one year in [Radio series episode]. *Talk of the nation.* Washington, DC: National Public Radio. Retrieved from http://www.npr.org/templates/story/story.php?storyId=122701272

Ott, B. L., & Mack, R. L. (2010). *Critical media studies: An introduction.* Malden, MA: Wiley-Blackwell.

Pager, D., & Shepherd, H. (2008). The sociology of discrimination: Racial discrimination in employment, housing, credit, and consumer markets. *Annual Review of Sociology, 34,* 181–209.

Pettigrew, T. F. (2009). Post-racism? Putting President Obama's victory into perspective. *Du Bois Review, 6*(2), 279–292.

Picca, L. H., & Feagin, J. R. (2007). *Two faced racism: Whites in the backstage and frontstage.* New York, NY: Routledge.

Plaid, A. J. (2008, July 14). The New Yorker and hipster racism. *Racialicious.* Retrieved from http://www.racialicious.com/2008/07/14/the-new-yorker-and-hipster-racism

Tannenbaum, R. (2012, December 1). Playboy interview: John Mayer. *Playboy.* Retrieved from http://www.playboy.com/playground/view/playboy-interview-john-mayer?page=2

Tatum, B. D. (1992). Talking about race, learning about racism: The application of racial identity development theory in the classroom. *Harvard Educational Review, 62*(1), 1–24.

Tatum, B. D. (1997). *Why are all the Black kids sitting together in the cafeteria? And other conversations about race.* New York, NY: HarperCollins.

Trotta, D. (2012, March 25). Joe Oliver, George Zimmerman's friend, defends shooter in Trayvon Martin case. *Huffington Post.* Retrieved from http://www.huffingtonpost.com/2012/03/25/joe-oliver-george-zimmerman-trayvon-martin_n_1378390.html

Valbrun, M. (2012, April 2). Rewriting the script won't change the facts in the Trayvon Martin case. *Slate.com.* Retrieved from http://www.slate.com/blogs/xx_factor/2012/04/02/trayvon_martin_zimmerman_s_black_friend_and_hispanic_defenses_won_t_work_.html

Welp, M. (2009). Vanilla voices: Researching White men's diversity learning journeys. In A. Ferber, C. M. Jimenez, A. O. Herrera, & D. R. Samuels (Eds.), *The matrix reader: Examining the dynamics of oppression and privilege* (pp. 622–628). New York, NY: McGraw-Hill.

West, L. (2012, April 26). *A complete guide to "hipster racism."* Retrieved from http://jezebel.com/5905291/a-complete-guide-to-hipster-racism

Wise, T. (2009). *Between Barack and a hard place: Racism and White denial in the age of Obama.* San Francisco, CA: City Lights Books.

Wise, T. (2010). *Colorblind: The rise of post-racial politics and the retreat from racial equity.* San Francisco, CA: City Lights Books.

About the Editors

Stephanie M. McClure is an associate professor of sociology at Georgia College. She teaches classes on racial stratification, social theory, and the sociology of education. Her research interests are in the area of higher education, with a focus on college student persistence and retention across race, class, and gender, and a special emphasis on postcollege student experiences that increase student social and academic integration. She has published in the *Journal of Higher Education, Symbolic Interaction*, and *The Journal of African American Studies*.

Cherise A. Harris is an associate professor of sociology at Connecticut College. She specializes in race, class, and gender and teaches classes on the sociology of ethnic and race relations; the sociology of inequality; race, gender, and the mass media; and middle-class minorities. Her book, *The Cosby Cohort: Blessings and Burdens of Growing Up Black Middle Class*, was published in 2013. She has also published in *Teaching Sociology, Sociological Spectrum, and Journal of African American Studies*.

⊛SAGE research**methods**

The essential online tool for researchers from the world's leading methods publisher

Find exactly what you are looking for, from basic explanations to advanced discussion

More content and new features added this year!

"I have never really seen anything like this product before, and I think it is really valuable."

John Creswell, University of Nebraska–Lincoln

Discover Methods Lists—
methods readings suggested by other users

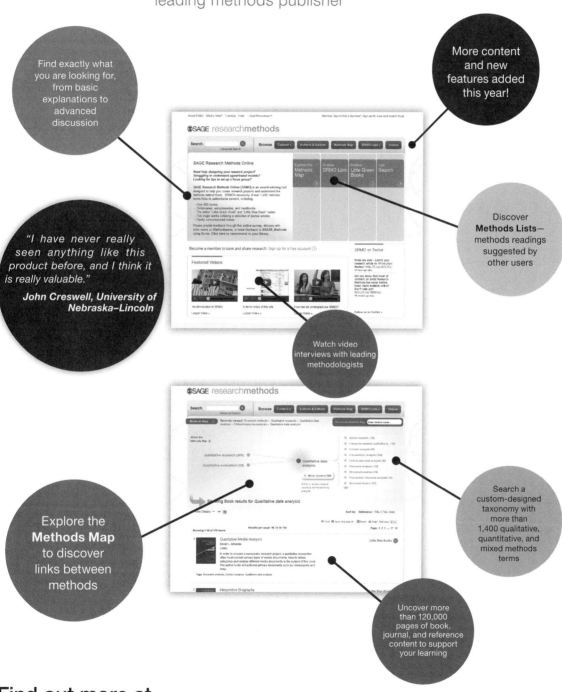

Watch video interviews with leading methodologists

Explore the Methods Map to discover links between methods

Search a custom-designed taxonomy with more than 1,400 qualitative, quantitative, and mixed methods terms

Uncover more than 120,000 pages of book, journal, and reference content to support your learning

Find out more at
www.sageresearchmethods.com